CISCO SWITCHED INTERNETWORKS

McGRAW-HILL CISCO TECHNICAL EXPERT TITLES

Fisher *Configuring Cisco Routers for ISDN* *0-07-02273-5*
Gai *Internetworking IPv6 with Cisco Routers* *0-07-022836-1*
Held and Huntley *Cisco Security Architectures* *0-07-134708-9*
Lewis *Cisco TCP/IP Routing Professional Reference* *0-07-041140-1*
Parkhurst *Cisco Router OSPF Design and Implementation* *0-07-048626-3*
Parkhurst *Cisco Multicast Routing and Switching* *0-07-134647-3*
Rossi *Cisco and IP Addressing* *0-07-134925-1*
Rossi *Cisco Catalyst LAN Switching* *0-07-134982-0*
Sackett *Cisco Router Handbook* *0-07-058097-9*
Slattery/Burton *Advanced IP Routing in Cisco Networks* *0-07-058144-4*
Van Meter *Cisco and Fore ATM Internetworking* *0-07-134842-5*

Cisco Switched Internetworks

Chris Lewis

McGraw-Hill
New York San Francisco Washington, D.C.
Auckland Bogotá Caracas Lisbon London
Madrid Mexico City Milan Montreal New Delhi
San Juan Singapore Sydney Tokyo Toronto

McGraw-Hill 

A Division of The McGraw-Hill Companies

1 2 3 4 5 6 7 8 9 0 AGM/AGM 9 0 4 3 2 1 0 9

ISBN 0-07-134646-5

The sponsoring editor for this book was Steve Elliot, the editing supervisor was Scott Amerman, and the production supervisor was Clare Stanley. It was set in New Century Schoolbook by Don Feldman of McGraw-Hill's Professional Book Group composition unit in cooperation with Spring Point Publishing Services.

Printed and bound by Quebecor/Martinsburg.

This book is printed on recycled, acid-free paper containing a minimum of 50% recycled, de-inked fiber.

CONTENTS

ACKNOWLEDGMENTS

First, I must acknowledge my wife, Claudia, whose love and support were again essential in helping me comple a task of this kind. I also wish to put a mention in for my son Ben, who was born during the writing of this book. He has seemed most understanding when he lost his play partner on weekends during the writing of this book; I promise to make up for all the missed playtime now.

I must also acknowledge Thomas Astuto and John Matula for doing such a fine job of transforming my random scribblings into clear diagrams for this book. Thanks, guys. Finally, I would like to thank Steve Elliot for his encouragement and acknowledge that without his support, this book would not have come into being.

INTRODUCTION

This book is essentially a second volume on networking Cisco equipment, a continuation of the *Cisco TCP/IP Routing Professional Reference,* also published by McGraw-Hill. That book covered the theory and operation of routed networks, along with their implementation on Cisco equipment. Using the concepts in that book, one could construct an IP-based network that would service the vast majority of corporate network requirements.

The one constant in the world of networking is, however, change, and we find the world of routed networks being complemented with, and in some cases supplanted by, switched networking. With the world of routed networking delivering reliable, scalable solutions at a cost that the legacy networks could not match, one might wonder what additional benefits the switched network will provide. Also, armed with a few years' experience in this industry, you will recognize the value in finding out what the problems are with this technology before you try to implement it on your network. As always, you should weigh the pluses and minuses beforehand.

This books focuses on the practical implementation issues and device configurations necessary when introducing switching technology to an existing network infrastructure. This is not another book that rehashes the standards documentation; instead, it will take you through a practical understanding of the theory of operation of these new technologies and show how they are implemented using Cisco equipment. This book assumes that you have a clear understanding of the first four layers of the OSI seven-layer model—the physical, data-link, network, and transport layers—as well as IP addressing and subnet masks. If you do not have at least 1 year's experience implementing routed networks, it is recommended that you read the *Cisco TCP/IP Routing Professional Reference* first.

Now, for an overview of the book:

Chapter 1 will provide the background knowledge required to appreciate the topics covered in the rest of the book. Experienced network engineers may wish to skim this chapter, as it reviews repeater, bridge, router, and switch operation. The chapter explains the concepts of layer 2, 3, and 4 switching and discusses how each network device handles and, in some cases, alters a packet's contents as the packet travels through it. Chapter 1 also introduces the essential concepts to switched Ethernet networking: the collision and broadcast domains.

Chapter 2 presents a practical view of the theoretical background of LAN switching in both Ethernet and token ring environments. This chapter discusses the operation of VLAN trunks, along with features such as VTP, VMPS, and STP optimization. The essential role of CGMP and PIM in multicast deployment is presented, and an introduction to Gigabit Ethernet is given.

Chapter 3 provides a practical view of WAN switching technologies, with particular reference to ATM as a transport for the IP protocol. Options for carrying IP over ATM, such as RFC 1577 (CIOA), LANE, and NHRP as it is used in MPOA, are discussed. This chapter also discusses the operation of ATM UNI and NNI, including frame access to cell-based services by FUNI and DXI and how tag switching (now the MPLS standard) can be used in ATM.

Chapter 4 is the first chapter to show how these technologies can be implemented on Cisco equipment, beginning with a description of the switch command-line interface. VLAN creation and management is illustrated on the 2916XL platform. For the 2916XL, hardware description and software optimization are presented. Additionally, this chapter shows how to implement voice over IP services via the MC3810 product, which can switch voice over existing IP links. Implementation options for the MC3810 are fully discussed, including real-world examples of using this platform to emulate PBX to PBX tie lines.

Chapter 5 covers the hardware modules and software configuration for the 5000 and 5500 series switches. Specific examples cover multiple VLAN support, VTP, VMPS, the Route Switch Module, trunk options, and supervisor channels.

Chapter 6 illustrates configuration of Cisco products that support ATM networking, particularly the router AIP and NPM cards and the LightStream1010 switch. Configuration of both SVC and PVC operation is illustrated, and complete examples of CIOA, PPP, IISP, PNNI, LANE, MPOA, and class of service implementations are given.

Chapter 7 discusses issues of switched network implementation, with reference to network design as an ongoing part of network operations. The focus of this chapter is to look at how different devices in the overall design impact traffic flows and packet construction. Within this chapter a blueprint that can be used in most switched network implementations is presented, along with a discussion of how this could be migrated to by a company currently using a traditional router-based network.

This book was not designed to be read as a novel, although it can be read from cover to cover, if you so choose. Because of this, there is some duplication of information among chapters where it is necessary to make a section carry complete information.

CISCO SWITCHED INTERNETWORKS

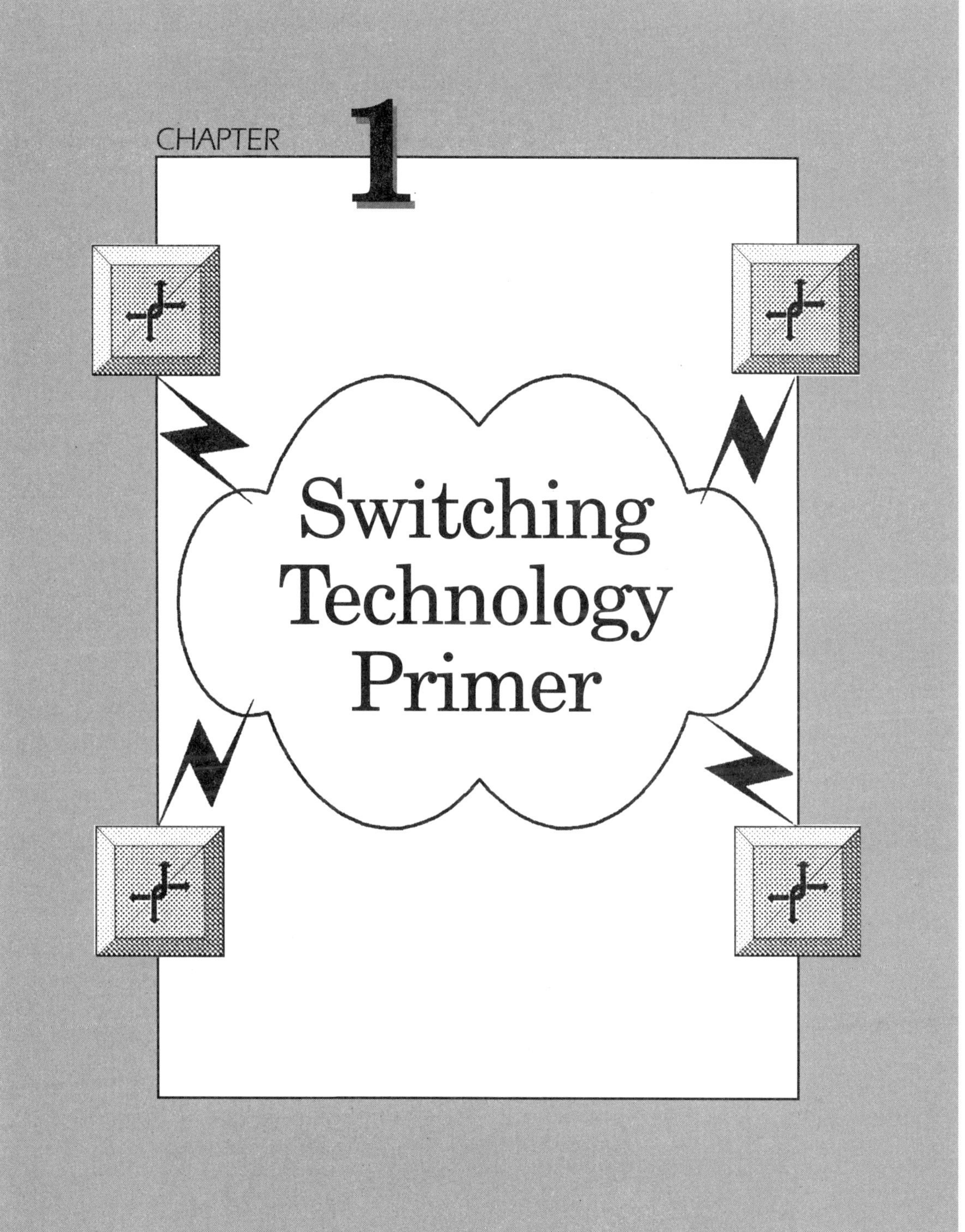
CHAPTER 1
Switching Technology Primer

Objectives

This chapter introduces network devices such as repeaters, bridges, routers, and switches, as well as the concepts of layer 2, 3, and 4 switching. The focus is on understanding how the different devices alter the traffic, packets, performance, and cost of a network. The concepts presented in this chapter form the foundation for the remainder of the book. The concepts of Asynchronous Transfer Mode (ATM) are also introduced, and an explanation of the most common ATM terms is provided.

Network Devices

A network exists to get packets of information from a sender to the receiver or receivers in the quickest possible way, with the least cost. To achieve these goals, various addressing mechanisms are employed, and protocols are implemented to deal with different network media, conditions, and fault scenarios. At its simplest, devices that operate at the lower end of the OSI seven-layer model are quickest and cheapest, while devices operating at the upper layers of the OSI model are more expensive and take more central processing unit (CPU) to achieve the same throughput. Put simply, a repeater, which is a physical layer device (OSI layer 1 device) will only affect the level of electrical signals that form the 1s and 0s that constitute frames of data. Therefore, it is relatively cheap. Alternatively, an application layer firewall (which will typically operate at several of the higher layers of the OSI stack) will examine in detail the meaning of the 1s and 0s of a frame. This device, therefore, costs a lot more than a repeater.

What adds to the cost and slows a device down is the complexity of what it is trying to do to the information within a packet as it is received. Let's review what each of the major network devices do to the packets they receive, and how that impacts the speed of operation and the cost of the device.

Repeater Operation

As its name suggests, a repeater merely repeats whatever it receives. A repeater is used just to extend the distance a signal can be transported over a given medium, by regenerating the electrical signal. As such, it is not an interesting network device. The repeater is an OSI level 1 device and does not understand anything other than voltage levels; it knows nothing about the electrical signals it is repeating representing 1s and 0s in a network message.

Bridge Operation

The venerable bridge was the mainstay of many corporate multisegment local area networks (LANs) in the mid-1980s; however, its time has come and gone. The switch is a very similar device that has gained significant popularity in today's LANs, and we will discuss the switch a little later on. I do recommend that when you consider switch implementations, you also consider the shortfalls of the bridge, as many can still apply. I'm not suggesting that a switch is no better than a bridge, just that poorly chosen and improperly implemented switches will give you the same problems that bridges used to.

So let's get back to bridges. The most common form of bridge was the *transparent bridge*; it was called "transparent" because it could be placed in a network and not alter any of the media access control (MAC) addresses in packets that flowed through it. At first, this may seem a violation of what the MAC addresses are there to do—namely, identify the source and destination addresses of the devices sending and receiving frames. That is the conundrum of a networking device that operates purely at OSI layer 2 (in many ways a contradiction in terms). Layer 2 devices only understand physical addresses, and in an Ethernet LAN environment, those are the 6-byte MAC addresses we are all familiar with. The source MAC address is supposed to identify the machine sending the packet out on to the LAN. However, the transparent bridge does not alter the MAC address of any packet that passes through it (unlike a router). The result is that a packet will pass through a bridge from one segment to another, and when the destination device receives the packet, it will be able to determine the MAC addressing of the station originating the packet.

The basic job of a bridge is to receive packets, store them, and retransmit them on the attached LANs connected to the bridge. A bridge was useful for extending simple LANs, by restricting traffic to only the cable segments necessary. Bridges "learn" which MAC addresses of workstations are on which LAN cable and either forward or block packets according to a list of MAC addresses associated with interfaces kept in the

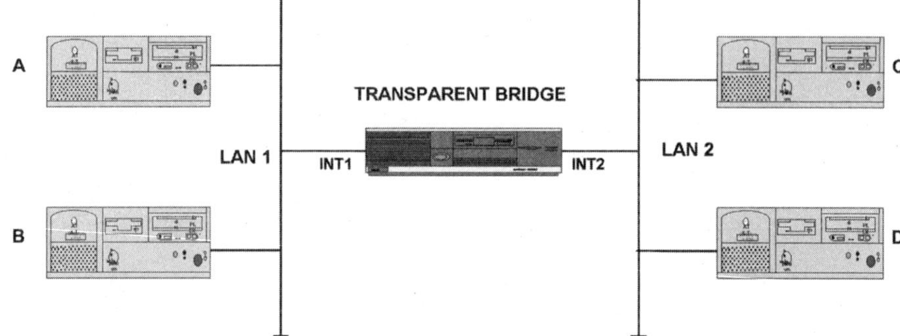

Figure 1-1 Transparent bridge operation.

bridge. Let's look at how a bridge would handle a very simple multi-LAN environment as depicted in Figure 1-1.

First, it must be noted that as far as any layer 3 protocol, such as Internet Protocol (IP) or Internet Packet Exchange (IPX) are concerned, LAN 1 and LAN 2 are the same network number. The process operated by the transparent bridge is as follows:

- Listen to every packet on every interface.
- For each packet heard, keep track of the packet's source MAC address and the interface from which it originated. This is referred to as the *station cache.*
- Look at the destination field in the MAC header. If this address is not found in the station cache, forward the packet to all interfaces other than the one on which the packet was received. If the destination MAC address is in the cache, forward the packet to only the interface the destination address is associated with. If the destination address is on the same bridge interface as the source address, drop the packet; otherwise, duplicate delivery of packets will result.
- Keep track of the age of each entry in the station cache. An entry is deleted after a period of time if no packets are received with that address as the source address. This ensures that if a workstation is moved from one segment to another, its old location is deleted from the station cache after time.

Using this logic, and assuming that workstations A, B, C, and D in Figure 1-1 all communicate with each other, the bridge will produce a station cache that associates workstations A and B with interface 1, then C and D with interface 2. This potentially relieves congestion on a network. All traffic that originates at and is destined for LAN 1 will not be seen on LAN 2 and vice versa. As well as reducing the amount of traffic on each segment, we have created two collision domains as a result of implementing the two segments. By this I mean that a collision on one segment will not affect workstations on another segment.

This form of bridging works well for any LAN topology that does not include multiple paths between two LAN segments. We know that multiple paths between network segments are desirable to maintain connectivity if one path fails for any reason. Let's look at what a simple transparent bridge would do if implemented in a LAN environment such as that shown in Figure 1-2.

Let's say the network is starting up and the station caches for both bridge A and bridge B are empty. Suppose workstation X on LAN 1 wants to send a packet. Bridges A and B will hear the packet, note that workstation X is on LAN 1, and queue the packet for transmission on to LAN 2. Either bridge A or bridge B will be first to transmit the packet on to LAN 2; for argument's sake, say bridge A is first. This causes bridge B to hear the packet with workstation X as the originator on LAN B. We have already run into problems. Bridge B will note that workstation X is on LAN 2 and forward the packet to LAN 1. Bridge A will then forward the packet on to LAN 2 as before, and a very vicious circle is established.

This all occurs because bridges do not alter MAC addresses and have their LAN interfaces set to what is known as "promiscuous mode," so that they take in all packets transmitted on the LAN connected to each interface. To enable bridges to work in the above scenario, bridge suppli-

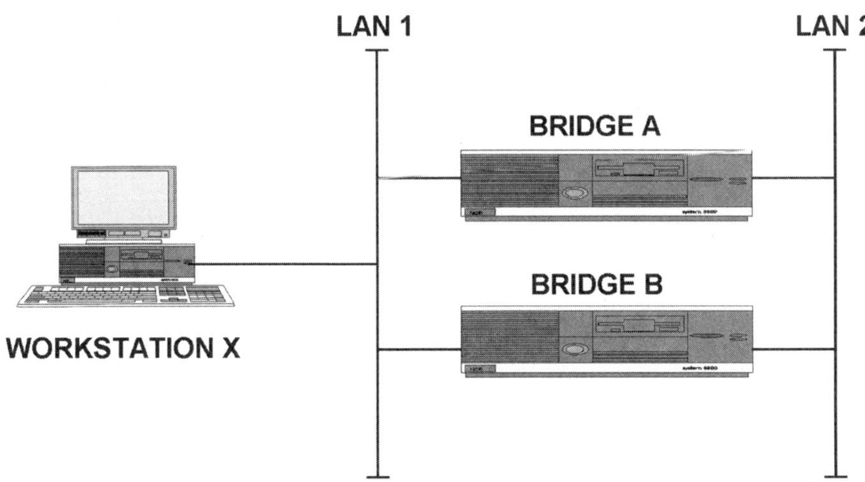

Figure 1-2 Network with multiple bridge paths between LANs.

ers implemented the Spanning Tree Protocol. Essentially, this protocol identifies a loop-free path and temporarily disables bridge interfaces to keep that loop-free topology in effect. If there is a link failure, spanning tree will recalculate a new loop-free path and change the interfaces that are temporarily disabled. The following is an overview of the spanning tree operation.

Spanning Tree Bridges operating spanning tree dynamically select a subset of the LAN interfaces available on each bridge. These selected interfaces form a loop-free path from any LAN to any other LAN. This avoids the nasty packet duplication problems we discussed in relation to Figure 1-2. A spanning tree–enabled bridge will both send out bridge protocol data units (BPDUs) and listen to BPDUs of other bridges. The BPDU configuration contains enough information so that all bridges can perform the following:

- Select a single bridge that will act as the "root" of the spanning tree.
- Calculate the distance of the shortest path from itself to the root bridge.
- For each LAN segment, designate one of the bridges as the closest one to the root. That bridge will handle all communication from that LAN to the root bridge and will be known as the "designated bridge."
- Let each bridge choose one of its interfaces as its root interface, which gives the best path to the root bridge.
- Allow each bridge to mark the root interface—and any other interfaces on it that have been elected as designated bridges for the LAN to which it is connected—as being included in the spanning tree.

The result is a tree structure, originating from the root bridge, that spans connectivity to all LAN segments. Packets are then forwarded to and from interfaces included in the spanning tree. Packets received from interfaces not in the spanning tree are dropped. Packets should never be forwarded onto interfaces that are not part of the spanning tree.

This setup improved the operation of a LAN built with multiple bridges, because the topology could automatically recover from link failures. However, all those interfaces blocked by spanning tree does waste a lot of potential bandwidth that could be used to carry traffic on the network. We'll discuss how to make use of this closed-off bandwidth in a network with switches later. For now, however, just know that as a plug and play device that did not require any configuration, spanning tree had its uses.

Conceptually, spanning tree enabled the layer 2 bridge to perform functions that were really meant for layer 3 devices, like directing traffic between network segments. As such, spanning tree and learning bridges were useful for smallish LANs (up to a couple of hundred nodes), because congestion on segments was reduced and the network could recover from link outages. Where the layer 2 bridge failed was in its handling of broadcasts. A layer 2 bridge always forwards a broadcast to all interfaces in the spanning tree and, therefore, does not give you the opportunity to control broadcasts within a network. Additionally, spanning tree is not as configurable as Routing Information Protocol (RIP), Interior Gateway Routing Protocol (IGRP), or other routing protocols that allow you to reduce the size of routing updates. This makes spanning tree inappropriate for scaling to larger networks.

Layer 3 networking allows the concepts of address hierarchy to reduce the size of routing tables (equivalent to a bridge station cache) and route updates (equivalent to BPDUs). Layer 2 switches also rely on spanning tree but implement virtual LANs (VLANs) to manage broadcast domains. Implementing VLANs also provides the opportunity to assign interface priority on switches, so that different instances of spanning tree (one per VLAN) will select a different interface to be blocked than other instances of spanning tree. The advantage here is that all links on the physical network can be utilized. However, before we look at that technology more closely, let's see what came next chronologically, the router.

Router Operation

The Cisco TCP/IP Routing Professional Reference covered router operation in some detail; however, for the sake of completeness, we'll cover the pertinent details here also. A router does a much more thorough job of examining and modifying the contents of packets than a bridge. That is what makes a router more intensive in its use of software, memory, and processing power. In essence, routers in a network do the following:

- Keep track of layer 3 (by this I mean IP- or IPX-type protocol) network numbers and work out the best way to route packets through the network from source network to destination network. Within routers this is known as the *routing table* and is updated either by automatic processes [like RIP, IGRP, and Open Shortest Path First (OSPF)] or by hand using static routes.

- When it comes time to deliver a packet to its destination host, a router will use its ARP table to obtain the layer 2 address of the specific host that the ARP table associates with the destination IP (or other layer 3 protocol) address.
- Each time a packet comes in to a router and is forwarded on to another network segment, the layer 2 information is changed by the router. This is illustrated in Figure 1-3.
- A router will look at the layer 2 (MAC) address, the layer 3 (IP, IPX, or other network protocol) address, and optionally, the layer 4 (application port) address. Layer 4 ports can be thought of as addresses of different applications running within the host. For example, if a workstation needs to establish a telnet session with a host, it will set the layer 4 destination port to 23, as that is known as the port that a host will receive calls on for telnet sessions. FTP, rlogin, and other applications accept calls on different port numbers.

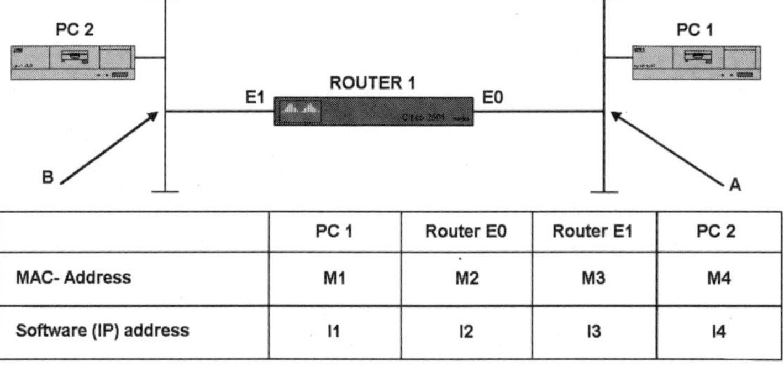

	PC 1	Router E0	Router E1	PC 2
MAC- Address	M1	M2	M3	M4
Software (IP) address	I1	I2	I3	I4

Figure 1-3 How the MAC address used in addressing a packet changes as travel an internetwork.

A packet sent from PC1 to PC2 will look like this at point A:

destination MAC	source MAC	destination IP	source IP	data
M2	M1	I4	I1	1001001

A packet sent from PC1 to PC2 will look like this at point B:

destination MAC	source MAC	destination IP	source IP	data
M4	M3	I4	I1	1001001

Note that the source and destination IP address remain constant as the packet traverses the internetwork.

Figure 1-4 shows how each layer of network software encapsulates the information it receives from the layer above it. This encapsulation includes the addressing information used by the layer itself. In layer 2 the Mac address is added, in layer 3 the protocol address is added (like an IP address), and in layer 4 the port numbers are added.

All of the traditional router's functions are implemented on general-purpose hardware by software programs. This places a considerable load on the hardware to execute the instructions issued by the software as the traffic to be handled by the router increases. This has led to some manufacturers implementing router functions in hardware.

Note: The terms "implemented in hardware" and "implemented in software" can be somewhat confusing, as software of some description needs to be there for any decisions to be made, and hardware needs to be there for any device to exist. Implemented in hardware means that the software functions have been built in to special-purpose hardware that is optimized to perform that function. Currently, these hardware-specific devices are known as Application Specific Integrated Circuits (ASICs).

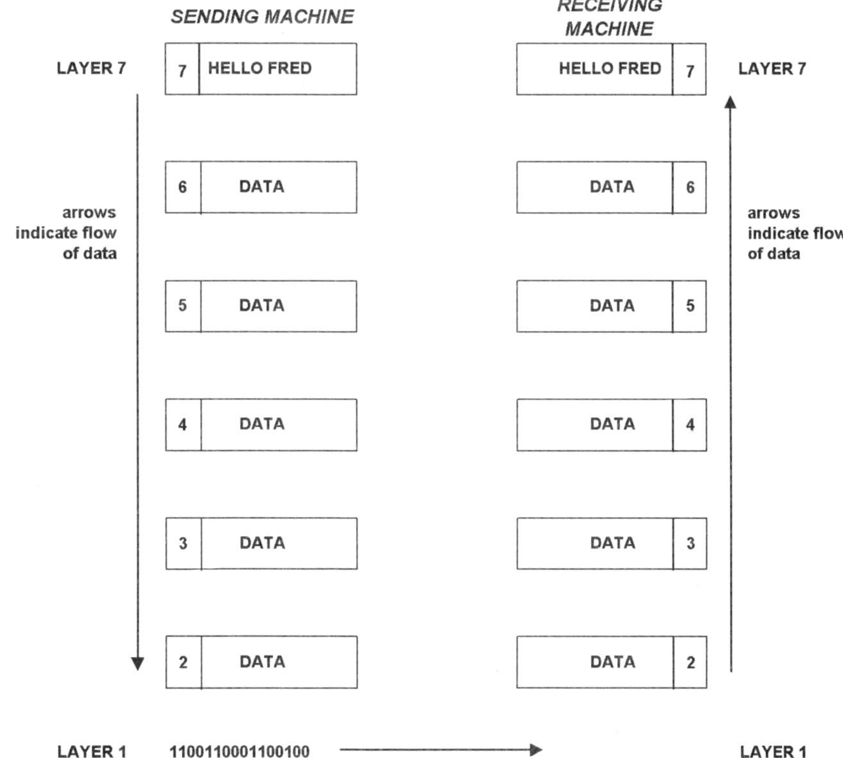

Figure 1-4 Encapsulation through the layers of the OSI model.

What causes the software router to require more processing power than a bridge to perform adequately under the same load is that the router performs table lookup for both IP address (the routing table) and MAC address [the Address Resolution Protocol (ARP) table] before a packet can be forwarded through an interface. Of course, in most live networks, a routing protocol of some kind is deployed, such as RIP or OSPF, which adds to the processing burden of the router. Even though a routing protocol for a router is in many ways equivalent to spanning tree for a bridge, it does take more processing power than spanning tree.

Switches

The topic that will constitute the majority of the text in this book concerns the various switching technologies available to us today. When we look at a simple LAN switch that has no VLANs defined, explaining why it is not a bridge in a new box is really very difficult. A simple LAN switch creates a station cache, runs the Spanning Tree Protocol, and does not utilize layer 3 network protocol information or change the MAC addresses as the packet passes through it. This is identical to the operation of a transparent bridge. When pushed, some manufacturers simply state that its switches are faster than a bridge. This is just a function of the software being implemented on special-purpose hardware, rather than on general-purpose hardware. I suspect the real reason in these cases is marketing; it is unlikely that a manufacturer will sell a bridge these days. A better definition is that a LAN switch provides the ability to implement VLANs—something that a bridge never could. If you choose to implement switches without VLANs, you really are implementing a bridged network. You, therefore, need to recall the problems that existed with them.

So, for the purposes of introduction, a switch is a network device that will forward packets between network segments based on logic built in to specialized hardware chips, with a minimum of recourse to table lookup. Beyond that rather general statement, we have to consider what type of switching we are referring to, which is the topic of the next section.

Switching Concepts

Switches were originally introduced as layer 2 devices operating essentially in the same manner as a bridge. However, once the advantages of purpose-built hardware were observed, manufacturers started to make available layer 3 and even layer 4 switches. In many ways these distinctions are becoming artificial; the lines between which layer a device operates at are becoming more and more blurred. I have already said that a layer 2 switch is separated from a bridge by the fact that it supports VLANs, but we will see that in order to support VLANs, some type of routing function is necessary. This has led to many switches offering a simple internal routing device, thus giving it some layer 3 functionality. On the flip side, router manufacturers have seen the benefits of switching and are enhancing their router devices with switch-type features. Silicon switching and tag switching are Cisco features we will overview later in this section and cover in more detail in later chapters.

The key to managing these devices in the future is to have a solid understanding of how a device forwards packets within a network and not necessarily with its label as a switch, router, or whatever else. Having stated that, it must be conceded that categorization makes it easier to explain how devices function, so for the next few subsections, we will consider each layer 2, 3, and 4 function in isolation.

Layer 2 Switching

Layer 2 switches first came to the marketplace in the guise of layer 2 bridges implemented in hardware. These early devices provided the same benefits and drawbacks of the layer 2 bridge, in that they could introduce multiple collision domains but were limited to the single broadcast domain. Collision and broadcast domains are illustrated in Figure 1-5.

A hub forwards all packets out all ports whether the attached workstation wants the packet or not. The switch will decide to send packets only to the workstation requiring the data; however, it still sends broadcasts out all ports. With VLANs, broadcasts are only sent out of the ports that belong to the VLAN the broadcast originated from.

Simple layer 2 switches differed from layer 2 bridges by generally operating in one of three modes with regard to packet forwarding. Layer 2 bridges only operated in the *store-and-forward mode,* which meant they would have to receive the complete packet, read the source and destination MAC address, perform the cyclic redundancy check (CRC), and apply filters before forwarding it on to any other segment. This, of course, introduced some latency into the network. Switches introduced two more modes of packet forwarding, called cut-through and frag-free.

Figure 1-5 Collision and broadcast domains.

On a shared hub all workstations share a single collision and broadcast domain.

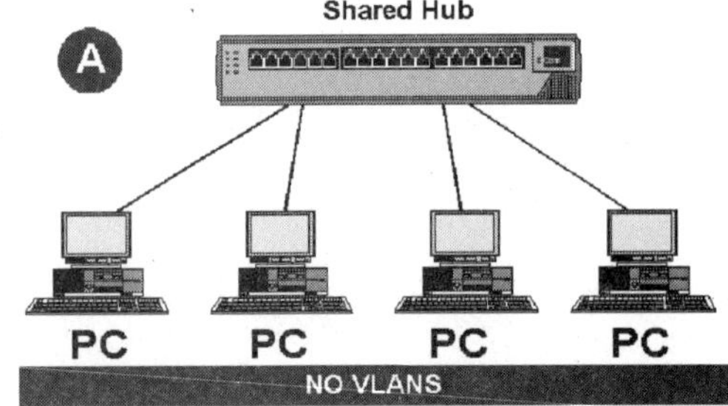

Each switch port is its own collision domain, however all PC's are still in the same broadcast domain.

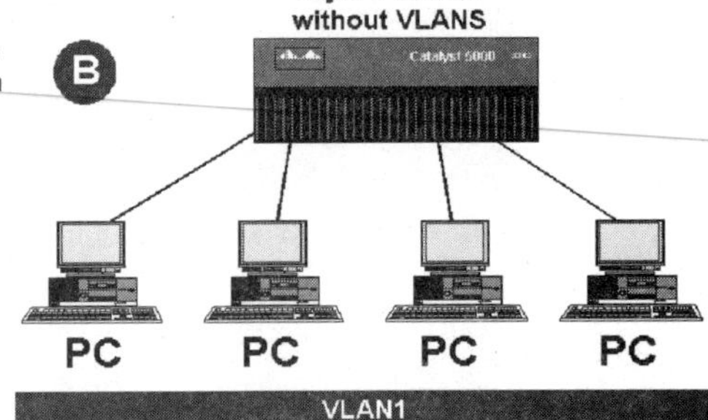

With VLANS implemented, each switch interface has its own collision domain. On this switch two VLAN's are present here two broadcast domains are defined.

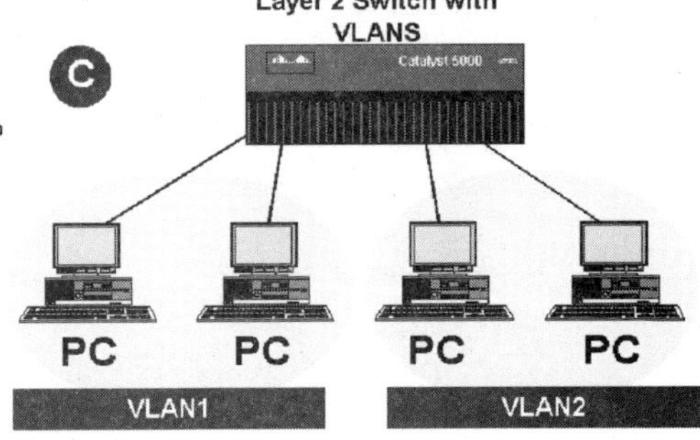

In *cut-through mode,* the switch checks the destination MAC address and starts to forward the packet immediately, which significantly reduces latency. *Frag-free mode* is a kind of middle ground; the switch will take in more than just the destination MAC address, before forwarding the packet, but will not take the whole frame and perform the whole CRC. The aim of this is to identify fragmented frames on the network that appear as the result of collisions and enable the switch to drop these packets before they are forwarded unnecessarily on to another segment.

The other difference we have mentioned between a bridge and a switch is the virtual LAN, or VLAN. Virtual LANs really came into existence to help with moves, additions, and changes on a network. In a typical LAN, 30 to 40 percent of the users will move within the year, which gives rise to a lot of cabling changes. With VLANs there is no need to move users' cables ever again; users can be moved from one VLAN to another purely in the configuration of the switch. Prior to this, users would need their network cables moved from one LAN to another, effectively moving them from one router interface to another. Cisco's VLAN implementation associates an interface with a VLAN. Although some other manufacturers work on the basis of assigning workstations to VLANs via a MAC address, in my opinion the interface assignment that Cisco uses will lead to the best results. Figure 1-6 illustrates how this looks in physical terms. Note that interfaces are assigned to VLANs that are classified according to color. This has become the standard notation for identifying different VLANs on a network.

Figure 1-7 shows how VLANs could be assigned on some other manufacturer's hardware. In this figure we see different-colored VLANs on the same switch interface. This works well for packets originating from these PCs, but the drawback is that any broadcast (or multicast) that originated elsewhere in the network on any of the three VLANs (red, blue, or green) will result in a broadcast coming onto the interface 1 segment and interrupting all the PCs on that segment irrespective of the VLAN they are assigned to. This somewhat negates the benefit of VLANs in the first

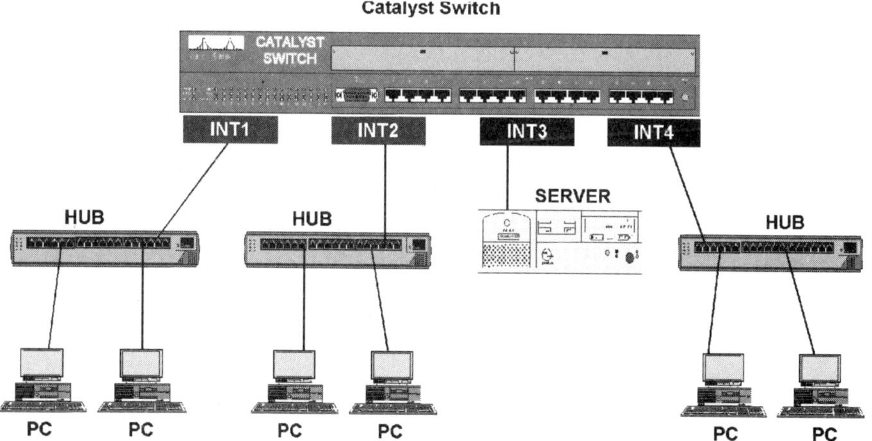

Figure 1-6
Int1 and Int2 are in the red VLAN; Int3 and Int4 are in the blue VLAN. This network has four collision domains and two broadcast domains.

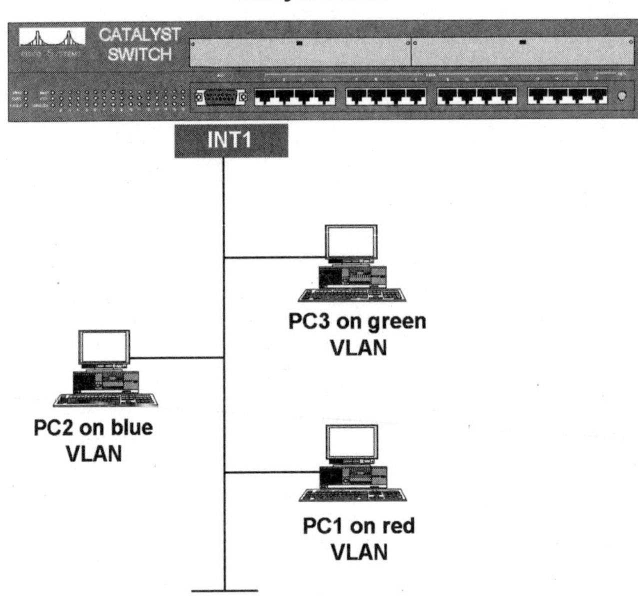

Figure 1-7 Multicolored port on a switch.

place. The only time it really makes sense for multicolored ports is in the case of trunking, which will be covered later.

In summary, simple layer 2 switches give you two main benefits. First, each port has the full Ethernet bandwidth available, dedicated on a per-interface basis. If you connect just one endstation to a switch interface, that one station will receive the full Ethernet bandwidth available, which is in stark contrast to the bandwidth supplied by shared hubs that effectively divide the available bandwidth between all endstations. Second, collisions are local to the switch port only and are not carried forward to other ports.

Layer 3 Switching

The definition of what a layer 3 switch does and why it is different from a router is troublesome. The fact that most manufacturers identify a layer 3 switch as operating much faster than a traditional router does not help. I find it difficult to draw the line in terms of packets-per-second throughput that will differentiate a device as a switch rather than a router. In terms of forwarding packets from one interface to another, the decision process followed by a layer 3 switch and a router are for all intents and purposes the same; the only difference being in physical implementation. Layer 3 switches use the popular ASIC, whereas routers use general-purpose microprocessors. So both a layer 3 switch and a router will forward packets based on IP destination, manipulate MAC addresses, decrement the Time To Live (TTL) field, and perform a frame check sequence.

As well as packet forwarding, routers are responsible for creating and dynamically maintaining routing tables, usually via some routing protocol such as IGRP or OSPF. It needs to be the same for layer 3 switches; by one method or another, a layer 3 switch must operate from a current routing table. This can be achieved in practice by a layer 3 switch participating in the routing protocol process or by the layer 3 switch receiving its routing table from a traditional router.

Another, more interesting difference between the layer 3 switch and a router is the concept of "route once, switch many." We will visit this concept in more detail in Chapter 3 when we discuss tag switching, but for now just know that Cisco has implemented a scheme that will allow a layer 3 switch to discover the correct route from the routing table the first time a remote destination needs to be contacted, then it will use a "shortcut" switching process for subsequent packets to the same destination. This shortcut usually takes the form of an identifier that is appended to the packet. The identifier identifies the packet as part of a particular flow. The benefit is that by switching packets according to the simple identifier, the device does not need to examine each and every packet in its entirety. This mode of operation provides a clear differentiation between a layer 3 switch and a router because the switch is doing something distinctly different than a traditional router. In the Catalyst 5000 range that we will be exploring later, layer 3 switching is provided via a combination of the Route Switch Module for handling routing protocols and the NetFlow feature card that does the high-speed layer 3 packet switching.

Layer 4 Switching

Layer 4 switching is a relatively new concept that refers to a layer 3 switch whose ASIC hardware has the capability of interpreting the layer 4 Transport Control Protocol (TCP) or User Datagram Protocol (UDP) information and applying different levels of service to different applications. Interpreting this information allows the device to assign individual priority to different applications (identified via port number). When implemented in Cisco hardware, the NetFlow feature card caches flows based on source and destination port, as well as source and destination IP address. This has little if any impact on performance of the switch, as all the processing takes place in ASIC hardware, which is in contrast to the implementation of layer 4 control functions in traditional routers. Traditional routers can take significant performance hits through complex access lists and custom queuing to provide layer 4 switching functionality.

In practice, layer 4 switching is most beneficial when controlled by a central policy server that will manage priorities for applications across the entire network.

Integrating Switches and Routers

The first implementations of switches in networks were to operate basically as fast layer 2 bridges. This introduced multiple collision domains and enabled network performance to remain constant, or even improve, while reducing the number of router interfaces used. This implementation created subnet masks that had many more usable IP addresses in them than was previously the case, because each switch interface delivered the full Ethernet bandwidth to the connected workstation or workstations. Figure 1-8 shows a before and after depiction of a network, first

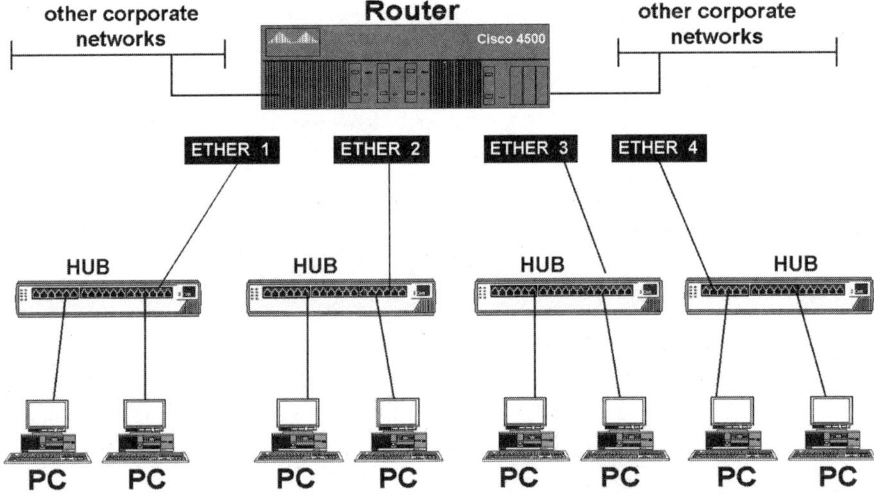

Figure 1-8a Using a router to segment a network.

Figure 1-8b Using a switch to segment a network.

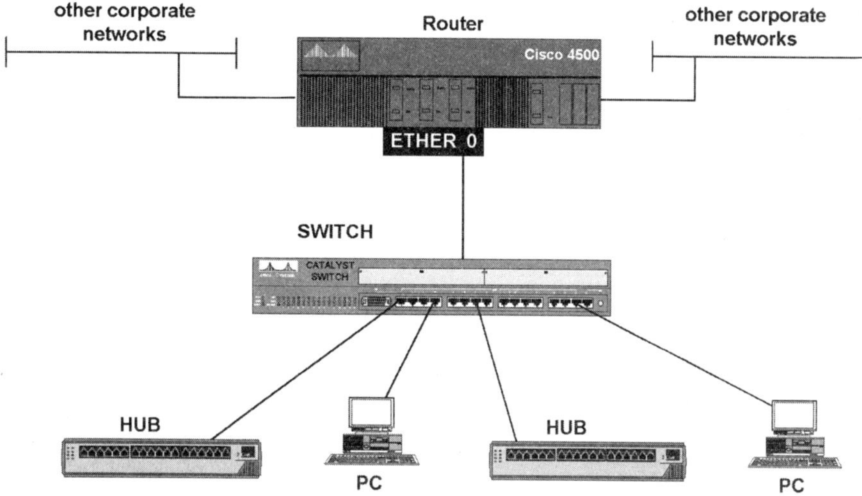

using multiple router interfaces to achieve segmentation, then using switches to reduce the number of router interfaces necessary. The main advantage of this procedure is that the overall cost of the network is reduced, since router interfaces are very costly. Additionally, one could argue that switch interfaces operate faster than router interfaces, resulting in improved network performance.

This first method of introducing switches into a network really did not take advantage of switch capabilities to the greatest extent possible. Switches really start to make sense when we add VLAN capability, as we are then introducing multiple broadcast domains as well as multiple collision domains. Adding VLAN capability, however, means that we need some type of routing function to communicate between VLANs, because each VLAN needs to be its own subnet. Fortunately, we do not need to grow the number of router interfaces on a network to make use of VLANs.

The first way multiple subnets were introduced into a VLAN environment was by subinterfaces on what is commonly termed a *one-armed-router (OAR),* illustrated in Figure 1-9. In this setup, router subinterface 0.1 is associated with the red LAN, which in the figure has switch 1, interface 1, 2, 3, and 4 assigned to it. In practice this means that router subinterface 1 will have an IP address in the same subnet as the devices connected to switch 1, interface 1, 2, 3, and 4 and that the PCs on this VLAN have the IP address of subinterface 0.1 defined as its default gateway. Any packet that needs to travel from one VLAN to another will

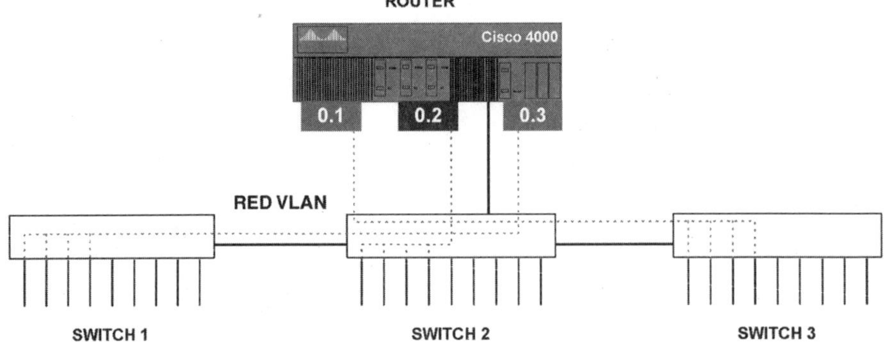

Figure 1-9 Associating router subinterfaces with VLANs.

be routed between subinterfaces in the router. Some switches, like the Catalyst 5000, can have a Route Switch Module inserted that performs the function of the OAR.

With the introduction of simple switches, we saw IP subnet masks allocate more hosts per subnet. Now that VLANs are more common, we are seeing subnets being reassigned to allow fewer hosts per subnet.

One last topic to introduce in this brief introduction to switches is the Cisco Group Management Protocol (CGMP). CGMP is designed to enable Cisco routers and switches to communicate configuration information. This is particularly useful for enabling switches to deal more effectively with multicasts.

Multicasts are sent to special IP addresses (224.0.0.1 and above). Hosts that wish to receive a particular multicast will take in packets destined for the multicast address of interest, while hosts on the same subnet that are not interested in the multicast will not take the packet in. Cisco switches do not automatically learn broadcast or multicast addresses and treat a multicast address the same as a packet destined for an unknown MAC address: it is flooded out of all interfaces within the VLAN it originated from. This may not sound bad, but if several video streams are present on the network, having all of those packets forwarded out of each interface will severely limit the performance of the network. It is possible to program the Catalyst manually with the multicast addresses in use, effectively associating a static set of interfaces with a multicast group.

This is not a particularly satisfactory solution, however. Most multicast applications use IGMP at the host, sending signals to a multicast router and dynamically joining and leaving multicast groups. Clearly, static tables are not only cumbersome to administer but also ineffective in some situations. The answer is CGMP, which allows the multicast router to signal to the switch which interfaces should be part of which multicast group in a dynamic fashion.

Router Switching Modes

It should be becoming apparent that the distinction between layer 2 switches and layer 3 devices is getting less and less clear. It should also be clear that routing is a form of switching—all we are really talking about are different methods for a device to decide which interface to forward a packet out of. In fact, traditional software routers had many types of switching, which we will take a brief look at now.

The default mode of switching in Cisco routers is *fast switching,* which relies upon a cache in main memory created by previous packets. Basically, the router creates a table of where packets with given destinations get routed to and then uses this table, when possible, to switch future packets to the same destination. The benefit is that all the routing and ARP table lookups do not need to be performed every time a packet moves through a router.

The mode that is often invoked on a router that connects fast LANs to much slower WANs (for example, a router connecting a 10-Mbit/sec Ethernet to a 64 K leased line) is called *process switching.* This is done by inserting the `no ip route-cache` command into the configuration of the interfaces in use. The benefit of doing this is to slow down packets coming from a fast media onto a slow media to prevent overwhelming the slower media interface. *Autonomous switching* is available in the 7000 series routers and uses a cache that is similar in concept to the cache used for fast switching but is resident on the interface processor. This has the added benefit of not generating any interrupts to the system processor when switching packets.

The fastest mode is *SSE switching,* which is sometimes referred to as "silicon switching." (SSE stands for "silicon switching engine.") SSE switching again uses a cache to perform lookups, but the cache is held in specialized hardware in the silicon switching engine of the Silicon Switch Processor Module. Silicon switching is only available on Cisco 7000 routers equipped with the Silicon Switch Processor. One point to note is that if header compression is enabled (as is often the case on dial-up asynchronous links to save bandwidth), fast switching is not available.

The Briefest of Introductions to ATM

Asynchronous Transfer Mode (ATM) as we know it is a small but very important part of the broadband ISDN scheme. Broadband ISDN (Integrated Services Digital Network) refers to ISDN at rates over 2 Mbit/sec, as opposed to the narrowband ISDN that supplies two 64-Kbit/sec channels and one 16-Kbit/sec channel. ATM was really designed as a WAN technology for carriers to transport all types of traffic on the one physical network, rather than have separate voice, data, and video systems. As such, it operates most efficiently over the WAN and only really comes into difficulty when it has to emulate a LAN, as ATM is really a point-to-point technology.

ATM is a connection-oriented protocol, which means it will contact the destination node and initiate a call sequence before it sends any data from source to destination. If the intended destination is not online, or the network cannot guarantee the required level of service requested in the call setup, the connection is not made and the source will not send any packets on to the network.

The A in ATM Stands for Asynchronous

Most communications people think of *asynchronous* as it relates to a PC communications port, as in "dial-up asynchronous modem." Asynchronous here means that timing signals are sent with every character, as opposed to synchronous systems, which have a separate clock signal and use timing signals for groups of characters. With this mode of operation, asynchronous means "I'll only send a timing signal when I need to send data."

Asynchronous in ATM refers to a different concept. The current generation of synchronous networks (typified by the well-known T-1 and E-1 circuits) consists of fixed channels; for example, an E-1 consists of 32 individual 64-Kbit/sec channels. Even if there are no packets to be transmitted, a channel will carry a keep-alive or idle poll in every timeslot to maintain synchronization. By contrast, an ATM network will only send data that is associated with a connection when there is live data to send. A synchronous network will identify whose traffic belongs to whom by position in the data stream, typically a time-division timeslot (illustrated in Figure 1-10).

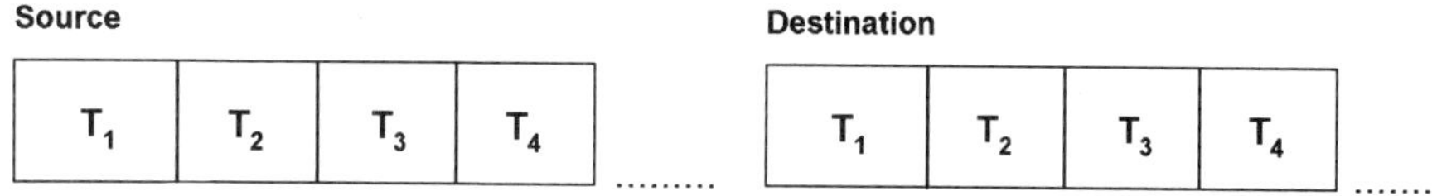

Figure 1-10 In a time-division multiplexed synchronous network (like current E-1/T-1 technology), individual timeslots (channels) are identified by their position in the data stream. T1 will carry the data associated with channel 1.

ATM is not based on position in the data stream. A header identifies whose traffic it is, which also defines where the traffic goes. All ATM traffic is sent on demand, and no bandwidth is wasted on idle channels. There are essentially two types of ATM device (we'll cover all the LANE servers necessary in Chapter 3): a client and a switch. To have an ATM network, you need at least one device that acts as a switch, much the same as a Frame Relay network. Indeed, if you are just trying to understand ATM for the first time, thinking of ATM PVCs as the same as Frame Relay DLCIs is a good start.

Within the ATM network, there are two interfaces of prime importance: the user-to-network interface (UNI) and the network-to-network interface (NNI). These interfaces are depicted in Figure 1-11.

With such a network it is possible to accommodate all traffic types on the one media and finally move away from the dedicated voice, data, and video networks of the present. However, getting all traffic on the one physical path is one thing; to effectively replace all the different types of networks prevalent today, ATM has to accommodate the different types of service delivery each network currently delivers. For example, the telephone network is connection-oriented and sensitive to delay variations, whereas data networks are either connection-oriented or connectionless (meaning they send out data with no knowledge of whether the recipient is available) and relatively insensitive to variations in delay. In addition to differences in tolerance of delay, some networks have to support constant bit rate traffic (like cable TV) and others have to support variable bit rate traffic (like Internet access). The challenge to ATM is to support all these different demands equally well, and the way ATM does this is via the ATM cell.

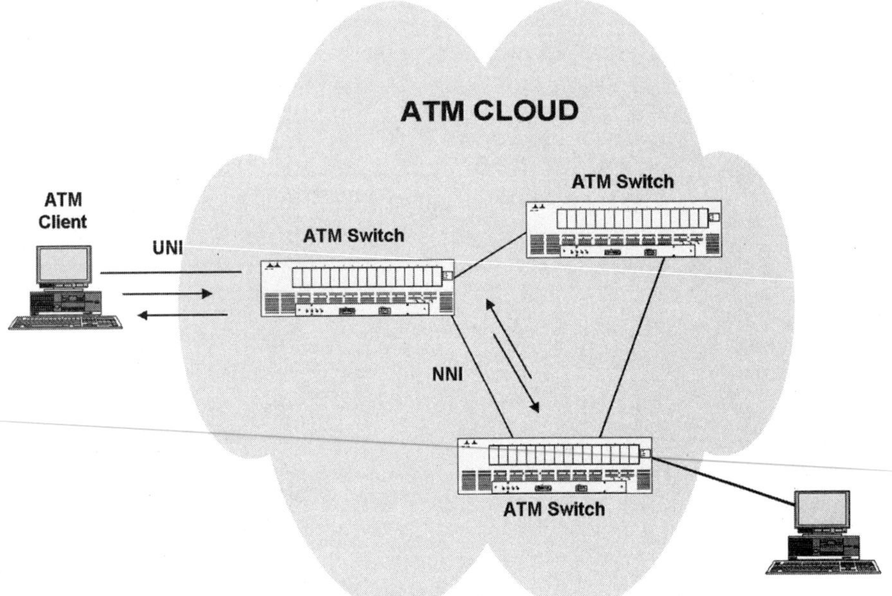

Figure 1-11 The use of UNI between client and switch and NNI between switches.

The ATM Cell

The cell header is defined in Figure 1-12. Before we look at the function of each field, note that the most glaring difference between the header format of ATM and other encapsulations (like Ethernet, IP, or token ring) is that there is no source or destination address. So how does traffic get moved from one location to another? Within an ATM network, all communication is associated with individual connections. These connections are termed *virtual circuits* and in practice are almost exclusively of the switched virtual circuit (SVC) type.

When an ATM device wants to contact another ATM device across an ATM cloud, it will ask the ATM switch it is connected to for a connection identifier that it can use to contact the specified ATM address. The ATM switch will set up the call and assign a call identifier to the virtual circuit associated with the end destination. From that point on, the endstation uses the connection identifier to address packets, not the ATM destination address. The connection identifier is valid for the duration of the call and is then reusable for other calls once the original call is finished. Therefore, the ATM address is only used at call setup time and is not transmitted over the ATM cloud. During data transfer, the ATM addresses are not seen in the traffic stream between source and destination. We'll examine the call setup procedures in more detail in Chapter 3.

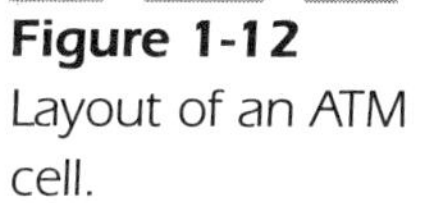
Figure 1-12 Layout of an ATM cell.

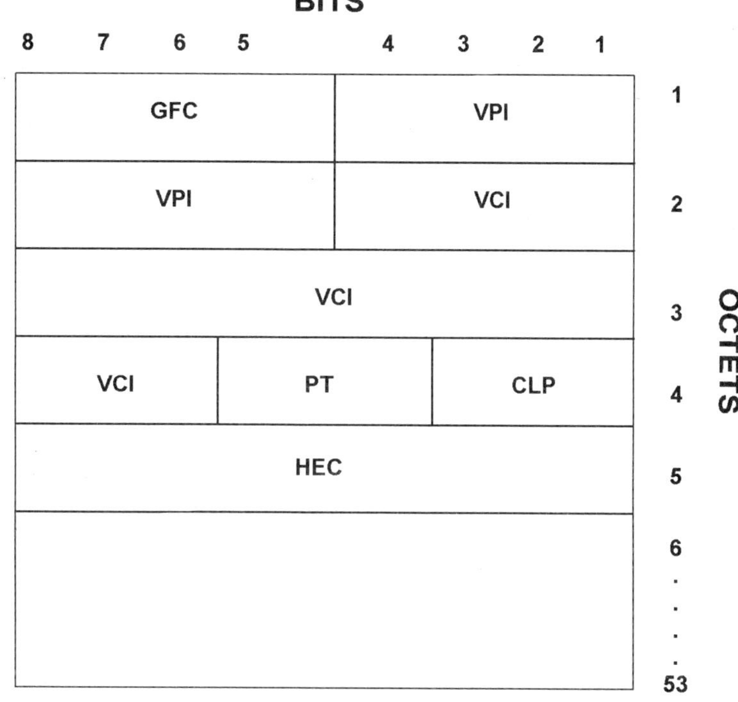

The following is a description of the ATM cell header fields:

GFC The Generic Flow Control field has local significance only, meaning it is used by the device originating the cell and is not understood by receiving devices. At the moment, no specific definition exists for the GFC field.

VCI The Virtual Channel Identifier identifies the virtual circuit that has been established to carry traffic to the required destination. The VCI is actually half of the identifier; the other half is the VPI, which is discussed next. The value has local significance only on the UNI. Each ATM switch will map an incoming VCI to an outgoing VCI through its switching process.

VPI The Virtual Path Identifier is the second half of the definition of a connection in the ATM world. The VPI can be thought of as a superset of VCIs, in that several VCIs can be grouped together and addressed via one VPI. The advantage is that a switching node in an ATM cloud can forward all the VCIs associated with a VPI with one switching decision (this is known as "VP switching").

PT The Payload Type field is of limited value and is used to identify what type of data is being transported.

CLP The Cell Loss Priority can only have values 0 or 1 and indicates the likelihood that a cell will be dropped. This value can be set either by the ATM access device (the client) or an ATM switch. The ATM access device will set the CLP based on the current congestion on the network, and the ATM switch will set the CLP based on the access device's adherence (or lack thereof) to the traffic contract established at call setup time.

HEC The Header Error Check is a value that is calculated based on the first 4 bytes. Single-bit errors in these bytes can be corrected and multiple-bit errors can be detected by this value.

The key differentiation between a cell and an IP packet is that a cell is always fixed length. This may not seem such a big deal, but it is huge. In fact, it is a complete departure from the way things used to be done with pre-ATM protocols. In TCP/IP networking, IP is responsible for fragmentation (at routers) and reassembly (at hosts) of data, which takes place on a hop-by-hop basis. As packets travel through a network, they will be fragmented by routers needing to send them over segments that are incapable of handling such large packets (for example, a packet originated on a token ring can be over 4 Kbytes in size, whereas Ethernet only handles just over 1.5 Kbytes). This is seen as efficient in that no space in the packet is wasted: If you only need to send a small amount of data, a small packet is sent; if you need to send lots of data, large packets are sent. This has the added benefit that with larger packets, the fixed size of the packet header constitutes a smaller protocol overhead in percentage terms.

However, this mode of operation presents significant difficulties to devices that must manage constant bit rates and constant delay services. If a device never knows the size of an incoming packet, it is very difficult to deliver a specific level of service to other traffic also using the device. Essentially, a network device does not know how much resource any given incoming packet will present to either bandwidth or processing requirements.

Having a fixed cell length gets around these problems. Given that a device only receives fixed-format, fixed-length cells, its switching logic can be programmed into fast ASIC hardware that allows the device to forward packets as fast as the connected bandwidth allows. In this mode of operation, the device will know its capabilities in terms of attached bandwidth and be able to commit to specific levels of service for new connections made through it.

Once we acknowledge that having fixed-length cells rather than variable-length packets provides the opportunity for delivering constant bit rate and delay services using a packet switching device (a cell is only a specific form of packet), the question arises of how big should that packet (cell) be? In ATM the answer is 53 bytes, which breaks down in to a 5-byte header and a 48-byte payload—a 10 percent header overhead, but one that is worth it. There are rumors that 48 bytes was a compromise between one camp in the ATM Forum wanting 32 bytes and another wanting 64 bytes for the payload. The arguments are obvious: The smaller the cell, the more that is wasted in header overhead. The larger the cell, the more payload that is potentially wasted each time a partially loaded cell is transmitted. However, there was no disagreement on payload size; the figure of 48 bytes is a statistically derived figure that provides optimum results for carrying voice, data, and video traffic over the one physical network.

ATM Multiplexing

There are two important concepts that we have discussed already that contribute to ATM's ability to provide fixed services to both voice and data systems: the fixed-length cell and the idea of ATM devices transmitting data in an asynchronous fashion on an as-needed basis, rather than having specific streams of data dedicated to specific- and fixed-capacity channels. What pulls this together and enables ATM to work its magic is the way ATM multiplexes data from several logical connections onto one physical network. Before looking at the ATM multiplex model, let's review traditional time-division multiplexing (TDM), the kind that's still in use to supply many services, such as T-1s and E-1s.

Figure 1-13 shows how a traditional TDM device works on the basis of having a fixed-length timeslot allocated to each input channel. This means that several physical connections are multiplexed onto one wire, effectively creating a parallel-to-serial conversion. If B is the only channel with data to transmit, all four timeslots are used, with only timeslot 2 carrying data. The ownership of the data is defined by the position in the data stream. If channel B has more data to transmit, even if no other channels have data to transmit, it must wait its turn in the data stream to come around again.

In contrast, in ATM multiplexing, shown in Figure 1-14, timeslots are assigned to whichever channel needs to transmit. As the timeslot in the data stream no longer identifies which channel the data belongs to, there needs to be some other identification in the timeslot to associate it with a channel. This association is made by the VPI/VCI number in the cell header. Effectively, fixed-length timeslots have been replaced with fixed-length cells, with each cell having the information in it that associates it with a channel.

This mode of operation allows ATM to support both circuit mode and packet mode. Circuit mode is there to support guaranteed bit rate services, enabling an ATM connection to emulate a T-1 type of service. Figure 1-15 shows how an ATM connection supports both fixed and variable bit rate services on the one physical link.

Before we can truly understand how this works, we must first look at how ATM cells are transported over SONET (Synchronous Optical Network), as that is the most common medium for ATM. SONET allocates 8000 timeslots a second, which equates to 125 microseconds to transmit one timeslot (1/8000). For an OC-3 (sometimes referred to as STS-3) circuit, with a potential bandwidth of 155.52 Mbits/sec, each timeslot (confusingly referred to as a "frame" in SONET parlance) fits about 44 ATM cells. Effectively this gives 135.168 Mbits/sec of throughput, calculated as 44 cells per frame, times 8000 frames per second, times 48 bytes of data per cell, times 8 bits per byte. This is interesting, but the point is that ATM over SONET still involves some use of fixed timeslot technology. This is what allows ATM to offer circuit mode operation. To do this, an ATM device will dedicate a specified number of

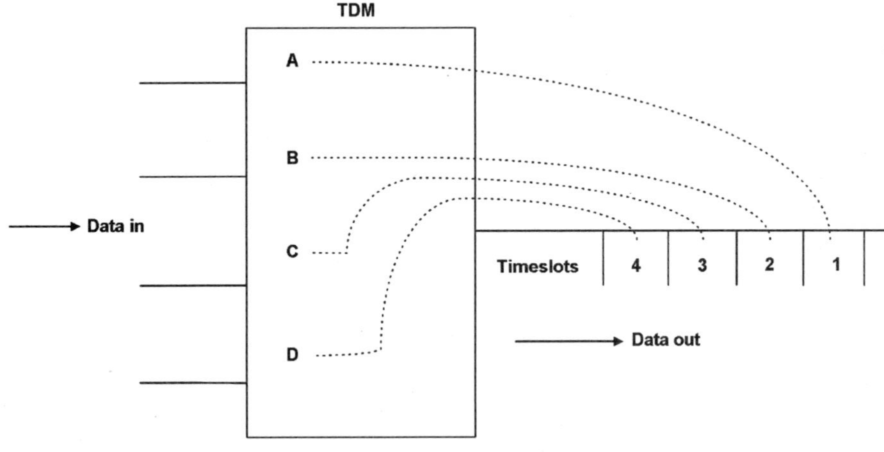

Figure 1-13
TDM takes a parallel input and converts it to a serial output by assigning fixed-length timeslots to channels A, B, C, and D.

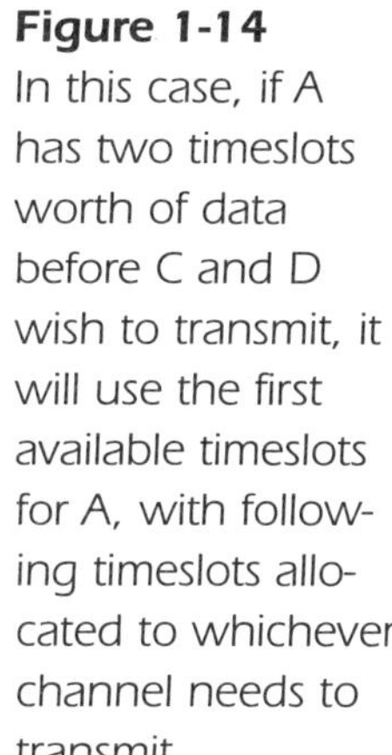

Figure 1-14 In this case, if A has two timeslots worth of data before C and D wish to transmit, it will use the first available timeslots for A, with following timeslots allocated to whichever channel needs to transmit.

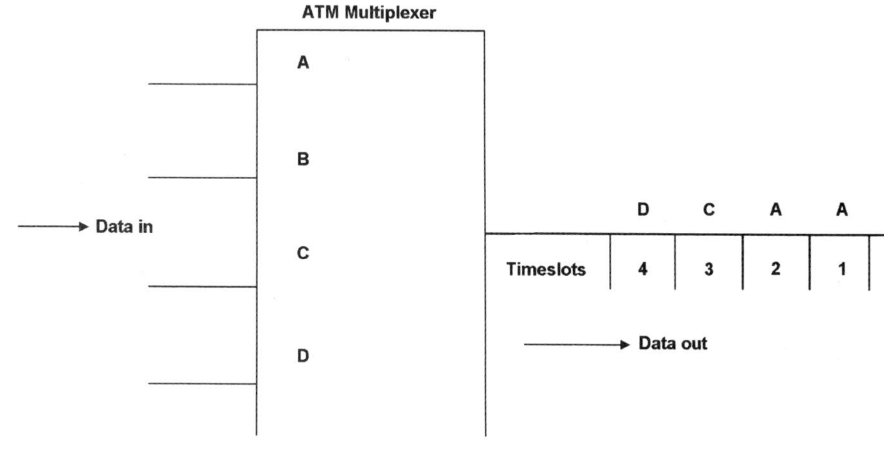

Figure 1-15 ATM supporting both fixed and variable bit rate services on the same connection.

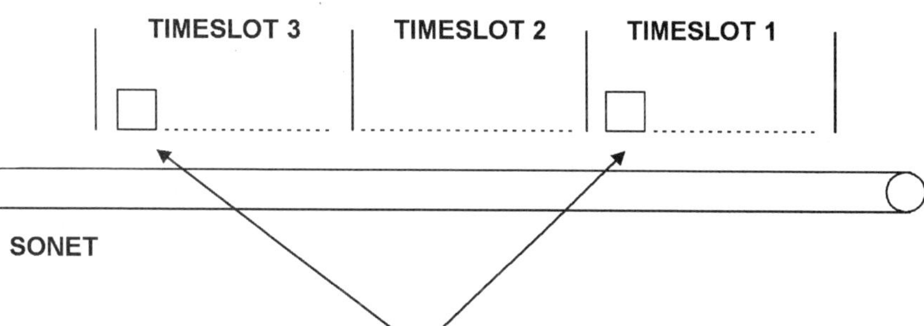

SONET timeslots to the user requesting circuit mode service. Let's look at some simple math that will illustrate how this works. Let's say that a user wants a T-1 circuit-emulated service over ATM running on SONET. We can get 1.536 Mbit/sec by dedicating one cell every other timeslot. This comes to 48 bytes in the ATM cell payload times 8 for the number of bits, which equals 384. Multiplying this by 4000, for the number of cells transmitted per second (half of the 8000 timeslots per second of SONET), yields the 1.536 Mbit/sec. So by committing one cell every other timeslot, the user gets an emulated T-1. Note that as we have 44 cells per timeslot; this is not much of the bandwidth available. The rest of the cells are available for packet mode connections, which will contend for the remaining (and very significant) bandwidth.

The ATM Communications Reference Model

In Chapter 6, we will be looking at Classic IP Over ATM (CIOA), which is one way of utilizing ATM that effectively views ATM as just another data-link layer protocol. This use places ATM and the adaptation layers as shown in Figure 1-16.

In this implementation, cell services are only available (via the adaptation layers) to the network layer; however, the IP layer is still doing all the routing and path selection functions. CIOA does not take full benefit of all ATM's features. Implementations that do take advantage of ATM fully must adhere to a different model. The familiar seven-layer OSI model does not really accommodate the ATM modes of communication, so

Figure 1-16 CIOA model.

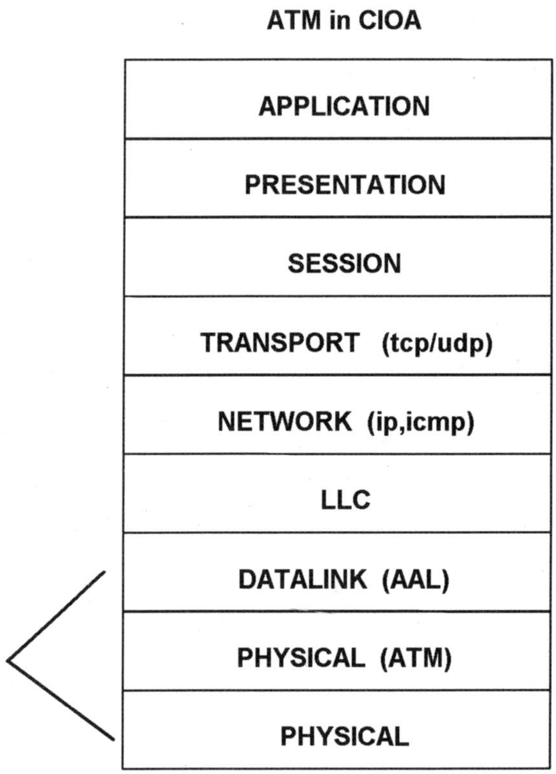

ATM has its own communications reference model, which is actually defined in three dimensions as a cube. This cube is based on the concept of three planes: user, control, and management.

The *user plane* defines flow control, error detection, and correction and transfer of data. The *control plane* defines signaling functions, for example, call setup and termination. The *management plane* is split into two subplanes: plane management and layer management. Plane management is there to arbitrate between two or more entities trying to use the same channel at the same time. Layer management defines how to manage resources and negotiate parameters.

This talk of a reference model operating in three planes might be a bit confusing, at least initially. All it represents is a way of viewing the standards and procedures that go into defining the operation of ATM. The three-dimensional cube is shown in Figure 1-17.

If this model does not make sense, there is no need to worry about it. This book will proceed in a step-by-step fashion to build simple CIOA and other ATM networks, as well as the overly complex LANE networks, without referring once to this "magic" standards cube. The most important thing to recognize at this stage is that the ATM documentation specifies how ATM switches data, signals for connections, transmits bits of data, and manages faults and traffic flow, and how it provides services (such as circuit or packet mode). All of these features are made accessi-

Figure 1-17
The ATM reference cube.

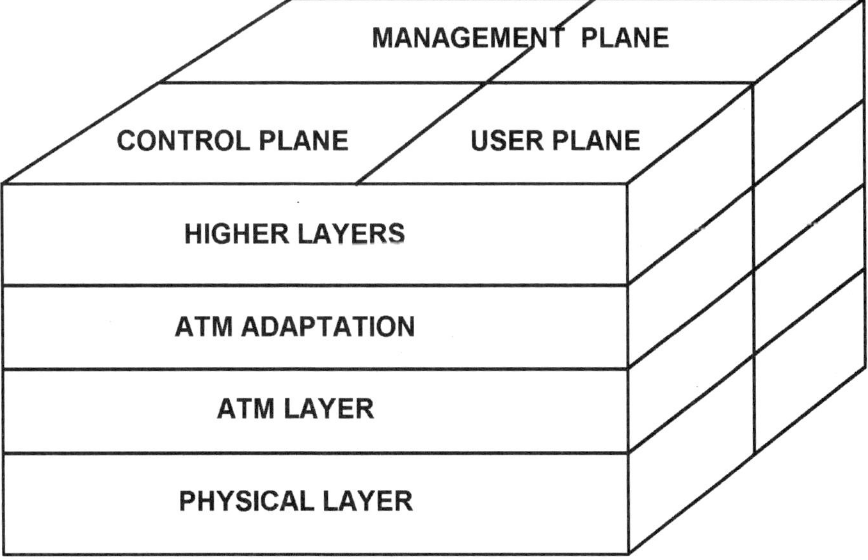

ble to legacy communication methods via the adaptation layers that define how legacy voice and data systems take advantage of cell services.

The ATM Adaptation Layers

The first of these adaptation layers is ATM Adaptation Layer 1 (AAL1), which details how ATM works with traditional time-division multiplexed services, such as T-1 services. AAL3 and 4 were defined for SMDS. With different AALs for different services, it was getting difficult to manage, so AAL5 was defined as the Simple Effective Adaptation Layer (referred to as SEAL) that now covers most interfaces. AAL5 offers lower overhead and therefore better bandwidth utilization at the expense of error recovery (much the same as Ethernet in this respect, as both leave error recovery to a higher layer, like TCP, or the application layer).

The goal of these adaptation layers is to prepare data, coming from upper layers, into 48-byte segmentation and reassembly (SAR) protocol data units (PDUs). As most applications tend to use AAL5, and selecting the AAL is not normally the responsibility of a network engineer, we'll just briefly review the AAL5 operation rather than look at all AAL types.

The operation of AAL with respect to converting upper-layer data to fixed-length cells is illustrated in Figure 1-18.

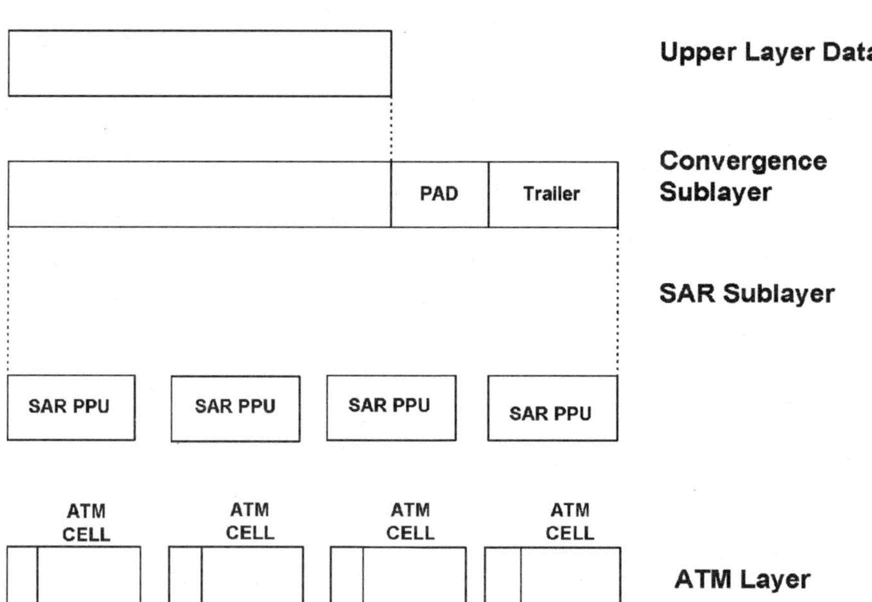

Figure 1-18 Generating ATM cells from upper-layer data rid the SAR and convergence sublayers.

Within the convergence sublayer of the adaptation layer, upper-layer data frames are appended with an 8-byte trailer, which includes payload length, CRC, and between 0 and 47 bytes of padding to ensure that the SAR sublayer will be able to cut up this unit into 48-byte chunks. These 48-byte chunks are passed down to the ATM layer, prepended with the 5 bytes of ATM header, and delivered to the physical layer for transmission onto the network cable. The upper-layer data discussed will typically be an IP datagram, containing IP source and destination addresses, UDP or TCP port numbers, and all the other header information, as well as the actual application data we wish to transmit.

Cisco-Supported ATM Interfaces

Earlier we mentioned the two main interfaces UNI and NNI that are present within an ATM network. To finish this chapter, we'll look at these interfaces in a little more detail and how they are supported on Cisco hardware.

There are two flavors of UNI: one for connecting to private networks and one for connecting to public networks. The UNI is a specification for how an endstation, such as a switch or router, can connect to an ATM switch. The latest version of UNI is 4.0. The endstation-to-switch interface always has two permanent virtual circuits active. (We'll look at how to view these connections on a Cisco endstation in Chapter 6.) The first connection is 0/5 (VPI 0, VCI 5), which is used for signaling—for instance, requesting a VPI/VCI number to use when connecting to a remote ATM address. This connection uses Q.2931 signaling, which is very similar to the Q.931 signaling used in narrowband ISDN connections.

The second PVC is 0/16, which is used for the Integrated Local Management Interface (ILMI). ILMI performs a similar function to the LMI used in Frame Relay, enabling an endstation to obtain configuration and status information from an ATM switch. ILMI is really SNMP under another name (the ATM specifications excel at renaming all kinds of standards). The difference between SNMP and ILMI is that ILMI uses AAL5 as the transfer mechanism, as opposed to UDP and IP as in SNMP. When an endstation connects to an ATM switch, the endstation acts as the SNMP client and the switch as the SNMP server. ILMI MIBs (Management Information Bases) exist in both the endstation and the ATM switch and use an Interface Management Entity (IME) to communicate MIB information between devices. This facility allows for a base level of plug and play for ATM endstations, in that they can be plugged in with no configuration and obtain most of what they need from the ATM switch. These concepts are illustrated in Figure 1-19.

Support for UNI as an endstation is available in the LightStream 1010 (when connecting to a public network), the Catalyst 5000 switch, and both the ATM Interface Processor for 7500 series routers and the ATM Network Processor Module (NPM) for the 4x00 series routers. The LightStream 1010 also supports the UNI function on the network side that endstations connect to.

The NNI also comes in two flavors: plain NNI, which specifies the interface between switches in a public network, and private NNI (PNNI), which describes the interface between switches in a private network. Prior to version 1 of the PNNI being released, this interface was known as the Interim Inter-switch Signaling Protocol (IISP). IISP is really a way of statically configuring ATM routes within an ATM network, whereas PNNI does it dynamically. The LightStream 1010 currently supports PNNI version 1.

On the physical side, Cisco supports ATM transmission rates over various media, as specified in Figure 1-20. Note that this is only a guide; these rates are constantly subject to change by the standards bodies. The most recent information can be obtained from www.atmforum.com.

Although it is likely that in the future all WAN-based ATM traffic will be carried over SONET, there still exists the digital signaling system in

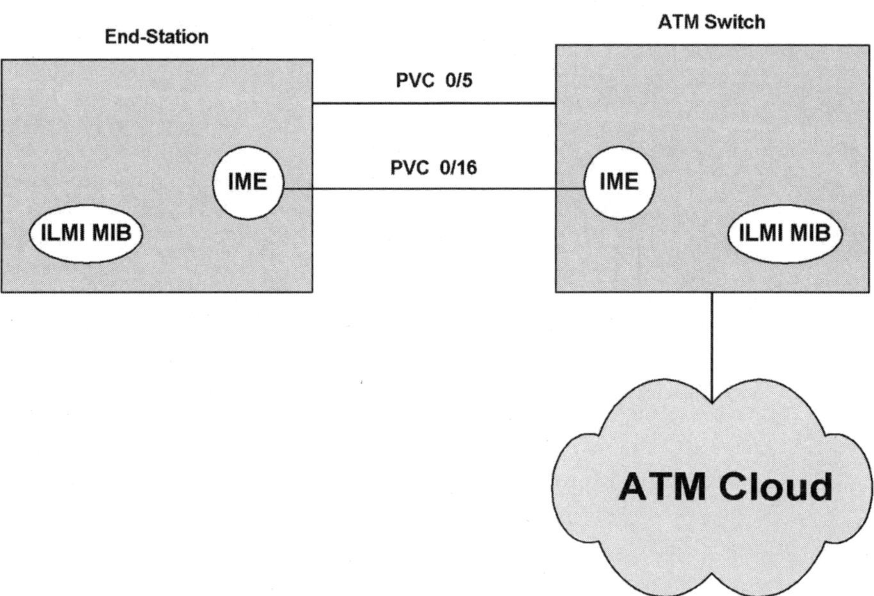

Figure 1-19 ILMI and signaling connections

Figure 1-20
ATM transmission rates.

Transmission Rate	Frame Formats	Media Supported
2.5 Gbit/sec	OC-48	SMF
622 Mbit/sec	STJ-12, OC-12	MMF, SMF
155 Mbit/sec	STS-3c, 8B/10B	MMF, UTP5
100 Mbit/sec	4B/5B	MMF
51.8 Mbit/sec	STS-1, OC-1	UTP-3
45 Mbit/sec	DS3, T-3	TWISTED PAIR
34 Mbit/sec	E-3	COAX
25 Mbit/sec	ATM25	UTP
6.2 Mbit/sec	J2	COAX
2.048 Mbit/sec	E1	TWISTED PAIR, COAX
1.544 Mbit/sec	T1	TWISTED PAIR

use today on T-1 and E-1 circuits. In the same way that DS1 has the same transmission rate as T-1 (DS is the generic term, and T refers to transmission over copper), OC (optical carrier) and STS (Synchronous Transport System) rates are equivalent. OC-3 and STS-3 each have a transmission rate of 155 Mbit/sec. For both OC and STS, the number that follows—for example, 3—is the multiple of 51.84 Mbit/sec that comprises the bandwidth of the link. The key lesson from this figure is that you must be sure the interface framing and the transmission media match between the Cisco equipment and the telco, as well as the transmission rate, before equipment is ordered.

Summary

This chapter provided a brief overview of the operation of traditional repeaters, bridges, and routers, and discussed how these devices altered packets that travel though them. Layer 2, 3, and 4 switches were discussed, and the similarities between switching and routing were identified. The concepts of broadcast and collision domains were introduced, along with the concept of different layers encapsulating data with their own headers.

Spanning tree and VLANs were explained, and the blurring of the differences between current-day switches and routers was discussed. It is now difficult to identify single devices as layer 2 or layer 3 devices, since switches have routing functions and routers perform switching.

ATM was introduced as a connection-oriented protocol that uses fixed-length cells to deliver both constant and variable bit rate and delay services. ATM is asynchronous, as it only transmits data when necessary, uses connection identifiers to route packets in a network, and has an LMI function similar to Frame Relay to autoconfigure endstations.

CHAPTER 2

Switched VLANs

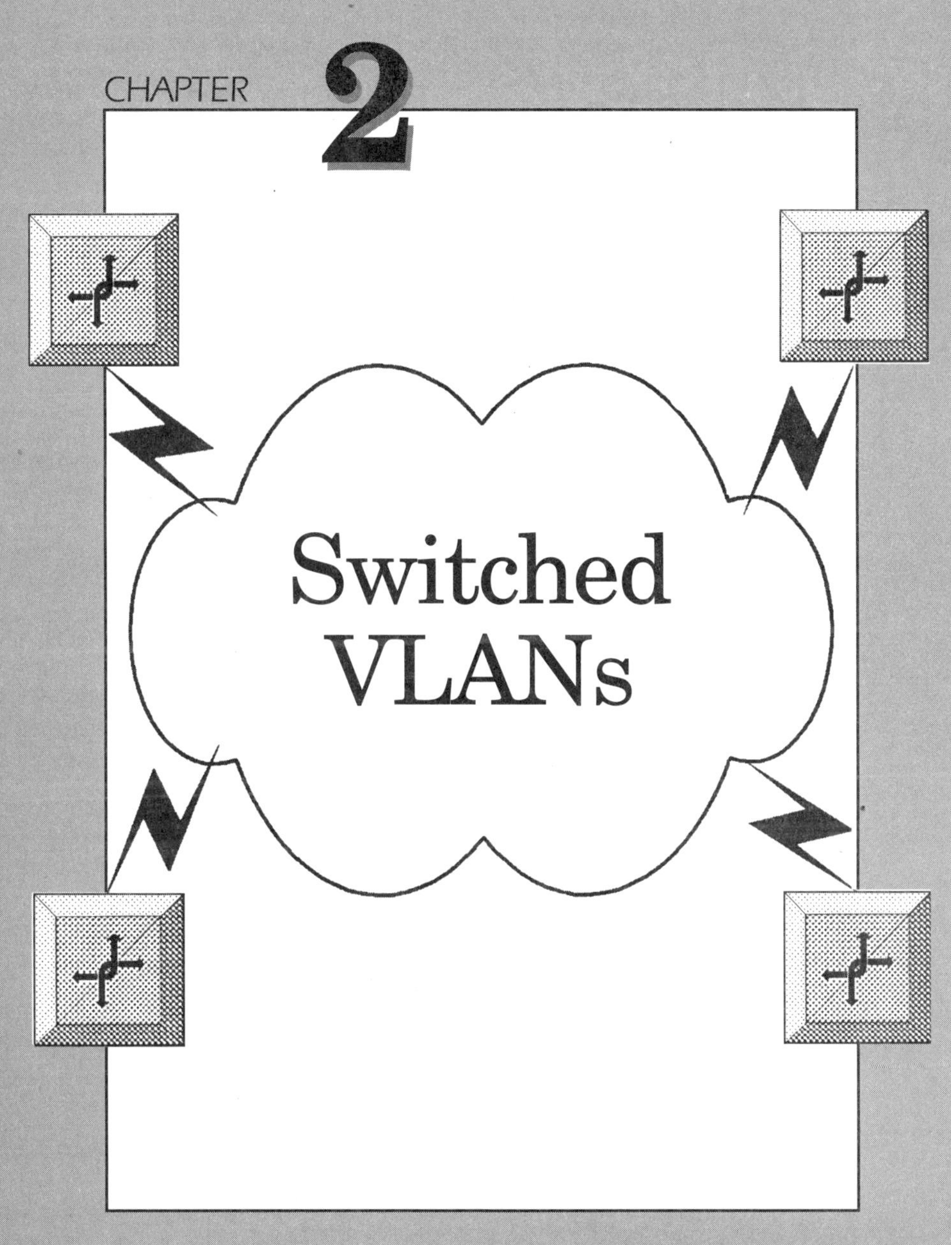

Objectives

In this chapter we'll look at VLANs in more depth. We'll look at the differences between switched VLANs in Ethernet and token ring environments and at trunking VLANs between switches using FDDI and ISL (trunking over ATM is covered later). We'll cover VMPS and VTP, along with how to customize spanning tree. We'll also examine how full duplex can be incorporated into a network and the role that CGMP plays in optimizing multicast capabilities. This chapter forms the theoretical background for the router and switch configurations used in later chapters.

VLAN Environments

Several concepts and technologies have come together to compose the switched VLAN environments we see today. In this section we'll look at multiswitch Ethernet VLANs, full-duplex Ethernet, and token ring in a switched environment.

Multi-VLAN Ethernet Switches

In Chapter 1 we saw that each interface on a switch was a collision domain and each VLAN defined within the switch is a broadcast domain. The question arises of how a switch identifies a packet as belonging to one VLAN or another. The answer is VLAN tagging. Internal to a switch, all packets coming in on an interface are tagged with the VLAN ID of that interface. This VLAN ID is then used within the switch to associate this packet with the VLAN in question. This is clearly of most benefit to incoming broadcast packets that will be confined to the switch interfaces associated with that VLAN. The VLAN ID added to the packet is removed prior to the packet being sent out of the switch to an endstation. The only time a packet leaves a switch with the VLAN ID still appended is when the packet is traversing an interswitch trunk, as shown in Figure 2-1.

The ability of VLANs to segment traffic, localize collisions, and control broadcasts has been discussed. VLANs can also improve security, in that packets sent on the network are not visible to everyone, as is the case in a shared network. It is simple to create a VLAN for users with high security needs; all the packets they send on their VLAN will not appear on

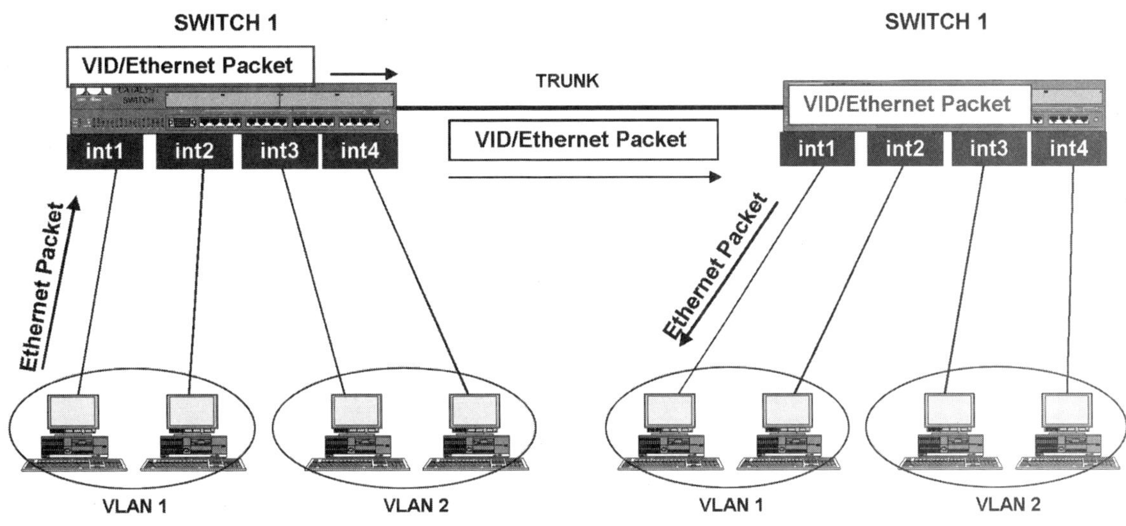

Figure 2-1 The switch-to-switch trunk link carries traffic between switch 1 and 2 with VLAN ID information appended. The VID is the VLAN ID header.

any other segments, making it impossible for other users to capture and decipher their data. With switched Ethernet leading to instances when a switch interface has only one endstation connected to it, changing the half-duplex nature of Ethernet becomes possible. Of course, implementing full duplex only works for interfaces that are dedicated to one endstation, but if that endstation is a server of some kind, significant benefits can arise.

Full-Duplex Ethernet

Full-duplex Ethernet connections use point-to-point cabling, such as you could use between switches or between a switch interface and a single server—no hubs are involved in the process. By definition, *full duplex* means that both ends of the point-to-point link can transmit at the same time; therefore, collisions are completely eliminated in a full-duplex connection. Full-duplex connections can use 10BaseT, 100BaseTX, 100BaseFX, and ATM as the point-to-point link, as illustrated in Figure 2-2.

Within a standard half-duplex Ethernet Network Interface Card (NIC) only the transmit or receive circuitry will be active at any time. For example, when a station is not actively transmitting data onto the

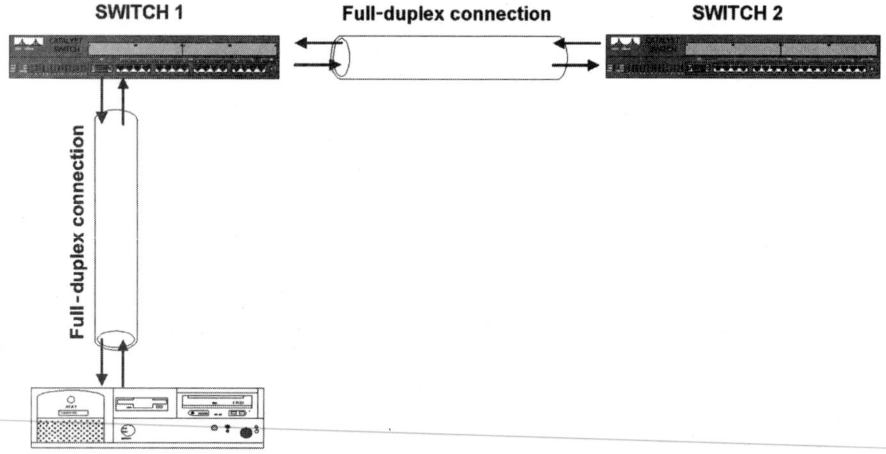

Figure 2-2 Full duplex is only available on point-to-point connections.

network, the receive circuitry is active, performing the carrier sense function of Ethernet. Effectively, both the transmit and receive circuitry share the same logical network cable and can therefore only operate independently of each other. In a full-duplex Ethernet NIC, there is no collision detect circuitry, and the cabling provides a direct path from the transmit circuitry of the NIC at one end of the point-to-point connection, in order to the receive circuitry of the NIC at the other end.

With this arrangement, as shown in Figure 2-3, there is no multiple access possible on the same media as in half-duplex Ethernet. Half duplex normally starts to reach its limit at around 50 percent utilization. Full duplex can happily operate at 100 percent utilization in both directions without significant performance implications.

By now you should have a clear understanding of the theory of switching Ethernet packets, using full-duplex Ethernet, and incorporating VLANs into Ethernet networks. Later chapters will cover how to config-

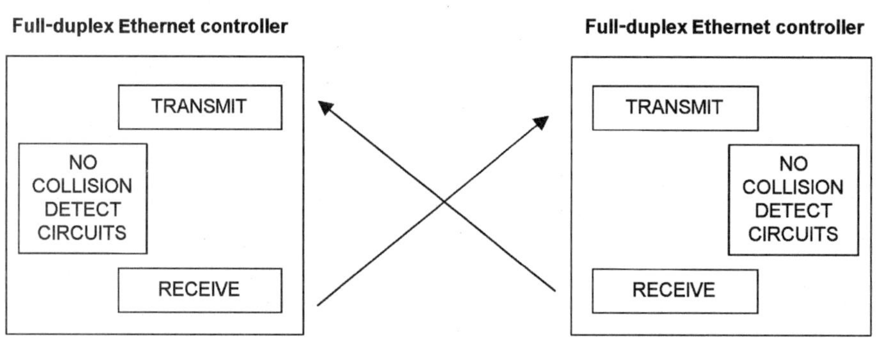

Figure 2-3 Full duplex is point-to-point, with transmit circuitry directly connected to receive circuitry.

ure these features on Cisco hardware. Switched token ring and VLANs for token ring are a whole other story and are covered next.

Switched Token Ring

Token ring refuses to die. Despite all the advances with Ethernet technology and the leadership in market share, there are still a significant number of token ring installations. Indeed, with new advances like switched token ring and token ring at 100 Mbit/sec, along with some of the inherent benefits of token ring's technology, such as its ability to set different priorities, it looks like token ring is here to stay—at least for the immediate future. Let's review some of the basics of traditional token ring operation before we look at the newer features.

Traditional Token Ring Operation Token ring is based on the IEEE 802.5 specification. Although the physical appearance of token ring wiring is that of a star, the physical path is a ring, as illustrated in Figure 2-4. Priority values 0 to 3 are set by the user. Priority value 4 is for bridge transmissions, 5 is for non-real-time multimedia, 6 is for real-time multimedia, and 7 is for critical MAC frames. Switches typically use two priority queues, one high and one low. Commonly, priority 0 to 4 are assigned to the low queue and 5 to 6 to the high queue. Priority 7 frames use the system queue for the highest priority.

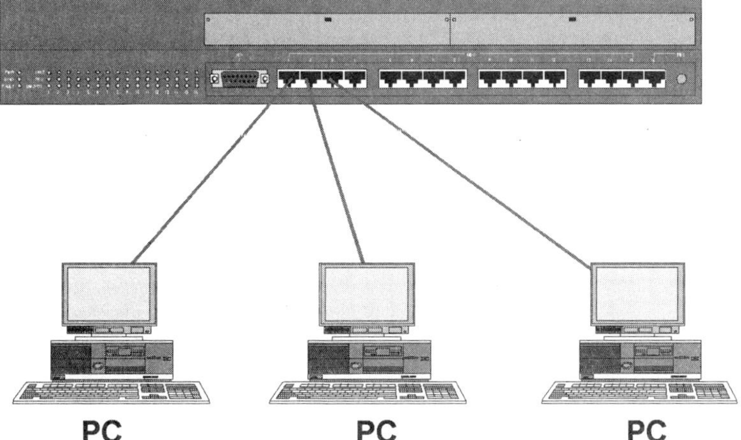

Figure 2-4 Each cable contains out and back cabling, maintaining a ring connection.

On each ring, a continual process of LAN monitor election is in effect. Essentially, every few seconds all stations on a ring will try to determine who should be the LAN monitor. The LAN monitor makes sure that the token is intact and that there are no duplicate tokens, and performs other general housekeeping tasks. The token itself is a packet containing a special bit pattern that each workstation needs to receive before it can transmit onto the network. By this method of passing the token around the ring, token ring networks eliminate collisions. As the token traverses the ring, each station repeats the data, performs error checking, and if the station is the destination, passes the data to the higher-layer protocols within the workstation. When the token gets back to the originating station, the data is removed from the ring and the token is passed on to the next in line. Because the token is necessary to send data on the network, it is possible to alter an individual station's priority so that it gets the token more often than others.

Token ring networks were extended by the use of source route bridges (SRBs) in much the same way Ethernet networks were extended by the use of transparent bridges. SRBs, however, appear to be a standard endstation on the ring to other endstations (as opposed to transparent bridges, which are unseen by other endstations). They forward packets destined for other rings and copy packets from other rings onto the local ring. SRBs end up having similar limitations as transparent bridges in the Ethernet world and experience difficulty when scaling to larger environments and dealing with multimedia applications.

We'll now take a look at how token ring handles source routing. In particular, we'll examine how explorer packets are used to determine routes. This is necessary to understand the benefits of the switched token ring environment and will be useful in later chapters when we discuss ATM's routing, which is based on a form of source routing.

Source Routing The goal of source routing is to generate a packet header containing a route that is inserted by the endstation. That route consists of a sequential list of bridges and LAN segments that form the path from source to destination. The traditional mechanism by which the source determines the route to get to the destination is through the all-routes explorer packet. Assume a source endstation wishes to send a packet to a remote (i.e., located on another segment) destination MAC address of unknown location. First, a local test frame is sent on the local segment, which will be returned, indicating that the destination address is unrecognized. Then the source endstation will send out a single all-routes explorer packet that will be replicated at each potential route choice on every possible path. These explorer packets keep a diary of their travels, and when they reach the destination station, they are returned to the source. The first explorer packet to return to the source endstation has its route information selected, and a cache of discovered routes is kept in the endstation for future reference.

To insert this information in a packet header obviously requires additional fields that are not used when a packet is sent to an endstation on the local segment. The indicator that marks whether this additional information is present is the Routing Information Identifier (RII). The RII is the multicast bit in the source address that is not used in normal circumstances, as nobody ever sends from a multicast address. If an RII is present, a RIF (Routing Information Field) is next, shown in Figure 2-5, which contains the following fields:

- *Type.* 3 bits are used to identify whether the packet already contains routing information, is an all-paths explorer, or is a spanning-tree explorer (sometimes referred to as a single-route explorer).
- *Length.* 5 bits are used to identify the number of bytes in the RIF.
- *Direction.* 1 bit specifies whether the route should be read from left to right or right to left.
- *Largest Frame.* A 3-bit value represents the maximum packet size.
- *Route.* A sequence of 16-bit route designators, split between 12 bits for the LAN number and 4 bits for the bridge number.

In addition to this all-routes broadcast, there is a single-route broadcast, which is also known as the spanning-tree explorer. This mechanism relies on spanning tree to create a loop-free path to all LANs for explorer packets, so that the replication of an all-routes broadcast explorer does not happen.

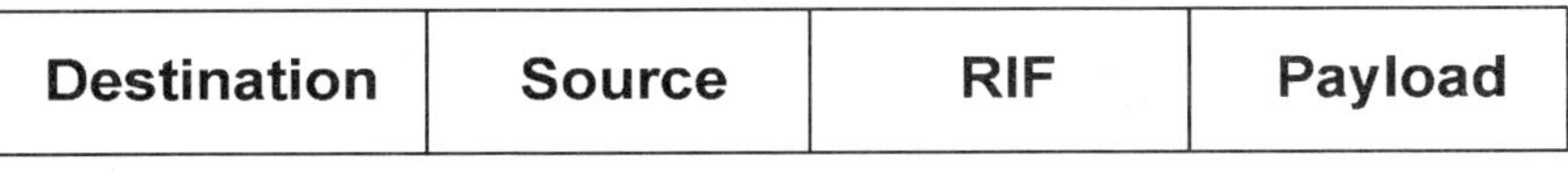

Figure 2-5 Routing information field.

Token Ring Bridge Types Cisco token ring switches support source route bridging (SRB), transparent bridging (TB), and source route transparent (SRT) bridging. Source route bridges operate as described in the previous section, and token ring transparent bridges operate much the same as Ethernet transparent bridges, in that forwarding decisions are based purely on the MAC address (that is, the bridge refers to a station cache to determine which interface to forward the packet to). The source route transparent bridge can operate as either a source route bridge when a RIF is present or as a transparent bridge when no RIF is present.

One problem with the normally desirable SRT bridging is that it does not allow the same MAC address to appear on different rings. At first this may seem a reasonable restriction; however, in an SNA configuration utilizing the load-balancing and fault-tolerant features of 3745 controllers, the lack of duplicate MAC address support is troublesome. The 3745 controller allows all of its interfaces to utilize the same MAC address; this enables multiple source route paths to be defined for the same MAC address, thus providing load balancing and automatic recovery in the event of an interface failure. For this purpose it is preferable to maintain a pure source route environment when IBM controllers are present. However, the issue arises of how to support Ethernet LANs in that environment, as Ethernet frames do not support a RIF. (*Note:* The following discussion is only relevant if you need to bridge Ethernet and token ring together. Routing between Ethernet and token ring does not present these problems; typically, the only time Ethernet and token ring need to be bridged is if nonroutable protocols like NetBIOS need to be supported across both media.)

Source route token ring networks are bridged to Ethernet LANs using source-route translational bridging (SRTLB). We will discuss the operation of this type of bridging with reference to Figure 2-6. In practice, Ethernet segments are assigned a virtual ring number that the source route LANs can use to identify it with. This LAN number only exists within the switch or router being used to connect the two segments (in this case, the Ethernet segment is assigned a token ring LAN number of 100). If a source route packet comes in to the switch or router connecting the token ring and Ethernet, the RIF is terminated in that device and the packet is transparently bridged onto the Ethernet segment.

Besides the adding or deletion of a RIF as packets traverse the Ethernet to token ring boundary, the two other prime reasons for translational bridging are bitswapping and handling of NetBIOS name queries. Bitswapping arises because Ethernet networks transmit bytes

Figure 2-6 Bridging between source routed token ring and an Ethernet network.

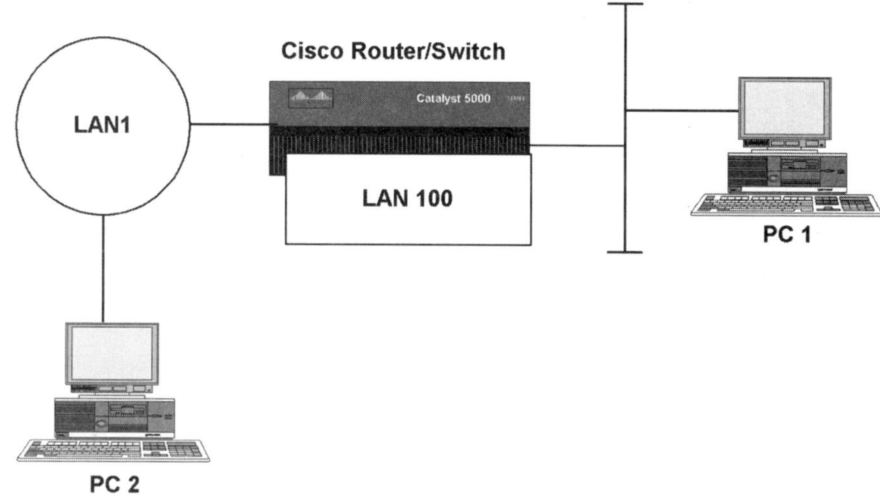

on the wire starting with the least significant bit first (canonical), whereas token ring networks start with the most significant bit (non-canonical). This means the device connecting token ring and Ethernet must reverse the bit order for each byte in sequence. An example with reference to Figure 2-6 is if PC 1 wants to send a packet to PC 2. Supposing PC 2 has a token ring MAC address of 00-00-C0-00-00-02, the router/switch device in this figure must actually tell PC 1 that PC 2 has a MAC address of 00-00-03-00-00-40. This is achieved by converting the address to binary and reversing the order of bits in each byte.

Handling NetBIOS name queries is also difficult. Suppose PC 1 wants to determine the NetBIOS name of PC 2. Within the NetBIOS protocol, this is handled via broadcasts, which in the Ethernet environment are sent to MAC address FF-FF-FF-FF-FF-FF. However, in the token ring environment, PC 2 listens to MAC address C0-00-00-00-00-80 for name queries. To accommodate this, the router/switch must recognize that PC 1 is sending a name query, generate a RIF (if there is additional bridging in the path to PC 2), and change the destination address. Fortunately, most of this is hidden from the configuration details. All that really needs to be completed is to create the pseudo-ring that is identified with the Ethernet LAN, which is done by the `source-bridge transparent` command.

Source Route Switching Source route switching (SRS) can be used to segment an existing token ring in a source route bridge network. SRS

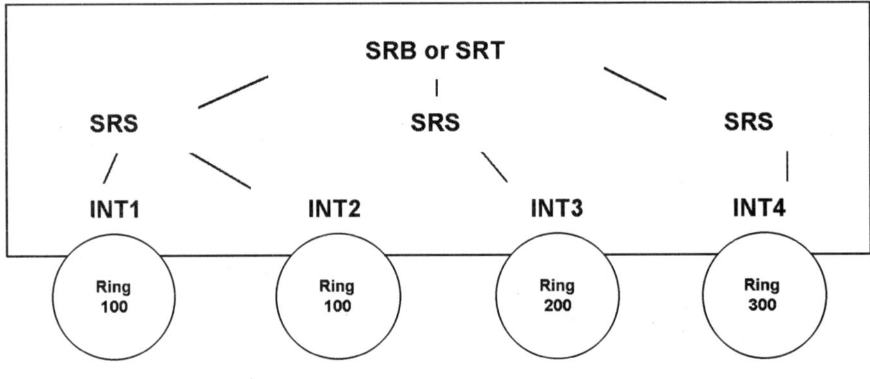

Figure 2-7 Source route switching allows workstations connected to different interfaces to be part of the source ring. Either SRB or SRT can be used to forward packets between rings.

allows several switch interfaces to be configured as part of the same ring number, as illustrated in Figure 2-7.

In this figure the interfaces that are part of the distributed ring (interface 1 and interface 2) use SRS to carry packets between these interfaces, and either SRT or SRB to send packets to other interfaces that are configured for different ring numbers. SRS operates by switching packets based on MAC address, in much the same way as an Ethernet transparent bridge does with a station cache. (Given that this is the way it operates, maybe a better name would be "plain token ring switching," as no source routing is going on. However, we have to live with what we are given.)

Token Ring VLANs In concept, token ring VLANs are the same as Ethernet VLANs: They are a layer 2 broadcast domain. Whereas routers were used to internetwork between different bridged networks (in a bridged network, all stations are on the same IP subnet), switches are used to internetwork between different VLANs. In transparent bridging (as used on Ethernets), there is only one type of broadcast, and therefore only one type of broadcast domain. In token ring there are broadcast types that are confined to a single ring and broadcast types that traverse the entire bridged network. In traditional token ring LANs, individual bridge interfaces identify separate rings. Typically, endstations were connected to multistation access units (MSAUs) that were chained together to form a ring. With this topology, it was simple to see that ring-specific broadcasts did not travel through bridge interfaces.

With the switched token ring VLAN environment, it is a different story. We have seen that with SRS, a single ring can span multiple interfaces on the switch. To see how to accommodate the two broadcast domains present in a token ring VLAN, we encounter the first terms that differentiate a token ring VLAN from an Ethernet VLAN: CRF and BRF. CRF is an IEEE term that stands for concentrator relay function. The IEEE consider the familiar multistation access unit (previously referred to as a MAU, now an MSAU) a concentrator. The CRF is merely a way of identifying interfaces on a switch that should be considered part of the same ring. With reference to Figure 2-7, interface 1 and 2 would be associated with the same CRF, as they are configured for the same ring, number 100. It should be noted, however, that a CRF cannot have physical token ring switch ports directly assigned to it. When configuring the switch, VLAN numbers are assigned to CRF names with the `set vlan` command, and VLANs are associated with physical interfaces via a separate `set vlan` command. Thus, the association between a CRF and a physical interface is a two-step process.

The second token ring–specific VLAN term is a BRF, or bridge relay function. The BRF is used to transport broadcast packets between different rings. In Figure 2-7 the bridge relay function facilitates broadcast communications between interfaces 3 and 4. Both the CRF and BRF are internal functions of the switch. The best way to think of BRF is in the order of the configuration tasks that we will explore in Chapter 5. A BRF is given a VLAN ID number that identifies the bridge (SRB or SRT) that connects all logical rings (CRFs) together. Multiple CRFs end up belonging to the single parent BRF. For a clearer picture of this concept, refer to Figure 2-8. In this figure, CRF 1 groups together interfaces 1, 2, and

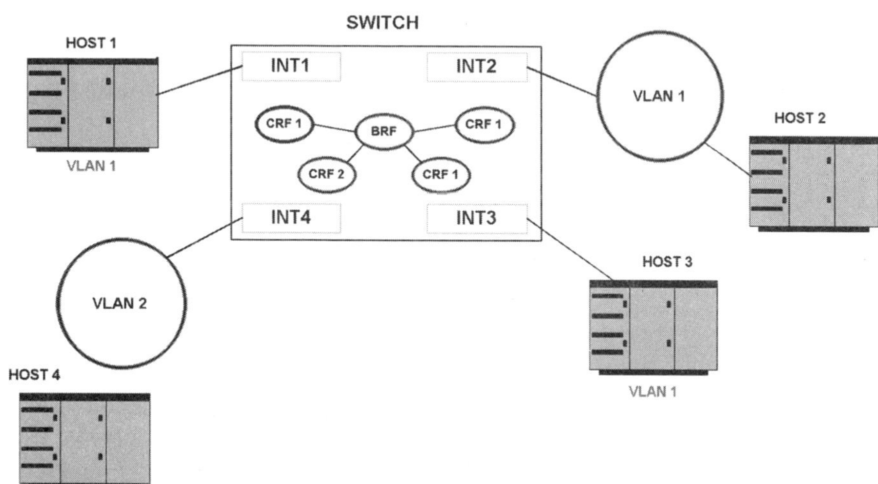

Figure 2-8 Hosts 1, 2, and 3 are in the same VLAN and use the same CRF. If they are the same ring number, they will use SRS to switch packets between interfaces.

3, and the BRF is used to communicate between these interfaces to interface 4, which is part of CRF 2.

In summary, a CRF identifies an interface, or a group of interfaces, that belongs to the one ring. Within a CRF, SRS is used to switch packets between interfaces. Multiple CRFs are connected with one BRF that uses either SRB or SRT to forward packets between CRFs.

Dedicated Token Ring Just as shared hubs in the Ethernet world are half-duplex devices, so too are token ring adapters that connect to MSAUs. Similarly, with regard to switching, Ethernet can support full-duplex communication for endstations connected directly to switch ports. Token ring can also support full duplex in the same configuration. The traditional operation of token ring adapters involves a passing of the token from NIC to NIC around the ring; this is sometimes referred to as TKP (token passing). Dedicated Token Ring (DTR) is specified in a new IEEE standard, 802.5r. This standard defines how a switch interface can look like a concentrator (MSAU) port to an endstation NIC. Also, the DTR specification defines a new method of communication that bypasses the need for a token to be passed between endstations, which is known as Transmit Immediate (TXI). With TXI in effect, the switch-to-endstation communication is full duplex, enabling the switch interface and endstation NIC to transmit simultaneously. DTR with TXI is really only appropriate for server connections in a token ring environment, much the same as full-duplex Ethernet.

An interesting question though is whether a point-to-point connection with TXI is really a token ring, since there is no token and no ring. I don't really know—maybe, if that link can be part of a source route scheme. The real point is that the traditional distinctions between all classes of network technology are blurring and becoming less meaningful.

VLAN Trunking

VLAN trunking describes how switch-to-switch traffic can be encapsulated to support multiple VLAN traffic being transported over the one switch interface. This is useful when you have more than one Catalyst in a switched network and want to have interfaces on different Catalysts as part of the same VLAN. The most important encapsulation that supports multiple VLANs over the one segment, at least from the Cisco point of view, is the Inter-Switch Link (ISL) protocol. Both 802.10 FDDI and

LANE across ATM can be used to transport VLANs through a backbone, as well as ISL on Fast Ethernet.

ISL

ISL is currently private to Cisco, but in many ways, it is similar to the 802.1q specification. Deploying ISL on a server requires an ISL-aware NIC. This is a good idea to implement, as it enables multiple VLANs to communicate with a server directly via a switch interface without recourse to a router interface. For example, Figure 2-9, assuming the server is equipped with an ISL-capable NIC, packets from multiple VLANs will be sent directly to the server by the Catalyst.

The key enabler for this technology is the VLAN ID in the ISL header. A different encapsulation is required for this facility, since adding a VLAN ID to an already maximally sized Ethernet packet would cause devices to recognize the packet as a giant (i.e., an oversized packet) and discard it. For this reason, the VLAN IDs inserted by switches are removed prior to transmission onto non-ISL links. The ISL frame format is shown in Figures 2-10 and 2-11.

Although the ISL specification allows an ISL frame payload (identified as the "encapsulated frame" in Figure 2-10) to be up to 24.5 Kbytes, the maximum packet size is currently never reached. ISL currently encapsulates Ethernet, FDDI, or token ring frames, and the size of the payload is limited by the maximum packet size of each of these technologies. The ISL frame encapsulation is 30 bytes, split between the 26-byte header and the 4-byte CRC. Of the technologies encapsulated within ISL, FDDI has the minimum packet size, set at 17 bytes; therefore, the minimum ISL encapsulated packet is 47 bytes. Token ring now has a theoretical

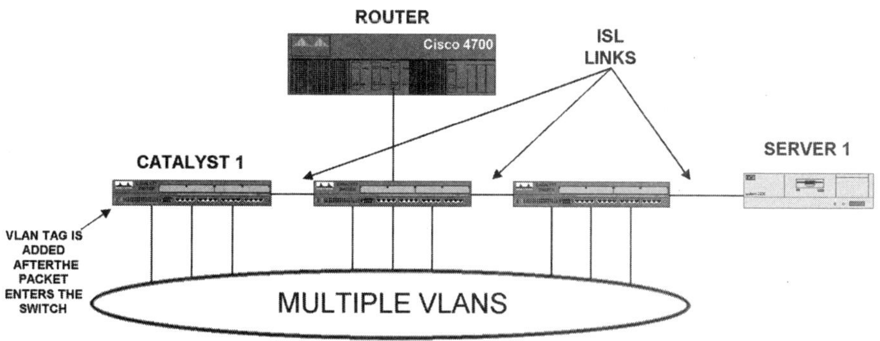

Figure 2-9 ISL enables traffic from all VLANs to travel directly to the server, without having to go to the router for routing between subnets.

ISL HEADER	ENCAPSULATED FRAME	CRC

Figure 2-10 The ISL packets encapsulate Ethernet frames with an ISL header and CRC for transmission over an ISL trunk.

DA	TYPE	USER	SA	LEN	AAAA03	HSA	VLAN	BPPU	INDEX	RES	PAYLOAD

Figure 2-11 ISL header in detail.

maximum packet size of 18,000 bytes, yielding a maximum ISL packet size of 18,030 bytes.

Multiple frames are not encapsulated within the one ISL packet at the moment. If at some point in the future multiple frames could be encapsulated together, they would have to be destined for the same VLAN, as there is only one VLAN identifier in the ISL header.

The following describes the individual fields within the ISL header:

- *DA—Destination address.* The DA field of the ISL packet is always set to the same 40-bit address. This address is a multicast address and is currently set to be 01-00-0C-00-00. This indicates to the receiver that the packet is in ISL format.
- *TYPE—Frame type.* The TYPE field value indicates the type of frame that is encapsulated. The values currently defined are 0000 for Ethernet, 0001 for token ring, 0010 for FDDI, and 0011 for ATM.
- *USER—User defined bits.* The USER bits are there as an extension of the TYPE field and usually have a value of 0000, which is the default. For Ethernet frames, two USER field values have been defined, which are 0 and 1. These indicate the priority of the packet as it passes through the switch.
- *SA—Source address.* The SA field is the source address field of the ISL packet and contains a 48-bit MAC address of the switch interface transmitting the frame. As ISL is a point-to-point link, the receiving device may ignore the SA field of the frame.
- *LEN—Length.* The LEN field represents the packet size in bytes, excluding the DA, T, U, SA, LEN, and CRC fields. It is stored as a 16-bit value.

- *AAAA03.* The AAAA03 field is an 18-bit constant value of AAAA03.
- *HSA—High bits of source address.* The HSA field is the upper 3 bytes, the manufacturer's ID portion, of the MAC source address. It must contain the Cisco prefix 00-00-0C.
- *VLAN—Virtual LAN ID.* The VLAN field is the virtual LAN ID of the packet, which identifies the VLAN membership of the encapsulated packet.
- *BPDU.* The BPDU referred to here is the BPDU used by spanning tree; the bit is set if the encapsulated packet is of this type.
- *INDX.* The INDX field is used for diagnostic purposes only and may be set to any value by other devices. It is a 16-bit value and is ignored in received packets.
- *RES.* The RES field is used to accommodate specific fields in token ring or FDDI packets that are not present in Ethernet (in which case the field is all zeroes). When token ring packets are encapsulated with an ISL packet, the AC and FC values appear here. For FDDI packets, this field contains the content of the FC field.
- *Payload.* Payload is the encapsulated frame, including its own CRC value, completely unmodified. The internal frame must have a CRC value that is valid once the ISL encapsulation fields are removed. The payload can, in theory, vary from 1 to 24.5 Kbytes. Once a switch receives an ISL frame, the ISL header is stripped off, and the payload is associated with the VLAN in question on the receiving switch. It is possible that the payload may be reencapsulated in ISL for transport on to another switch, if the VLAN exists there.
- *CRC.* The CRC is a standard 32-bit CRC (cyclical redundancy check) value calculated on the entire encapsulated frame, including the payload. The receiving switch will check this CRC and can discard packets that do not have a valid CRC on them. Note that this CRC is in addition to the one at the end of the payload data.

VLAN Trunk Protocol

The VLAN Trunk Protocol (VTP) is used to distribute VLAN information to switches across connecting trunks. In concept, it is like a routing protocol that advertises VLANs and provides reachability information across the interswitch connections. VTP-enabled switches send summary advertisements every 300 seconds to VLAN1 (the default management domain), only on trunk interfaces. The advertisement contains a configuration revision number (starting at 0 and incrementing by one each time), a list of the VLANs this switch knows about, and some configuration information for each VLAN. The advertisements are sent to a multicast address so that all neighboring switches receive them; however, they are not forwarded by switches. Routers, unless they are configured for bridging, will ignore these advertisements.

The prime benefit of this protocol is that all switches within the same management domain learn about new VLANs created on the switch sending the VTP advertisements. Additionally, as VLAN configuration only has to be entered once, you get the benefit of no retyping errors. Once VTP is operational within a switched network, new switches can be brought online with a minimal VTP configuration and can learn about the VLAN configuration of the network via VTP, thus reducing the configuration work necessary.

When we show how to configure VTP in Chapter 5, we'll show the configuration of all Catalysts in the switched network as the server for VTP. It is possible to configure one Catalyst as the server and others as clients; however, Catalysts configured as VTP clients can lose their VTP configuration when power-cycled. This is because VTP servers keep their configuration in nonvolatile memory or can access it across the network via TFTP when required.

Even with VTP configured for each Catalyst, it is still necessary to configure the VLAN membership for individual interfaces on each Catalyst. Through VTP, each Catalyst will know about the VLANs that exist and the Catalysts they are on, but not the individual interface membership within a Catalyst.

We have already mentioned management domains in passing, but we need to define exactly what this means. The management domain is set by using the `set vtp` command, which establishes (among other things) the management domain name and the VTP operation as client or server. A *management domain* is a collection of VLAN numbers that are all configured for the same domain name. Several VLAN domains can exist within a network and can be thought of as equivalent to separate routing domains in a routed network; however, a switch can only be in one domain at a time.

VTP Pruning It is possible to optimize VTP by enabling pruning on certain interfaces within the domain. Cisco switches have single-colored interfaces, meaning that each interface only belongs to one VLAN. This makes the management of broadcasts within VLANs on a single switch effective, as broadcasts for one VLAN are not forwarded out of an interface belonging to another VLAN. But what about multicolored ports used as VLAN trunks between switches? They carry traffic for multiple VLANs, as shown in Figure 2-12.

Without VTP pruning, broadcast information will be sent for both the red and green VLANs to switch 2, which will forward that on to switch 3 via the trunk link. As switch 3 only has red VLAN interfaces defined, it will drop the broadcasts belonging to the green VLAN. This, however, has wasted bandwidth on the switch 2-to-switch 3 trunk. It is possible to stop this wasting of bandwidth by pruning the green VLAN traffic at the switch 2 trunk connection that leads to switch 3.

To enable this type of facility, each trunk interface keeps the status of a variable on a per-VLAN basis. This variable can either be in the joined state, indicating the interface will send broadcast and other flooded frames for the VLAN, or the status will be pruned, in which case the interface will not send broadcasts (other than STP, CDP, and VTP packets) originating from that VLAN.

VLAN Membership Policy Server

VLAN Membership Policy Server (VMPS) is a mechanism that allows a new endstation to be introduced to the network and for it to be automatically configured to a specific VLAN. This is done by reference to a VMPS database that lists MAC address-to-VLAN membership. This list of associations is really a text file that resides on the VMPS. The process is initiated when an interface on a switch is configured as dynamic. The only real restriction in the network design when using VMPS is that VMPS servers and clients must be configured for the same management VLAN

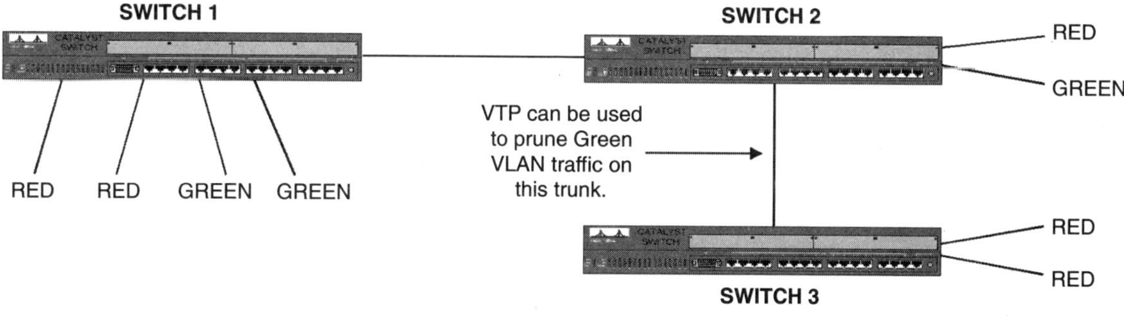

Figure 2-12 Network illustration of VTP pruning.

and that security features are limited on interfaces that want dynamic VLAN assignment.

The configuration commands to set up VMPS vary from switch to switch, but generically they must include the following configuration:

- Define an IP address for a TFTP server and a filename for the VMPS database that resides on that TFTP server
- Enable VMPS for the switch being configured
- Define the interfaces that will be obtaining their VLAN membership dynamically

VMPS has some attractions for a centrally managed network, although it does require some work to set up initially. The trade-off is with VMPS; all you need do is add MAC-to-VLAN membership entries on a central text file database to bring a new device online. Without VMPS, each interface on the network needs to be assigned to its VLAN by logging in to that switch and configuring the interface manually. Of course, typing MAC addresses by hand is a problem and needs alteration if the device gets a new NIC. We'll look at this more in Chapter 5.

FDDI VLANs

FDDI (Fiber Distributed Data Interface) has been around for many years and has become a popular LAN backbone technology, with its ability to supply 100-Mbit/sec bandwidth before 100-Mbit/sec Ethernet was available. FDDI is defined by ANSI X3T9.5 and is implemented as a token-passing network. Specifically, FDDI has two simultaneously counter-rotating tokens, each operating at 100 Mbit/sec to provide redundancy. FDDI implemented on multimode fiber-optic cable can span a distance of 2 kilometers between endstations, with single mode fiber capable of supporting links up to 32 kilometers between endstations.

CDDI (Copper Distributed Data Interface) uses the same protocols as FDDI but is implemented on copper cables and has become popular as a way of providing 100-Mbit/sec throughput with STP or UTP cables, for distances of up to 100 meters.

At the time that FDDI was put together, it was very expensive to support circuitry that would generate a 200-MHz clock signal to support 100-Mbit/sec throughput (with the type of Manchester encoding used by Ethernet and token ring, there are two clock transitions for every bit of data). To avoid the cost of 200-MHz circuitry, the FDDI designers went with 5-bit encoding of 4-bit data. This all comes about through having to maintain synchronization between endstations when transmitting a constant stream of 0s or 1s. With Manchester encoding, voltage transitions, rather than voltage levels, represent data. This assures that even if a constant stream of 0s or 1s is transmitted, there are always transitions occurring in the data stream to maintain synchronization. With 5-bit encoding of 4-bit data, it is possible to assign 5 bits for each 4 bits of data and maintain transitions within the data stream even when continuously sending 0s. By this mechanism, it is possible to have circuitry running at 125 MHz that supports throughput of 100 Mbit/sec.

Interestingly, ATM shows its roots in being designed for optical networks for delivering 25-Mbit/sec ATM to the desktop over token ring cabling. Token ring cables support 16-Mbit/sec throughput, which with Manchester encoding requires a clock speed of 32 MHz. Therefore, if we use 5-bit encoding of 4-bit data, we can get an effective data rate of four-fifths of 32 Mbit/sec, which yields 25.6 Mbit/sec, the speed at which ATM to the desktop operates.

Encapsulating or Translational Bridging

The method of getting packets across a FDDI backbone to Ethernet networks is usually implemented via routing between the two topologies. However, when we come to look at mapping Ethernet VLANs across a FDDI backbone, we have to look at some form of bridging to allow the two Ethernet segments connected via FDDI to belong to the same subnet. This is necessary, since the same subnet cannot appear at two physical locations within a network because it would confuse the routing tables.

Ethernet and FDDI frame types are different, so there are two ways of bridging Ethernet to FDDI: by translating the packet information or by encapsulating Ethernet frames within FDDI frames. Translational operation (in accordance with IEEE 802.1H) is the default and does introduce more latency because of the translation process, which can become a concern particularly for connection-oriented protocols. Currently, however, a Cisco switch using the encapsulation method is only compatible with another Cisco switch and limits the interoperability of devices on your network. With FDDI interfaces, there are multiple encapsulation types available, just as there are for Ethernet. Examples include `encapsulation snap` for 802.2 mode and `encapsulation snap` for subnetwork access protocol operation, which happens to be the default. The interface command `fddi encapsulate` changes the mode of bridging from the default translational to encapsulation.

APaRT and fddicheck

An important part of translational bridging is Automated Packet Recognition and Translation (APaRT). APaRT uses a lookup table (referred to as a CAM for content addressable memory) that maps a specific layer 2 frame type, such as Ethernet II or Subnetwork Access Protocol (SNAP) to a MAC source address. An FDDI module can be configured to use this feature with the `set bridge` command.

Another feature of the FDDI module on Cisco switches is the `fddicheck` command. This feature is available to counter the operation of some older FDDI devices that do not conform to the most recent specifications. What should happen is that an FDDI interface should wait until it receives a token before transmitting onto the fiber cable. The specifications also state that two frames marked as void frames should be sent immediately after any data frame is sent. Because the FDDI interface maintains possession of the token until it receives one of the void frames it sent following the data frame, it does not expect to see any other endstation use the FDDI ring. If any other packets are seen on the ring while the interface holds the token, they are stripped off the ring. However, problems occur if another station erroneously sends a void frame on to the ring without possession of the token.

Consider Figure 2-13. Let's say station 1 on the Ethernet needs to send a packet via the FDDI ring, which is delivering backbone service. First, the switch receives the packet, and when int 1 on the switch receives the FDDI token, it sends the packet received from station 1. Then the two void frames

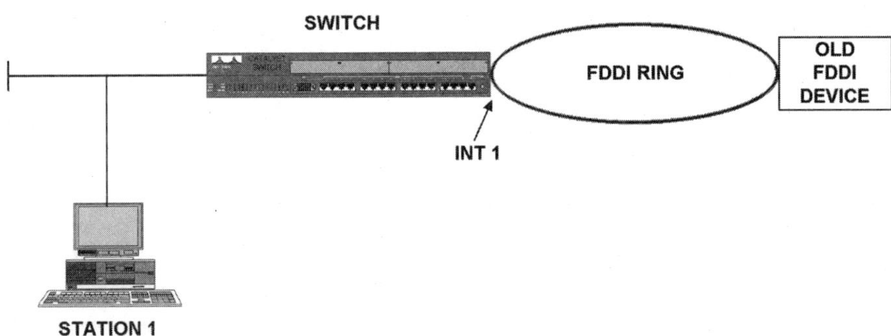

Figure 2-13 Network configuration where `fddicheck` is required.

as before. In normal operation, the sent packet will travel the FDDI ring and return to int 1, which will then remove the packet from the ring. The void frames are then received by int 1, which then takes these frames as the signal to stop removing frames from the ring.

Problems occur if the old FDDI device sends void frames without having possession of the token. This is particularly problematic if these erroneous void frames are sent out before the switch int 1 interface has removed its packet from the ring. In Figure 2-13, station 1 sends a packet destined for a device on the other side of the FDDI ring to the switch. The switch will insert an entry in its CAM listing the source address and the frame type (in this case, the MAC address of station 1 and a frame type of 802.3). Assuming the switch is performing translational bridging, it forwards the frame on to the FDDI ring with the Ethernet address of station 1 as the source. If the old FDDI device now sends a void frame before this packet returns to int 1 on the switch, the switch will take this as a signal to stop removing packets from the network. Therefore, when the packet int 1 did send on the ring returns, it will be forwarded on again instead of being removed. Without `fddicheck`, the situation gets even worse, since the packet appears to have originated on the FDDI ring, the CAM on the switch is now updated with the source address of station 1. So the result is loss of connectivity and loss of bandwidth due to continually circulating packets on the FDDI ring.

What `fddicheck` does to prevent this happening is to check the source address of all incoming packets against the CAM before the CAM is updated. If a packet coming into the FDDI side of the switch has a source MAC address that has already been associated with the Ethernet side of the switch, the CAM will not be updated and connectivity is maintained.

Since `fddicheck` uses the CAM, APaRT must be enabled for `fddicheck` to be enabled.

802.10 VLAN Tagging

In the section on VLAN trunking we said we could use ISL, FDDI, or ATM links as trunks. To enable FDDI to be used as a VLAN trunk, we must implement 802.10 frame tagging.

802.10 is now implemented as an open standard that enables LAN traffic to carry a VLAN identifier. 802.10 was originally conceived to improve security on shared LANs, providing encryption and authentication features. As a layer 2 protocol, 802.10 is suitable for use in switched

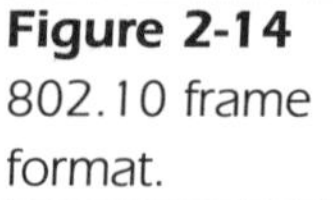

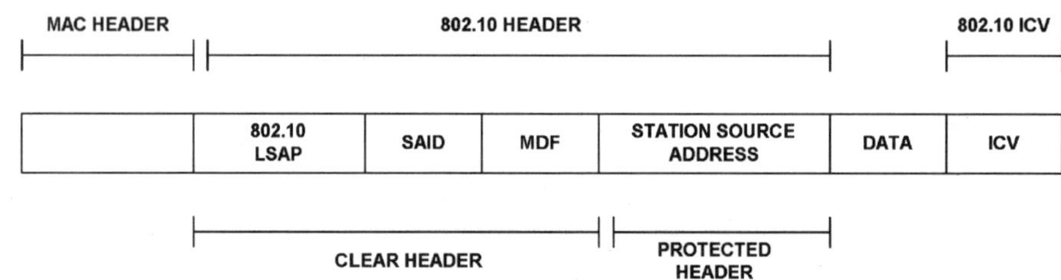

Figure 2-14 802.10 frame format.

LANs and enables fast switching of frames by layer 2 addressing. This standard is implemented by the 802.10 header appearing after the MAC header but before the frame's data, as illustrated in Figure 2-14.

The frame format shown in Figure 2-14 is referred to as a Secure Data Exchange unit (SDE) and is the encapsulation type that needs to be configured on an FDDI interface to enable 802.10 frame tagging. The 802.10 header is split into clear and protected sections. The clear header comprises the 802.10 LSAP, which identifies the frame as an 802.10 VLAN frame; the SAID (Secure Association Identifier), which provides the VLAN ID; and, optionally, the MDF (Management Defined Field). The protected header is a copy of the source address for validation purposes, in order to ensure that the frame is from the advertised source address. The ICV (Integral Check Value) is a secure form of FCS; it enables a receiving station to check that the data contained in the packet has not been modified in transit. When using 802.10 to facilitate VLAN frame tagging, switches must minimally support the clear header portion.

In an environment where a VLAN is distributed between two switches that are interconnected via an FDDI ring, as in Figure 2-15, the switches maintain a VLAN-to-SAID association.

In this setup, if an Ethernet endstation on VLAN 1 is connected to switch 1, which wants to send to an endstation on switch 2, VLAN 1, it will want to send the normal 802.3 frame on to the Ethernet.

When the packet reaches switch 1, an 802.10 header is appended for transporting the frame over the FDDI ring. Once switch 2 gets this packet, with the appended header, it examines the SAID to see if it is destined for one of its VLANs. If it is, the frame has the 802.10 header removed and the frame is forwarded to the appropriate VLAN interfaces; otherwise, the frame is dropped.

This association between VLAN and SAID number is defined using the `set vlan` command, which we will examine further in Chapter 5. However, VTP does advertise these VLAN mappings.

It should be noted that there is no direct relationship between a VLAN number and a SAID number. They can be selected independently of each

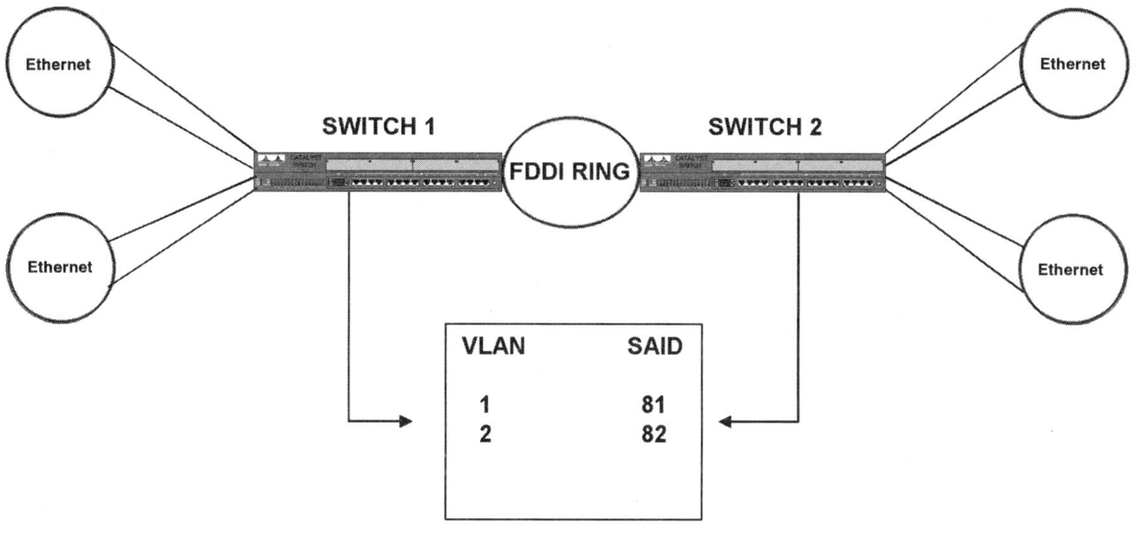

Figure 2-15 Both switches maintain a VLAN-to-SAID association.

other, and any VLAN value (up to 1000) can map to any SAID number (up to 4.29 billion). One implementation issue that should be considered here is that when multiple VLANs are mapped across a backbone FDDI, it is advantageous that a separate instance of the Spanning Tree Protocol runs for each VLAN. This makes better use of the available links, as the paths that each spanning tree will take through the network can be customized so that different VLANs use different trunk connections, thus maximizing the available bandwidth.

Spanning Tree Optimization

Spanning Tree Protocol (STP), as incorporated in the 802.1D standard, is a necessary part of providing loop-free paths in a bridged network. The benefit of STP is that it allows bridged networks to continue functioning with multiple physical paths between LANs. The downside is that STP does not load-balance between equal paths, and in a large environment, it is slow to converge to a new path after a link failure.

It is possible to optimize STP operation, but before we discuss the options, we should first recap some of the terms that will be used, with reference to Figure 2-16. The root bridge is elected according to the bridge ID value. On the root bridge, all interfaces are placed in the for-

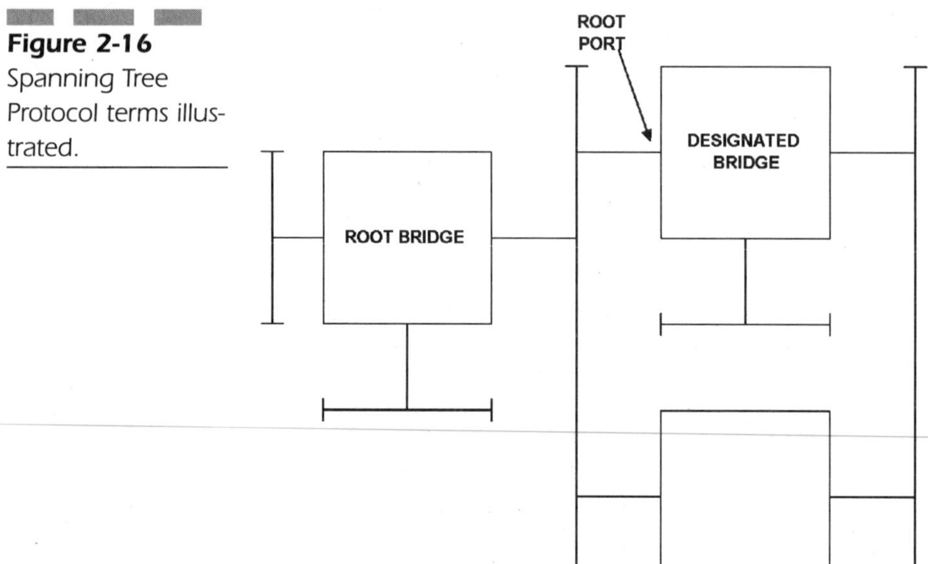

Figure 2-16 Spanning Tree Protocol terms illustrated.

warding state. For each segment that has more than one bridge connected to it, a designated bridge is selected that will forward frames to the root. Each bridge selects a root port that will be used to forward frames toward the root bridge. Ultimately, STP selects all the designated bridges and root ports necessary and identifies a loop-free path between the root bridge and all LANs, placing the selected bridge interfaces into a forwarding state and all others in a blocked state. The spanning tree is maintained by the root bridge, transmitting BPDUs every 2 seconds by default. Upon receipt of a BPDU from the root bridge, the other bridges transmit their own BPDU (BPDUs were covered in Chapter 1).

Within large networks, this operation is suboptimal and has subsequently been replaced by routed networks. However, with VLANs, the opportunity to run several instances of STP on the network is now available, thereby optimizing STP operation to provide better utilization of network resources.

Optimizing Timers

The first place to look to optimize STP in a switched network is at the timers used to send BPDUs and those that determine when a missing BPDU indicates a link failure. The original designers of STP set conservative levels for timers, and rightfully so, as they were unsure of the topologies that network administrators would build with STP bridges. However, in a well-designed switched network, there is plenty of scope to speed up the convergence time of STP by trimming timers. The key timer values—hello time, max age, and forward delay—are set at the root bridge (we'll cover how to get the switch you want selected as the root bridge in the next section).

The max age timer has a default value of 20 seconds and is tunable down to 4 seconds on the 2900XL range of switches from Cisco. Using a default hello time of 2 seconds with a 4-second max age timer is probably too tight. This means that only two BPDU packets can be missed before a switch will be forced to recompute its spanning tree. In routing distance vector routing protocols, we normally allow the timers to be set for three missed packets before any recalculations occur. This would imply a minimum max age of 7 seconds, to be on the safe side. This setting is still much quicker than the 20-second default. Of course, if the hello timer (which is settable for between 1 and 10 seconds) is reduced, the max age timer can be reduced in step; however, by doing this you do pay the penalty of more bandwidth being consumed by BPDU traffic.

The forward delay timer sets the amount of time a switch interface will be kept in both the listening and learning state when making the transition from blocked to forwarding as a result of a spanning tree recalculation. This value has a default of 15 seconds and a range of 4 to 30 seconds. If the minimum 4 seconds is selected, a total of 8 seconds will pass before an interface transitions from a blocked to a forwarding state if the spanning tree has selected it as part of the tree. The potential problem is that the switch has only 8 seconds to identify all the possible BPDUs that would prevent it from placing the interface into forwarding mode. If an essential BPDU is not received within this time, the interface may be erroneously put in a forwarding state, which could cause a loop. Chapter 1 discussed the horrendous possibilities of a loop existing in a transparently bridged network—clearly something to be avoided.

Root Bridge and Interface Priorities

The root bridge should be as near to the center of your network as possible, in order to approximately synchronize the delivery of management BPDUs to bridges on the edge of the network. The STP selects a root bridge among the available switches in the network based on the bridge ID; the bridge with the lowest bridge ID will be selected as the root. In the event of a tie, the switch with the lowest-value MAC address is selected. The default value for all switches is 32,768, and a range between 0 to 65,535 is allowed. For Catalysts, it is a simple matter of using the `set spantree priority` command to set the switch bridge ID priority (remember, 0 will be higher priority than 65,535). The bridge priority needs to be set on a per-VLAN basis, as each VLAN will be running its own STP and selecting its own root bridge.

Once the switch that will serve as the root bridge has been selected, it is beneficial to look at the individual interface priorities on a per-VLAN basis to make sure you are making the most of your available network bandwidth. This is illustrated in Figure 2-17.

The command to define the interface priority per VLAN is `set spant portvlanpri`. The goal here is to set the link between the two 1/1 interfaces as the preferred link for VLAN1 and to set the link connecting the 1/2 interfaces as the preferred link for VLAN2. By setting the priority appropriately, we can still have the other link available to the VLAN as a backup, should its preferred link fail.

So if we use the command `set spant portvlanpri 1/1 31 1` on switch 1 in Figure 2-17, we are setting the priority for VLAN1 on interface 1/1 (the first interface in the first module) to 31. The priority can be set to a value between 0 and 63, with 0 indicating highest priority. Assuming that interface 1/2 has a priority of 32, this will make 1/1 the preferred interface for VLAN1. One point of interest is that if we have set switch 1 as the root bridge, we will not see interface 1/2 blocked for VLAN1; to see this link blocked, we have to log in to switch 2, which will show interface 1/2 as blocked for VLAN1.

Performing a similar configuration for VLAN2 to use the link connecting interfaces 1/2 will separate the traffic from each VLAN and send

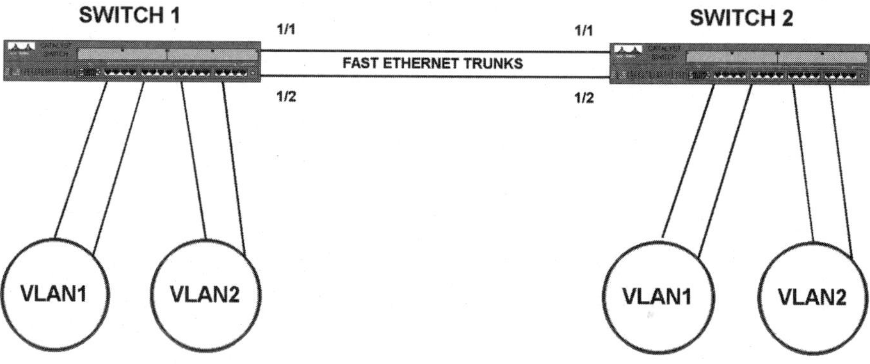

Figure 2-17 Configuration for setting trunk priority on a per-VLAN basis.

each over a different link. The setting of port priority on a per-VLAN basis is available on the Catalyst 5000 range, but not on the 2900XL range, which currently only allows the setting of an interface priority, irrespective of its VLAN membership. By making these adjustments to priority, each of the links in this figure will be the preferred route for different VLANs.

The final priority setting feature to look at is the interface cost per VLAN (referred to in the Cisco documentation as the "port cost"). This is set by default according to the type of media in use on the link. For example, a 10-Mbit/sec interface will have a default cost of 100, whereas a 100-Mbit/sec interface will have a default cost of 10. As with most interface-specific commands, there are options to set this for all VLANs present on the interface or on a per-VLAN basis. The cost of an interface is used in the STP calculation that selects which interface will become the root port. The root port is the one that provides the lowest cost path back to the root bridge.

The two commands discussed here are the `set spantree portcost` for setting the cost on the interface for all VLANs and the `set spantree portvlancost`, which defines the cost per VLAN on each interface selected in the command.

STP Uplink Fast Groups

The Uplink Fast feature is made available on the Catalyst 5000 range by software releases starting at 3.1.1. It is there to speed up the convergence time of STP switched networks, in the presence of redundant links. The method used groups interfaces together and identifies them as specific uplink groups. This is most easily explained with reference to Figure 2-18, which shows part of what a switched network that employs Uplink Fast groups might look like. The key feature is that both the switch configured as the root bridge and the switch configured as the backup bridge have physical links to each switch that is used to connect to users in the network. In this instance, the root bridge and its backup only connect to other switches, not LAN segments that have endstations on them.

With this configuration, the blocked links to switch 3 and 4 are shown as dotted lines. For Uplink Fast groups to work, Uplink Fast must be enabled on each non-root bridge switch and each switch must have at least two connections (one to the root bridge, one to its backup). One of these two links has to be in the blocked state. Uplink Fast also only provides backup for the links from the distribution switches (switches 3 and

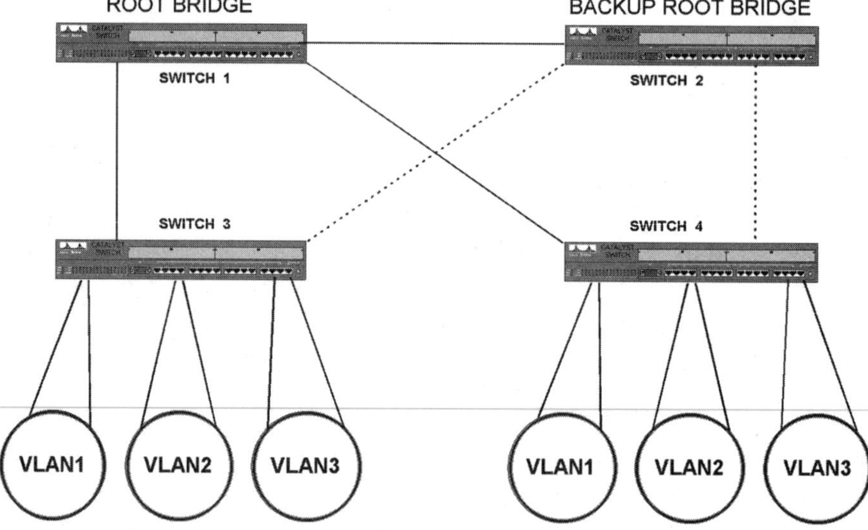

Figure 2-18 Switch interconnections to support Uplink Fast groups.

4 in Figure 2-18) back to the root bridge and its backup. Uplink Fast is not an appropriate technology to provide for the backup of user VLAN links (such as those to VLAN1, 2, or 3 in Figure 2-18). It is also not appropriate to enable Uplink Fast on the root or backup root bridge, as fast transitions of the root bridge location will cause problems for the rest of the spanning tree to converge.

To understand how this works in practice, assume the link from switch 1 to switch 4 is failing. Immediately switch 4 detects the link failure and will unblock the connection to switch 2. Because the switch 1-to-switch 2 link is no longer present, no loops are generated by this unblocking, and connectivity to a root bridge (even though it is the backup root bridge) is restored without the need to go through the listening and learning phases. Convergence is therefore completed within seconds rather than minutes, since it is not necessary for the max age timer to expire.

One last point on the tasks for configuring this setup is that there is a simpler way to set the root bridge and its backup for a VLAN. Instead of manipulating bridge IDs, you can use the `set spantree root` command. This command lets you designate the bridge as the root or secondary. This will allow you to specify the VLANs for which this is to be effective, the diameter of the network (in terms of bridge hops) that will be acceptable, and the hello timer. An example is `set spantree root 1-3 dia 10`, which will set the switch as the root bridge for VLANs 1,

2, and 3, accepting a maximum bridge hop count of 10 between endstations. The benefit of using this command is that the switch will start off with a priority of 8192 (as reflected in its bridge ID) and test to see if that is low enough to make it the root. If not, the switch will lower its priority on each VLAN until it is selected as the root.

Fast EtherChannel

Fast EtherChannel is the next step up in bandwidth provision from full-duplex Ethernet. With full-duplex Ethernet implemented on a Fast Ethernet link (by *Fast Ethernet,* I just mean a 100-Mbit/sec Ethernet link), we could get 200-Mbit/sec data rates if you assume that both directions on the point-to-point link are transmitting at the maximum 100 Mbit/sec. Fast EtherChannel is a technology that groups these full-duplex Fast Ethernet links together to provide increments of 200-Mbit/sec bandwidth, as depicted in Figure 2-19.

Fast EtherChannel is, of course, a point-to-point link technology, since it relies upon similar circuitry as used for full-duplex Ethernet. I realize all the marketing literature talks of full-duplex Fast Ethernet providing 200-Mbit/sec throughput, but having worked extensively with digital WAN links during my career, I find this claim a bit misleading. When you buy a 64-Kbit/sec leased digital circuit from a telco, you get 64-Kbit/sec in both directions on the point-to-point link. The telco does not advertise it as a 128-Kbit/sec link, because you can transmit 64 Kbit/sec in both directions simultaneously. I concede that the marketers had to differentiate full-duplex Ethernet within the marketplace, and what better way than to say it is capable of twice the throughput? In reality, there are very few occasions when both directions on a full-duplex point-to-point link are simultaneously saturated. Having said that, full-duplex Ethernet does provide some benefits, and particularly for server connections, it is a reliable mode of communication.

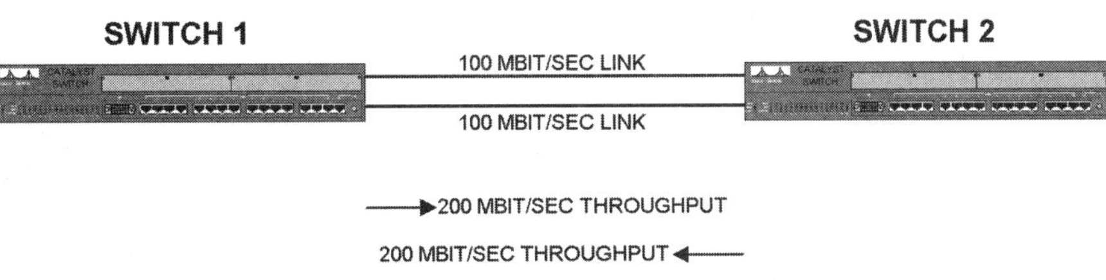

Figure 2-19 Fast EtherChannel aggregates full-duplex Fast Ethernet links.

Fast EtherChannel Concepts

Being a multilink technology, Fast EtherChannel provides the expected benefits of being able to load-balance across multiple links and provide resiliency in the event of link failure. An added benefit is that all of this is transparent to applications, and no network APIs need to be rewritten (as would be necessary if we were to move from IP to native ATM at the desktop). When implemented on Cisco technology, Fast EtherChannel interoperates with protocols like ISL and provides an upgrade path to Gigabit Ethernet.

The technology used in Fast EtherChannel trunks was first developed by Kalpana, before it was acquired by Cisco. The basis of this technology is that between two and four separate trunks can be grouped together to appear as one link with the combined bandwidth of the component links. When implemented on router links (such as the Fast Ethernet Interface Processor or Versatile Interface Processor), the router uses layer 3 principles to load-share. This means the router looks at the source and destination IP addresses and load-balances across the EtherChannel links based on that information. Fast EtherChannel does not require the use of 802.1D STP to converge, as it has its own peer-to-peer protocol that only considers the device on each end of the point-to-point link.

Fast EtherChannel Network Design

The most typical applications of Fast EtherChannel are shown in Figure 2-20. In this figure, three links are aggregated to produce a throughput of 600 Mbit/sec between the central switch and the server, and there are two 400-Mbit/sec links connecting distribution switches to the central switch. If support for transporting multiple VLAN traffic across Fast EtherChannel links is required, all that need be done is to use ISL encapsulation on each link within the EtherChannel.

An alternate configuration is to use Spanning Tree Protocol to provide resilience within the network connections, as shown in Figure 2-21. However, this does require Catalyst software 3.1 or later, as early versions of Fast EtherChannel do not support STP. Of course, this has the disadvantage of wasted bandwidth because of STP blocked ports.

In Figure 2-21, the central switch has three 400-Mbit/sec links configured, two of which connect to the same switch. Spanning Tree Protocol is enabled on these links and will select one of the two links to switch 1 to

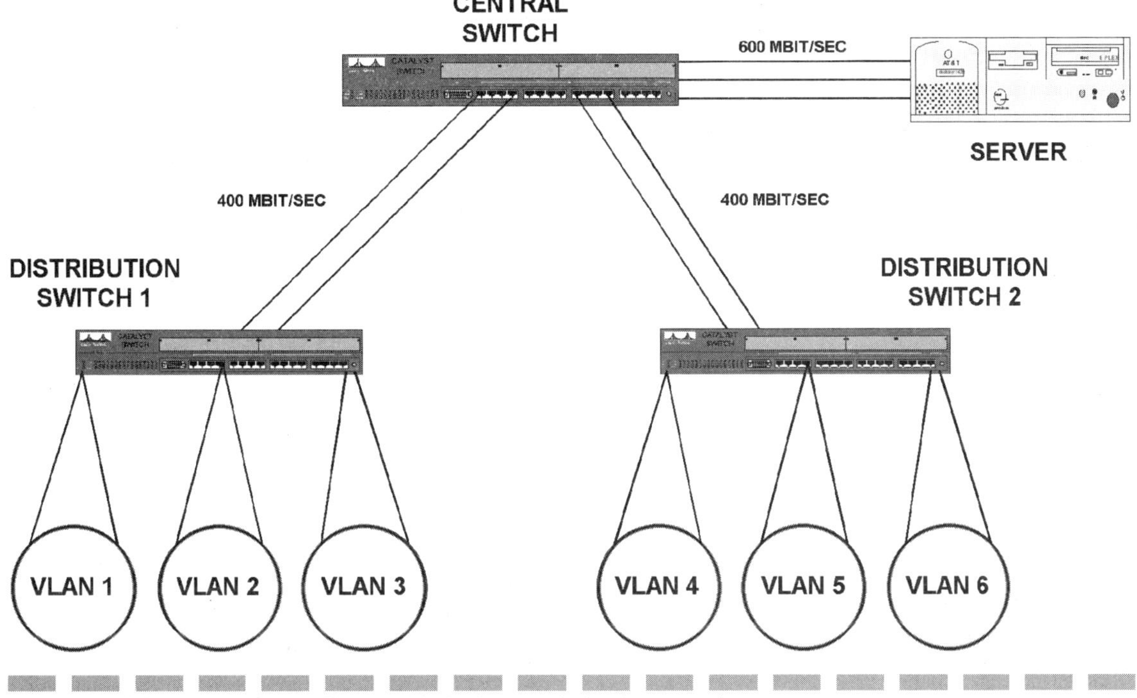

Figure 2-20 Fast EtherChannel links in a switched network.

be placed in the blocking state, ready to take over should a failure occur in the unblocked link. Currently these Fast EtherChannel links can be implemented on 100BaseTx and 100BaseFx on the Catalyst 5000 series, and soon on the 2900XL series. It is also expected that when the Gigabit Ethernet standard (802.3z) gains acceptance in the marketplace, Gigabit EtherChannel will be available to provide aggregate throughputs in the region of 8 Gbit/sec.

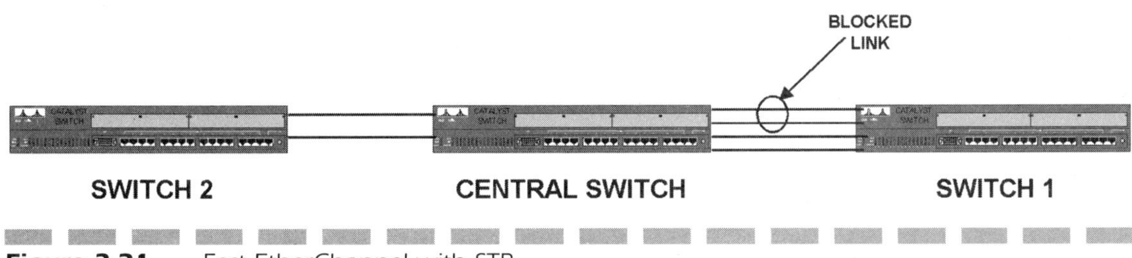

Figure 2-21 Fast EtherChannel with STP.

The normal operation for a Catalyst switch to forward packets is upon receipt; the packet is sent to all interfaces in readiness to be sent out. A separate process decides if the packet will be dropped from the interface (if it does not need to be forwarded) or forwarded out onto the network wire. This mechanism provides the opportunity to implement an exclusive OR operation for the interfaces belonging to the Fast EtherChannel link. What this means is that for those interfaces configured to be part of the Fast EtherChannel, the packet will be forwarded out of only one of them. In this mode, the switch is allowed to forward a packet out of interfaces to MAC addresses learned from a different interface. Of course, this is in contrast to normal switch operation, whereby the switch learns to forward packets to MAC addresses it has learned the existence of from source MAC addresses in incoming packets.

The exclusive OR operation just mentioned is based on a comparison of the source and destination MAC pair. If there are four links in the Fast EtherChannel bundle, the exclusive OR operation will be performed on the last 2 bits of the source and destination MAC addresses within the packet waiting to be forwarded. With 2 bits being used, there are four possible answers to the exclusive OR operation (00, 01, 10, 11), which are associated with each of the links. This method of distributing load between links does not directly use a determination of the comparative load on each of the links within the bundle, but it has proven to deliver acceptable load splitting in the Fast EtherChannel environment and is much faster than some real-time load analysis. Similar operations occur for the 2 and 3 links in a bundle case.

This analysis of source and destination MAC addresses works well in an Ethernet switch environment, since the switch transparently bridges packets without altering the MAC addresses of the packet as it is forwarded out of an interface. The only time when this logic is not appropriate is if it is used to connect two routers together, when the source and destination addresses will always be the same. If it is required to link two routers together with Fast EtherChannel technology, it is better to use a layer 3 routing protocol, like IGRP or OSPF, to load-balance across equal-cost links.

The latest release of Fast EtherChannel utilizes the Port Aggregation Protocol (PAgP), sometimes referred to as Fast EtherChannel II. It supports Uplink Fast (as discussed in the previous section) and STP. PAgP eases the creation of Fast EtherChannel bundles by automatically identifying multiple direct links between switches, exchanging parameter information, and grouping the links into a channel. If STP is running, a bundle is then identified as a single-bridge interface for the purpose of

STP blocking or forwarding. One implementation issue to consider is that PAgP does not allow any of the links in the bundle to use dynamic VLANs. Either all the links must belong to the same VLAN or be configured as a trunk to carry multi-VLAN traffic.

These options are set via the `set port` command. Typically, Fast Ethernet is set to the "desirable" option for automatic configuration of bundles; however, using the keywords "on" and "off" either sets or clears the assignment of Fast EtherChannel bundles, respectively. When using the "on" option, the links that will form the bundle need to be explicitly identified. We will look at specific configuration examples in Chapter 5.

Gigabit Ethernet

Proponents of ATM networks always point to the scalability, quality of service (QOS) aspects, and suitability to multiple traffic types (voice, data, and multimedia) that ATM offers and say that, ultimately, ATM will rule everywhere. At the desktop, the reason that Ethernet and other data-oriented technologies have had trouble with audio and video traffic concerns how the network behaves during time of congestion. When an Ethernet LAN is busy, there are variable delays that can destroy a video stream. There have been schemes such as RTP (Real Time Protocol) and RSVP (Resource reSerVation Protocol) that enable multimedia over Ethernet to some extent. However, there is no substitute for having massive amounts of available bandwidth to make multimedia applications work well in an Ethernet environment. With Gigabit Ethernet, we certainly are getting into the realm of massive available bandwidth for real-time applications to the desktop.

It is most probable that early implementations of Gigabit Ethernet will be within backbones and server connections. However, as the price of this technology falls, there is no reason to assume that it will not work its way to the desktop, with server connections making use of gigabit links in Fast EtherChannel bundles.

Gigabit Ethernet Basics

The Gigabit Ethernet standard is based upon the merging of two technologies: the 802.3 frame formats and the physical interface of Fibre Channel. This was done to maintain backward-compatibility with legacy

Ethernet technologies and make use of the gigabit speeds available in the Fibre Channel physical interface. Figure 2-22 shows the pertinent layers borrowed from these two standards to form the basis of Gigabit Ethernet.

You should familiarize yourself with two key issues regarding Gigabit Ethernet operation. The first is that the initial standards identify fiber-optic cable as the primary cabling system, with a new specialized balanced and shielded copper cable as a short-haul alternative. UTP (unshielded twisted pair) is not an option at present, although there are investigations into Gigabit Ethernet over UTP (it is conceivable this may be available by time of printing). The second is that the encoding of data bits onto the cabling system uses 10-bit encoding of 8-bit data, which is similar in concept to the 5-bit encoding of 4-bit data used in FDDI networks. The presentation of the 8-bit data encoded into 10 bits to the upper layers is handled by the serializer/deserializer, illustrated in Figure 2-22. The Fibre Channel specification sets out a signaling rate of

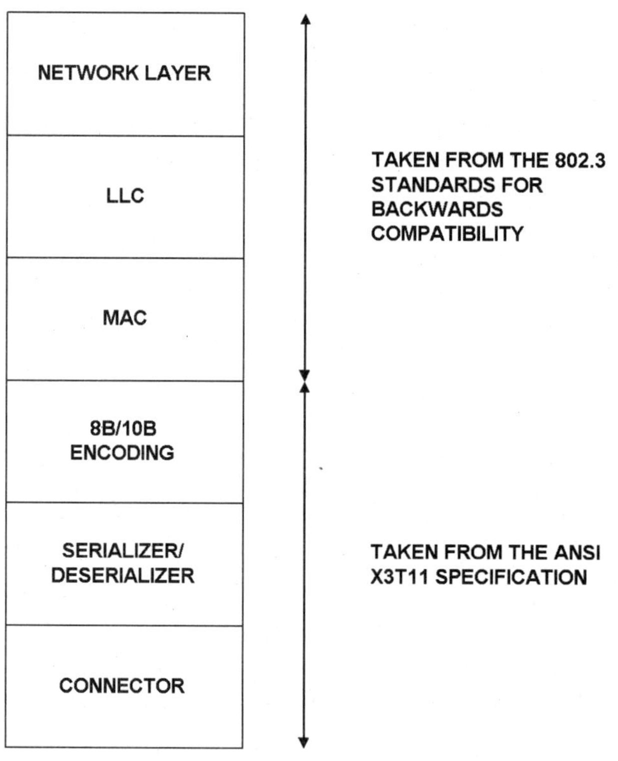

Figure 2-22 Meshing 802.3 and Fibre Channel to form the Gigabit Ethernet standard.

1.062 Gbit/sec, which has been upped by Gigabit Ethernet to 1.25 Gbit/sec. This, as we know from the FDDI specification, yields 1-Gbit/sec throughput, due to the encoding of 8 bits of data into 10 bits for transmission onto the cable. The encoding of 8 bits of data into 10 bits not only allows synchronization to be maintained, but the potential of a DC bias, which is present in the FDDI encoding mechanism to be eliminated.

Gigabit Ethernet Standards

At the physical layer, the connector for Fibre Channel is the SC optical connector that is used for both single-mode and multimode fiber. This is also the fiber connector used for Gigabit Ethernet. There are two fiber specifications for Gigabit Ethernet: 1000BaseLX for long-wave lasers over single- and multimode cable, and 1000BaseSX for short-wave laser over multimode fiber. 1000BaseCX is the standard for Gigabit Ethernet over the new specialized copper cable connector.

When looking at whether to deploy short-wave or long-wave lasers, the choice is fairly simple, depending on the physical constraints of the network you have to implement. Short-wave lasers are used in CD players and are therefore relatively cheap. However, short-wave lasers will only cover distances up to 250 meters on 62.5-micron multimode fiber, whereas long-wave lasers will cover up to 550 meters on the same fiber type. Long-wave lasers will span a distance of 3 km using single-mode fiber.

By contrast, the 1000BaseCX standard will only support distances of up to 25 meters on the two-pair shielded twisted-pair cable.

To handle all these options (multimode fiber also comes in 62.5-micron or 50-micron diameter), the IEEE 802.3z committee has provided a Gigabit Ethernet interface carrier layer that will allow network managers to configure individual interfaces on a gigabit switch for different media types. At the MAC layer, half-duplex Gigabit Ethernet implements the usual CS/MA/CD of 802.3, and full-duplex Ethernet is the same as that implemented for both 10-Mbit/sec and 100-Mbit/sec Ethernet. In order for Gigabit Ethernet to be compatible with the collision detect mechanisms of standard 802.3, a facility called *carrier extension* has been added to the specification. Carrier extension increases the size of small packets by adding bits to the frame. This is necessary because as the speed of putting a frame onto the network cable increases, the time available to handle collisions decreases, particularly for small packets.

The second change to the 802.3 standard is frame bursting, when an endstation can send several frames onto the network cable without relinquishing control of the network. This is achieved by adding extension bits between frames, so that to listening stations, the cable will always appear busy for the duration of the frame burst.

The frames that are sent on the network cable are fully compatible with the standard 802.3 format, and, therefore, no frame translation is required when going from standard 802.3 to Gigabit Ethernet (unlike the 802.3-to-FDDI translation necessary when connecting those two topologies together). This has the added benefit of reducing latency when implementing Gigabit Ethernet as a backbone technology, as no translation is required.

Gigabit Ethernet Deployment

The initial deployment of Gigabit Ethernet is expected to be used to relieve packet congestion on backbones, in much the same way that 100-Mbit/sec Ethernet did. In time, gigabit switches will be available to replace the 10/100 switches currently in use. It is unlikely that nonblocking gigabit switches will be available immediately after the first gigabit devices come to market. The issue is that a switch with multiple Gigabit Ethernet connections could be faced with demands of over 15 to 25 Gbit/sec, which is a throughput level that no vendor in the industry offers at the moment. "Nonblocking" means that a packet never has to wait in a queue to be forwarded out of an interface, allowing a device to forward packets at wire speed on all interfaces simultaneously.

Gigabit Ethernet has value in short-haul connections of up to a few kilometers that require high bandwidth. The technology is familiar and the complexities of ATM implementation are avoided.

CGMP and Multicasts

IP multicasting is becoming more popular as a means of efficiently delivering multimedia traffic over LANs and WANs. The goal is for a host to send a stream of traffic out once and for it to be received by multiple clients. This is achievable by broadcasting, but multicasting adds a measure of intelligence by dynamically routing the data stream to subnets where it is required and stopping it from reaching subnets where it is not needed. In a classic routed network, the existing specifications for IP multicast (RFC1112 for IGMP, RFC 1584 for MOSPF, and RFC 1075 for DVMRP) work well. However, when combined with the increasingly popular layer 2 switches that are being deployed across corporate networks, its benefits are easily negated. In this section we'll review multicasting, look at why switches can negate the benefits of multicasting, and see how the Cisco Group Multicast Protocol (CGMP) can restore those benefits in a switched environment.

Multicast Basics

Multicasts use Class D IP addresses (those that start at 224.0.0.1 up to 239.255.255.255) to address a subset of hosts within the network. Typical well-known multicast addresses are 224.0.0.2 for all routers on a subnet, or 224.0.0.5 for all MOSPF routers. The Internet Group Management Protocol (IGMP) administers the dynamic joining and leaving of hosts to a multicast group, and multicast routing protocols like MOSFP (Multicast Open Shortest Path First) direct multicast traffic to the hosts belonging to a particular multicast group.

Classic multicast in a routed environment is illustrated in Figure 2-23, which shows host 1 multicasting to hosts 4, 7, and 8 on remote networks (*remote* meaning on the other side of one or more routers). To achieve this, hosts 4, 7, and 8 must have used IGMP to register membership with host 1, and routers 1, 2, and 3 must have used a multicast routing protocol to route the multicast packets across the network to the appropriate hosts. This can be quite efficient for the distribution of video or audio traffic across a network and requires minimal administration after the initial setup of IGMP and, say, MOSPF.

We have stated what multicasts use at the IP level, but what is used at layer 2? For example, what MAC address would router 3 use to forward the multicast packet on to hosts 7 and 8? Sending two packets point-to-point using the MAC address of each host would somewhat defeat the objective. Likewise, sending a MAC layer broadcast to all ones is not the aim, either. In fact, special multicast MAC addresses are used. The way it works is that the low-order 23 bits of the 32-bit destination multicast IP address are mapped to the low-order 23 bits of the MAC address. Hosts that are members of the multicast group in question will recognize the destination MAC address as the MAC address of the multicast group and pass the packet up through the layers for processing.

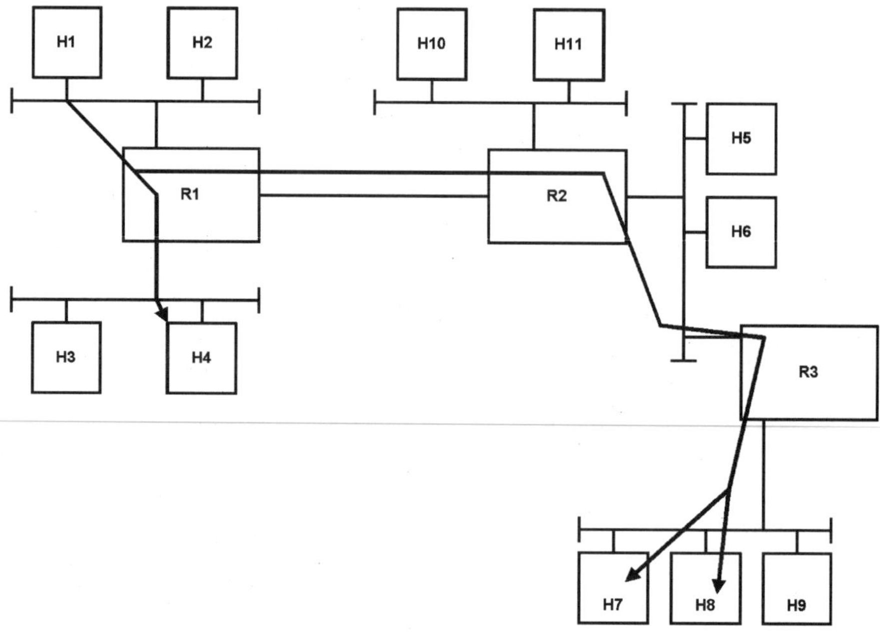

Figure 2-23 Classic multicast in a routed environment.

Ethernet addresses used in multicast packets range from 01:00:5e:00:00:00 to 01:00:5e:7f:ff:ff.

We have already mentioned DVMRP and MOSPF, but with Cisco routers there is a more flexible solution for routing within a multicast environment: Protocol Independent Multicasting (PIM). PIM offers two modes of operation, dense mode and sparse mode, which are appropriate in different circumstances. Dense-mode PIM is best for applications like distributing real-time video over a LAN. The characteristics of this traffic are that there are a few senders but many receivers, the multicast traffic is fairly constant, and the senders and receivers are in close proximity. Dense-mode PIM uses a mechanism to distribute the multicast traffic that is very similar to the Reverse Path Forwarding (RPF) technique used within DVMRP (the Distance Vector Multicast Routing Protocol, as specified in RFC 1075). The basis of Reverse Path Forwarding is that the router starts off by flooding the multicast packet out of every interface except the one on which the packet was received. This process ensures that the datastream will reach all LANs within a network. If one of the routers in the network has a LAN attached that has no clients on it that wish to receive the multicast stream, it will send a prune message upstream to stop further multicast packets from being sent to it.

In the instance when the first host on a LAN wants to receive the multicast, it has to wait until RPF performs one of its periodic floods of all networks to receive its first packet of the stream. The router that had been sending a prune message back upstream will no longer send a prune message for the LAN that now has a host wishing to receive the multicast stream, and the host is now online. There is obviously a trade-off here between the frequency of RPF floods and the amount of time it takes a new host to come online to a multicast stream. Additionally, one would not want to perform RPF floods too frequently, as the bandwidth penalty can become quite high.

The difference between DVMRP and dense-mode PIM is that dense-mode PIM can use any unicast routing protocol for the unicast route update messages (like IGRP or OSPF), rather than the DVMRP-specific unicast routing protocol (which is a lot like RIP version 1).

Dense-mode PIM is illustrated in Figure 2-24. The LAN TV host sends one multicast packet to router 1, which floods the packet to R2, R3, and R4. R2 and R4 have hosts that wish to receive this multicast stream and do not send a prune message back. R3 has no hosts wishing to receive the multicast stream and sends a prune message back to router 1.

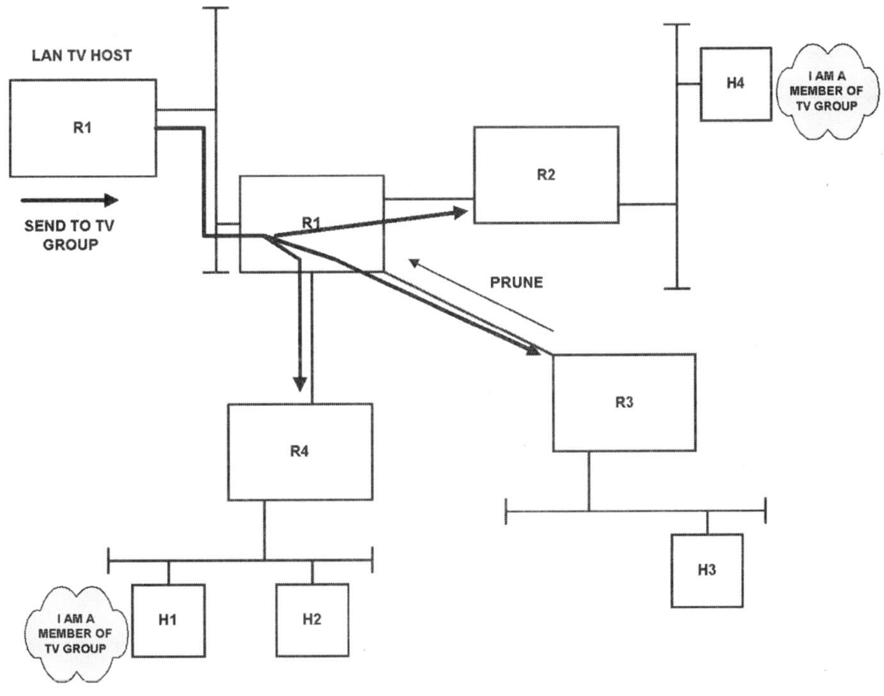

Figure 2-24 The operation of multicast traffic flooding and pruning within a dense-mode PIM network.

Subsequent packets in that multicast stream from the LAN TV host are only sent to R2 and R4 by router 1. This situation persists until R3 has a host wanting to receive the LAN TV multicast and a flood occurs, at which time R3 will not return a prune message.

Sparse-mode PIM is more suited to data applications that traverse WAN links. An example might be regional offices of a stockbroker company that has many news services distributed over a WAN. Not all offices want to receive all news services. Each news service could be defined as a discrete multicast group, and only the offices that have hosts (broker workstations) that register for a specific news service actually get the data sent to them. A possible setup for this scenario is given in Figure 2-25.

This setup fits the design goals of sparse-mode PIM, because the traffic is intermittent (headlines for news stories that pop up on broker workstations are only sent out as generated by the news service) and bandwidth utilization is more of a concern, as senders and receivers have to communicate via WAN links. Sparse-mode PIM is also beneficial when

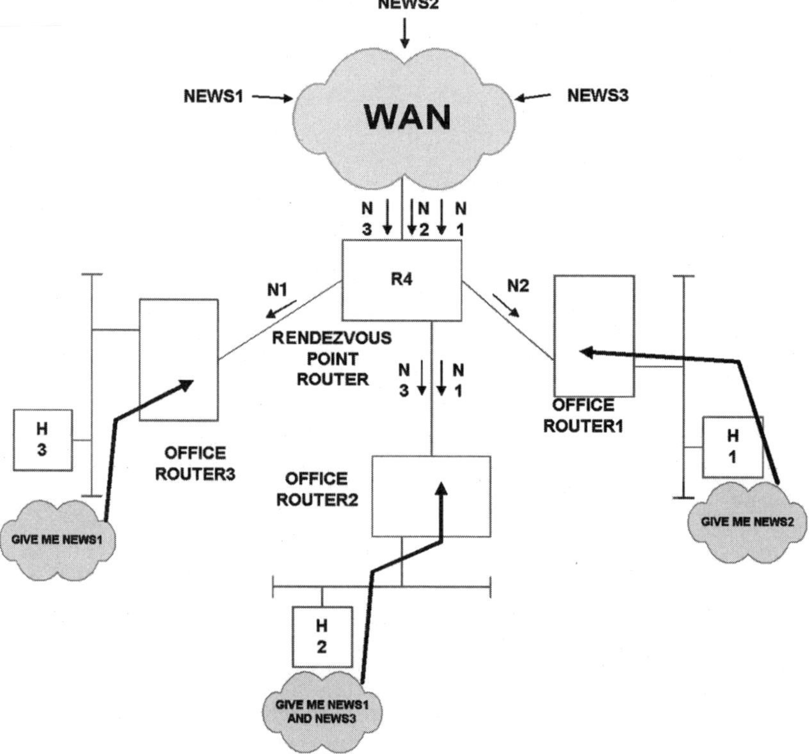

Figure 2-25 Rendezvous point operation of sparse-mode PIM.

there are many streams, each taken by a small number of receivers. The application depicted in Figure 2-25 would work very poorly with the RPF mechanism of dense-mode PIM; the WAN links would suffer from the regular flooding, which would be mainly unnecessary, since the membership of groups at the remote branches should not change very frequently.

By contrast, sparse-mode PIM forces receivers to register their interest in a particular multicast group with a rendezvous point (not just the next hop router, as in dense-mode PIM). Senders also register the groups they are willing to service with the rendezvous point. Once a sender/receiver pair has been identified, the routers along the path between the sender and receiver optimize the path for subsequent packets in the multicast group in question. The basis of sparse-mode PIM is that a host has to make a request before it receives any data from the multicast sender.

Multicasting clearly has sound solutions for a routed environment. Things are not so rosy when it comes time for multicast traffic to traverse a switched network. The reason for this is that switches learn where workstations are in the network by examining source MAC addresses. For example, in Figure 2-26, the switch will generate the listed table, and every time a packet is to be sent to one of the known MAC addresses (MAC A through F), it will refer to this table to decide which interface to send the packet out of.

Now when the time comes to send a packet destined for a multicast MAC address, the switch will refer to its MAC address-to-interface lookup table and see that the destination address is not listed. This is clearly the case, since no station will have used the multicast address as its own source address at any time. By default, a switch will assume that the destination multicast address belongs to a workstation that it does not know about and flood it out of every interface. Because of this logic,

Figure 2-26
MAC address-to-interface mapping.

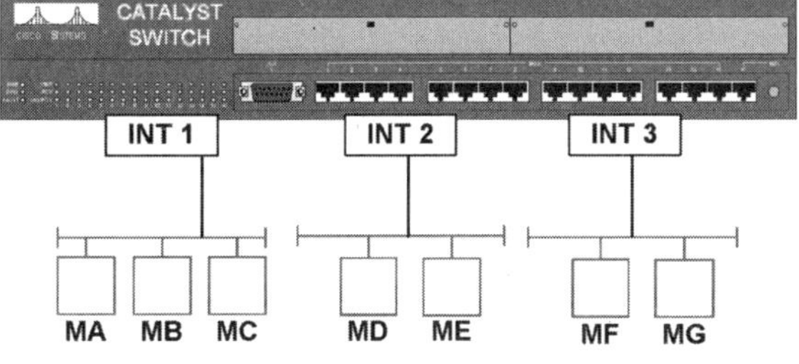

SOURCE ADDRESS	INTERFACE
MA	INT 1
MB	INT 1
MC	INT 1
MD	INT 2
ME	INT 2
MF	INT 3
MG	INT 3

the switch treats multicasts in the same way as broadcasts, and multicast benefits are therefore negated. At this stage, every workstation on the switch will receive the multicast packets, when what we really want is for the switch to only send the multicast stream out of the interfaces that have workstations registered for the multicast traffic. If a multicast stream is a real-time video application requiring between 1 and 2 Mbit/sec of bandwidth, this is clearly a problem in terms of wasted bandwidth on the segments attached to the switch interface that do not need the traffic.

CGMP to the Rescue

To deal with this problem of a layer 2 switch treating a multicast as a broadcast, Cisco has developed the Cisco Group Multicast Protocol (CGMP). Prior to CGMP, one could program specific-destination multicast addresses to be sent out of only specific switch interfaces. This, however, becomes an administrative inconvenience, particularly with a large and continually changing network. Also, by utilizing a manual process, the IGMP join process that is meant to automate the delivery of multicast traffic is negated.

An alternate solution that was employed to manage the level of broadcasts and multicasts was setting the maximum percentage of broadcast traffic on a segment. All broadcast/multicast traffic above that percentage was dropped. This brute-force method does allow you to ensure that a link does not become overburdened with broadcast traffic, but one assumes the broadcasts are there for a reason. If a multicast application is used to send stock price data, you may not want the switch to drop multicast packets during times of heavy market trading. CGMP is there to resolve many of these problems and to retain broadcast/multicast traffic on the network.

The goal of CGMP is to enable a switch to make use of a layer 3 router's intelligence and thus have the switch treat multicasts in a more efficient way. What CGMP does is to make use of the fact that to receive a multicast stream, an endstation must issue an IGMP join message (this is true for either dense-mode or sparse-mode PIM). The segment that has the workstation on it that issued the join message is then added to the multicast distribution tree. When an endstation makes a request to join a multicast group, CGMP notes its source MAC address. A CGMP join message is then sent from the router to the switch (as illustrated in Figure 2-27) that adds an entry to the switch's switch table identifying

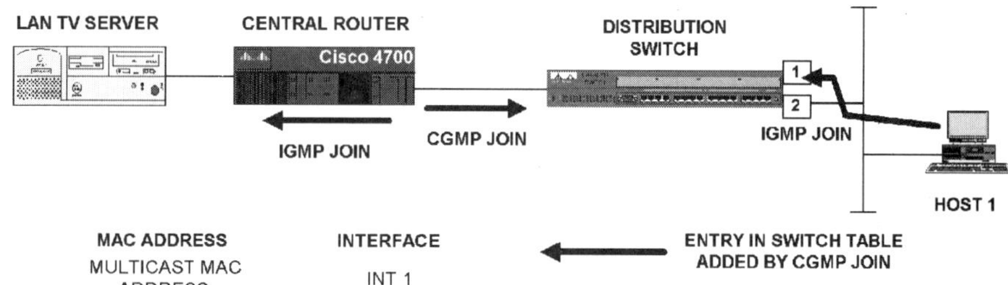

Figure 2-27 The process of CGMP adding an entry to a switch table for efficient multicast operation.

the endstation requiring the multicast stream. With this entry in place, any incoming traffic destined for the multicast address in question is sent to the segment where the join message originated from. By this mechanism, packets belonging to the multicast stream are only sent to the switch interfaces that require them.

Because CGMP works its magic by making entries in the switch's switching table, no additional processing overhead is experienced by the switch and it can continue to operate without any performance implications. Put simply, once the extra entry is in the switching table, all multicast packets are switched the same way as other packets. This is in stark contrast to some other competitive protocols that require the switch to examine the layer 3 data for each incoming packet to identify the packet as multicast and determine which interface it should be forwarded out of.

A final word about CGMP is that as it facilitates communication between a router and a switch, it can enable RSVP priorities to be communicated between these devices. For example, say that a multimedia stream is headed for a particular interface on a switch. Assuming a router is feeding this stream to the switch, the router can use CGMP to tell the switch that a multimedia stream is headed for a particular interface. Upon receipt of this information, the switch can choose to increase the interface priority to ensure that the multimedia stream is not disturbed by other activity within the switch.

Summary

This chapter introduced the main concepts relating to switched VLANs that are necessary to design, build, and troubleshoot these types of networks. We reviewed VLAN tags within a switch, noting that these tags that associate a packet with a particular VLAN are never sent out on segments where endstations are located. They only exist within switch backplanes or connections used as VLAN trunks. We discussed full-duplex Ethernet as a point-to-point technology useful for server connections. We covered the basics of token ring switching, which allows us to access the inherent prioritization mechanisms of token ring (something missing in Ethernet) that make token ring attractive in a switched environment.

We also covered the basics of source route bridging, source route transparent bridging, source route switching, along with the concentrator relay function, and bridge relay function inherent in switched token ring networks. We also looked at the new dedicated token ring, a point-to-point token ring technology that requires neither a token nor a ring. We then covered trunking, or the transport of VLAN data across multiple switches with ISL encapsulation on Fast Ethernet links. The VLAN Trunk Protocol was discussed as a means of advertising VLAN information throughout a switched network to reduce manual configuration, as was the operation of VLAN Membership Policy Server to enable a device to be connected to a network and assume membership of the correct VLAN.

We discussed the operation of both encapsulating and translational bridging across FDDI networks, noting that the simplest solution was to route across these backbones, but conceding that if VLANs were to traverse the FDDI backbone, bridging was necessary. We covered how `fddicheck` can deal with void frames that are generated in error and how that relies on a facility called APaRT that sets up a memory-resident table of destinations and associated frame types.

802.10 VLAN tagging was discussed as an alternate to ISL that can be used on FDDI trunks. Optimization of the Spanning Tree Protocol was discussed, as was how to set the root bridge for a VLAN and assign trunk priorities on a per-VLAN basis to provide load balancing. The mechanics of Uplink Fast were discussed in an environment that has redundant links between the root bridge and distribution bridges.

Fast EtherChannel was discussed as a means of bundling multiple Fast Ethernet links together to provide increased throughput for point-to-point links and as a path to Gigabit Ethernet. Gigabit Ethernet was described as a marrying of the physical layer standards of Fibre Channel to the data-link layer standards of 802.3. This allows the speed of Fibre Channel to be used without the need for translation within an 802.3 environment. Finally, we looked at multicasts, PIM, and CGMP (along with CGMP's interaction with IGMP) as a way of efficiently implementing multicast applications within a switched environment.

CHAPTER 3

ATM Operation and WAN Switching

Objectives

Chapter 1 provided an overview of ATM by introducing the fixed-length cell as the foundation for ATM networking. ATM was defined as a connection-oriented protocol, with an asynchronous form of multiplexing multiple traffic streams onto the one physical cable that could equally accommodate traffic with variable bandwidth requirements and fixed latency requirements. The basics of the user-network interface and the network-network interface were also discussed, and the operation of the integrated local management interface was also outlined.

This chapter covers the operation of ATM in a number of environments, including Classic IP Over ATM (CIOA), Next Hop Resolution Protocol (NHRP), ATM and Frame Relay interworking, LAN Emulation (LANE), Multi Protocol Over ATM (MPOA), and call setup procedures. We will also cover the concepts of tag switching as it relates to switching performed in the WAN. Chapter 6 covers the device setups needed to implement all these technologies in real-world networks.

Introduction to UNI Signaling

User-network interface (UNI) signaling has simple goals, but the issues can get complicated in implementation. ATM UNI signaling procedures are there to support the dynamic provision of ATM connections within a single network. The important word here is *dynamic*. In technologies like Frame Relay, the signaling is simpler, since the network is designed to provide static connections at the user interface, as represented by DLCI (Data Link Connection Identifier) numbers. Although traffic throughout the Frame Relay network may be dynamically rerouted, at the user interface, destinations are each presented with the same and permanent identifier. At each access point to a Frame Relay cloud, each DLCI (which have local significance only) represents a specific destination and always the same one, as represented in Figure 3-1.

In ATM networking, the UNI is there to dynamically allocate connection IDs to connections that are continually being established and torn down. In fact, because UNI IDs are reused after the connection is terminated, an ID used for one connection at the UNI can lead to a totally different location when used for a different connection.

ATM does support permanent virtual circuits (PVCs) as well as the switched virtual circuits (SVCs) that require a UNI ID to be allocated

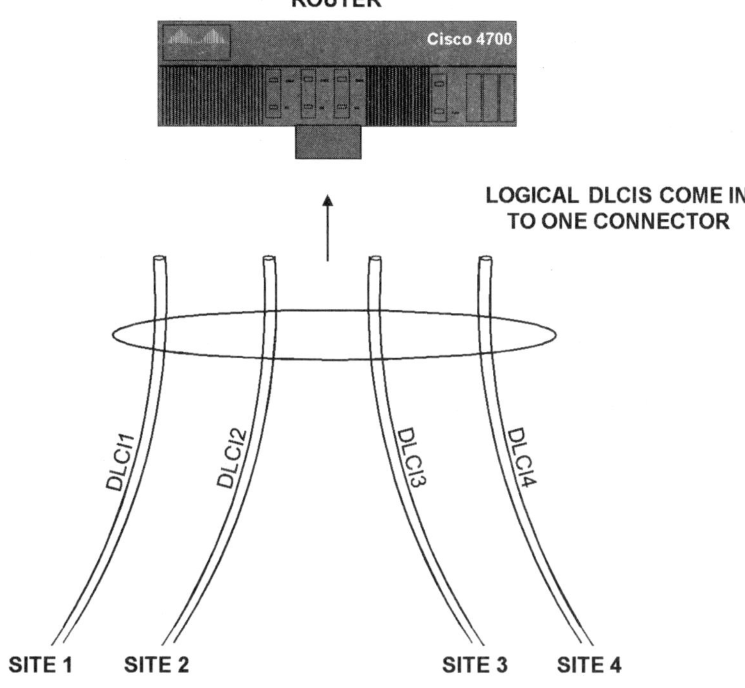

Figure 3-1
At a router interface, several DLCIs are delivered on one physical connector, each representing access to a specific remote location.

each time a connection is established. PVCs, however, are usually set up via manual commands outside of the UNI's automated processes.

UNI Signaling Procedures

Within the specifications, there are ATM endpoints (in our scenario, they are typically Catalysts) and both private and public ATM networks (an ATM network requires one or more switches, which equates to one or more LightStream 1010 switches). With these entities, there are a number of possible interconnections via ATM links, which are listed below and shown graphically in Figure 3-2.

- Endpoint to endpoint (Catalysts to Catalyst) uses UNI signaling.
- Endpoint to either a public or private ATM network uses UNI signaling.
- Private ATM network to public ATM network uses UNI signaling.
- Private ATM network to private ATM network uses PNNI.
- Public ATM network to public ATM network uses BICI (Broadband Inter-Carrier Interface), which is out of the scope of this book.

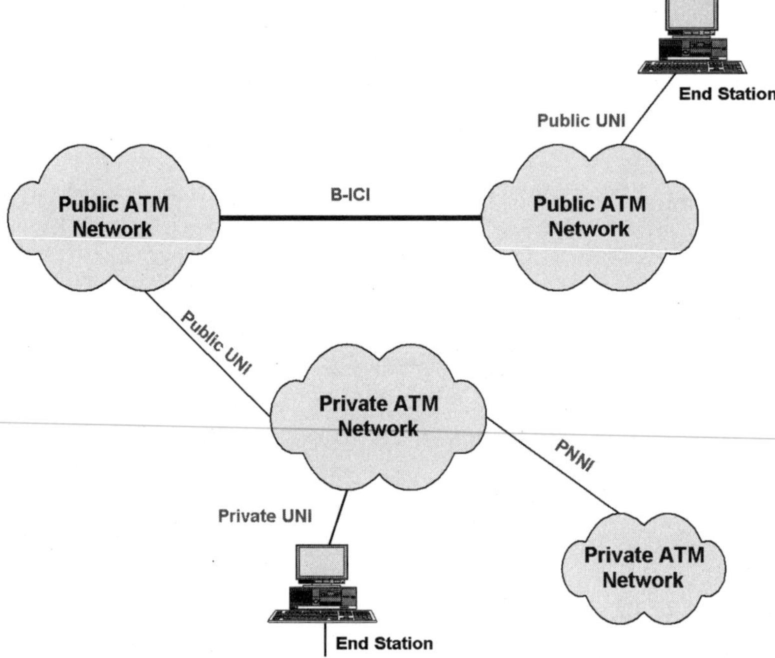

Figure 3-2 Interconnections via ATM link.

The UNI signaling that we will be discussing is based on the current revision, which is the ATM forum's UNI 4.0. UNI 4.0 is closely aligned to the ITU Q.2931 standard. These UNI specifications bear an uncanny resemblance to the Q.931 signaling of ISDN. This is a positive, as the designers of ATM excel at sensibly making use of existing proven technology.

Specifically, these signaling processes are based on connection requests and responses. Common functions that ATM signaling deals with is the identification of call initiated, call proceeding, and call released states. The whole signaling process is there to generate a connection and its identifier, thus bypassing the need to carry ATM addresses in cells used to transmit end user data. This is a good thing when you look at the size of ATM addresses, as illustrated in Figure 3-3.

As a connection-oriented protocol, connection request messages must be replied to with an acknowledgment from the destination prior to the commencement of a connection. The following two sections look at how point-to-point connections and point-to-multipoint connections are established.

Figure 3-3 ATM address structure.

IDP		DSP		
AFI	LCD or DCC or E.164	user defined hierarchy	ESI	SEL
1 byte	2 bytes	10 bytes	6 bytes	1 byte

IDP=Initial Domain Part
DSP=Domain Specific Part
AFI=Authority and Format Identifier
LCD DCC and E.164 are different formats for the Initial Domain identifier
ESI=End System Identifier
SEL=Selector

Point-to-Point ATM Connections The process described below is illustrated in Figure 3-4. In the explanation of the call setup procedure below, the calling and called user equate to a Catalyst on the end of an ATM link, and the network refers to one or more ATM switches, like the LightStream 1010.

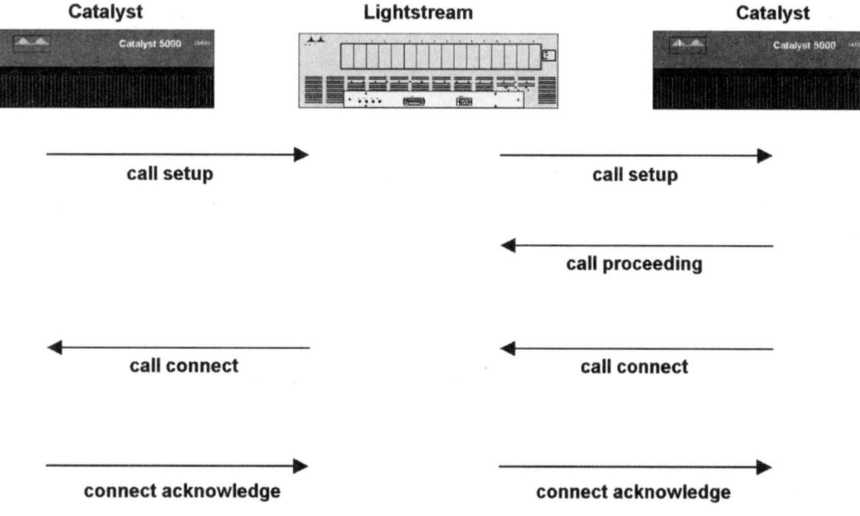

Figure 3-4 Call setup procedures for point-to-point ATM communication.

1. The calling user sends a call setup message to the network, which passes this request on to the called user.
2. A call proceeding message is sent from the called user to the network, indicating that until the present call setup request is serviced, it will accept no more call requests.
3. Assuming all is well, the call proceeding message is rapidly followed by a call connect message, sent from the called user to the network, which is passed back to the calling user. This indicates acceptance of the call by the called user.
4. Finally, a connect acknowledge notifies the network and the called user that the setup has been completed and the transfer can begin.

Knowledge of this procedure is not essential to set up a simple ATM connection; however, as knowing about the existence of a three-way handshake within TCP is beneficial when designing and troubleshooting TCP/IP networks, so too is knowledge of the ATM call setup process. Connection-oriented protocols like TCP and ATM allow firewall and other security procedures to be put in place that allow connections to be originated from within the internal network, but not from an external network.

Point-to-Multipoint Connections At first glance, point-to-multipoint communication for a connection-oriented protocol is difficult to perceive. After all, the whole idea behind connection-oriented protocols is that there is a call setup sequence that checks to see if the recipient is ready, willing, and able to receive. What happens in a point-to-multipoint communication if only one of the intended recipients is unable to respond? Should no packets be sent? Or should only packets to those that are able to receive be transmitted? If so, given that the sender is sending to one multicast address, how will it know which of the potential recipients is unable to receive? It was these sorts of issues that made TCP point-to-multipoint communications unworkable. Fortunately, the ATM design bypasses these problems and presents a framework that does allow point-to-multipoint communications with a connection-oriented protocol. Point-to-multipoint communication in an ATM network is illustrated in Figure 3-5.

As can be seen, one stream of traffic is sent from the sender across the ATM network. Once the stream has reached the location where multiple receivers of that stream are resident, multiple point-to-point connections are established to deliver the multipoint data. At first this may seem that it generates much more traffic than current multicast or broadcast systems, but in fact, that is not true. With current multicast systems, a

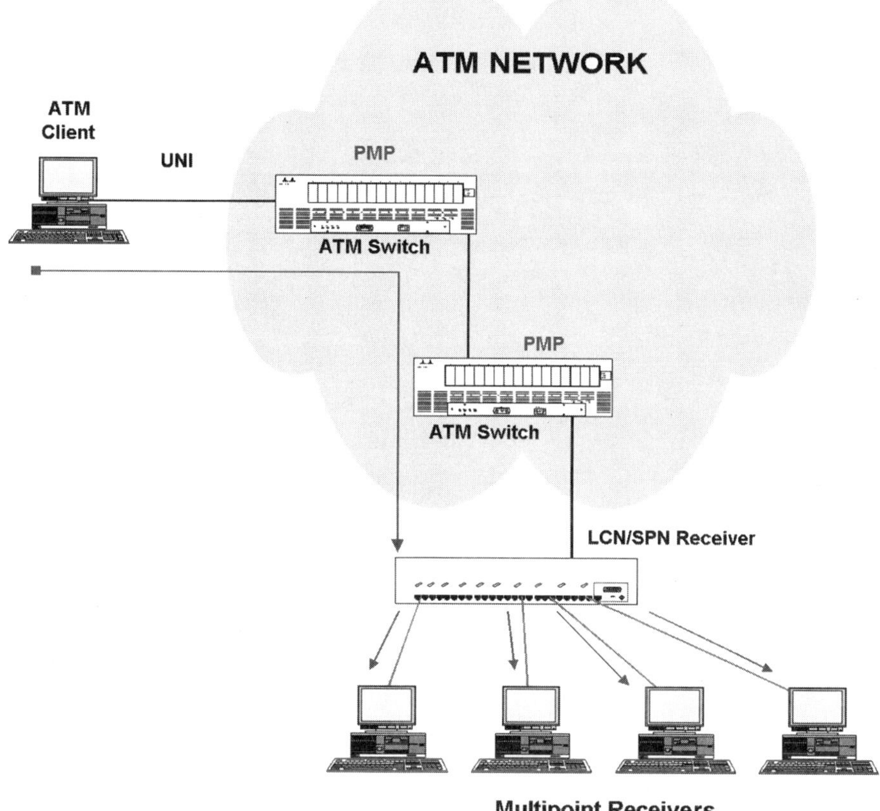

Figure 3-5 The traffic streams generated in a point-to-multipoint communication.

packet is sent to a specific multicast address, and all endstations registered to receive that multicast get it. In the days of 10Base2 LANs, it would be true that a multicast or broadcast packet would only travel once on the network cable for multiple endstations to receive it. However, as soon as we moved to 10BaseT and each endstation had its own cable back to a hub, multicast or broadcast packets were generated for each endstation receiving them. This is just as true with switches: One multicast or broadcast packet comes into the switch and an identical multicast or broadcast packet is generated out of each interface that has an endstation requiring that data. When viewed in that light, it can be seen that the ATM method of dealing with multicast and broadcast packets is no less efficient than the methods we employ today.

As you can imagine, the call setup procedure is a little more complicated in the point-to-multipoint environment, and there are some special names associated with the various parties involved in an ATM point-to-

Figure 3-6 ATM multipoint connections with separate LCN and SPN.

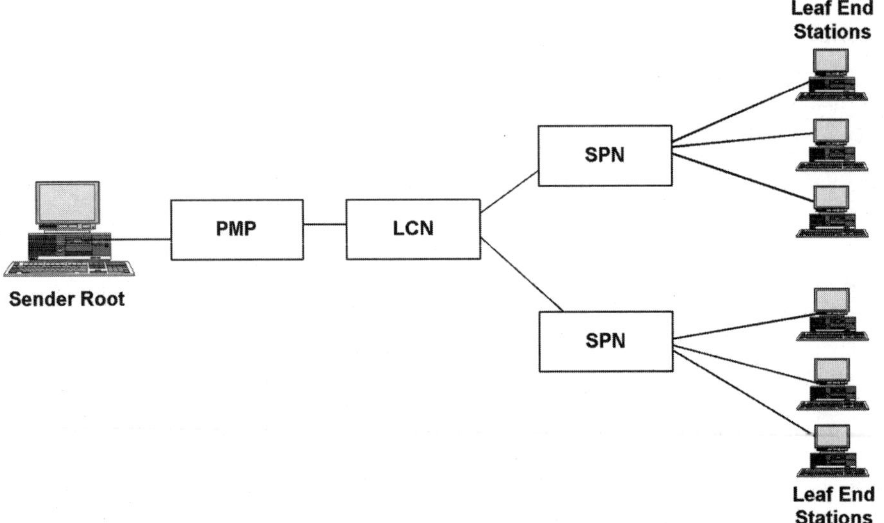

multipoint connection. Each of these terms is identified in Figure 3-6 and are defined as follows:

- Root is the sender.
- PMP node is a switch in the path from sender to receiver that has just one incoming stream and one outgoing stream for the multipoint connection.
- Last common node (LCN) is the first location in the ATM network where one incoming stream leads to more than one outgoing stream for the multipoint connection.
- Single-party node (SPN) is the node that connects the LCN to leaf nodes.

The LCN and the SPN may be the same device, which is the case in Figure 3-5. Figure 3-6 shows a situation when the LCN and SPN are different.

To support point-to-multipoint, all leaf endstations need to be added to the connection, which can either be initiated by the root or the leaf stations themselves. One potential call setup sequence for a point-to-multipoint connection is illustrated in Figure 3-7 and described below.

Let's say the root is aware it needs to add an endstation to receive the multicast (this will have come from a leaf endstation, possibly as the result of the leaf setup request message). The first thing that happens is that an add party message is sent out by the root and forwarded by any PMPs in the path to the leaf nodes. Once the LCN for that multicast

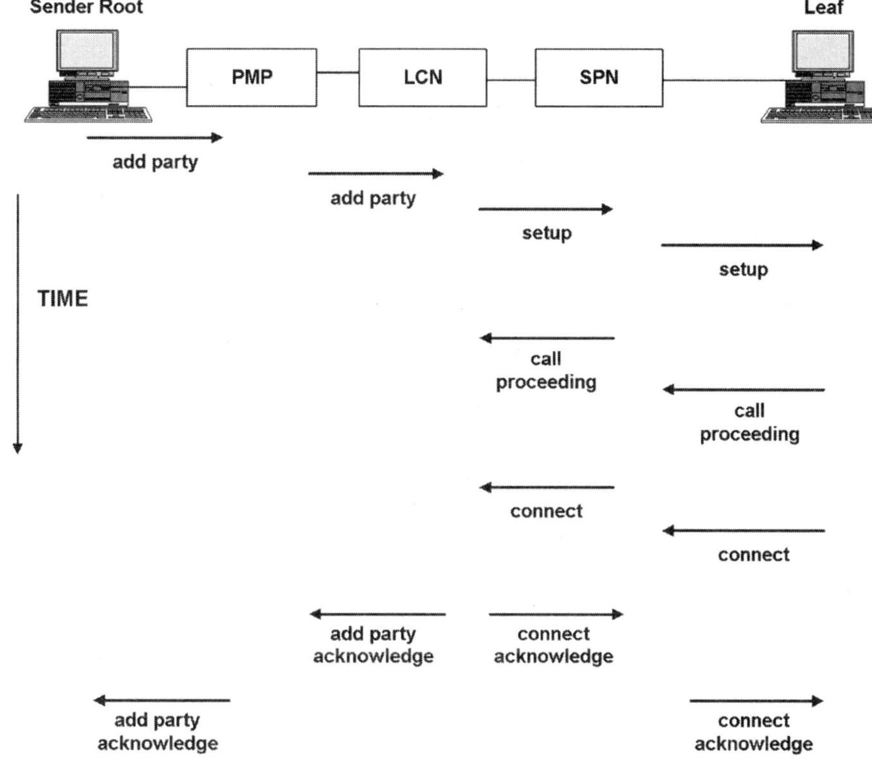

Figure 3-7 Point-to-multipoint call setup sequence.

stream is reached, the add party call is changed to a regular point-to-point setup call, which is forwarded to the SPN (if any) and on to the leaf nodes. Both the SPN and leaf node will respond with call proceeding messages followed by connect messages. The LCN will pass the connect message back via any PMPs in the connection to the root in the form of an add party acknowledgment. The LCN relays to the SPN, and the SPN replies to the leaf node with a connection acknowledgment.

This rather complex process is performed only at the initiation (or cancellation) of a leaf node joining a multipoint connection. After the connection has been made, a multicast packet will be sent once by the root, and only replicated when it reaches the LCN; it then can potentially be further replicated by any SPNs in the delivery path to leaf nodes.

ATM Addresses

ATM addresses are what the network uses to identify devices and end-stations within the network, similar to IP addresses within an IP network. As we showed in Chapter 1, the cell used in ATM communications does not carry any ATM addresses. The only time ATM addresses are used on the network is during call setup. Once a call is set up, all transfers take place via the VPI/VCI number assigned for the duration of that connection. For private ATM networks, ATM addresses use the 20-octet OSI format. When we configure an ATM network in Chapter 6, we will be illustrating this 20-octet format for private networks. This private network addressing scheme splits the address in two: the initial domain part (IDP) and the domain-specific part (DSP). The structure of ATM private network addresses is shown in Figure 3-3.

The IDP contains the Authority and Format Identifier and the Initial Domain Identifier, which can be an International Code Designator (assigned by the British Standards Institute), a Data Country Code (assigned by the ISO), or an E.164 address (assigned by the ITU). The DSP contains address information that is supplied by the domain administrator, plus an End System Identifier (commonly a 6-byte MAC address) and a 1-byte Selector field. For a private network, the domain administrator will be the network administrator. These addresses are supplied to ATM endstations via ILMI from an attached switch that is the first hop in the ATM network. As previously discussed, the cell has no address information and carries data between source and destination purely by the VPI/VCI number assigned for the duration of the established connection.

ATM Routing and NNI Signaling

This covers two main areas: (1) ATM routing, which discusses how ATM networks choose the route that traffic will take through an ATM network, and (2) the signaling used between networks when establishing connections. ATM routing has to provide the same functions that are found in IP routing: There has to be some database of address locations, there has to be a way to select the best route for a connection, and the network must react to topology changes like link-downs.

The ATM forum PNNI protocol is an open protocol that will be implemented by all the major ATM switch manufacturers. The lure of PNNI is that it will allow switches from different vendors to interoperate, much like using OSPF will allow Cisco and non-Cisco routers to share topology and routing information, whereas using IGRP restricts you to Cisco equipment only. PNNI is, in fact, based on OSPF link-state routing principles.

The basis of PNNI deployment, and the key to it being able to support very large ATM networks, is its ability to logically divide the network into interconnected multilevel peer groups, as illustrated in Figure 3-8. The scalability comes from route aggregation, by assigning some form of common addressing to each group and containing that uniqueness to be within the group. This is the same concept as CIDR (classless interdomain routing) or the route aggregation property of OSPF.

IP route aggregation reduces the number of entries a router needs to have in its routing table in a subnetted network. Suppose a router receives advertisements for 10 consecutive remote subnets that are all reachable via the same next-hop router. Instead of placing 10 entries in the routing table, route aggregation allows the router to place just one entry that points to all 10 subnets. CIDR takes this concept a step further by allowing a router to, for example, place one entry in its routing table for all Class C networks that have 194 as the first octet. This, of course, only works when all the 194.x.x.x Class C networks are reachable via the same next-hop router and hence requires all 194 networks to be located in the same area of the network.

Referring to Figure 3-8, note that each of the address areas, A through G, will have its own common prefix within the ATM address scheme.

Figure 3-8
Hierarchy in ATM addressing.

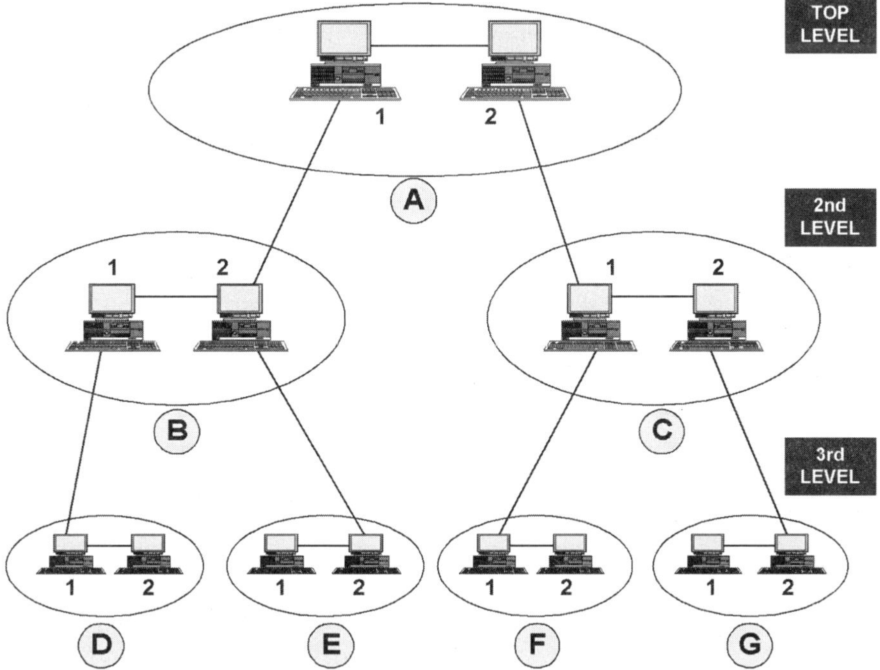

This reduces the number of entries each ATM device needs to keep in its routing table to be able to communicate with all other devices.

Essentially, the routing side of PNNI makes use of link state routing, based on a hierarchical implementation, and source routing to select specific routes for connections. Link state routing was preferred to distance vector routing due to its better scalability. Source routing enables a switch to define the intermediate nodes to pass through so that there is no possibility of a connection request getting caught in a loop. Additionally, source routing helps with ensuring connections travel through the nodes that have committed to provide them with the requested quality of service.

Constructing ATM Address Hierarchy

The key to understanding ATM routing tables (referred to as a *topology database*) and address hierarchy is that the ATM address structure, as outlined in Figure 3-3, consists of a 13-byte network prefix and a 7-byte endstation-specific ID (the 6-byte ESI and 1-byte selector). An endstation constructs its address from the ESI and SEL (which it knows) and the network prefix that it gets from a switch. The ESI is generally a MAC address for LAN-attached endstations and the selector byte generally relates to the subinterface in use on the endstation.

Just as in IP networking, where there was a netmask that defined hierarchy within a given network address, ATM addresses use a level indicator, which can range in length from 0 to 13 octets (0 to 104 bits). Each bit represents a level; therefore, there are a possible 105 levels within PNNI.

To discuss this area fully and to illustrate the concepts with a few examples, we need to define a few terms. The first term is a *peer group,* which is simply a group of nodes that are at the same level in the hierarchy, such as nodes 1 and 2 in area A in Figure 3-8. This group will be identified by a combination of the prefix (the first 13 bytes of the address) and the level, which will define how much of the prefix is reserved for use by this group. This level indicator is 1 byte in length, ranging from 0 to 104 in value, and is manually configured on the switch. All members of the peer group share the same topology database and hence have the same view of the network.

Once a peer group is established, a *peer group leader* is elected, somewhat similar to a designated router in an OSPF area (OSPF is discussed more fully in the *Cisco TCP/IP Routing Professional Reference*). The peer group leader is elected based on priority, with the ATM address acting as a tie-breaker, and is responsible for communicating route information to the rest of the ATM network. Typically the peer group leader will summarize topology information from groups lower in the hierarchy and it will pass that information up, and it will pass information from higher in the hierarchy down. Peer group leaders are also known as *logical group nodes* (LGNs). Note that there is a routing control channel on VPI = 0—VCI = 18—which is used for nodes to exchange routing information on.

In Chapter 6 we will go through assigning ATM addresses and prefix level identifiers, and look at topology databases on LightStream equipment. For now, though, we need to be sure we understand how this works on theoretical ATM addresses. Take, for example, the ATM address 11223344556677889900, which has the expected 20 bytes (each character represents 8 bits of data, which is 1 byte). Let's say that for our network we want to define the first 10 bytes as the network prefix. To achieve this, we have to give the level indicator a value of 80. This is a similar concept to setting a netmask to 255.255.255.0 for a Class B network address to split the available network address space between subnets and host portions. In the ATM world, we are assigning the first 10 bytes to identify this peer group, with the remaining 3 bytes of the network prefix for group lower down in the hierarchy.

So the following illustrates the effects we have been discussing:

ATM address 11223344556677889900

Level Indicator 72

Peer group identifier 112233445XXXX

The peer group identifier is always 13 bytes long (the length of the network prefix). The level indicator, however, tells us that the last 4 bytes can be of any value, and we will still reach the destination ATM address via this peer group. Whether the destination ATM address is within this peer group or one lower in the hierarchy below this peer group depends on the value of the last four digits.

As with netmasks in IP, where there were acceptable values for the netmask (255.255.255.240, 255.255.255.224, 255.255.255.192, etc.) based on what the netmask represented in binary, so too there are acceptable values for the level indicator. The level indicator indicates the number of bytes in the network prefix that are associated with peers at a particular level within the hierarchy and therefore have to be a multiple of 8. Clearly, the higher the value of the level indicator, the lower the peer group identified is in the hierarchy. Put another way, the higher the value of the level indicator, the more specific is the location in the hierarchy that you are specifying.

To clarify this concept, refer to Figure 3-9. This figure equates a netmask in a link state routed network to the level indicator in an ATM network. It is important to use a link state routed network for this comparison, as regular distance vector routing protocols like RIP and IGRP do not support variable-length subnet masks (VLSM). (If you are unfamiliar with VLSM, please refer to the *Cisco TCP/IP Routing Professional Reference.*)

In Figure 3-9, the different value for netmask within the IP network identifies subnetworks at different levels within the address hierarchy. This type of hierarchy would allow a router in a different Class B network to have one entry in its routing table to direct all traffic to any endstation within the 172.8.0.0 Class B address space. Routers within the 172.8.0.0 address space, however, would have many entries for all the 172.8.0.0 subnets listed in their routing tables.

The level indicator performs a similar function in the ATM network in Figure 3-9. Here we are looking at the 13-byte network prefix, and the initial level 56 indicator identifies all the network prefixes that start with 1234567 as belonging to the same level in the hierarchy. The level 72 indicator looks at the first 9 bytes and will therefore use 123456789 to place network prefixes in the hierarchy. As you can see, the higher the value of the level indicator, the more specific (or lower down) we are iden-

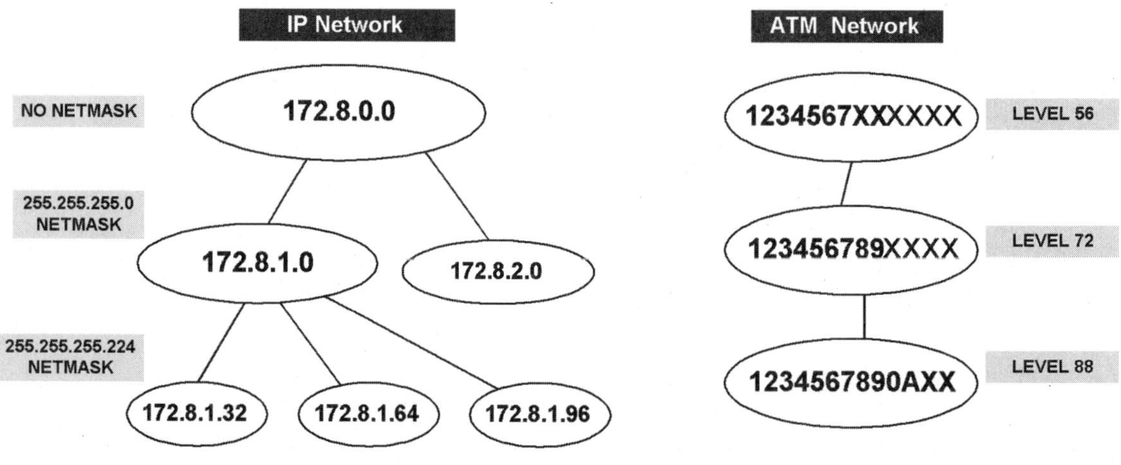

Figure 3-9 Equating a netmask and level indicator to define hierarchy in networks.

tifying network prefix in the ATM hierarchy. Just as a router in the top level of the IP network in Figure 3-9 can advertise reachability to all the 172.8.0.0 network to routers in other Class B networks, an ATM switch in the top level of the ATM network in Figure 3-9 can advertise reachability to all network prefixes that start with 1234567 to other ATM switches. Whereas a router's view of the network was contained within the routing table, an ATM device's view is kept within a topology database. Before we look at what one of those topology databases looks like in a LightStream 1010, we need to discuss just a few more concepts.

ATM Topology Database Updates Just as OSPF uses the Hello protocol for neighbor discovery and as a keep-alive, so does PNNI within ATM. Hello runs on all active interfaces on an ATM switch and is used just to communicate with directly connected neighbors, even if there are multiple links to that neighbor. Once the Hello protocol is exchanged, adjacent nodes will determine if they belong to a common peer group. If they do, they will synchronize their topology databases. Unlike link state routing protocols, the contents of the node's view of the network (the routing table or topology database) is not sent unless the content of that view has changed. Hello packets do not regularly advertise topology database information; that is left to other mechanisms.

PNNI Packets As well as the hello packet type, PNNI supports the PNNI topology state packet (PTSP), the PNNI topology state element (PTSE), database request, and PTSE request. In essence a PTSP contains multiple PTSEs. Consider a PTSE as the basic element of data within a PNNI network. Each PTSE is itself a self-contained piece of data that contains reachable ATM addresses, horizontal and uplink information, and link resource utilization.

Database summary packets are used during the initial connection of peers to synchronize the peers' topology databases. Initially, one peer does not send all its topology information to the other; all that is exchanged is summary information. The receiving peer uses specific PTSE requests to get the full information on PTSEs that it does not know about.

Convergence within an ATM peer group (note that the goal of PNNI is to converge topology databases within a peer group, not the whole network, which is one of the features that enables ATM to scale so well) is achieved through a flooding technique. After two nodes synchronize, either node that has had to update its PTSE information with newer data as a result of the database synchronization will flood those newer

PTSEs to all its neighbors within the peer group. The speed of convergence is therefore dependent on the number of nodes within a peer group. It is expected that the most common maximum number of nodes with a peer group will be 50 (this refers to switching nodes, not end-stations).

PNNI Topology Databases Now we can preview the PNNI topology database, an example of which can be displayed on a LightStream 1010 by issuing the command `show atm pnni database detail`, as shown in Figure 3-10. This figure leaves out some of the display for clarity.

The important points to note from the display at this stage are that:

- Each PTSE is sequentially numbered by the node (that is, PTSEs are identified starting with number 1 onwards).
- ATM addresses are represented by 40-digit numbers, two digits per byte of the 20-byte address, and each PTSE lists the level indicator (in this case, 56). Previously in this text we had been writing ATM addresses with 20 digits; that was somewhat of a shorthand notation

Figure 3-10 Output of the `show atm pnni database detail` command.

```
1010# show atm pnni database detail ««==========-

Node I ID 33:124:63.00987654321000123456789ab.0123456789a.00 (name: LSIOIO)
PTSE ID Length Type Seq no. Checksum Lifetime Description

1 88 224 21951 20711 56 Int. reachable address
Time to refresh 2, time to originate 0

Type 224 (Int.Reachable address), length 32, Port 0
ATM address 24.0123410000001234567108 1.00410BOA6541.00
priority 0, leader bit NOT SET
preferred PGL 0:0:00.00000000000000000000000.000000000000.00

2 56 97 21948 47472 59 Nodal info
Time to refresh 6, time to originate 0

Type 97 (Nodal info). Length 48

Scope (level) 56, Address info length (ail) 16, Address info count    2
Pfx: 24.0123.4100.0000.0123.4567.6541..., length 104
Pfx: 24.0123.4100.0000.0123.4567.9871..., length 104

3 52 256 21958 60341       54            Ext. reachable address
Time to refresh 6, time to originate 0

Type 256 (Ext.Reachable address), length 32, Port 0
Scope (level) 56, Address info length (ail) 12, Address info count    I
Pfx: 24.0123.4100.6542.432.eOl..., length 84
```

used for convenience. The real-world convention is to represent each 4 bits with one hexadecimal character.

- Internal and external addresses (with respect to the peer group) are identified via different PTSE types, as are horizontal links, if any. Horizontal links are links between peer groups that are at the same level in the address hierarchy.
- The network prefix is associated with the switch, the ESI identifies the individual interface, and the SEL byte identifies the subinterface, if any. In this respect, ATM addressing mimics IP addressing in that it is an address of an interface, rather than an address of a switch as a whole.

In IP systems that used OSPF as the routing protocol, topology databases were formed as the basis for selecting routes to enter into the routing table. The topology database here is used for the initiation of connections that will have a VPI/VCI number, leading to the desired ATM address. Connections are initiated through PNNI signaling that uses a form of source routing to define the connection path through the network. The endstation initiating the connection will compute the source route information based on the available PTSEs in the topology database.

Next, we will look at the PNNI signaling used to establish connections and connection identifiers between PNNI nodes and networks.

PNNI Signaling

PNNI signaling is used to set up connections between two private ATM networks or two private ATM network nodes. The call setup computation has two elements. First, the route (in terms of nodes and links) to use to get from source to destination is determined. Second, each node along the route must commit to provide the necessary type and quality of service requested by the connection.

Perspective is required here to realize that connections are only established as the result of two hosts needing to communicate. Given that connections are initiated from hosts, PNNI connections that carry user data are always initiated as the result of a UNI connection request. The first stage of PNNI connection setup is that the route is selected, which leads to the creation of designated transit lists (DTL). This is the ATM networking name for a source route descriptor that lists the nodes and links to use from source to destination. Unlike IP, where the return path could be very different from the outbound path, ATM connections use a symmetric approach in that both directions of the connection are serviced through the same route. A DTL only has significance within the peer group in which it was created. As the connection setup progresses from peer group to peer group, a new DTL is computed that takes the connection through the current peer group to the next peer group in sequence. This process is illustrated in Figure 3-11.

In Figure 3-11, host A wants to contact host B. When host A sends data to Catalyst 1, which is destined for host B, Catalyst 1 initiates a connection with LS1 in peer group 1 via UNI signaling, requesting a connection to Catalyst 2. Once LS1 knows that a connection to Catalyst 2 is required, it will examine its topology database. From this it will determine that LS6 will provide access to the destination Catalyst and that LS6 is in peer group 2. LS1 will also find from its topology database that LS3 is the border node for peer group 1. At this stage a DTL is generated for the peer group that lists LS1>LS3, as well as a next-level DTL that lists PG1>PG2. When LS5 in peer group 2 gets the connection setup request, it realizes it is the final destination peer group and sets up the DTL to be LS5>LS6.

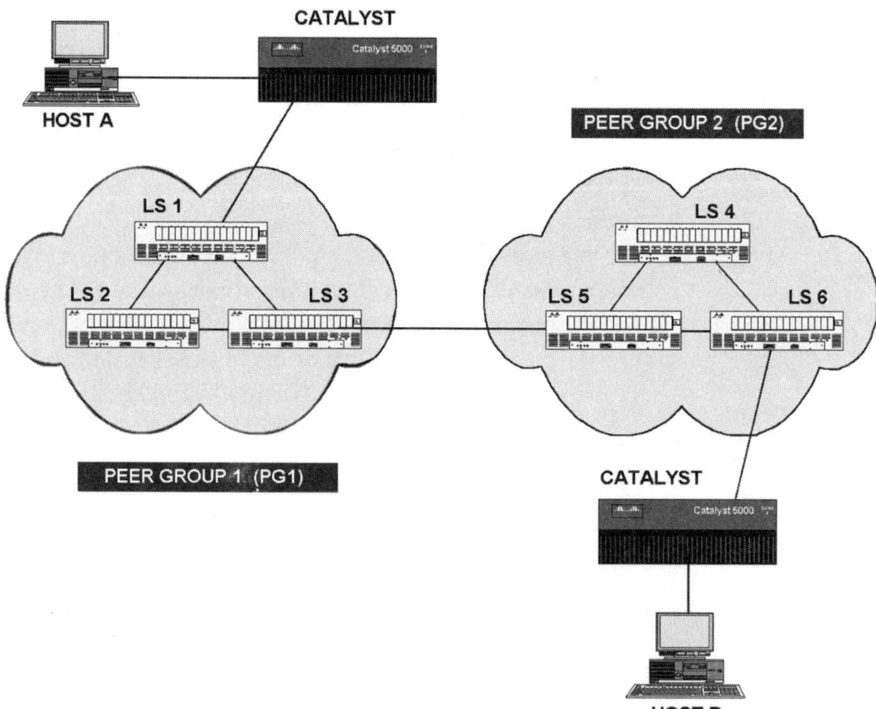

Figure 3-11 PNNI call setup in a simple ATM network.

In the event of link or other network component failure, each border node saves the DTLs so that an alternate path can be selected should that be necessary. In PNNI, this is referred to as "crankback." Crankback is useful because the DTL (i.e., the selected path through the ATM network from source to destination), based on the topology database that is common to all peer group members, is calculated at the time of connection initiation. There is the potential that an event occurs elsewhere within the peer group and a node defines the DTL prior to having its topology database synchronized with other members of the peer group. This may mean that the path selected may not have the resources available to meet the demands of the connection. If this occurs, the originating node will try to find an alternate path. If that is not possible, the call is returned back to the UNI with an indication that the call setup was unsuccessful.

The benefit of using the DTL for the crankback process is that the call does not have to go all the way back to the device originating the connection; it merely has to go back to the source of the DTL for that peer group.

Assuming that there is physical connectivity between the source and destination at the time of call setup, a good DTL will be generated. That is stage one. Stage two is to check that the selected route has the required resources to meet the demands of the connection. ATM can support the following types of service:

- Constant bit rate
- Real-time variable bit rate
- Non-real-time variable bit rate
- Unspecified bit rate
- Available bit rate

The call setup procedure does not specifically state that it wishes to set up one of these types of services specifically. Instead, values for specific information elements (IEs) are set that relate to one of these types of service. These are IEs based on the type of carrier, a traffic descriptor, and QoS requirements.

ATM and Frame Relay

It is unlikely that end-to-end ATM networks will form much of the corporate network environment for many years, if ever. However, ATM does have a place in the WAN and is already popular when used as a corporate WAN backbone with Frame Relay used to connect to branch sites. This is illustrated in Figure 3-12.

The interworking function (IWF) is responsible for encapsulating Frame Relay packets in AAL5, then cutting these up into ATM cells for transmission over the ATM backbone. The reverse is true for communication in the other direction. There are generally two generic forms of interworking: encapsulation (as used here) and translation (as used in some Ethernet-to-FDDI switches).

Frame Relay to ATM Connectivity Issues

It is not worth going through a full explanation of Frame Relay here; the *Cisco TCP/IP Routing Professional Reference* covered Frame Relay implementations on Cisco equipment in some detail. What is worth considering is how ATM and Frame Relay should operate, given that in the environment described above, both will be used to transport information from source to destination. However, we will review the relevant features of Frame Relay here.

The ITU (International Telecommunications Union) and the ATM Forum have defined two types of interworking for ATM and Frame Relay, which are network interworking and service interworking.

Frame Relay Review Frame Relay basically sets up permanent virtual circuits (PVCs) that are identified as DLCI numbers to a device connecting to the Frame Relay cloud. Frame Relay works on the basis of

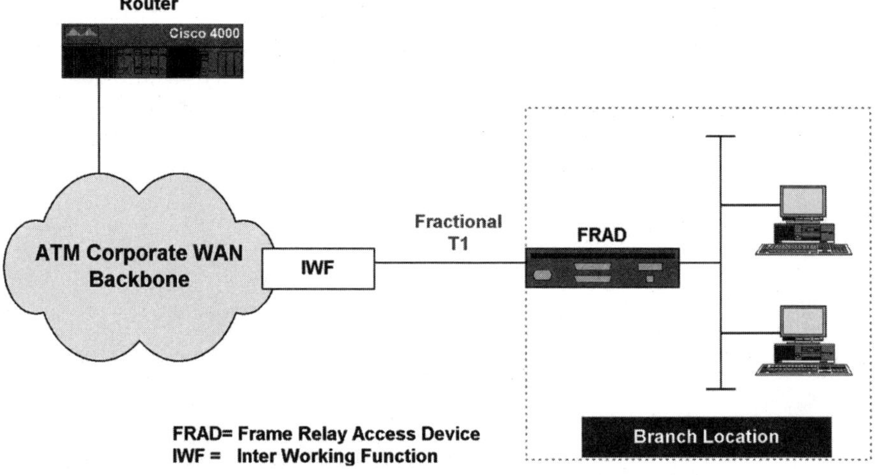

Figure 3-12 Interconnecting ATM and Frame Relay.

guaranteeing a certain amount of throughput, and making more available to an endstation if the network can support it. The key elements of this process are the CIR (committed information rate), DE (discard eligible), FECN (forward explicit congestion notification), BECN (backward explicit congestion notification), Bc (committed burst size), Be (excess burst size), and the committed time interval.

The most common specification network engineers have to make when buying a Frame Relay connection from a carrier is to size the CIR. Typically a Frame Relay connection will be bought with something like a 128K link, having a CIR of 64 Kbit/sec or so. The concept is that the purchaser will always be able to get at least 64 Kbit/sec and occasionally something more.

Whether this whole concept is real or not is a matter of some debate. It is extremely difficult for Frame Relay providers to monitor in real time the bandwidth utilization of each client and guarantee that they will each get their CIR, particularly during periods of severe congestion. What is more usual now is that the CIR is guaranteed during "normal" operation and as an average for the committed time interval (discussed next).

The second important service specification relates to the Bc and Be parameters. The Bc defines the number of bits that can be sent during a committed time interval, based on the CIR. In reality, the Bc merely states that for a specific time, you will get the maximum throughput your CIR allows. For example, if the Bc is 384K, with a CIR of 64 Kbit/sec, you get 6 (calculated by 382/64) seconds at Bc guaranteed (the 6-second value is the committed time interval). The Be is a separate number of bits, which specifies the maximum amount of uncommitted data in excess of Bc that the Frame Relay network can attempt to deliver during the committed time interval.

In practice this means that you are only guaranteed the CIR as an average over the length of your committed time interval and that you may burst above that, but that burst data may not get through. So with a committed time interval of 6 seconds, for any 6-second time interval, you may get 30 Kbit/sec for the first 2 seconds, followed by higher than 64 Kbit/sec for the next 4 seconds, so that over 6 seconds you average 64 Kbit/sec throughput, leaving the CIR intact.

The primary mechanism that leads to frames being discarded on a Frame Relay network during times of heavy load is the DE (discard eligible bit). This is normally set on the Frame Relay network access device for specific types of traffic, so one could define all Web traffic discard eligible, but not in-house application traffic. In addition, frames in the Be size range are normally marked as DE.

The DE bit really comes into play when FECN and BECN start to kick in. The FECN bit is set by a switch in the Frame Relay cloud that is experiencing congestion. This FECN bit is set in packets sent in the direction of the data flow to the recipient of the data. Once the recipient of the data flow receives FECN bits, it sets a BECN bit in packets going back to the source of the data, telling it to back off. If congestion continues even with the setting of FECN and BECN bits, packets marked with the DE bit will be discarded first. If congestion still persists, regular packets will be dropped also. This is illustrated in Figure 3-13.

This is all very unpalatable to the ATM world, which is geared toward producing guaranteed end-to-end delivery. Next, we'll look at network interworking and service interworking, which have to mesh together these disparate technologies.

Network Interworking Network interworking enables a Frame Relay endstation to communicate with an ATM endstation. In this model, ATM is really just used as a transport mechanism, with the real data being carried within frames. Of course, the frames are encapsulated within AAL5 and segmented into cells for transmission over the ATM network, but the receiving endstation still has to decode frames. This requires the receiving ATM endstation to be able to understand frames. Essentially, the interworking function and ATM endstation have Frame Relay protocols running on top of the ATM and ATM segmentation/reassembly layer.

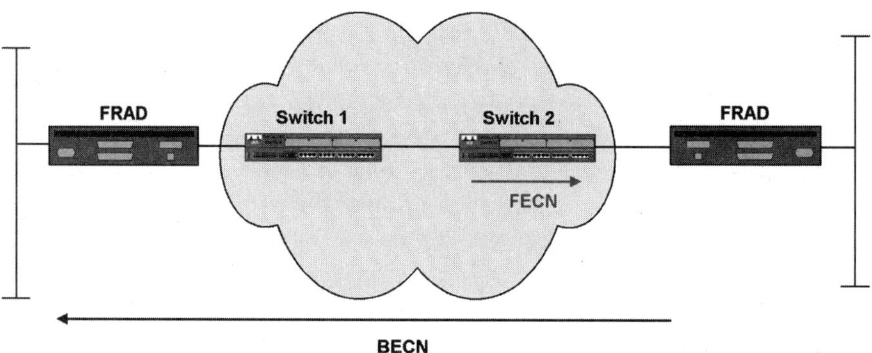

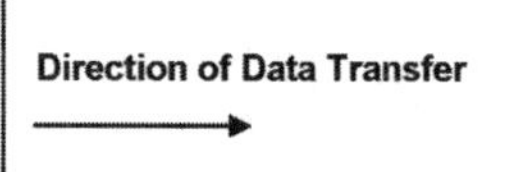

Figure 3-13 FECN and BECN in a Frame Relay network.

The detail of this operation is contained within the ITU-T recommendation I.555 and the ATM forum implementation FRF.5. These specifications mandate the use of AAL5 adaptation, the mapping of a DLCI to one VPI/VCI ATM connection, mapping DE to ATM Cell Loss Priority, and mapping of the FECN/BECN to the ATM EFCI congestion field.

Service Interworking This is a more complete function than network interworking. In service interworking neither the Frame Relay endstation nor the ATM endstation knows anything about being connected to an endstation of the other persuasion. In this case, the service interworking function handles all conversions between the two technologies, delivering full translation between the protocols. The following outlines the main features of service interworking:

- Cell Loss Priority (CLP) and DE are translated. For traffic traveling from Frame Relay to ATM, the DE is either mapped to CLP if present or all cells are given a preset CLP value.
- Congestion is again handled by an FECN to EFCI mapping and vice versa in the reverse direction.
- DLCIs are mapped one-to-one to VPI/VCI numbers.

As can be seen, service interworking is basically bidirectional protocol translation performed within the ATM network, whereas network interworking is Frame Relay frames encapsulated within ATM and requires ATM endstations to reassemble Frame Relay frames from cells and pass those frames up to higher protocol layers.

Frame-Based UNI (FUNI) and DXI

For either of the interworking functions described above, the Frame Relay endstation knows nothing of ATM communications. With Frame-Based UNI (FUNI), however, a frame-based endstation may make use of an ATM network via the regular ATM-UNI interface, as a FUNI-enabled endsystem is ATM-aware. Although a FUNI endsystem uses frames instead of cells, it is still able to access the key ATM-UNI functions. A FUNI endstation can assign VPI/VCIs and make use of UNI signaling but has limited address range and does not support all types of ATM traffic (no CBR or ABR types).

Within the FUNI header, 10 bits are used for the frame address, 4 bits for the VPI, and 6 bits for the VCI. The FUNI frame does carry both a

Congestion Notification field, which is used to relay the ATM EFCI bit value, and the usual CLP, which is copied from the FUNI frame to the ATM cell directly.

A similar interface is the data exchange interface, or DXI for short. The DXI interface specifies the connection between a DTE, such as a Cisco router serial interface and a circuit termination device, such as an ATM DSU. The benefit is that the router interface can send DXI format variable-length packets at slower speeds, such as T-1 speeds, then the ATM DSU can cut up the frames into cells.

This is beneficial for slower-speed links because of the percentage protocol overhead in variable-length frames compared to fixed-length cells. With ATM cells, the header is 9.4 percent of the data transmitted, which is OK when you have plenty of available bandwidth. However, on the slower links, bandwidth is at more of a premium and the cell overhead is too great. With variable-length frames, the header overhead is generally far less. DXI and FUNI are contrasted in Figure 3-14.

DXI is currently more widely deployed than FUNI, as the latter is a newer specification and there are far more DXI-capable devices avail-

Figure 3-14 DXI connections to an ATM network.

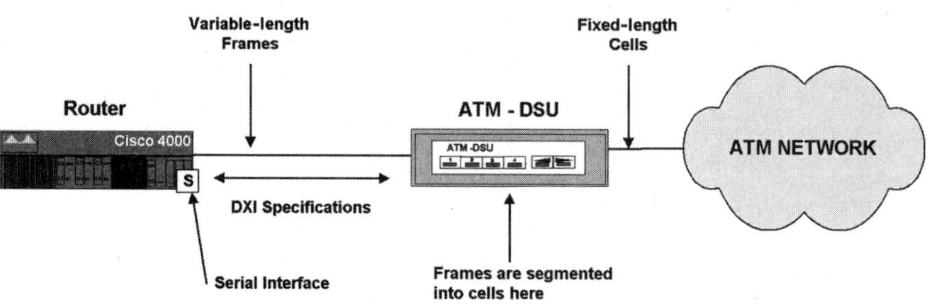

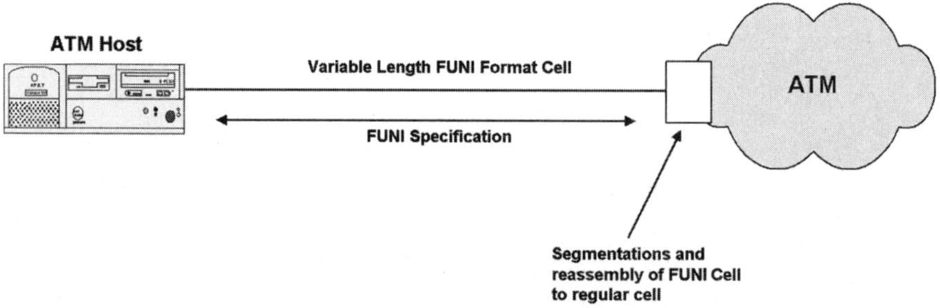

able. As ATM becomes more widely deployed, it is expected that FUNI will replace DXI.

ATM and IP Integration

The most popular network layer protocol of the present time, and for the immediate future, is the TCP/IP suite of protocols. When ATM networks are deployed, the likelihood is that they will have to transport IP datagrams. We then have to consider how we mesh these two technologies that have considerable overlap and, in many ways, opposing design goals. As an example, whose routing mechanism do we use, IP with OSPF and IGRP protocols or ATM with its own OSPF-derived mechanism? Also, how do we support the ARP (Address Resolution Protocol) of IP across an ATM network? There are various solutions to all the issues that face using both IP and ATM within the same network. Some are simple; some are complex. In the next few sections we'll cover the theory necessary to understanding these options, and in Chapter 6, we'll show the Cisco device configurations necessary to support them.

Review of IP Over ATM Issues

We have already hinted at some of the issues with running TCP/IP and ATM together. The problems exist as the protocols overlap in what they are trying to do. The picture is complicated further when you consider that the IP model is connectionless, whereas ATM is connection-oriented. True, TCP is a connection-oriented protocol, but establishing TCP connections relies on the IP layer, which is connectionless and allows it to utilize broadcast mechanisms like ARP to locate host addresses. ATM is a nonbroadcast multiple-access (NBMA) network like Frame Relay (the operation of NBMA networks was discussed in the *Cisco TCP/IP Routing Professional Reference*). As such, one of the key integration issues is how to provide support for these connectionless broadcast-reliant mechanisms within the connection-oriented ATM network.

We also have the opportunity to utilize ATM's ability to establish direct connections between devices that are on different IP subnets, without recourse to a router. The most common way of integrating IP and ATM is termed Classic IP Over ATM (CIOA) and maintains the IP rules of communicating between subnets via a router. This method reduces ATM to a link layer protocol (albeit a potentially very fast one) and does not enable endstations to take advantage of the sophisticated features of ATM as a network protocol. We will look at CIOA next.

Classic IP Over ATM

CIOA is formally defined in RFC 1577 and was developed by the IETF so that ATM technology could be introduced to existing routed networks with as little disruption to the existing operation as possible. Proceeding with the CIOA approach enables network engineers to gain familiarity with ATM operation and equipment without changing their view of their network too dramatically. Once familiarity with CIOA is gained, operations staff can move on to look at utilizing enhancements like the Next Hop Resolution Protocol (to be discussed next) and gradually migrate to using more and more ATM facilities.

As we have said, CIOA uses ATM as a link layer protocol within the overall IP communications scheme; however, this is done for unicast (i.e., point-to-point) communications only. As such, hosts on the subnet are allocated an IP address and an ATM address. Therefore, when a host communicates with another host on the same subnet, an address resolution has to be performed to resolve the destination IP address to a destination ATM address. With this communications method, the router is making all the routing and filter/security decisions based on the IP rules of communication.

To discuss CIOA further we need to introduce a new term, the LIS, which stands for the logical IP subnet. All this refers to is the collection of ATM interfaces that are assigned to the same IP subnet in the network and communicate with each other directly using ATM. In Figure 3-15, examples are interfaces A, B, and C, which are all in LIS 3. The other key points to note on Figure 3-15 are that each router has a physical connection into two subnets and each subnet has its own ATM ARP function. In this mode, if host 3 wishes to contact host 1, the path for communication routes via R3 and R2, even though there is a direct ATM path from host 3 to host 1.

There are two types of virtual circuits within ATM: a switched virtual circuit (SVC) and a permanent virtual circuit (PVC). The ATM ARP service is used for SVC connections, whereas inverse ATM ARP is used for PVC connections.

SVC operation with ATM ARP operates in much the same way that ARP does in a LAN environment. In the LAN environment, if an IP endstation wants to contact another IP endstation within the same subnet

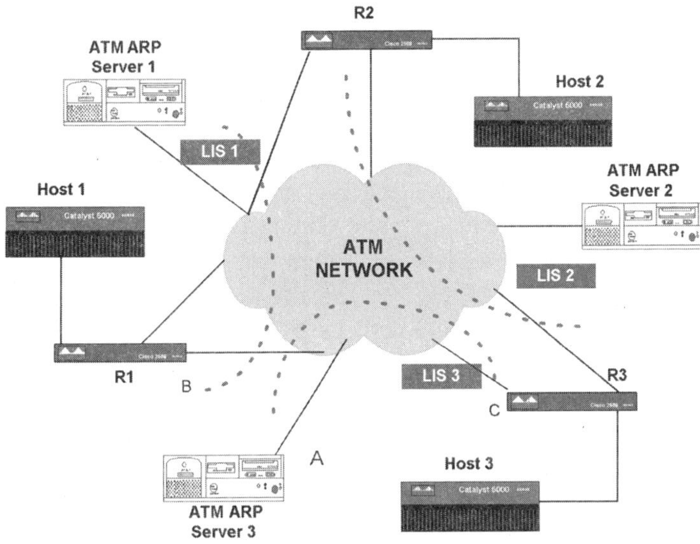

Figure 3-15 CIOA using ATM ARP to resolve IP addressing to ATM addresses within the single subnet.

that it does not know the MAC address of, a broadcast ARP packet is issued by the first IP endstation, asking for the endstation with the desired IP address to reply with its MAC address. The endstation that possesses the destination IP address picks up the broadcast and replies with its MAC address, and then connectionless point-to-point unicasts can proceed on the LAN between the source and destination endstation.

The only difference between how this operates and how ATM ARP operates when establishing an SVC connection is that instead of the source node issuing an ARP broadcast, it makes a request of the ATM ARP server for the ATM address of the destination IP node. This assumes, of course, that the ATM ARP server has a complete map of ATM-to-IP address for all nodes within that LIS. The ATM ARP server may be defined on a router and not need a separate device to support this function.

In multicast environments, the ATM ARP principle is extended in a MARS, or Multicast Address Resolution Server. The most significant difference between a MARS and an ATM ARP server is that the MARS server contains a table that maps IP group addresses (the Class D multicast addresses) to a list of ATM addresses that consists of the devices registered for each multicast group. (MARS is discussed further in Chapter 6.)

There is no mechanism by which a client (such as host 1 in Figure 3-15) can dynamically learn the ATM ARP server address. Each device in the LIS needs to be manually configured with the address of the ATM ARP server. When each client starts up, it will use the preconfigured

ATM ARP server address to signal for a connection. The ATM ARP server then uses inverse ARP to obtain the ATM/IP server address pair from the new client and inserts that pair in its server table. Each client will send periodic updates to the ATM ARP server to refresh its address pair in the server tables.

So, with CIOA, we are using ATM as a potentially high-speed link layer protocol, with the classic IP routing between subnets intact. To do this, routers need to connect to the ATM network using something like an ATM Interface Processor to support the higher speeds of the ATM network. With this model the ATM network looks like just another interface on the router that provides point-to-point communication.

In a PVC network, the connection across the ATM network is already defined, and what is needed is to determine the protocol (IP) address that exists at the other end of that PVC. This is essentially how Frame Relay operates, with the DLCI providing a local connection identifier for access to a specific IP address. With a PVC network, the client does not need to contact an ATM ARP server; all it does is issue an inverse ATM ARP request down each PVC to obtain the IP address of the remote connection.

CIOA does provide access to the higher transmission speeds of ATM and may be useful for a small campus network, possibly where high-resolution video images need to be transferred between workgroups in separate buildings. With a small number of subnets, this mode of operation can provide the benefits of ATM transmission speeds, without network operations staff facing a whole-scale change in network operation. It does, however, have problems retaining optimal operation and scaling to a network that contains large numbers of hosts and subnets. It is clear to see even from the small network in Figure 3-15 that as host 3 is directly connected to the ATM network, it would be beneficial to take advantage of ATM's ability to connect directly to host 1 should it wish to, rather than be forced to route through router 2. The mechanism developed to enable this type of communication is the Next Hop Resolution Protocol (NHRP) and is the next stage in IP/ATM integration. The key point about NHRP is that it breaks the normal rules of communication between IP subnets by allowing direct communication between devices that are not on the same subnet.

NHRP—The Next Hop Resolution Protocol

The key difference between CIOA and NHRP networks is the method used to resolve a destination IP address to an ATM address. In CIOA, the

ATM ARP server delivers ATM addresses for hosts within one subnet. NHRP, however, allows hosts to get destination ATM addresses across multiple subnets. As such, NHRP is an address resolution protocol, rather than another form of routing protocol. However, as the ATM address resolved for the next hop is often outside of the IP subnet of the originating host, the endstations need modified stacks to work with NHRP.

Because NHRP allows address resolution across multiple subnets, it can be considered a superset of ATM ARP. The network we will use to describe NHRP is illustrated in Figure 3-16.

At first glance, it may appear that all we have done is replace the ATM ARP server per LIS with a Next Hop Server (NHS) process per LIS. That is all that has changed in physical terms, but the operation of the NHS is radically different from the ATM ARP server. Whereas the ATM ARP server provided ATM addresses for IP interfaces within the one subnet, the NHS obtains the ATM address of the final destination, not just the next hop router.

An NHS has two modes of operation. The first is *server mode,* which supports manual configuration of ATM-IP address pairs from remote subnets. The second is called *fabric mode.* Fabric mode enables an NHS to retrieve information about remote subnets automatically, by querying routing tables generated by inter- and intradomain routing protocols (like IGRP and BGP, respectively).

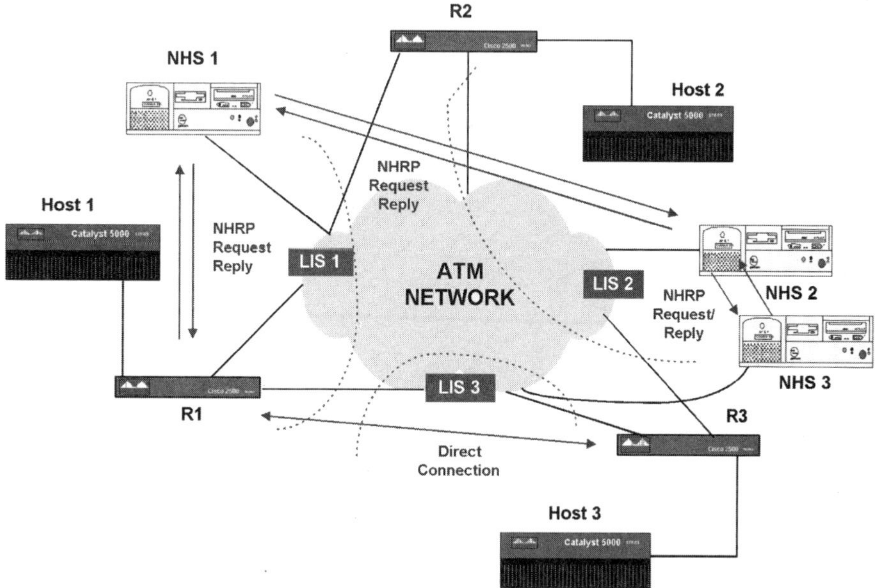

Figure 3-16 NHRP connection being established across subnet boundaries.

The following describes how the NHS works in Figure 3-16. Supposing host 1 wants to contact host 3, the shortest route is for router 1 to establish a direct connection with router 3. However, router 1 does not have an interface connected to LIS 3. So router 1 makes a request to NHS 1 for the ATM address of the next hop machine to get to router 3. If NHS 1 recognizes the destination IP address of router 3, the corresponding ATM address is returned to router 1 immediately. If the address pair is unknown, NHS 1 will consult other NHS servers via the NHRP request/reply path shown, which will pass the request on until an NHS with the required information is found. The information is passed back along the path it came from, so that all NHSs on the path can update their tables with the new information. Once router 1 has the destination ATM address of router 3, a direct connection is established, as shown.

So we have moved from using ATM as just a link layer protocol with CIOA to making use of ATM's ability to cut across subnet boundaries with NHRP. The next level of using ATM within a network is LAN emulation (LANE) to generate emulated LANs across an ATM switching fabric.

LANE

LANE was designed to connect remote LANs together over an ATM backbone. A significant advantage of this approach is that LAN applications can run unchanged over a LANE connection and have no idea they are running over ATM. With several hundreds of megabits per second available, it is possible to emulate full LAN bandwidth and connectivity across the wide area. The wide area links that use LANE to extend LANs across the wide area are termed *emulated LANs* and provide LAN services for both Ethernet and token ring. It should be noted that LANE does not support connection of an Ethernet to a token ring segment, or any support for FDDI. Additionally, an endstation equipped with an ATM NIC can become a member of either a token ring or Ethernet emulated LAN.

LANE operates exclusively at the data-link layer, and as such, ATM stations on the LANE connection appear as if they were on the same LAN as the associated Ethernet LANs on the ends of the LANE connection. The emulated LAN that extends across the ATM network and the two LANs it joins together all form one subnet and one broadcast domain—in effect, as if they were all part of the same VLAN. As with VLANs, it is necessary to connect via a router for two ELANs to communicate.

Compared to CIOA or even NHRP, LANE is complex. Understanding this technology is further hindered by the arcane and overlapping terminology used in the specifications. So before discussing LANE operation, we'll need to define a few terms.

LANE Terminology

LEC This is the LAN emulation client, a LANE endstation where the LANE protocols run. Most commonly this is implemented in a Catalyst LANE module that is optimized for that purpose. The LANE client connects directly to the ATM switch, which in the Cisco environment is a LightStream 1010.

LECS This term does not refer to a collection of LAN emulation clients; that term is LECs, the plural of LEC. LECS refers to the LAN Emulation Configuration Server, which is a server that contains configuration information for several ELANs. One LECS per domain, or collection of ELANs, has to be configured. The sort of information a LECS contains is the ATM address of the LES.

LES This is the LAN Emulation Server, which provides address resolution services within the LANE environment. The resolution is supplied to an endstation that knows the MAC address of the device it wishes to contact but does not know the ATM address. This service uses LE_ARP, or LAN Emulation ARP, which is different from IP ARP. IP ARP resolves IP (layer 3) addresses to MAC (layer 2) addresses. LE_ARP resolves MAC to ATM addresses, which in this model are both at layer 2.

BUS The Broadcast and Unknown Server is used when a LEC wants to send a broadcast or contact an as-yet unknown ATM address. The BUS handles sending data to multiple locations, thus emulating the effect of broadcasts. In an emulated LAN environment, the LES and BUS functions are mostly implemented on one unit, referred to as the *LES/BUS,* which is configured on one Catalyst.

Overview of LANE Communications

Figure 3-17 illustrates what we are trying to achieve with the LANE protocols, in terms of trying to extend an Ethernet or token ring LAN across ATM. Each ELAN is considered a separate broadcast domain, and in the Cisco implementation, each ELAN is referred to by name rather than

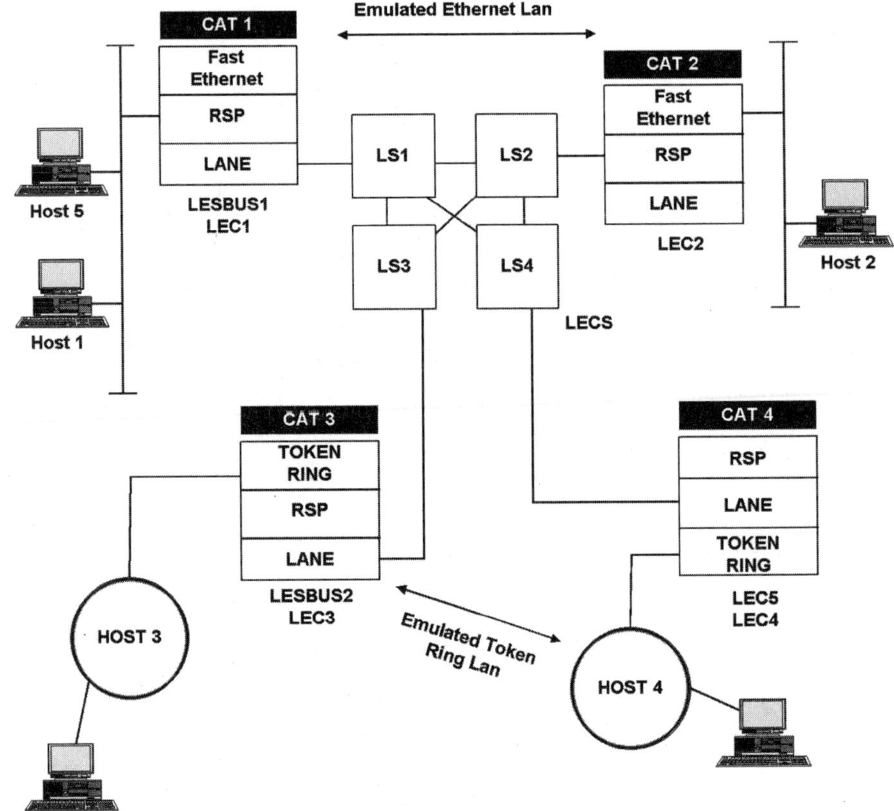

Figure 3-17 Emulated Ethernet and token ring LAN.

number in device configurations. ELANs are connected to each other via router functions just as VLANs were, and as such, LANE conforms to the normal IP subnet rules.

Figure 3-17 shows both an emulated Ethernet and token ring being implemented across an ATM network. An ATM network consists of ATM switches, such as the LightStream 1010, represented by LS1 through 4. The device that accesses the ATM network from the local Ethernet or token ring segment is generally a Catalyst, or a router ATM Interface Processor in the Cisco environment. So in Figure 3-17, Cat 1 uses its Fast Ethernet interface to connect to local stations and the LANE module for transmission through the ATM network across the emulated Ethernet LAN. There is one LECS per LANE domain, which is implemented in Cat 4, and each emulated LAN has its own LES/BUS. As can be seen, each Catalyst runs its own LAN Emulation Client software to communicate with the ATM network. In fact, if there were several

VLANs on Cat 1, each would need its own LEC configured for it to communicate across a VLAN.

As stated initially, LAN applications do not know that they are using ATM, and the whole business of LANE communication connections is hidden from them. So, for host 1 to communicate with host 2, the first hop is to Cat 1. We now have to work out how Cat 1 will forward data to Cat 2 for the data to reach host 2. At this stage, host 1 thinks that host 2 is on the same LAN, and therefore sends out the Ethernet packet with the destination IP and MAC address of host 2.

Cat 1 will be configured to associate the VLAN that host 1 is on with the appropriate ELAN to get the packet to the destination LAN. Through the LANE processes that we will describe, Cat 1 will set up a direct connection with Cat 2 and send the data to Cat 2, which will deliver the packet to host 2.

The exact process for the Cat 1-to-Cat 2 connection to be made across LANE is a lengthy and complex one, so it may help to break this down into two phases. First, we'll look at achieving the initial state for Cat 1, whereby all the configuration information is available to the devices that need it and control connections are established. Second, we'll see how the LANE facilities are used to establish the data transmission connection between Cat 1 and Cat 2.

For the first phase of reaching the initialized state, let's summarize the main points of what is going to happen before considering them in detail:

- LEC (in this case Cat 1) connects to LECS and finds the LES address.
- LEC joins ELAN.
- MAC address-to-ATM address map is registered with the LES.
- A connection to the BUS is established to support broadcast and multicast.

The first thing a LEC (in this instance Cat 1) does when it comes up on the ATM network is contact the LECS to find out the address of its LES. Once the LES has been found, the LEC uses the LES to resolve all MAC addresses to ATM addresses through LAN Emulation ARP (LE_ARP).

The first question is how does the LEC know the address of the LECS? There are several options. Given that the attached LightStream has the address of the LECS for that LANE domain configured, each attached Catalyst can use ILMI to retrieve the LECS address, or connection 0/17 (VPI = 0, VCI = 17), which will initiate a connection directly to the LECS.

Failing that, the LEC will try a well-known address for the LECS, which is kind of a default ATM address for the LECS that all LECs know about. Of course, your LECS will have to be configured to have this specific address (47007900000000000000000000A03E00000100). Cisco provides a proprietary option also, which is to configure the LECS address directly into the LEC.

If we assume that one of the methods above works for the LEC to contact the LECS, the LEC will get the address of the LES for its ELAN and connect to it. Once established, this SVC is referred to as the *configure direct VCC* (virtual circuit connection). The LEC will then move on to join the ELAN phase where the LEC registers with the LES. As part of this join phase, the LEC may register one or more MAC addresses and the corresponding ATM address with the LES. In the case where the LEC registers multiple MAC addresses, it is registering MAC addresses on behalf of attached endstations. This would occur if Cat 1 were registering MAC addresses with the LES for host 1 and host 5 in Figure 3-17. When the addresses of host 1 and host 5 are registered with the LES, they are registered as being via a proxy. That is, the LES knows that to get to them it has to connect via Cat 1.

Next, the LEC will send an LE_ARP request to the LES to obtain the ATM address of the BUS (in Cisco, this will be the same address as the LES). Once the BUS address is determined, the LEC establishes a connection with the BUS (known as the *multicast send VCC*), which connects the newly joined LEC to the point-to-multipoint broadcast channel (the *multicast forward VCC*), thus emulating a LAN's broadcast capabilities. The effect is that the ATM ELAN looks like an extension to the Ethernet LAN to the hosts on the physical Ethernet network. In essence, host 1 and host 2 will be configured for the same IP subnet. Figure 3-18 shows how VLANs and ATM ELANs are connected on a LANE network.

We are now ready to move on to the second phase, which consists of Cat 1 establishing an ATM connection to Cat 2, to support host 1 communicating with host 2. Given that host 1 knows the MAC address of host 2, the job of Cat 1 is to get the ATM address that corresponds to this MAC address and set up a connection to support data transfer between Cat 1 and the destination ATM address. First, Cat 1 issues an LE_ARP request to the LES to determine the ATM address to go to, in order to reach the destination MAC address (the MAC of host 2). While Cat 1 is waiting for this reply, it also sends frames destined for host 2 to the BUS. The BUS then forwards these frames to all members of the ELAN. If the LES knows the ATM address for the required MAC address, it replies fairly quickly to the Cat 1 LE_ARP. If the destination MAC address is unknown, the LE_ARP request is sent to all ELAN members that registered as proxies to see if the MAC address is known by them. Ultimately, Cat 1 will get a reply to its LE_ARP request and have the ATM address to send to.

Armed with the destination ATM address, Cat 1 can now establish a data direct VCC to Cat 2. We now have a potential problem of the frames that have been delivered by Cat 1 to the BUS and passed on to Cat 2 being received out of sequence with the frames being sent directly to Cat 2. This is a problem, as a LAN does not deliver out-of-sequence frames (remember the lengths we went to with Spanning Tree Protocol to ensure a single loop-free path) and we have to emulate the operation of a LAN here. The way we get around this problem in LANE is to make use of the Flush protocol.

The operation of the Flush protocol is as follows. When Cat 1 establishes the data direct VCC with Cat 2, it also sends a special flush packet to the BUS and stops sending the BUS any more data. When Cat 2 receives the flush packet, it returns it to Cat 1, which in effect tells Cat 1 that all the packets it sent via the BUS to Cat 2 have been received by Cat 2. Now that Cat 1 has a connection to Cat 2 and all the frames passing through the BUS have been flushed, full-speed communication between Cat 1 and Cat 2 can now take place. Once packets destined for

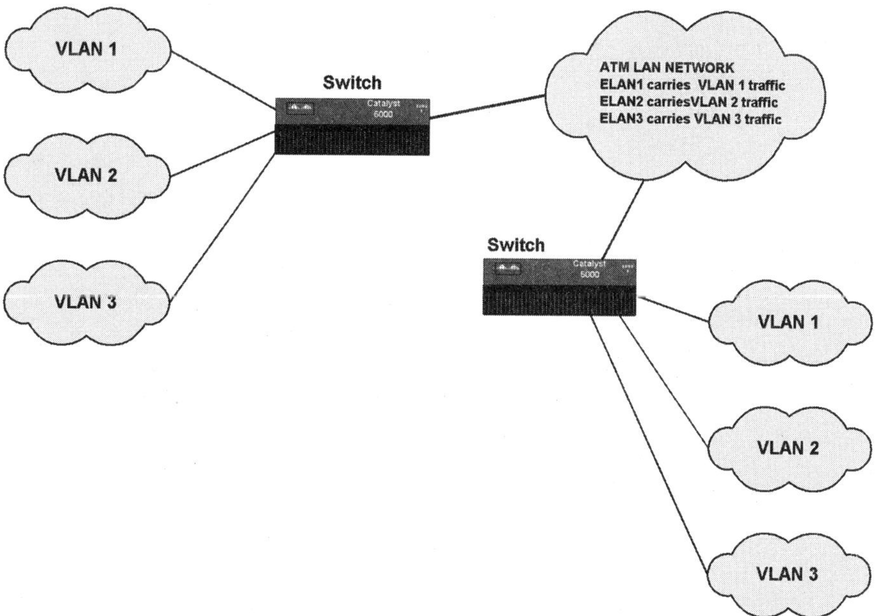

Figure 3-18 ATM VLANs extend VLANs across an ATM network.

host 2 are received by Cat 2, Cat 2 forwards them on to host 2 as it would any other packet received from any other segment belonging to that VLAN.

Implementing LANE and using an ELAN to connect two parts of a VLAN that are physically separated across an ATM network can be thought of as a form of VLAN trunking. LANE, however, provides more functionality than trunk links like ISL, which we covered earlier. Particularly, LANE allows an Ethernet host to communicate directly with an ATM host on the associated ELAN. ISL did not allow any host connectivity on the VLAN trunk. With ISL, the VLAN tag was kept in the frame for transmission across the trunk, which is not the case with LANE. Essentially, with LANE we are giving all the ATM devices MAC addresses that are addressable directly from the associated VLAN.

In the example depicted in Figure 3-17, host 1 will address packets to host 2 via MAC address, which Cat 1 will forward on to the ELAN, knowing that the MAC address of host 2 does not reside on the same LAN as host 1. If host 1 needs to resolve a destination IP address to a destination MAC address prior to commencing communication, it will issue the usual IP ARP broadcast, which will be forwarded by Cat 1 to the BUS, which will send it on to all ELAN members.

LANE has some definite advantages, but it is extremely complex in comparison to other ATM technologies and is still bound by the normal IP subnet rules. In addition, because the BUS maintains a separate connection for all members of the VLAN, the scalability of LANE to large numbers of hosts per ELAN has to be in question.

Just as with CIOA, where we had NHRP to make full use of ATM's ability to cut across subnet boundaries, we now have MPOA (Multi-Protocol Over ATM), which combines LANE and NHRP to take advantage of LANE, allowing it to be more efficient across the ATM network.

MPOA

Multi-Protocol Over ATM is the ultimate level of complexity currently available in deploying an ATM network. Because this standard is still very new and quite complex, we will only illustrate specific implementations of this protocol in overview in later practicals. However, a brief theoretical overview is appropriate here.

As with nearly all the different ways of implementing ATM on a network, there are some new and unique terms that need to be defined:

MPC Multi-Protocol Client; this takes an equivalent place in the network to the LEC in LANE.

MPS Multi-Protocol Server; this is resident on the same machine as the NHS (MPOA is basically LANE with NHRP). The MPS accepts connections from the MPC and provides ATM address resolution services. When drawing an MPOA network, you can regard the MPS as taking the place of an NHS in an NHRP network.

IASG Internetwork Address Subgroup, which is a fancy name for an IP subnet.

Edge device A physical device that connects legacy networks to ATM networks. It is referred to as an edge device because it is placed on the logical edge of the ATM network cloud.

Virtual router An MPOA term that refers to router functions implemented in software that may be distributed throughout the ATM network. A virtual router provides path computation and packet-forwarding services. In effect, a virtual router performs path computation and routing table maintenance in one location (typically an ATM switch), then uses the ATM network as the router bus to transport packets; the router ports are defined on ATM edge devices.

The main MPOA system components are illustrated in Figure 3-19.

So far we have considered intrasubnet (meaning within the one subnet) ATM address resolution using ATM ARP and intersubnet address resolution (between subnets) using NHRP that allows ATM devices to communicate directly across subnet boundaries. With intersubnet address resolution, the ATM address supplied will be the ultimate destination node, not an interim router, even if the source and destination nodes are assigned to different IP subnets. As MPOA utilizes NHRP, it provides cut-through capabilities and does not conform to the standard IP subnet rules. Thus, the MPOA facilities will allow a host on IASG1 in Figure 3-19 to communicate with hosts on IASG2 via a connection between LS1010a and LS1010b, without having to route via LS1010c.

MPOA Operation

In MPOA operation, physical routers and other edge devices use LANE to connect to an ELAN on the network. So, an MPC will go through the normal LANE initialization procedures when it first joins an ELAN.

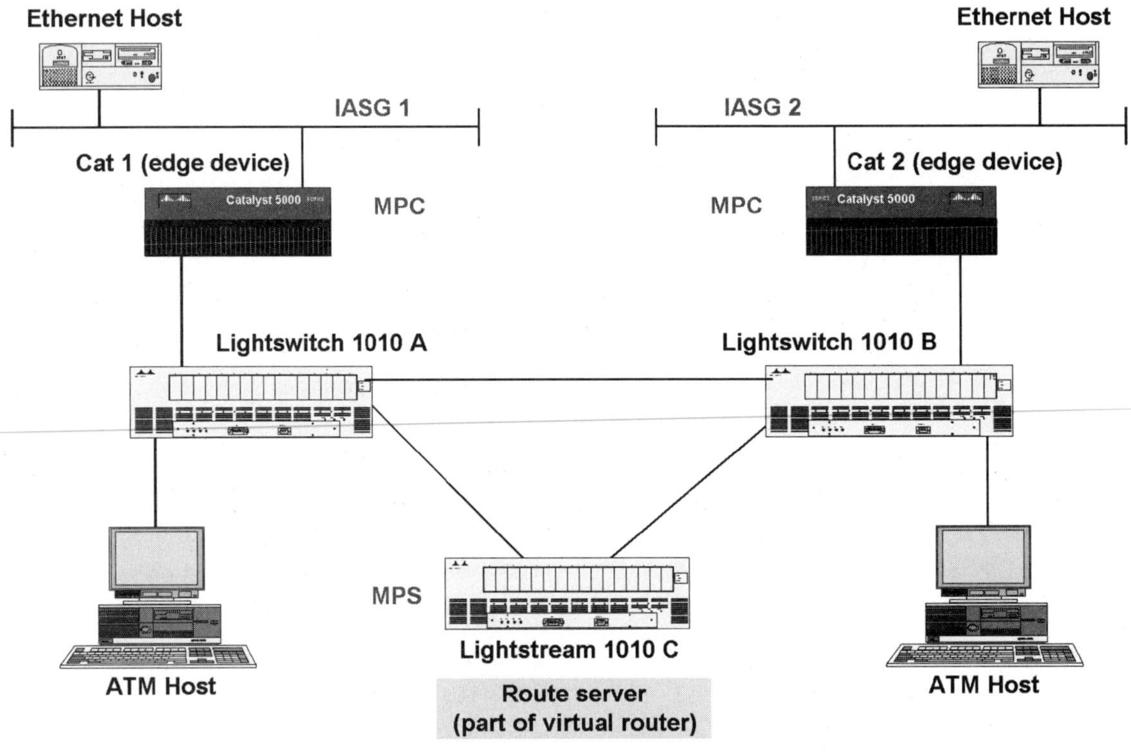

Figure 3-19 Main MPOA system components.

Within the MPC, however, is a layer 3 forwarding function that operates under the normal IP subnet rules. It is at the MPS (implemented in a router that contains an NHS function) where we provide the cut-through functionality for ATM-connected edge devices to establish connections across subnet boundaries. Essentially, the MPS routing function (running either in a physical or virtual router) will use the NHS to obtain the cut-through ATM address to establish a direct connection from source to ultimate destination without passing through a router.

A Word on RFC 1483

In all of the discussions of NHRP, LANE, MPOA, and CIOA (RFC 1577), we have made no mention of how the frames generated by legacy Ethernet or token ring hosts are encapsulated for transmission over the cell-based ATM network. In fact, they all use a common encapsulation technique that is specified in RFC 1483. RFC 1483 is termed Multi-Protocol Encapsulation Over ATM, not to be confused with the ATM Forum's specification for MPOA.

RFC 1483 actually describes two methods for connectionless protocols to communicate over an ATM network: LLC/SNAP encapsulation and virtual connection-based multiplexing. We will only consider the LLC/SNAP encapsulation, as this is the one used by CIOA and ARP over ATM. This specification can be thought of as a precursor to CIOA in that it is static (no ATM ARP) and it also conforms to the usual IP subnet rules. RFC 1483 calls for local virtual circuits to be associated with destination IP addresses, much the same as a DLCI does in a Frame Relay network. With PVC connections, these associations need to be manually applied. With SVCs the associations are supplied by whatever signaling procedures are in place.

With LLC/SNAP encapsulation, the layer 2 DSAP, SSAP, CTRL, and SNAP header fields are encapsulated along with the IP packet into an AAL 5 PDU, which is padded to bring it up to an appropriate number of bytes that will allow the whole to be split into cells without any leftover.

Plain RFC 1483 encapsulation by itself is not promoted for use in many places anymore, as it requires lots of manual configuration and reduces the functionality of an ATM link to a fast leased line. However, this encapsulation is still important, since it forms the basis for the enhanced techniques such as CIOA and LANE that followed.

Tag Switching

Tags and tag switching are another layer 2 feature that is promising to deliver faster switching performance to routed networks. As we shall see, although I classify tag switching as a layer 2 feature, it does rely upon a layer 3 being present and actually works by combining layer 2 and layer 3 functionality. The idea behind this technology is that there is a database of IP address destinations mapped to tag IDs, which is maintained within a switch/router that allows the switch/router to use the tags rather than resort to layer 3 mechanisms to forward the frame. By swapping tags that are small data elements and only performing a single lookup for the tag, performance in forwarding frames is enhanced.

The importance of this idea to ATM is that within ATM we already have tags assigned for destinations in the form of VPI/VCI numbers.

Thus, it is perceived that tag switching will become very important for the future of high-speed packet forwarding between IP and ATM networks. The benefits of going to all the trouble with tags is that, particularly for large internetworks, layer 3 scalability through hierarchy is maintained and combined with very simple and therefore speedy switching logic.

From our knowledge of legacy networks (by this I mean a classic IP network based on routers) and of VLANs, we can understand the two most important features of tag switching. First, in legacy networks, we know that an ARP table is used to reassign source and destination MAC addresses to a packet each time it traverses a router. We also know that VLAN IDs (which can be thought of as a kind of tag) are appended to a frame as it enters the VLAN switching cloud (the cloud consists of a single switch if there are no trunks defined). These VLAN IDs are then stripped off as the packet exits the cloud on its way to its final destination.

These two operations summarize how tags are used. Tags are assigned and changed at each passage through a switch/router in the tag switching cloud as the tag switch/router refers to its tag database and looks up what tag it should apply to the packet to move it on to the next hop in its journey. These tags are assigned at the entry point to the cloud and stripped off at the exit point of the tag switching cloud and are therefore transparent to endstations that are communicating over the tag switch cloud.

Tag Switching Elements

As with all technologies examined in the switching arena, tag switching has its own terms that need definition before we can look at the protocol in more detail. The first term is a *tag edge router* (TER). These devices are routers that participate fully in the routing mechanism of the legacy IP network that they are attached to, using routing protocols like EIGRP or OSPF to generate routing tables. The TER assigns a tag to each packet it sends into the tag switches. This assignment of tags is made by reference to a tag database (we'll discuss how this is generated and maintained by the TER and tag switches soon). The TER is also responsible for exchanging tag information with the tag switches it is connected to. For packets exiting the tag switch portion of the network, TERs remove tags so that the legacy devices can understand the frame.

Next, we need to examine tag switches a little further. These devices forward packets based on tag IDs rather than a layer 3 network address. Performing switching based on short tags (also referred to as "labels" within the literature—why use one term when you can use two?) allows the switching logic to be simple and, hence, economically implemented in specialized and therefore fast hardware chips. Tag switches must also maintain their own tag and route information and exchange tag information with other tag switches and TERs. In the Cisco implementation, all tag switches are, in effect, tag switch/routers rather than straight tag switches, as they do need to maintain some routing functionality.

Finally, we need to introduce the *Tag Distribution Protocol* (TDP). The TDP is a topology-driven protocol in that a change or discovery of network topology is required before an update to the tag assignments via the TDP is effected. TDP uses point-to-point communication between routers to maintain tag associations.

As seen in Figure 3-20, tag switch/routers form the core of the network and assist in scaling internetworks to support very large numbers of nodes in an efficient manner. Data flows from many, many source loca-

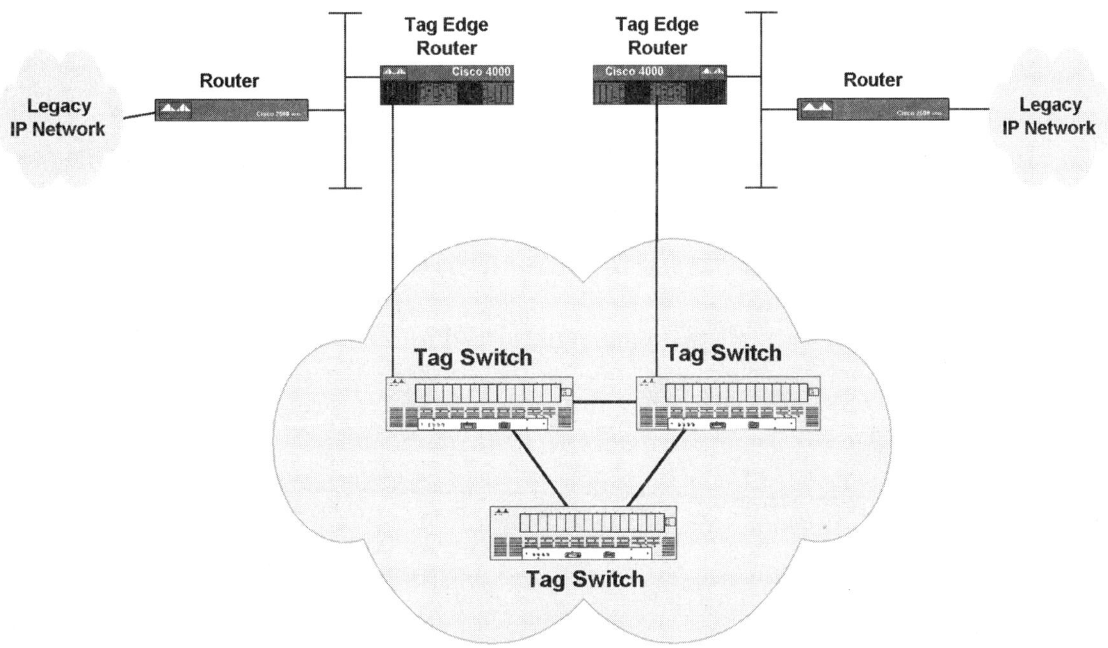

Figure 3-20 Tag switching network devices.

tions can be switched using the one destination tag ID in a very efficient manner. To understand the mechanics of this, let's look at tag allocation in a bit more detail and review a theoretical example of how tags are used to get a packet from one legacy network to another via a core tag switched network.

Tag Allocation

Tag allocation mechanisms actually depend to some extent on the underlying networks that are attached to them. If, for example, we use tag switching in a totally routed network purely as a mechanism to speed up the packet-forwarding process (as may be done within some of the higher-end Cisco routers), tags are assigned based on destination IP address. However, if the TER uses an ATM interface to connect to an ATM switch (which forms part of the tag switched network), the value of the tag assigned can be the VPI/VCI value for the connection established between switches participating in the tag switch procedures.

Tags can be allocated by either downstream or upstream devices. In downstream allocation, every tag switch generates an incoming tag for each route in its routing table, which are then advertised to tag-aware neighbors. For downstream allocation, each tag switch generates an outgoing tag for each route in its routing table, which is then advertised to all tag-aware neighbors. The net effect is the same; it just requires consistent operation within the tag-aware network.

In the Cisco implementations of ATM switches that perform tag switching, there is a critical difference between straight ATM forum operation and tag switching using an ATM interface. Tag switching uses standard IP routing tables and TDP to generate and distribute tag information. The benefit here is that ATM switches with tag switching capability have no call setup overhead when they come to transport IP traffic over ATM. In practice, this has two implications, one for the tag switch and one for the TER. First, the tag switch (for example a LightStream 1010) will implement a standard layer 3 routing protocol as well as TDP, so that the routing table is maintained by a routing process on the 1010. Second, in the situation where a TER is connecting a legacy network to an ATM network, the TER will place the tag in the VPI/VCI field of the ATM cell. This enables subsequent ATM switches in the path from source to destination to use VPI/VCI values to transport the cell. The concepts described above are best considered in the context of an example, which we will examine now.

Tag Switch Example

Let's start by looking at tag switch operation in the steady state, before we consider how the Tag Distribution Protocol works in practice. Figure 3-21 shows a simple network that could form part of a tag switch core of a large internetwork. A regular routing table will list the destination subnet, the IP address of the next hop router this is reachable by, and the interface through which to reach the next hop router—three pieces of information that we can refer to as the "destination triple." On routers that are tag switch-enabled, an additional entry is present in the routing table: the tag, which represents this destination triple.

So for Figure 3-21 we see a normal IP packet coming into interface 1, destined for 10.1.1.1, which happens to be reachable via the core tag switch section of the internetwork. Assuming no subnet masks, the router will examine its routing table and see that network 10.0.0.0 is reachable via the router with address 174.8.3.2, which is on the same segment as the router's interface 4. Given that this router is performing tag switching, the router will append tag 20 (this is an arbitrary figure chosen for illustrative purposes) as the identifier for future forwarding of the packet. Once the packet enters the tag switching core, it has the tag appended and will use that tag exclusively for forwarding decisions. After the tag switching core has used the tag to switch the packet to the

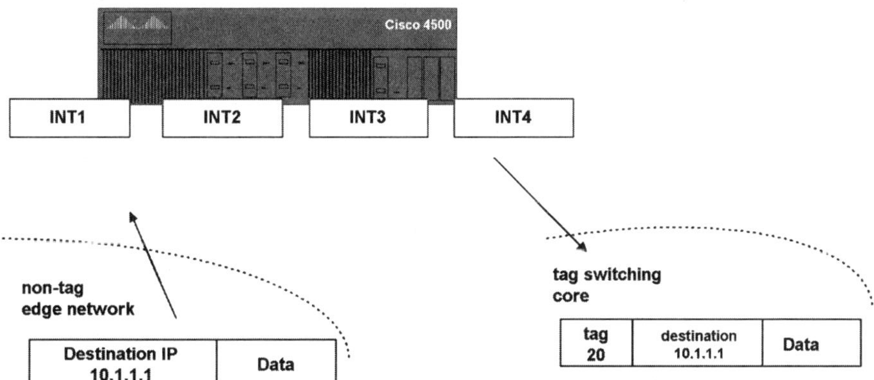

Figure 3-21 Routing table, including tag identifiers.

Routing Table

Destination IP	next hop	interface	tag
10.0.0.0	174.8.3.2	4	20

desired destination, the tag is taken off the packet for delivery to the host on a non-tag edge network.

Figure 3-22 illustrates what happens when this packet reaches the next hop router in the tag switch core. In this example, the packet destined for 10.1.1.1 that was prepended with the tag 20 when exiting interface 4 is arriving at interface 1 (presumably, this interface has IP address 174.8.3.2, as indicated by the routing table in Figure 3-21). The first thing that happens when this packet arrives at interface 1 is that the switching table is examined and the router sees that an incoming tag of 20 should be switched for an outgoing tag of 40. The packet is then forwarded out interface 2. As stated previously, this switching of tags can be referred to as *label swapping*. In fact, the IEEE are looking to standardize Cisco's proprietary tag switching under the name of Multi-Protocol Label Swapping (MPLS).

Once the new tag has been applied at the incoming interface, the router uses the new tag to switch the packet out interface 2, without resorting to routing table lookups. The speed benefit this delivers is that all the time-consuming table lookups have been performed prior to a packet needing to be switched, and the results are stored in a switching table that uses much smaller data elements than the routing table.

Figure 3-22 Routing table, including tag identifiers.

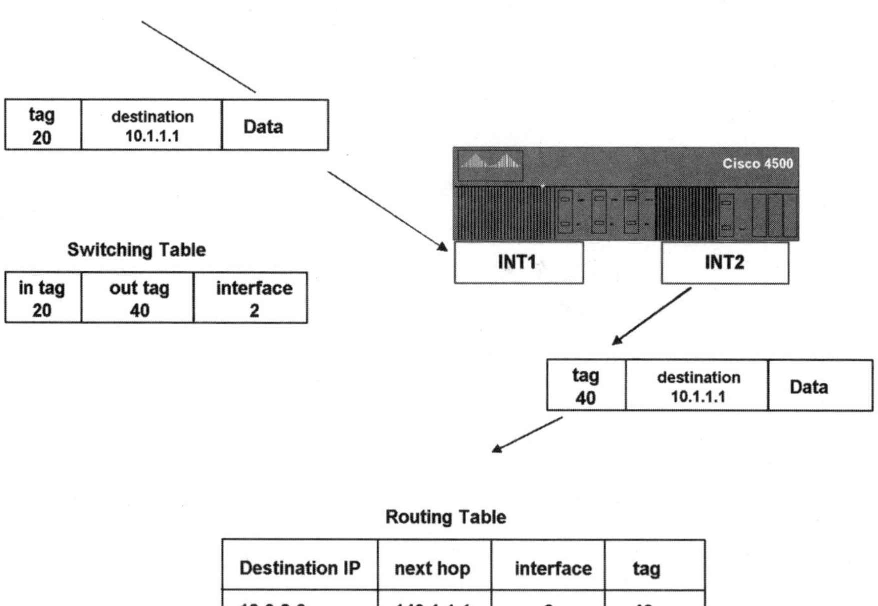

It should be noted that tags are of local significance only; therefore, the same tag value may appear on each router interface. This could give rise to the situation when a packet has the same tag value both inbound and outbound from a router. For the sake of clarity, this was not done in the example just discussed. Having discussed the case where all the destinations already have tags applied, let's look at an example of the Tag Distribution Protocol to see how tag associations are initially made.

TDP is, as we have stated before, a topology-driven protocol. Tag values are assigned when the topology is first discovered or when it changes. This differs from some other schemes that only assign labels when traffic appears for a given destination (like MPOA). So let's use the network in Figure 3-21 as the base for our examination of how tags are applied to a newly discovered destination network. Suppose the router in Figure 3-21 gets an IGRP routing update notifying it of network 120.4.0.0, a previously unknown destination network. In this instance, 120.4.0.0 will get entered into the routing table with a blank tag entry. TDP is now tasked with obtaining a tag for this new destination. Typically, this router will use TDP to ask the router that informed it of the new network to assign a tag value for the new destination network. Note that because tags only have local significance, it does not matter if a tag value is supplied that is already in use on another interface.

We can see by this example that tags are only present within packets traveling in the tag switch core, change on a hop-by-hop basis, and are only of significance to the interfaces they are received upon. We'll end this discussion of tag switching by reviewing some of the practical aspects of tag switch implementation on an ATM core network.

Tag Switching in an ATM Core

We'll conclude our discussion on tag switching by bringing together the points we have raised in the general discussion and applying them to what will most likely be one of the most common network configurations: classic IP edge networks interconnected via an ATM tag switch core. In this configuration, we need to define in a little more detail what the tag edge router and the tag switch router consist of.

In Figure 3-23, tag edge routers are implemented as regular routers with an ATM interface. On the Ethernet side of these TERs, there will be connections to other routers, and route information will be exchanged in the normal way using routing protocols like IGRP. On the ATM interface,

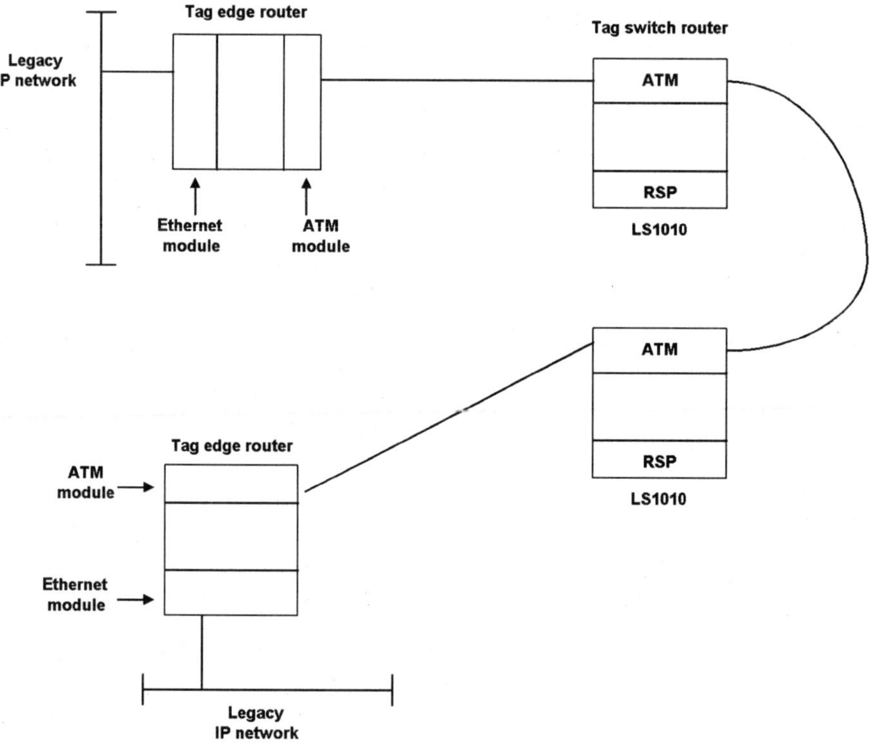

Figure 3-23 Possible tag switch network components.

both regular routing updates and TDP information are exchanged with the tag switch routers. From the TER point of view, it views a tag switch router as just another router with which it will exchange routing information.

The tag switch router also has its own routing table and runs a routing protocol, and therefore, each ATM switch will require a routing module. Between a TER and a tag switch router, the tag assignment for each destination network will be the VPI/VCI values for each destination location. This is an important point. It means that for a TER to assign tags for all entries in its routing table, it must have a corresponding VCC to each possible destination for there to be VPI/VCI values present. The implication is that each TER will create a VCC to all the other TERs in the network, creating a potential scaling problem as the numbers of TERs per network grows.

Summary

This chapter focused on the theory of ATM and specifically the theory of IP over ATM. We discussed the UNI and NNI interfaces in more depth and covered how the Private NNI Protocol provides services similar to link state routing protocols that are used in classic IP networks. We discussed how ATM initiates connections for both point-to-point and point-to-multipoint connections.

Like IP, ATM requires effective address hierarchy to maintain efficient routing by keeping topology database size to a minimum. ATM addresses were discussed as having sections relating to domain membership and a section that identifies the node within a specific domain. The level indicator was introduced as an ATM version of the IP subnet mask. The first method of integrating ATM and IP was presented as Classic IP Over ATM, which reduces ATM to a fast link layer protocol. CIOA uses an ATM network to establish point-to-point connections between devices that are configured for the same IP subnet. For a CIOA-configured device to access a host on another IP subnet, the connection needs to be routed through an intermediate router.

NHRP, or Next Hop Resolution Protocol, was presented as a way of improving efficiency over straight CIOA. NHRP allows an ATM connection to be established directly between the two endpoints that need to communicate whether they are on the same IP subnet or not. NHRP is therefore using the ATM network in a more efficient manner.

LANE was discussed as a way to extend local area networks over an ATM cloud. LANE provides the means to extend VLANS over what are termed emulated LANs in the ATM environment. The LANE components of LEC, LECS, and LES/BUS were described, and their role in enabling legacy LAN endstations to communicate with ATM hosts and LAN endstations on the other side of an ATM cloud was also discussed. The complexity of LANE is essential in emulating the broadcast capability of a LAN in what is the connection-oriented medium of an ATM network. LANE provides the trunking capability of ATM when operating in a VLAN environment.

Just as CIOA was bound by the normal IP subnet rules, so too is LANE. MPOA was introduced as a means of bringing NHRP functionality to LANE, but we left MPOA aside, as it is still early in its deployment.

RFC 1483 was identified as an important document that specifies how all the ATM methods above encapsulate IP traffic in an adaptation layer and segment that encapsulation into cells. In addition, ATM operation with Frame Relay networks was discussed, along with various methods of interworking these two technologies. Issues of interoperation between Frame Relay congestion notifications and frame loss procedures and the ATM equivalents were discussed.

A discussion of the two frame-based accesses to ATM was also delivered: FUNI and DXI. These methods allow variable-length frames to be input to ATM DSUs that then generate ATM cells for transmittal on the ATM network.

Finally, we covered tag switching and its application to both standard IP networks and those that incorporate an ATM core.

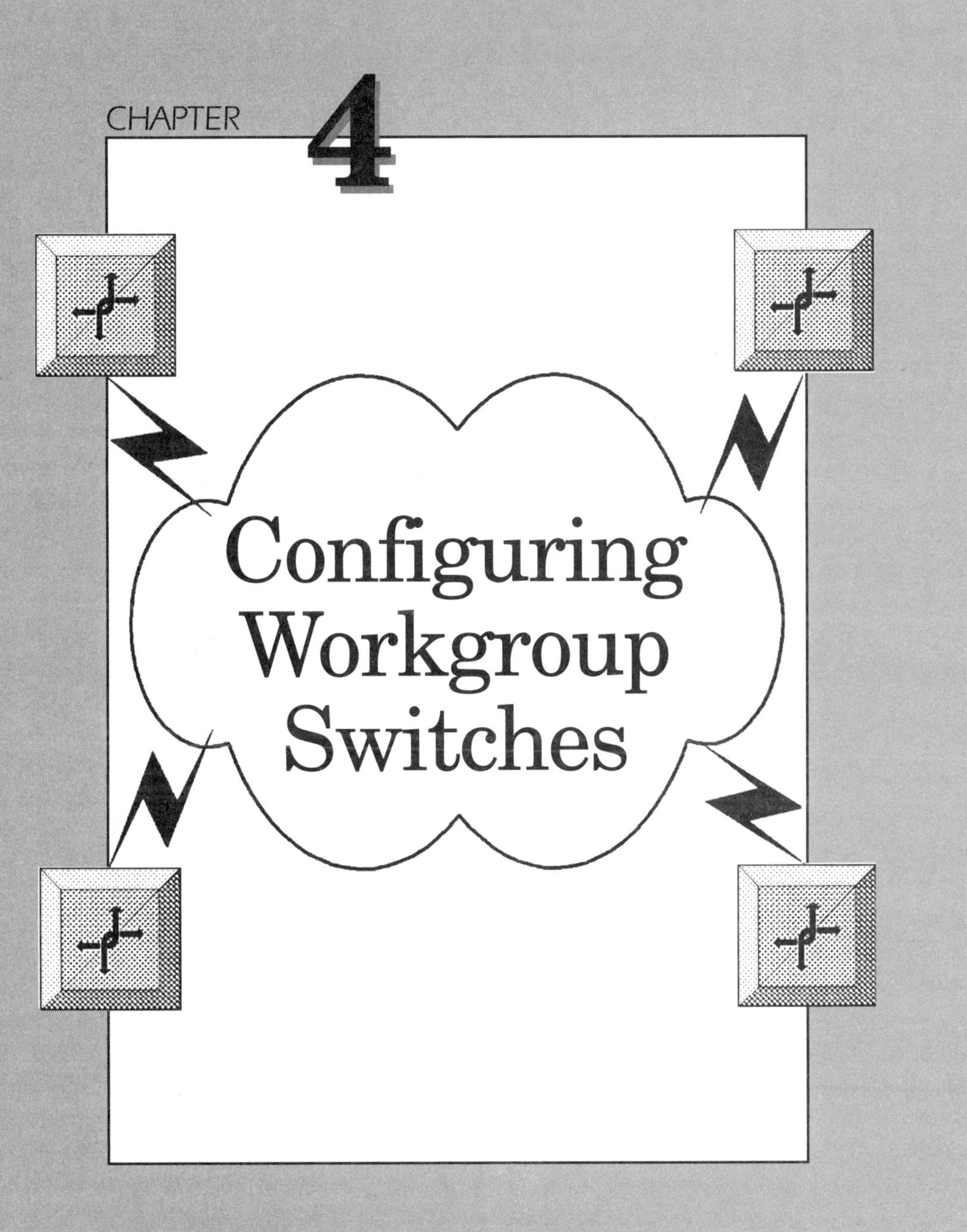
CHAPTER
4
Configuring
Workgroup
Switches

Introduction

The first three chapters covered the theory necessary to understanding what we are going to do when setting up and configuring switches in this and later chapters. From here on, I will leave out theoretical discussions so that the text can flow better as we build device configurations.

This chapter will cover what you need to do to introduce Cisco's entry-level switch range, the 2900, into an existing routed network. We will cover issues like how to connect to the device; using the command-line interface (CLI), which differs from regular router IOS; hardware modules available; upgrading the IOS; implementing CGMP; VLANs; routing between VLANs; and how to fine-tune the switch for optimum performance.

Connecting a 2900XL Series Switch into Your Network

The 2900 series Catalyst switches (we will use the 2916XL in this chapter) are relatively low-cost switches that actually do quite a lot for the money. These devices deliver a very low cost per port for 10/100 Ethernet operation, meaning that these ports can detect and operate with devices running at 10 or 100 Mbit/sec without you having to do anything. The most common initial application for these devices will be to introduce separate collision domains into a growing network. In this section we'll cover the physical connections necessary to connect the 2916 to individual workstations, hubs, and a terminal for CLI access, and for use of the Web-based management tool.

There are actually quite significant differences between the 2900 range and the 2900XL range. The 2900 series, which consists of devices like the 2901, 2902, and 2926, are derived from the 5002 Catalyst (with fixed configuration). The Catalyst 5000 is, of course, a modular device, and you can buy modules for that range to suit your needs. As the 2900 fixed-configuration switches are derived from the 5002, they run the same software and are thus able to support more-advanced switch software features, like trunking using ISL.

The 2900XL series, which includes the 2908XL, 2916XL, and 2924XL, is based on different hardware and thus supports a different software feature set. Unfortunately, the XL switches so far have not supported

ISL. The latest version of the software 11.2(8)SA3 now supports multiple VLANs within the switch, but an external router is needed to route between them. ISL will be supported soon on the 2916XL by a new module for that box, expected to be available some time in 1999. The options on this trunk module are a four-port 100BaseTX or two-port 100BaseFX. The trunking options supported will be ISL and 802.1q. It is unlikely that the 2900XL range will support trunking on any Fast Ethernet ports, like the Catalyst 5000-derived products.

The 2924XL and the 2908XL are fixed-configuration switches and, therefore, do not have an expansion slot for the new trunking module. Hence they will never support ISL.

Physical Connections to the Switch

The first thing to do is connect the rollover RJ-45 cable (supplied with the Catalyst) to the 9-pin adapter and connect it to a serial port on a PC. This is then connected to the console port on the switch. Using Windows HyperTerminal set to 9600 baud, 8 data bits, no parity, and 1 stop bit, you can power up the switch and see the display, shown in Figure 4-1.

The first thing to do is follow the initial dialog, as in Figure 4-1, and arrive at a base configuration. For those somewhat familiar with IOS configuration of Cisco routers, this command syntax should be familiar. For those more familiar with Catalyst 5000 operation, this is a little confusing. In Catalyst 5000 operation, the sc0 (system console 0) interface was used as a portable interface that could be associated with any VLAN when you wanted to configure that VLAN. This interface is no longer present on the 2900XL range.

Additionally, on Catalyst 5000 switches, the most significant difference between its CLI and a router's CLI was that no longer were there two modes for the CLI. With routers, there was a view mode and a configure mode. View mode enabled you to issue IOS `show` commands to view interfaces, routing tables, and the like. Configure mode (invoked by the `conf t` command) allowed you to change the router configuration, but not issue any `show` commands. With Catalyst 5000 switches, there is only one mode within which all view and configure commands can be issued. These commands fall into three categories: `show` for viewing switch status, `set` to configure the switch, and `clear` to erase parameters.

The 2900XL range reverts back to a two-level CLI, where there is one level for viewing status and another for making configuration changes, more like a Cisco router CLI. The sc0 interface has disappeared, and

```
C2900XL Boot Loader (C2900XL-HBOOT-M),
Version 11.2(8)SA, RELEASE SOFTWARE (fc1)Compiled Thu 11-Dec-97 11:06 by rheaton
Base ethernet MAC Address: 00:10:07:a1:88:c0
Xmodem file system is available.
Initializing Flash...
flashfs[0]: 62 files, 2 directories
flashfs[0]: 0 orphaned files, 0 orphaned directories
flashfs[0]: Total bytes: 1728000 flashfs[0]: Bytes used: 1252352
flashfs[0]: Bytes available: 475648 flashfs[0]: flashfs fsck took 3 seconds....done
Initializing Flash.Loading "flash:c2900XL-h-mz-112.8-SA"...##########################
##############################################################################################
File "flash:c2900XL-h-mz-112.8-SA" uncompressed and installed, entry point:
0x3000executing...

            Restricted Rights Legend

Use, duplication, or disclosure by the Government is
subject to restrictions as set forth in subparagraph
(c) of the Commercial Computer Software - Restricted
Rights clause at FAR sec. 52.227-19 and subparagraph
(c) (1) (ii) of the Rights in Technical Data and Computer
Software clause at DFARS sec. 252.227-7013.

          cisco Systems, Inc.
          170 West Tasman Drive
          San Jose, California 95134-1706



Cisco Internetwork Operating System Software
IOS (tm) C2900XL Software (C2900XL-H-M), Version 11.2(8)SA, RELEASE SOFTWARE (fc1)
Copyright (c) 1986-1997 by cisco Systems, Inc.
Compiled Thu 11-Dec-97 11:06 by rheaton
Image text-base: 0x00003000, data-base: 0x001A08D0


Initializing c2900 flash...
flashfs[5]: 62 files, 2 directories
flashfs[5]: 0 orphaned files, 0 orphaned directories
flashfs[5]: Total bytes: 1728000
flashfs[5]: Bytes used: 1252352
flashfs[5]: Bytes available: 475648
flashfs[5]: flashfs fsck took 3 seconds.
flashfs[5]: Initialization complete.
...done Initializing c2900 flash.
C2900 POST: System Board Test: Passed
C2900 POST: CPU Buffer Test: Passed
C2900 POST: CPU Notify RAM Test: Passed
C2900 POST: CPU Interface Test: Passed
C2900 POST: Testing Switch Core: Passed
C2900 POST: Testing Buffer Table: Passed
C2900 POST: Data Buffer Test: Passed
C2900 POST: Configuring Switch Parameters: Passed
C2900 POST: Ethernet Controller Test: Passed
C2900 POST: MII Test: Passed
cisco WS-C2916M-XL (PowerPC403GA) processor (revision 0x11) with 4096K/1024K bytes of memory.
Processor board ID FAA0212T0LJ, with hardware revision 0x00
Last reset from power-on
16 Ethernet/IEEE 802.3 interface(s)

32K bytes of flash-simulated non-volatile configuration memory.
Base ethernet MAC Address: 00:10:07:A1:88:C0
Notice: NVRAM invalid, possibly due to write erase.


Press RETURN to get started!


        --- System Configuration Dialog ---
```

Figure 4-1 Initial boot and configuration sequence for a 2916XL switch.

Figure 4-1
(Cont.)

```
At any point you may enter a question mark '?' for help.
Use ctrl-c to abort configuration dialog at any prompt.
Default settings are in square brackets '[]'.


Continue with configuration dialog? [yes/no]: y
Enter IP address: 200.200.25.79
Enter IP netmask: 255.255.255.0

Would you like to enter a default gateway address? [yes]: y
IP address of default gateway: 200.200.25.1

The following configuration command script was created:

interface VLAN1
ip address 200.200.25.79 255.255.255.0
ip default-gateway 200.200.25.1
snmp community private rw
snmp community public ro
!
end

Use this configuration? [yes/no]: y
Building configuration...
[OK]
Use the enabled mode 'configure' command to modify this configuration.

Press RETURN to get started.


Switch>enable
Switch#sho run
Building configuration...

Current configuration:
!
version 11.2
no service pad
no service udp-small-servers
no service tcp-small-servers
!
hostname Switch
!
!
no ip routing
!
interface VLAN1
 ip address 200.200.25.79 255.255.255.0
 no ip route-cache
!
interface FastEthernet0/1
!
interface FastEthernet0/2
!
interface FastEthernet0/3
!
interface FastEthernet0/4
!
interface FastEthernet0/5
!
interface FastEthernet0/6
!
interface FastEthernet0/7
!
interface FastEthernet0/8
!
interface FastEthernet0/9
!
interface FastEthernet0/10
!
```

Figure 4-1
(Cont.)

```
interface FastEthernet0/11
!
interface FastEthernet0/12
!
interface FastEthernet0/13
!
interface FastEthernet0/14
!
interface FastEthernet0/15
!
interface FastEthernet0/16
!
ip default-gateway 200.200.25.1
snmp-server community private RW
snmp-server community public RO
!
line con 0
 stopbits 1
line vty 0 4
 login
!
end

Switch#
```

VLAN 1 is configured by its own separate VLAN interface, rather than the roaming sc0 interface. Subsequent VLANs do not possess any IP information.

All these modifications to the CLI has left some anomalies present. When moving between routers, Catalyst 5000s, and 2900XL boxes, it is easy to get the wrong syntax when executing commands, particularly as the 2900XL will accept a `set` command but then puts you into a configuration dialog. My recommendation is to treat the 2900XL CLI more like the router CLI and use the two-level approach of one for `show` commands, and use `conf t` to go to configuration mode, forgetting about the `set` command altogether. The *Cisco TCP/IP Routing Professional Reference* discussed the router CLI in detail. All further discussion will assume familiarity with that interface.

Before we go any further, let's look at the initial configuration we have just generated in Figure 4-1 and list and explain each entry:

`no service pad`—Disables all packet assembler/disassembler (PAD) commands and connections between PAD devices and the switch. Unless you want to connect to an X.25 device, this service has no use.

`no service udp-small-servers`—Issuing the `no` form of the command here disables the device's ability to interact properly with some UDP services, like Echo. With this command entered, if an incoming packet is destined for the Echo port number, the packet is discarded.

`no service tcp-small-servers`—Similarly, disables the switch's ability to interact with some minor TCP services. Instead of just discarding the packet, as is the effect with the `udp` command, this command also sends a TCP reset to the device trying to use minor TCP services.

`hostname Switch`—This command sets the prompt to `Switch`.

`no ip routing`—This disables IP routing. As the 2916XL switch does not have any routing capability, there is no point in enabling IP routing.

```
interface VLAN1
ip address 200.200.25.79 255.255.255.0
no ip route-cache
```

These commands identify the only VLAN created by default, which is VLAN 1, and all interfaces are a member of this VLAN. The IP address assigned is for use by IP services like Telnet and SNMP. Switch interfaces, of course, do not have an IP address assigned. The `no ip route-cache` command forces all packets to be process-switched and is of no value here.

`interface FastEthernet0/1`—There are entries for each Fast Ethernet interface in the configuration, but I list only one here. This merely tells us that the interface exists and has no specific configuration.

`ip default-gateway 200.200.25.1`—Defines the default router to be contacted for routing to any other network, be that a physical or virtual LAN. With IOS 11.2 (8) SA3, the 2916XL supports multiple VLANs within the same switch but still requires recourse to a router to route between them. We'll illustrate switch and router configurations to support this later on.

`snmp-server community private RW`—Sets the SNMP read-write string to `private`. For security purposes it is a good idea to change this to something more obscure, as all hackers know this is the default value.

`snmp-server community public RO`—Sets the SNMP read-only string to `public`.

```
line con 0
stopbits 1
```

This major command and subcommand sets the console port to use 1 stop bit for the asynchronous communications.

```
line vty 0 4
login
```

This major command and single subcommand specifies that for the five terminal sessions possible, each one is required to supply a password, but none is set. With this configuration, no devices will be able to establish a telnet session with the switch until a password is configured.

`End`—Marks the end of the configuration file.

The first alteration I would make to the default configuration is to add the password for telnet sessions. There are, in fact, two options here to allow a telnet session to the switch. The first is just to remove the `login` subcommand, which allows a telnet session to be established without the user having to supply a password. Alternatively, we configure a password, which can be done as follows:

```
Switch>en
Switch#conf t
Enter configuration commands, one per line. End with CNTL/Z.
Switch(config)#line vty 0 4
Switch(config-line)#password test
Switch(config-line)#end
Switch#
```

Previously, if you tried to telnet to this switch, a message stating that a password is required but none set was echoed back, and access was not possible. Now you will be presented with a prompt to type in the password `test`.

Connecting via the Web Interface

The 2916XL range does, in fact, have a nice Web interface that allows all kinds of configurations to be performed via a graphical user interface. This is quite a friendly tool to use. In the default configuration no enable password is set, so any alterations made using the Web tool go straight through into the configuration of the switch.

To access the Web-based management tool, connections similar to those shown in Figure 4-2 need to be made. Of course, if the 2916 is being configured in a standalone environment, a PC LAN card can be connected to it using a straight-through cable.

With an enable password set, you are prompted for a username (which in this case will be `enable`) and a password. Once you have entered the username and password, that is stored within the browser for subsequent changes.

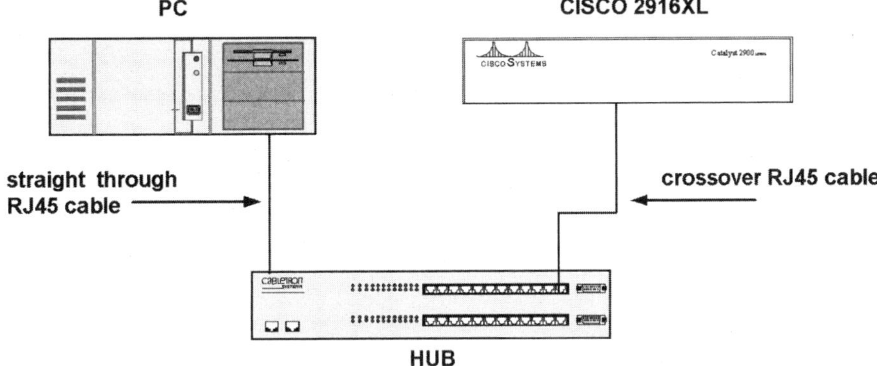

Figure 4-2 Connecting the 2916XL to an existing network.

The front screen for the Web tool is displayed in Figure 4-3. The most interesting of the options on this home page is the Web console, which shows a graphical representation of the switch, enabling you to click on each port to view and set its configuration, and to operate the mode switch on the front panel that shows port status, operating speed, and duplex setting. The other options on the home page are quite simple, showing the interfaces and log (which can be viewed by entering `show interface` and `show log` at the CLI, respectively). From this home page it is also possible to invoke a telnet session, show the technical support information, and have access to a command listing via the "monitor the switch" link.

Figure 4-3 Front screen for Web tool.

Cisco Systems
Accessing Cisco WS-C2916M-XL "Switch"

Web Console - Manage the Switch through the web interface.

Telnet - To the Switch.

Show interfaces - Display the status of the interfaces.
Show diagnostic log - Display the diagnostic log.
Monitor the Switch - Display the HTML command line interface.

Show tech-support - Display information commonly needed by tech support.

Help resources
CCO at www.cisco.com - Cisco Connection Online, including the Technical Assistance Center (TAC).
tac@cisco.com - e-mail the TAC.
1-800-553-2447 or +1-408-526-7209 - phone the TAC.
cs-html@cisco.com - e-mail the HTML interface development group.

2916XL Hardware Features

Before we start to expand upon the default configuration just generated and modify it to our needs, let's review the hardware aspects of the switch. The 2900XL range use flash memory to store both IOS files and configuration files. The configuration files are ASCII and can be stored to and retrieved from a TFTP server for offline editing and saving, just as router configuration files can be.

The 2916 gives you 16 autosensing 10/100 switched ports, with two expansion slots. The 2908 just has eight switched 10/100 ports, with no expansion slots. The 2916 expansion slots can house a four-port 10/100 Ethernet module or a two-port 100-Mbit/sec Ethernet over fiber module (100BaseFX), which uses the standard fiber-optic SC connectors and can be configured for half-duplex or full-duplex operation.

The LEDs are simple to understand and quite informative. The System LED is green when power is applied and everything is working. If there are operational problems, it will show amber. Next to the System LED is the Redundant Power Supply (RPS) LED. The redundant power supply is a separate module that takes two AC inputs and generates a single DC output. This DC output can be connected to the DC input connector on the rear of the 2916. When you are operating the redundant power supply, the AC power cord must be removed from the 2916. The RPS LED will tell you if anything is wrong with the RPS or the power connections in general. If the RPS light is flashing green, it means that both the redundant power supply and the AC power are connected (the obvious thing to do is remove the AC power). Amber indicates the RPS is correctly connected but not operating properly, and a green LED means the RPS is operational. Beneath the RPS LED are the Expansion Slot LEDs, which have the usual green for good and amber for bad operation.

The most interesting LEDs are the ones above each of the 16 Ethernet ports on the front of the switch. The function of these LEDs is controlled by the mode switch on the front of the unit. The mode switch can place these LEDs in one of four states. The first state (and the one in use after powering up the device) is status, which has the most variants in its display, as follows:

- Solid green means link established, but no traffic.
- Flashing green is the state of normal operation and indicates the link is up and receiving traffic.
- Solid amber is the next-most-common and indicates that the port is either administratively shut down, has been shut down because of an

address violation (one MAC address seen on two ports), or is in the blocked state as defined by spanning tree.

- Flashing green then amber is bad. This indicates that the port is experiencing Ethernet frame errors, like CRC, jabber, or alignment problems. The one caveat I have is that on some hardware versions, there are erroneous reports of errors when connecting a switch port directly via crossover cable to a router interface. This can be fixed by inserting a small hub between the two devices if it bothers you. Using a LAN analyzer will show the error reports are erroneous in this case.

To change the function of these LEDs, press the mode switch on the front panel. This will then cause UTL, FDUP, or 100 to be highlighted in rotation. FDUP refers to full-duplex operation, which is indicated by a green LED; half-duplex operation is indicated by the LED being off. 100 refers to 100-Mbit/sec operation, which is signaled by a green LED; 10-Mbit/sec operation is signaled by the LED being off. The UTL mode is interesting and gives an indication of the bandwidth utilization of the switch. This mode takes 50 percent utilization as the key level. The ports are numbered 1 through 16, left to right, and if all 16 LEDs are lit, it means that the switch is using more than 50 percent of its bandwidth. If the LED for port 16 is off, the switch is using less than 50 percent bandwidth. If the LED for port 15 is off, the switch is using less than 25 percent of available bandwidth. Each successive LED that is off indicates a further 50 percent reduction in the amount of bandwidth utilization.

If any mode other than status is selected, the switch will revert back to status after a short time.

Upgrading the IOS

It is a given that at some stage you will want to upgrade the IOS your Catalyst 2900XL is running. At time of writing, the latest version available is 11.2(8)SA3. The 2916XL we got was delivered with 11.2(8)SA. The SA3 version has a number of enhancements, most notably the opportunity to have multiple VLANs exist within the one Catalyst.

The most recent software available from the www.cisco.com Web-site section for switching products. To download the software, you need a TFTP server, which Cisco makes available. Alternatively, you can get any number of free TFTP server programs for most operating systems at www.shareware.com.

You download the new IOS as a binary and updated switch manager HTML files in TAR (tape archive) format. It is also possible to use FTP to the Cisco FTP site or, indeed, have the software sent to you by e-mail.

Once you have the software and TFTP server, you need to do the following to successfully upgrade. We will not upgrade the HTML files, as this text refers to configuring the switch via the command-line interface.

The first task is to rename the existing IOS in flash, as the flash in this switch can only hold one software image file. The process is to rename the existing IOS image to the name of the new image, so that when the new file is copied to the switch it overwrites the existing image. This way, the flash will not have to hold more than one image.

In this instance the filename is c2900xl-h-mz-112_8-sa3.bin. While connected at the console (or alternatively by a telnet session), type:

```
Switch#sho boot
BOOT path-list:  flash:c2900XL-h-mz-112.8-SA
Config file:    flash:config.text
Enable Break:    1
Manual Boot:     no
HELPER path-list:
NVRAM/Config file
  buffer size: 32768
```

Our task is to rename c2900XL-h-mz-112.8-SA to c2900xl-h-mz-112_8-sa3.bin (which is the new filename as given on the Cisco Web site) and then use TFTP to copy the new IOS image to the switch. The commands to complete this task are illustrated in Figure 4-4.

The key commands in this sequence are first the `rename flash:` command, followed by the `boot system flash:`, to change the name of the image file used as the default. To actually copy the new IOS image from the TFTP server to the switch, the `copy tftp:` command needs to have the correct IP address, path, and filename information. The example given in Figure 4-4 shows the TFTP host as IP address 200.200.25.13 (listening on UDP port 69 by default), with file c2900XL-h-mz-112_8-sa3.bin in the tftps subdirectory. For this to work, the TFTP server must be using the parent directory to the tftps subdirectory as its default. For example, if the TFTP server software is set to c:\ as its default, and the tftpf subdirectory is located directly below c:\, the command shown will work.

We have upgraded from the SA to the SA3 software image and to make that take effect, the switch needs a reload. Upon bootup with the new IOS in effect, the SA3 software will not recognize the `no ip routing` configuration command and deletes it from the configuration. The rest of the configuration remains as is.

The SA3 software can be run on any hardware version in the 2900XL range; however, there are some previous versions of IOS that will not run on some of the later 2900XL range motherboards. To see which mother-

Figure 4-4 Commands to rename file and copy new IOS image to the switch.

```
Switch#rename flash:c2900xl-h-mz-112.8-sa flash:c2900xl-h-mz-112_8-sa3
Source filename [c2900xl-h-mz-112.8-sa]?
Destination filename [c2900xl-h-mz-112_8-sa3]?
Switch#conf t
Enter configuration commands, one per line.  End with CNTL/Z.
Switch(config)#boot system flash:c2900XL-h-mz-112_8-sa3
Switch(config)#end
Switch#
%SYS-5-CONFIG_I: Configured from console by console
Switch#dir flash:
Directory of flash:

  2  -rwx      913008   Mar 01 1993 00:16:47  c2900XL-h-mz-112_8-sa3
  3  -rwx       59633   Dec 11 1997 19:07:53  c2900XL-diag-mz-112.8-SA
  4  drwx        3776   Dec 11 1997 19:07:55  html
 64  -rwx        2459   Mar 01 1993 00:19:37  config.text
 65  -rwx         177   Mar 01 1993 00:09:02  env_vars

1728000 bytes total (403456 bytes free)
Switch#sho boot
BOOT path-list:     flash:c2900XL-h-mz-112_8-sa3
Config file:        flash:config.text
Enable Break:       1
Manual Boot:        no
HELPER path-list:
NVRAM/Config file
      buffer size: 32768
Switch#copy tftp://200.200.25.13//tftps/c2900XL-h-mz-112_8-sa3.bin
Source IP address or hostname [200.200.25.13]?
Source filename [/tftps/c2900XL-h-mz-112_8-sa3.bin]?
Destination filename [c2900XL-h-mz-112_8-sa3]?
Loading /tftps/c2900XL-h-mz-112_8-sa3.bin from 200.200.25.13 (via
VLAN1): !!!!!!
!!!!!!!!!!!!!!!!!!!!!!!!!!!!!!!!!!!!!!!!!!!!!!!!!!!!!!!!!!!!!!!!!!!!!!!
!!!!!!!!
!!!!!!!!!!!!!!!!!!!!!!!!!!!!!!!!!!!!!!!!!!!!!!!!!!!!!!!!!!!!!!!!!!!!!!!
!!!!!!!!
!!!!!!!!!!!!!
[OK - 913008 bytes]

913008 bytes copied in 133.169 secs (6864 bytes/sec)
Switch#
```

board version you are using, enter the `show ver` command. This will display various software and hardware revisions. The pertinent entry in this case is the `Board ID` entry, which will have value 0x04, 0x07, 0x09, 0x06, or 0x0C. 0x04 and 0x06 will run all versions of IOS, 0x07 and 0x09 will not run the SA version, and the 0x0C board will not run the SA or SA1 IOS versions.

Modifying the Configuration

The initial configuration was explained in a previous section. Here, we'll look at expanding upon this base configuration to implement some of the features of switch operation we described in the earlier chapters. First, though, let's place this in some useful context in terms of why we would add these configuration commands to the switch.

Initial Placement of a 2916XL

With the base configuration, we have a device with 16 ports. All ports are in the same broadcast domain, but each port is its own collision domain. A typical application for this configuration of the switch is shown in Figure 4-5.

In this figure, one port is used to connect the switch to the corporate network via a router, with the remaining ports being split between individual PCs and a hub. All ports are within the one VLAN, which must be configured for the same subnet as the router interface it is connected to and the PCs connected to the switch. Each port will operate at either 10 or 100 Mbit/sec, depending on the operation of the NIC it is connected to, and also select half or full duplex on the same basis. Prior to introducing the 2916 to the network, it is likely that all PCs (and the server) were part of the same collision domain and connected to a hub that would typically be set at 10-Mbit/sec operation. Putting a 2916XL into a network

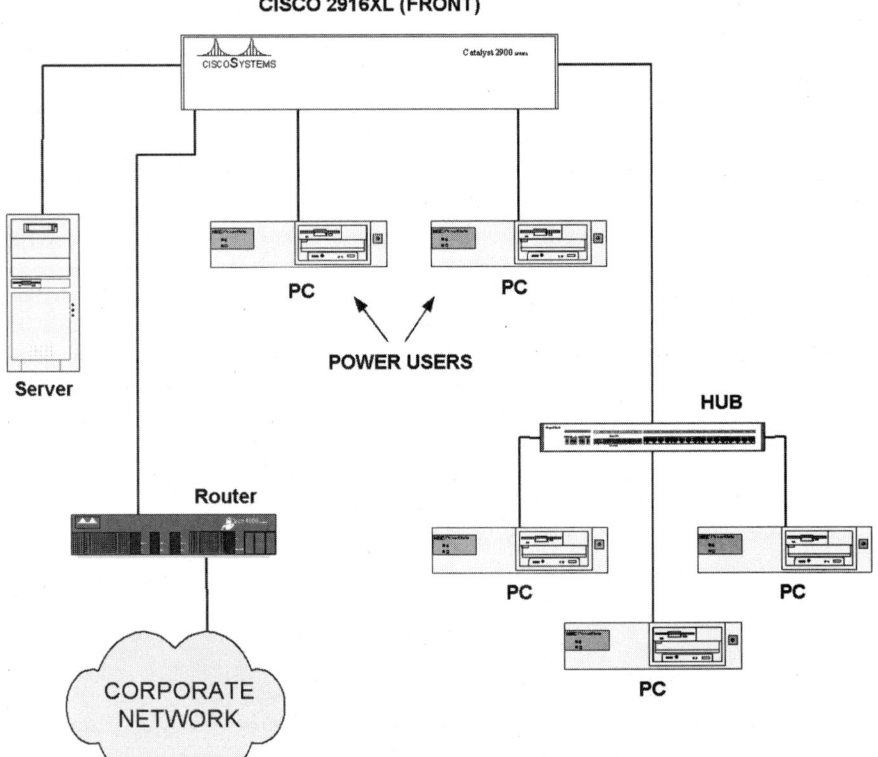

Figure 4-5 Introducing a 2916XL to create multiple collision domains in a network.

like this can significantly improve its performance, as the power users and the server now have dedicated full-duplex 100-Mbit/sec operation and are not affected by the collisions coming from the hub.

It is possible to connect switch ports to each other, in order to enable more ports for the one VLAN. There is some unique behavior that should be noted, however. The most common configuration for Ethernet ports to be in is set for auto on both speed and duplex. If a port that is set so is connected to a port set at 10 Mbit/sec with half duplex, the autosensing port will assume these settings. If, however, the port originally set to 10 Mbit/sec is then set to 100 Mbit/sec, the autosensing port does not adjust to 100-Mbit/sec operation. The reason for this is that 100-Mbit/sec fast idles look very similar to 10-Mbit/sec link pulses, and without a link-down state, a renegotiation of the link parameters does not take place. The thing to do is force a renegotiation by either shutting down one of the connected ports, physically disconnecting the link, or reloading one of the switches.

Adding Configuration Features

You may wish to place a port that is directly connected to a server in full-duplex mode. This is simply done. Just enter configuration mode, select the port you wish to turn on for full duplex, and save the configuration as follows:

```
Switch(config)#int fast 0/2
Switch(config-if)#duplex ?
 auto Enable AUTO-duplex configuration
 full Force full-duplex operation
 half Force half-duplex operation
Switch(config-if)#duplex full
```

This configuration sets the second port (slot 0 port 2 of the Fast Ethernet) to full duplex. As we can see from the `?` command, there are also options for setting half and autosense. This can often be useful if there are any difficulties with the NIC and the switch agreeing to use full duplex on startup.

The next modification that may be necessary is to add a second link to the server, forming a Fast EtherChannel connection to increase throughput to the server. In this illustration we'll configure ports 2 and 3 to be a Fast EtherChannel group. Our goal here is to increase the available throughput between a server and the rest of the network. We already know that by forcing the ports into full-duplex mode, we will allow the server to send data to the switch at the same time it receives data from the switch; however, adding multiple connections adds even more throughput. The server clearly needs multiple NIC interfaces, and in this example, we assume two. Each port in a port group belongs to the same VLAN and is in the same forwarding state (as decided by the Spanning Tree Protocol).

As each port in a port group must belong to the same VLAN, it is a given that the IP addresses of the attached devices must be within the same subnet, so the interfaces on the server used to connect to the port group need addresses within the same subnet. Within the one switch, as many as 12 port groups may be defined, each consisting of between one and four ports. It should be noted that a port assigned to a particular port group cannot be a secure port (to be discussed later) or a monitor port.

Let's discuss the consideration of whether to have the port group forward based on source or on destination address. At first, this may seem a strange consideration, as we know that a switch learns the location of devices by listening to the source address as packets come into the switch, puts those addresses in an address table, and forwards packets based on that table. We are, however, talking about the operation of the *port group,* which is different from the general switch. We have to consider how the port group is trying to communicate in order to decide whether to make the switch forward packets based on source or destination addresses within the port group itself. This really is a minor decision in the configuration process; the switch will always forward based on destination address. But within the links assigned to the group, the switch has to decide which link to send the packet over. Source-based forwarding is the default and the optimum for most network needs. It should be noted that this option did not become available until IOS 11.2 (8) SA3.

In most cases where Fast EtherChannel is deployed, it is as described above, when increasing the available throughput to a server. In that case, many workstations are communicating with one server, and source-based forwarding is best. In a case where we have many devices intercommunicating, destination-based port group forwarding can work best.

When we look at managing the address table later, we will examine how to enter static addresses into the switch address table. If this feature is appropriate (we will discuss this in the section on address management), you must configure the switch to forward to all ports in the port group if source-based forwarding is used, and to only one port in the group if destination-based forwarding is used in the group.

Figure 4-6 Configuration with two ports in a port group connected to a server.

```
Switch#conf t
Enter configuration commands, one per line.  End with CNTL/Z.
Switch(config)#int fast 0/2
Switch(config-if)#port group 2
Switch(config-if)#int fast 0/3
Switch(config-if)#port group 2
Switch(config-if)#end
Switch#
%SYS-5-CONFIG_I: Configured from console by console
Switch#sho port group
Group  Interface
----   ------------
   2   FastEthernet0/2
   2   FastEthernet0/3
```

A suitable configuration where we have two ports in a port group to connect to a server is generated in Figure 4-6 and, of course, assumes that the server is using Fast EtherChannel-aware NICs. Additionally, setting the ports to full-duplex and 100-Mbit/sec operation will give 200-Mbit/sec throughput between the switch and the server in both directions.

Configurations Specific to Single Workstation Attachment

We have documented that a switch will forward a packet destined for an unknown MAC address out of all ports. This is clearly unnecessary when a switch has a direct connection to one workstation only, as in the case where a server is attached directly to one or more ports. With that configuration, there is no chance of the unknown destination MAC appearing on the directly connected ports. It is therefore advantageous to block forwarding of unknown destination address packets to the server or other directly connected workstations. This is done using the commands displayed in Figure 4-7.

A key thing to note here is that even though the commands to block unicast and multicast frames destined for unknown addresses were entered on both Fast Ethernet 0/1 and 0/2, that entry is not shown in the running configuration if those ports are in a port group. For ports in a port group, port blocking for both unicast and multicast is enabled by default. For ports not in a port group, the configuration commands are seen in the switch configuration. The way to monitor status of port blocking unknown address frames is to use the `show port block unicast`

Figure 4-7 Commands used to block forwarding of unknown destination address packets.

```
Switch#conf t
Enter configuration commands, one per line.  End with CNTL/Z.
Switch(config)#int fast 0/1
Switch(config-if)#port block multicast
Switch(config-if)#port block unicast
Switch(config-if)#int fast 0/2
Switch(config-if)#port block unicast
Switch(config-if)#port block multicast
Switch(config-if)#end
Switch#
%SYS-5-CONFIG_I: Configured from console by console
Switch#wr t
Building configuration...

Current configuration:
!
version 11.2
no service pad
no service udp-small-servers
no service tcp-small-servers
!
hostname Switch
!
enable password winifred
!
no ip routing
!
interface VLAN1
 ip address 200.200.25.106 255.255.255.0
 no ip route-cache
!
interface FastEthernet0/1
 port group 2
!
interface FastEthernet0/2
 port group 2
!
end

Switch#sho port block unicast
FastEthernet0/1 is blocked from unknown unicast addresses
FastEthernet0/2 is receiving unknown unicast addresses
FastEthernet0/3 is receiving unknown unicast addresses
FastEthernet0/4 is receiving unknown unicast addresses
FastEthernet0/5 is receiving unknown unicast addresses
FastEthernet0/6 is receiving unknown unicast addresses
FastEthernet0/7 is receiving unknown unicast addresses
FastEthernet0/8 is receiving unknown unicast addresses
FastEthernet0/9 is receiving unknown unicast addresses
FastEthernet0/10 is receiving unknown unicast addresses
FastEthernet0/11 is receiving unknown unicast addresses
FastEthernet0/12 is receiving unknown unicast addresses
FastEthernet0/13 is receiving unknown unicast addresses
FastEthernet0/14 is receiving unknown unicast addresses
FastEthernet0/15 is receiving unknown unicast addresses
FastEthernet0/16 is receiving unknown unicast addresses
```

or `show port block multicast` command. Even then it is seen that only port Fast Ethernet 0/1 show up for blocking these frames.

An alternative to blocking packets destined for unknown addresses out each port that is directly connected to a workstation is to make use of the network port option. The idea behind this is illustrated in Figure 4-8. In such a network, all the ports on the 2916 are directly connected to PCs, except port 16, which is connected to the corporate LAN that is serviced by traditional shared media stackable hubs. It is simpler to define one port on the switch to be used for forwarding frames with unknown destinations, rather than deny all but one port for both unicast and multicast unknown frame address forwarding. This configuration can be executed by the following commands as long as you are running IOS 11.2 (8)SA3:

```
Switch#conf t
Enter configuration commands, one per line. End with CNTL/Z.
Switch(config)#int fast 0/16
Switch(config-if)#port network
```

Assuming that spanning tree is enabled on your 2900XL (as it is by default), switch ports directly connected to just one workstation benefit from the `spanning-tree portfast` parameter being set. Without this

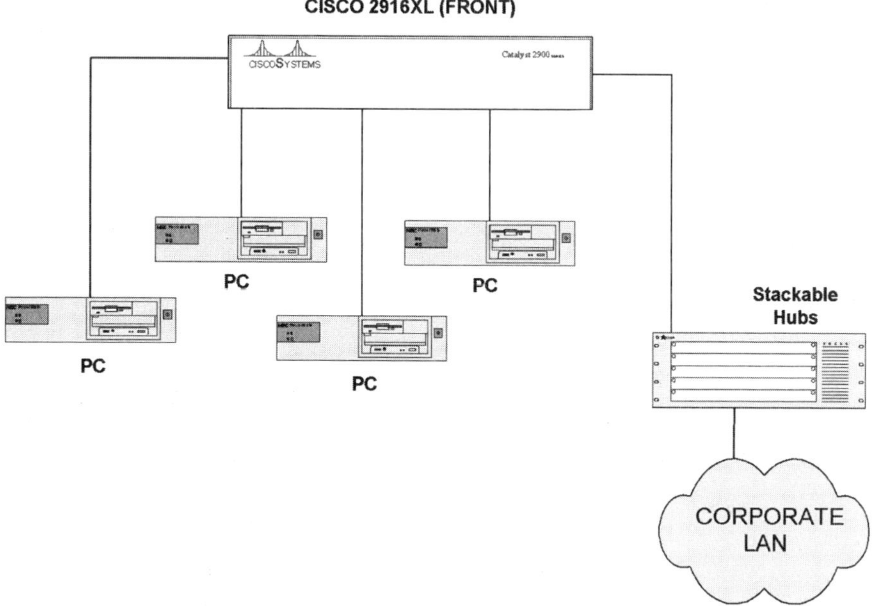

Figure 4-8 Network configuration that is appropriate for using the network port command.

option, it can take an extended period of time for the switch to bring the port into the forwarding state, and the workstation may time out and assume that a network connection is not available. Caution should be taken here. The effect on spanning tree calculations is quite dramatic, in that the port goes straight from a blocking state to a forwarding state without the associated learning phases. If the `portfast` command is active on a port that has a connection to a hub or other switch, or, in fact, anything other than a single workstation, the possibility exists that a potential loop will not be discovered by STP, with the expected disastrous results.

The commands to implement spanning-tree portfast are as follows:

```
Switch#conf t
Enter configuration commands, one per line. End with CNTL/Z.
Switch(config)#int fa 0/7
Switch(config-if)#spanning-tree portfast
Switch(config-if)#end
```

There are some further considerations to take into account when setting port groups. Some are fairly obvious, like no port group member can be configured as a SPAN port for traffic monitoring. The other restrictions are that ports in a port group cannot be set for port security and that all ports in the group must be set for the same `switchport access` mode, either all dedicated to one VLAN or all operating as multi-VLAN ports.

Because the switch treats port group members as a single port, VLAN membership settings and STP settings for portfast, port priority, and path cost values are automatically shared between all port group members. Configuration of the first port added to the group is used when setting these parameters for all other ports in the group. After a group is formed, changing any of these parameters changes the parameter on all other ports in the port group.

Other Port Features

The next area to look at is general enhancements to the basic configuration, and the first we will consider is setting up secure ports. Port security is defined by hardware address and could possibly be more appropriately named "address security." What you do is tell the switch that for a specific MAC address, all packets destined for that MAC address must be forwarded to one and only one port.

Figure 4-9 shows the configuration necessary to define a secure port, along with examples of the MAC address table both before and after the secure port commands are executed. The net effect is that we now have one secure address defined in the switch address table and that any packets destined for MAC address 0000.c0a4.0200 are forwarded out of Fast Ethernet port 0/3 and only that interface. We can add more addresses that can be addressed via that port by the same `mac-address-table secure` command. It should be noted that a secure address is only associated with one port per VLAN.

The practical implementation of this level of security is simpler than it sounds. What we are doing is manually manipulating the switch

Figure 4-9 Configuration used to define a secure port.

```
Switch#show mac-addre
Dynamic Addresses Count:                      27
Secure Addresses (User-defined) Count: 0
Static Addresses (User-defined) Count: 0
System Self Addresses Count:                  37
Total MAC addresses:                          64
Non-static Address Table:
Destination Address   Address Type   Destination Port
-------------------   ------------   --------------------
0000.0c47.42dd        Dynamic        FastEthernet0/1
0000.a701.fab0        Dynamic        FastEthernet0/1
0000.c00d.b8d0        Dynamic        FastEthernet0/1
0000.c013.b8d0        Dynamic        FastEthernet0/1
0000.c029.0300        Dynamic        FastEthernet0/1
0000.c02d.4200        Dynamic        FastEthernet0/1
0000.c02f.5a01        Dynamic        FastEthernet0/1

Switch(config)#mac-address-table secure 0000.c0a4.0200 fast 0/3

Switch#sho mac-address-tab
Dynamic Addresses Count:                      27
Secure Addresses (User-defined) Count: 1
Static Addresses (User-defined) Count: 0
System Self Addresses Count:                  37
Total MAC addresses:                          65
Non-static Address Table:
Destination Address   Address Type   Destination Port
-------------------   ------------   --------------------
0000.0c47.42dd        Dynamic        FastEthernet0/1
0000.a701.fab0        Dynamic        FastEthernet0/1
0000.c00d.b8d0        Dynamic        FastEthernet0/1
0000.c013.b8d0        Dynamic        FastEthernet0/1
0000.c029.0300        Dynamic        FastEthernet0/1
0000.c02d.4200        Dynamic        FastEthernet0/1
0000.c02f.5a01        Dynamic        FastEthernet0/1
0000.c0a4.0200        Secure         FastEthernet0/3
```

address table. When the interface command `port security` is entered into Fast Ethernet port 0/1 for example, the MAC address table merely changes the address type for each MAC address entry in the MAC address table from dynamic to secure and adds a `mac-address-table secure` entry in global configuration for every Mac address heard. If we now move the connection with all these MAC addresses to another port, say, Fast Ethernet port 0/4, the MAC address table does not change, as it will not learn the MAC addresses marked as secure and associated with Fast Ethernet port 0/1 when they appear on Fast Ethernet port 0/4. The thing to do is issue the `clear mac-address-table` command, which clears out the secure entries in the switch address table, along with all the automatically entered `mac-address-table secure` entries in the switch configuration. Once the address table has been cleared, the switch is free to learn the MAC addresses on this connection via Fast Ethernet port 0/4 and enters them in the address table as address type `dynamic`.

There is an option to limit the number of MAC addresses that will be learned on each port. This may be useful in an environment where network usage is charged back on a per-connection basis. Although this facility is implemented via a security command, it is not really much of a security measure, as the switch will just learn the first set of MAC addresses that comes along up to the limit set. The commands to implement this facility are as follows:

```
Switch#conf t
Enter configuration commands, one per line. End with CNTL/Z.
Switch(config)#int fast 0/4
Switch(config-if)#port security max-mac-count 5
Switch(config-if)#^Z
```

Before this can be done, you must make sure that there are no more than five secure addresses already defined on this port; otherwise, the command will not be accepted. The `max-mac-count` must always be equal to or greater than the number of secure MAC addresses defined for the port.

The effect of this command is to reduce the MAC address table to five entries, marked as type `secure`, which will generate corresponding `mac-address-table secure` entries in the configuration for the configuration file. For all the MAC addresses that try to use this interface, an entry similar to the following will be displayed on the console terminal:

```
%PORT_SECURITY-2-SECURITYREJECT: Security violation
occurred on module 0 port 4 caused by MAC address
0000.c076.b7d0
```

It is possible to customize the port to act further in the event of an unauthorized MAC address attempting to use the port. The port can be configured to either send an SNMP trap or shut down. This is accomplished via the `port security action` command that can either be followed by the keyword `shutdown` or `trap`.

It is also possible to enter static MAC address assignments. These addresses are entered via the CLI and accompanied with explicit instructions on how the switch should forward packets destined for the static address. An example of how to enter a static address is as follows:

```
Switch#conf t
Enter configuration commands, one per line. End with CNTL/Z.
Switch(config)#mac-address-table static 0000.2345.3456 fast 0/5 fast 0/6
Switch(config)#^Z
```

This specifies for the MAC address given the input port and the port to which it can be forwarded. This is shown in the MAC address table by a static section at the end of the usual `show mac-address-table` command as follows (note that for all examples so far, we have only considered the one VLAN, the default VLAN1):

```
Static Address Table:
Destination Address     VLAN   Input Port   Output Ports
---------------------   ----   ----------   ------------
0000.2345.3456             1      Fa0/5         Fa0/6
```

In this example, only one output port was identified. The description of how the packet is forwarded, as defined by the input ports and the output port list, describes how the switch forwards a packet destined for the static address based on the source port that the packet arrived on. In practice, what happens is if a packet destined for 0000.2345.3456 comes in on Fast Ethernet port 0/5, the static configuration as it stands will forward the packet out Fast Ethernet port 0/6. If more than one port was defined as an output port, the packet would have been forwarded to all those ports.

It is possible to change the aging time for dynamically learned addresses in the switch address table. The default is 300 seconds, which can be modified with the global command `mac-address-table aging-time 200`, which sets the aging time to 200 seconds. There should not be any need to alter this from the default in most installations. If you feel the need, though, the rule of thumb is that the smaller your network, the lower the aging time you can get away with. The effect of lowering the aging time too far is that MAC addresses that are still valid may disappear from the switch address table. However, the advantage in lowering the aging time is that if a PC moves from one switch to another, its entry in the first switch's address table will be removed more quickly and proper network operation will resume sooner.

In some networks, a phenomenon called "broadcast storms" can occur. Typically, this only occurs in networks containing a large number of switches or bridges that use spanning tree and experience rapid topology changes—for example, during some fault conditions with flapping ports. The broadcast can consist of spanning tree BPDU packets, or in some token ring configurations, spanning tree explorer packets can contribute. In any case, the effect on the user is slow or no response. It is possible to configure ports on the switch to contain broadcast storms by going into a blocking state when broadcasts reach a certain level and come out of blocking when the broadcasts have reached a more normal level. This is different from the condition we discussed earlier when we talked of setting a Catalyst 5000 port to drop broadcasts if they take up more than a given level of available bandwidth. I am more in favor of the method we are describing now to control broadcasts, as it deals with a situation that is only likely to arise under a fault scenario.

The port storm control feature is enabled on a per-interface basis, as in the following example:

```
Switch#conf t
Enter configuration commands, one per line. End with CNTL/Z.
Switch(config)#int fa0/9
Switch(config-if)#port storm-control threshold rising 2000 falling 500
Switch(config-if)#end
```

According to the Cisco documentation, the threshold rising and falling figures can be set to anything between 0 to 4294967295 packets per second.

We discussed in earlier chapters the benefits of Cisco's CGMP protocol that enables a router to send information to a switch to help it more efficiently forward multicast packets. CGMP is not enabled by default and needs to be added in global configuration mode. There are a couple of options with this command that are worth discussing. First is the `fast leave` parameter. CGMP exists for a router to tell a switch which ports to forward traffic to for a given multicast group. If a group is no longer active, the `fast leave` option speeds up the process of removing that group from the processing of the switch. The other option worth considering is the CGMP `holdtime` parameter, which defines how long a switch will maintain a connection to a router for the exchange of CGMP information. Following are examples of implementing these configuration options:

```
Switch#conf t
Enter configuration commands, one per line. End with CNTL/Z.
Switch(config)#cgmp leave-processing
Switch(config)#cgmp holdtime 300
Switch(config)#end
```

One operational issue to be considered is that when an STP topology change notification is received by the switch, the CGMP tables should be purged. If, for some reason, this does not occur and incorrect data is stored in the CGMP tables, it can be cleared with `clear cgmp vlan 1 group MMMM.MMMM.MMMM` (the M's represent MAC address numbers), which clears entries for this VLAN and group multicast address. If this error condition has occurred, the effect is that multicast packets will be sent to the wrong ports and workstations expecting the multicast stream may not get it. Once the `cgmp clear` command has been issued, its effects can be verified by entering the following:

```
Switch#sho cgmp
CGMP is running.
CGMP Fast Leave is running.
Default router timeout is 300 sec.
vLAN     IGMP MAC Address   Interfaces
----     ----------------   ----------
vLAN     IGMP Router        Expire    Interface
----     -----------        ------    ---------
```

This command shows the status of CGMP operation. The first table shows the interfaces that packets addressed to a particular group multicast address will be sent to, on a per-VLAN basis. The second table shows the expiry time for router connections when collecting CGMP data.

One final option in the general configuration of the switch that we will look at is the Cisco Discovery Protocol (CDP). This protocol exists to enable Cisco devices to exchange information with each other regarding neighboring devices. This is often not permitted in security-conscious installations. If CDP is enabled under a global configuration, it can be disabled on a port-by-port basis if you don't want to exchange that information with devices connected to specific ports. The commands to implement CDP globally, but disable CDP exchanges on port 5, are as follows:

```
Switch#conf t
%SYS-5-CONFIG_I: Configured from console by console
Enter configuration commands, one per line. End with CNTL/Z.
Switch(config)#cdp run
Switch(config)#int fa0/5
Switch(config-if)#no cdp enable
```

CDP itself is designed to be used for network management purposes. The type of information that is exchanged by CDP is the device type, its capabilities in terms of bridging or routing functions, and its network protocol layer functionality.

Spanning Tree Configuration

Spanning tree is enabled by default on 2900XL switches, and no specific action is necessary to have it operational, which is the recommended state. It is possible to view the spanning tree parameters by issuing the following command for individual interfaces:

```
Switch#sho span int fa0/1
Interface Fa0/1 (port 1) in Spanning tree 1 is FORWARDING
   Port path cost 100, Port priority 128
   Designated root has priority 32768, address 0010.07a1.88c0
   Designated bridge has priority 32768, address 0010.07a1.88c0
   Designated port is 1, path cost 0
   Timers: message age 0, forward delay 0, hold 0
   BPDU: sent 1160, received 0
```

For complete VLANs the following command will produce the display shown, plus the interface display for each port configured to be in the VLAN:

```
Switch#sho span vlan 1
Spanning tree 1 is executing the IEEE compatible Spanning Tree protocol
  Bridge Identifier has priority 32768, address 0010.07a1.88c0
  Configured hello time 2, max age 20, forward delay 15
  We are the root of the spanning tree
  Topology change flag not set, detected flag not set, changes 1
  Times: hold 1, topology change 35, notification 2
         hello 2, max age 20, forward delay 15
  Timers: hello 1, topology change 0, notification 0
```

Although it is possible to customize forward time, hello time, and others on a per-VLAN basis, mostly this is inadvisable. The only thing you may wish to do is change the switch priority so that you can be sure that the switch you want will be selected as the STP root bridge in your network. This is generally the switch located closest to the center (in terms of hops between switches) of the network. This is set via the `span priority` global command and can accept a value of between 0 and 65535, with a default of 32768. Lowering the bridge priority makes the switch more likely to be selected as the root bridge in the spanning tree.

Interface cost and priority settings are useful for trunk configurations where you have two trunks connecting two switched together. In this instance you can configure one trunk as the preferred link for one set of VLANs and the other trunk as the preferred link for the other VLANs. However, this is of little use to the SA3 version of software, since it does not support trunks at the time of writing, as discussed in the beginning of this chapter.

VLAN Assignment and Inter VLAN Communication

So far we have only configured one VLAN on the switch, the default VLAN 1, to which all ports are automatically assigned. That will give us 16 ports all within the one broadcast domain. We'll now discuss assigning ports to different VLANs, extending VLANs across multiple switches, and routing between different VLANs.

Extending VLANs Between Switches

Without expansion modules, the 2916XL has 16 Fast Ethernet ports available. This can be expanded to 24 ports with two expansion modules (each containing four Fast Ethernet ports), but to get any more ports in a VLAN, a crossover RJ-45 is necessary to connect a port on one switch to a port on another. This connection is illustrated in Figure 4-10.

In this scenario, switch 1 will see all the MAC addresses of the devices connected to switch 2 as reachable via interface Fast Ethernet port 0/16, and switch 2 will see the MAC address of all devices attached to switch 1 as reachable via its Fast Ethernet port 0/1. Assuming no expansion modules, this gives us a total of 30 ports in VLAN 1, as one port on each switch is used to connect them together.

Multiple VLANs on a 2916XL

The previous section discussed how to get around one of the limitations of the 2916XL not having trunking capability. The method of connecting two switches together by a crossover cable does expand the number of

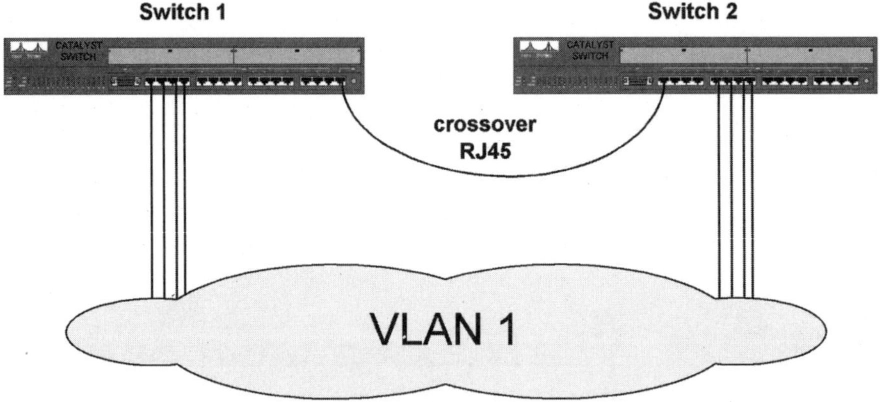

Figure 4-10 Connecting two switches together to extend the number of ports in a VLAN.

ports available to a VLAN, but it is a somewhat clumsy and inelegant mechanism. It does not support multiple VLAN traffic, as does ISL, and does not allow individual VLAN ports to be easily distributed between several switches.

A different requirement is how to route between two (or more) VLANs that may exist on the one 2916XL. We will examine the case with two VLANs first, as that allows us to use the one-armed router concept. The network configuration for this setup is shown in Figure 4-11.

What we have to achieve is assign one port on the switch to be in VLAN 1, one port to be in VLAN 2, and the port that is connected to the router to be in both VLANs. We also have to set the switch to use the router as its default gateway for its routing. There are only a few configuration changes that need be made to the switch, but they are not immediately obvious.

Initially, all ports are assigned membership of VLAN 1 by default. The first thing we will do is assign Fast Ethernet port 0/14 to VLAN 2. This is accomplished using the following commands:

```
Switch(config)#int fa0/14
Switch(config-if)#switchport access vlan 2
Switch(config-if)#end
```

In the configuration, ports assigned to VLAN 1 will not show any assignment; however, those assigned to other VLANs will show the switchport access designation. The `switchport` command has three options. The one we just used is the command to assign a switch port to a single VLAN. The next task is to assign port 0/13 to both VLANs, which requires two separate commands—the first to designate the port

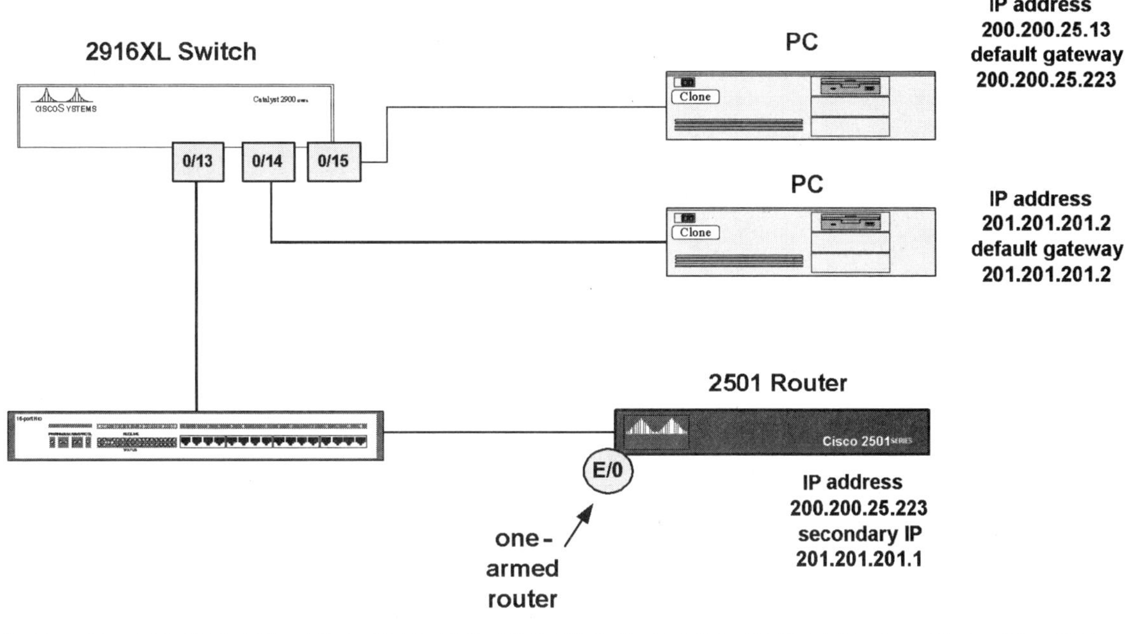

Figure 4-11 One-armed router configuration for routing between VLANs on a 2916XL switch.

as multi-VLAN capable and the second to define the VLANs to which it will become a member:

```
Switch#conf t
Enter configuration commands, one per line. End with CNTL/Z.
Switch(config)#int fa0/13
Switch(config-if)#switchport mode multi
Switch(config-if)#switchport multi vlan 1 2
Switch(config-if)#end
```

Note that a different command is required to make a port a member of multiple VLANs; one cannot simply keep adding VLAN membership by the `switchport access` command. The `switchport multi vlan` command is followed by the list for which you want this port to be a member. The only other configuration necessary is to make the default gateway for the switch, that of the attached one-armed router. The IP address of this default gateway entry has to be in the same network (or subnet, if netmasks are applied) as VLAN 1.

We are using a 2501 router in this example, and subinterfaces can only be supported on LAN media if part of an 802.10 or ISL trunk. As the 2916XL does not support these encapsulations, we have to use the primary and secondary IP address feature of the 2501 Ethernet interface. Of course, this limits us to being able to use this configuration only to route between two VLANs on the 2916XL, no more. What we are doing is setting up the Ethernet 0 interface on the router to respond to two IP addresses, each on separate network numbers, and route packets between those two networks. Clearly, the simplest way to set up the two PCs in this network is to have them use the respective address on the router Ethernet interface as the default gateway also. The configurations of the switch and router are given in Figure 4-12.

To verify the operation of this configuration, simply ping from one PC to the other. The ping message will be directed from the originating PC (let's say the PC on VLAN 1) to its default router through the switch. This packet will come out of interface 0/13 into the router interface. This router will route the packet from the IP network associated with VLAN 1 to the VLAN 2 IP network, sending the packet back out the same interface it was received on. The switch recognizes the MAC address of the router interface as belonging to both VLAN 1 and VLAN 2, and forwards the packet on to VLAN 2, enabling the destination PC to receive the ping request and respond.

The interesting thing is that you do nothing to explicitly define the second VLAN. Contrary to what you do for VLAN 1, there is no interface VLAN 2 section, for example. There are 1000 VLANs all waiting to be used in the 2916XL configuration. All that need be done to bring them into use is assign a port to one of the VLANs. These VLANs do not care what IP addressing scheme is used on the workstations attached to their ports. All the configuration that enables IP connectivity for these subsequent VLANs is done at the router and workstation level.

In the situation where you need to route between more than two VLANs on a 2916XL, the simplest thing to do is connect one port on each VLAN to a router interface and let the router route packets between VLANs. This is illustrated in Figure 4-13.

The interesting switch and router displays to view are shown in Figure 4-14. The first thing to look at is the `show vlan id` commands for both VLAN 1 and VLAN 2. This shows ports 0/13 and 0/14 in VLAN 2, but also all ports other than 0/14 in VLAN 1, illustrating the dual membership of port 0/13. Interestingly, the `show mac-address-table` command counts all MAC addresses that it has learned about via interface 0/13 as belonging to both VLAN 1 and 2, which leads to the total number of MAC addresses listed in that top part of this display as nearly double the number of devices in the network. The only devices with sin-

Figure 4-12
Configurations for switch and router.

```
Switch Configuration

Switch#sho run
Building configuration...

Current configuration:
!
version 11.2
no service pad
no service udp-small-servers
no service tcp-small-servers
!
hostname Switch
!
enable password winifred
!
!
!
interface VLAN1
 ip address 200.200.25.106 255.255.255.0
 no ip route-cache
!
interface FastEthernet0/1
!
interface FastEthernet0/2
 port group 2
!
interface FastEthernet0/3
 port group 2
!
interface FastEthernet0/4
!
interface FastEthernet0/5
!
interface FastEthernet0/6
!
interface FastEthernet0/7
!
interface FastEthernet0/8
!
interface FastEthernet0/9
!
interface FastEthernet0/10
!
interface FastEthernet0/11
!
interface FastEthernet0/12
!
interface FastEthernet0/13
 switchport multi vlan  1 2
 switchport mode multi
!
interface FastEthernet0/14
 switchport access vlan 2
!
interface FastEthernet0/15
!
interface FastEthernet0/16
!
ip default-gateway 200.200.25.223
snmp-server community private RW
snmp-server community public RO
!
line con 0
 stopbits 1
line vty 0 4
 password test
 login
!
end
```

```
Router Configuration

Router#sho run
Building configuration...

Current configuration:
!
version 11.3
service timestamps debug uptime
service timestamps log uptime
no service password-encryption
service udp-small-servers
service tcp-small-servers
!
hostname Router
!
enable secret 5 $1$dC./$HHcIF2wsHuQuA0L0fxghb1
enable password entest
!
no ip domain-lookup
!
!
interface Ethernet0
 ip address 201.201.201.1 255.255.255.0 secondary
 ip address 200.200.25.223 255.255.255.0
!
interface Serial0
 no ip address
 shutdown
!
interface Serial1
 no ip address
 shutdown
!
ip classless
!
!
line con 0
line 1 16
 transport input all
line aux 0
 transport input all
line vty 0 4
 password 3paths
 login
!
end
```

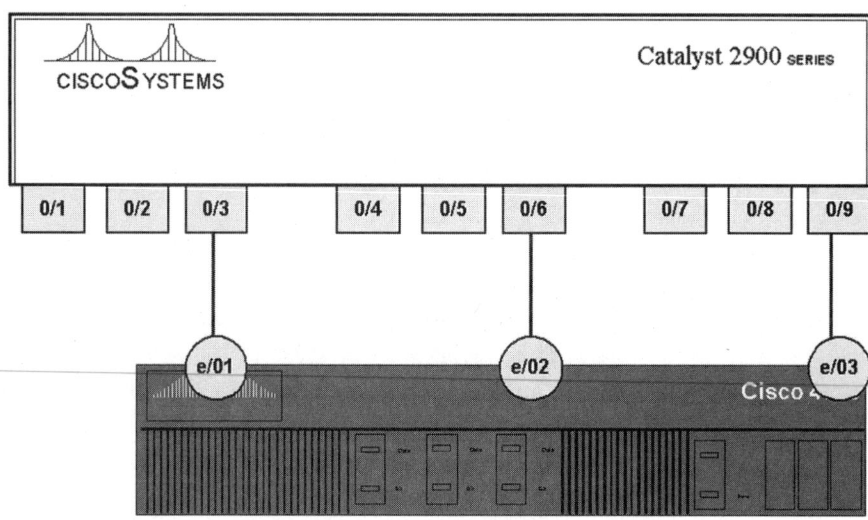

Figure 4-13 Network configuration to support routing between three VLANs all on the same 2916XL.

gle VLAN membership shown in this command are the PCs directly connected to 0/14 and 0/15.

Given this dual membership of VLANs by the router interface MAC address, it is interesting to further examine the flow of packets when a device on VLAN 1 pings a device on VLAN 2. We know the physical path is into the switch, out to the router, and back into the switch, but the question is that, given the router interface MAC address is a member of both VLAN 1 and 2, will the ping message coming out of the router interface on its way to the destination PC be forwarded to both VLANs? The answer is, of course, no. The router will reference its ARP table to determine the MAC address of the destination PC, and the switch will forward the packet to just the destination PC on the appropriate VLAN, since it forwards based on destination MAC address.

On the router it is interesting to look at the `show ip route` command, which shows that the two class C networks used in this example are directly connected to Ethernet 0. With this connection, no routing protocols or static routing statements are necessary to route between the two networks. Looking at the ARP tablc by the `sho ip arp` command shows that the router is able to detect the MAC address of all the IP addressed devices on both VLAN 1 and VLAN 2.

There is an interesting behavior associated with the use of secondary addresses and pinging from the router using an interface with a second-

Figure 4-14 Switch and router display.

```
Useful Switch show commands

Switch#sho vlan id 1
VLAN     Name                                  Status    Mod/Ports
-------- ------------------------------------- --------- ------------------------
1        VLAN0001                              active    Fa0/1 Fa0/2 Fa0/3 Fa0/4
                                                         Fa0/5 Fa0/6 Fa0/7 Fa0/8
                                                         Fa0/9 Fa0/10 Fa0/11 Fa0/12
                                                         Fa0/13 Fa0/15 Fa0/16
Switch#show vlan id 2
VLAN     Name                                  Status    Mod/Ports
-------- ------------------------------------- --------- ------------------------
2        VLAN0002                              active    Fa0/13 Fa0/14
Switch#sho mac-addr
Dynamic Addresses Count:                      44
Secure Addresses (User-defined) Count:        0
Static Addresses (User-defined) Count:        0
System Self Addresses Count:                  37
Total MAC addresses:                          81
Non-static Address Table:
Destination Address  Address Type  VLAN  Destination Port
-------------------  ------------  ----  --------------------
0000.0c35.0945       Dynamic          1  FastEthernet0/13
0000.0c35.0945       Dynamic          2  FastEthernet0/13
0000.0c47.42dd       Dynamic          1  FastEthernet0/13
0000.0c47.42dd       Dynamic          2  FastEthernet0/13
0000.a701.fab0       Dynamic          1  FastEthernet0/13
0000.a701.fab0       Dynamic          2  FastEthernet0/13
0000.c00d.b8d0       Dynamic          1  FastEthernet0/13
0000.c00d.b8d0       Dynamic          2  FastEthernet0/13
0000.c013.b8d0       Dynamic          1  FastEthernet0/13
0000.c013.b8d0       Dynamic          2  FastEthernet0/13
0000.c02f.5a01       Dynamic          1  FastEthernet0/13
0000.c02f.5a01       Dynamic          2  FastEthernet0/13
0000.c062.2c00       Dynamic          1  FastEthernet0/13
0000.c062.2c00       Dynamic          2  FastEthernet0/13
0000.c06b.d2e1       Dynamic          1  FastEthernet0/13
0000.c06b.d2e1       Dynamic          2  FastEthernet0/13
0000.c076.b7d0       Dynamic          1  FastEthernet0/13
0000.c076.b7d0       Dynamic          2  FastEthernet0/13
0000.c07b.26ee       Dynamic          1  FastEthernet0/13
0000.c07b.26ee       Dynamic          2  FastEthernet0/13
0000.c080.0200       Dynamic          1  FastEthernet0/13
0000.c080.0200       Dynamic          2  FastEthernet0/13
0000.c09c.69f4       Dynamic          1  FastEthernet0/13
0000.c09c.69f4       Dynamic          2  FastEthernet0/13
0000.c0a0.0100       Dynamic          1  FastEthernet0/13
0000.c0a0.0100       Dynamic          2  FastEthernet0/13
0000.c0a4.acdc       Dynamic          1  FastEthernet0/15
0060.b041.281b       Dynamic          1  FastEthernet0/13
0060.b041.281b       Dynamic          2  FastEthernet0/13
00a0.c909.7f46       Dynamic          1  FastEthernet0/13
00a0.c909.7f46       Dynamic          2  FastEthernet0/13
00a0.c968.e136       Dynamic          1  FastEthernet0/13
00a0.c968.e136       Dynamic          2  FastEthernet0/13
00aa.00c2.6927       Dynamic          1  FastEthernet0/13
00aa.00c2.6927       Dynamic          2  FastEthernet0/13
00e0.2902.6ee3       Dynamic          1  FastEthernet0/13
00e0.2902.6ee3       Dynamic          2  FastEthernet0/13
00e0.2902.a706       Dynamic          1  FastEthernet0/13
00e0.2902.a706       Dynamic          2  FastEthernet0/13
00e0.2906.3173       Dynamic          2  FastEthernet0/14
00e0.2910.1040       Dynamic          1  FastEthernet0/13
00e0.2910.1040       Dynamic          2  FastEthernet0/13
00e0.2910.162e       Dynamic          1  FastEthernet0/13
00e0.2910.162e       Dynamic          2  FastEthernet0/13
Switch#


Useful router show commands

Router#sho ip rout
Codes: C - connected, S - static, I - IGRP, R - RIP, M - mobile, B - BGP
       D - EIGRP, EX - EIGRP external, O - OSPF, IA - OSPF inter area
       N1 - OSPF NSSA external type 1, N2 - OSPF NSSA external type 2
       E1 - OSPF external type 1, E2 - OSPF external type 2, E - EGP
       i - IS-IS, L1 - IS-IS level-1, L2 - IS-IS level-2, * - candidate default
       U - per-user static route, o - ODR

Gateway of last resort is not set

C    201.201.201.0/24 is directly connected, Ethernet0
C    200.200.25.0/24 is directly connected, Ethernet0
Router#sho ip arp
Protocol  Address          Age (min)  Hardware Addr   Type   Interface
Internet  200.200.25.11          120  0000.c080.0200  ARPA   Ethernet0
Internet  200.200.25.13            8  0000.c0a4.acdc  ARPA   Ethernet0
Internet  200.200.25.223           -  0000.0c35.0945  ARPA   Ethernet0
Internet  201.201.201.1            -  0000.0c35.0945  ARPA   Ethernet0
Internet  201.201.201.2          165  00e0.2906.3173  ARPA   Ethernet0
```

ary address. Using the standard `ping` command from a Cisco sends a packet with a source IP address set to that of the primary address, not the secondary. When using the `extended ping` command in enable mode, there is the option to set the source IP address to something different, which in this case will be the secondary IP address. Given that there is a route between the two networks, the ping does work, but it may not follow the route you think you are testing.

Figure 4-15 shows the operation of the `ping` command with `debug ip icmp` set. As can be seen from the debug information echoed back to the console, the source address used for pinging either of the hosts is 200.200.25.223, the primary IP address of the interface. The effect this has on the path of the return ICMP ping packet is that it follows the route back to the 200.200.25.0 network. In this network configuration,

Figure 4-15 Operation of the `ping` command.

```
ICMP packet debugging is on
Router#ping 201.201.201.2

Type escape sequence to abort.
Sending 5, 100-byte ICMP Echos to 201.201.201.2, timeout is 2 seconds:
!!!!!
Success rate is 100 percent (5/5), round-trip min/avg/max = 4/5/8 ms
Router#
03:02:03: ICMP: echo reply rcvd, src 201.201.201.2, dst 200.200.25.223
03:02:03: ICMP: echo reply rcvd, src 201.201.201.2, dst 200.200.25.223
03:02:03: ICMP: echo reply rcvd, src 201.201.201.2, dst 200.200.25.223
03:02:03: ICMP: echo reply rcvd, src 201.201.201.2, dst 200.200.25.223
03:02:03: ICMP: echo reply rcvd, src 201.201.201.2, dst 200.200.25.223
Router#ping 200.200.25.13

Type escape sequence to abort.
Sending 5, 100-byte ICMP Echos to 200.200.25.13, timeout is 2 seconds:
!!!!!
Success rate is 100 percent (5/5), round-trip min/avg/max = 4/4/8 ms
Router#
03:02:45: ICMP: echo reply rcvd, src 200.200.25.13, dst 200.200.25.223
03:02:45: ICMP: echo reply rcvd, src 200.200.25.13, dst 200.200.25.223
03:02:45: ICMP: echo reply rcvd, src 200.200.25.13, dst 200.200.25.223
03:02:45: ICMP: echo reply rcvd, src 200.200.25.13, dst 200.200.25.223
03:02:45: ICMP: echo reply rcvd, src 200.200.25.13, dst 200.200.25.223

Now using the extended ping command

Router#ping
Protocol [ip]:
Target IP address: 201.201.201.2
Repeat count [5]:
Datagram size [100]:
Timeout in seconds [2]:
Extended commands [n]: y
Source address or interface: 201.201.201.1
Type of service [0]:
Set DF bit in IP header? [no]:
Validate reply data? [no]:
Data pattern [0xABCD]:
Loose, Strict, Record, Timestamp, Verbose[none]:
Sweep range of sizes [n]:
Type escape sequence to abort.
Sending 5, 100-byte ICMP Echos to 201.201.201.2, timeout is 2 seconds:
!!!!!
Success rate is 100 percent (5/5), round-trip min/avg/max = 4/4/4 ms
Router#
00:02:43: ICMP: echo reply rcvd, src 201.201.201.2, dst 201.201.201.1
00:02:43: ICMP: echo reply rcvd, src 201.201.201.2, dst 201.201.201.1
00:02:43: ICMP: echo reply rcvd, src 201.201.201.2, dst 201.201.201.1
00:02:43: ICMP: echo reply rcvd, src 201.201.201.2, dst 201.201.201.1
00:02:43: ICMP: echo reply rcvd, src 201.201.201.2, dst 201.201.201.1
```

that is the same as the return path to the 201.201.201.0 network; however, in a more complex network with more router hops, the return path may vary, which will mean without using the extended ping command, you will not be testing the return path you wish to. With the extended ping command, you can set the source address to that of the secondary, and the return path for the ping packet will follow the route mapped out to the 201.201.201.0 network.

Using the SPAN Port for LAN Analysis

If you are familiar with using a LAN analyzer on shared media Ethernet hubs, you will have connected the analyzer to a spare port on the hub and seen all the network traffic on that segment displayed on the LAN analyzer. This will not happen if you connect the same analyzer to a spare port on the 2900XL switch. Because the switch forwards packets out of ports based on destination MAC addresses, all you will see on the analyzer is broadcast traffic, or multicast traffic that is destined for a multicast group that has not yet registered port membership on the switch via CGMP.

The feature that the 2916XL switch supports to enable LAN analysis is the Switched Port Analyzer (SPAN) command. With this command you designate the port you will connect your LAN analyzer to (by going into interface configuration mode for that port), then tell the switch what traffic you want forwarded to that port for analysis. There are some restrictions to the ports that can be configured as a SPAN port, which are as follows:

- Port security cannot be enabled.
- The port must not be part of a port group.
- The port must not be a multi VLAN port.

A port is enabled for SPAN monitoring via the port monitor interface command, so in the following example, we will select Fast Ethernet port 0/1 as the SPAN port with the following commands:

```
Switch#conf t
Enter configuration commands, one per line. End with CNTL/Z.
Switch(config)#int fa0/1
Switch(config-if)#port monitor
FastEthernet0/1 and FastEthernet0/14 are in different vlan
```

As you can see, with no specification of the port to be monitored, the switch assumes that all ports on the device should be monitored but tells you that because Fast Ethernet port 0/14 is on a different VLAN, it cannot be monitored. This configuration command automatically puts several entries into the interface configuration, listing a `port monitor` entry for each port being monitored (in this instance, all the ports in VLAN 1).

To set up Fast Ethernet port 0/1 to monitor just one port (0/7 in this instance), use the following commands:

```
Switch(config)#int fa0/1
Switch(config-if)#port monitor fa0/7
```

Saving and Retrieving Configurations

In the *Cisco TCP/IP Routing Professional Reference* we covered how to save router configurations to a TFTP server and how to retrieve those configurations. The 2916XL works in a similar fashion as regards saving and retrieving configuration files. These files are ASCII, as with router configuration files, and can therefore be edited with any full-screen text editor prior to being uploaded to the switch. Saving the current configuration file to a TFTP server at address 200.200.25.13 using the filename switch-confg can be accomplished with the following commands:

```
Switch#wri net
Remote host []? 200.200.25.13
Name of configuration file to write [switch-confg]?
Write file switch-confg on host 200.200.25.13? [confirm]
Building configuration...
Writing switch-confg !! [OK]
```

Copying a configuration file from a TFTP server to a switch with a blank configuration can be accomplished using the following commands:

```
Switch#conf net
Host or network configuration file [host]?
Address of remote host [255.255.255.255]? 200.200.25.13
Name of configuration file [switch-confg]?
Configure using switch-confg from 200.200.25.13? [confirm]
Loading switch-confg from 200.200.25.13 (via VLAN1): !
[OK - 943 bytes]
```

As with a router, the `configure network` command combines the configuration elements of the configuration running in the switch at that time, with the configuration parameters in the file being loaded. If we attempt to do what we did with a router, by copying the configuration file on the TFTP server to the switch's startup configuration, this is the error we get:

```
Switch#copy tftp startup
Address of remote host [255.255.255.255]? 200.200.25.13
Name of configuration file [switch-confg]?
Configure using switch-confg from 200.200.25.13? [confirm]
Loading switch-confg from 200.200.25.13 (via VLAN1): !
[OK - 943 bytes]
Non-Volatile memory is in use[Failed]
Switch#
%SYS-3-CONFIG_NV_ERR: Nonvolatile store write error - configuration failed
```

At this stage a reload is necessary to free up the nonvolatile memory. The first thing to do is issue the `dir flash:` command to display the contents of the flash memory:

```
Switch#dir flash:
Directory of flash:
  2   -rwx    913008   Mar 01 1993 00:16:47  c2900XL-h-mz-112_8-sa3
  3   -rwx     59633   Dec 11 1997 19:07:53  c2900XL-diag-mz-112.8-SA
  4   drwx      3776   Dec 11 1997 19:07:55  html
 64   -rwx       969   Mar 01 1993 00:03:30  config.text
 65   -rwx       177   Mar 01 1993 00:09:02  env_vars
1728000 bytes total (404992 bytes free)
```

The file config.text contains the switch configuration, so one way of copying a configuration file from a TFTP server to replace an existing configuration file is as follows. Copy the new configuration file on the TFTP server to flash memory using the name bootfile. Then delete the existing config.text and rename bootfile as config.text.

After a reload, the configuration retrieved from the TFTP server will be the switch's new configuration. The commands to execute these changes are given as follows:

```
Switch#copy tftp://200.200.25.13/switch-confg flash:bootfile
Source IP address or hostname [200.200.25.13]?
Source filename [switch-confg]?
Destination filename [bootfile]?
Loading switch-confg from 200.200.25.13 (via VLAN1): !
[OK - 943 bytes]
```

So far we have copied the file named switch-confg from the TFTP server to a file named bootfile in the switch's flash memory. Next we need to delete the existing config.text and rename this bootfile to be the new configuration, which is achieved with the following:

```
Switch#delete flash:config.text
Delete filename [config.text]?
Delete flash:config.text? [confirm]
Switch#rename flash:bootfile flash:config.text
Source filename [bootfile]?
Destination filename [config.text]?
Switch#reload
```

After the reload, the new configuration file takes effect. Should it be necessary to wipe the configuration and start again, the `write erase` command followed by a `reload` will restore a blank configuration to the switch.

A Typical Base Configuration

In this section we'll put together a sample configuration that can be used for a typical initial placement of a 2916XL switch in a network. The physical layout is shown in Figure 4-16, with the configuration file displayed in Figure 4-17.

The idea is that VLAN 1 is used for connecting the server to the switch via a port group and for direct connections to power users. VLAN 2 is

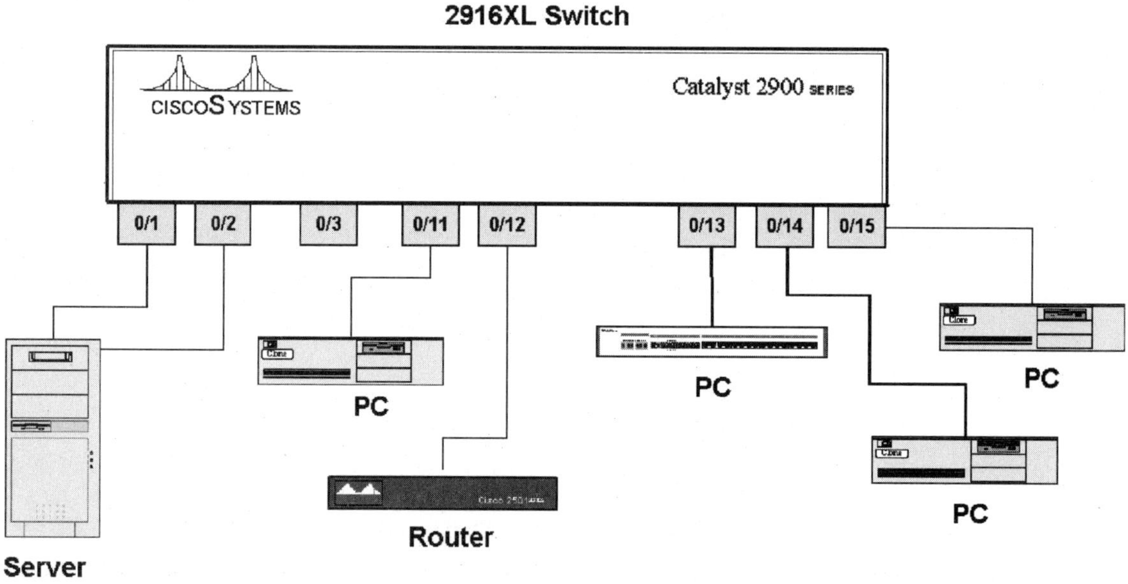

Figure 4-16 Typical workgroup connectivity for a 2916XL switch.

Figure 4-17 Configuration file for base configuration.

```
Switch#wr t
Building configuration

Current configuration
!
version 11.2
no service pad
service password-encryption
no service udp-small-servers
no service tcp-small-servers
!
hostname Switch
!
enable password 7 07182842470F0B0
!
!
spanning-tree vlan 1 priority 1000
spanning-tree vlan 2 priority 1000
cgmp leave-processing
!
interface VLAN1
 ip address 200.200.25.106 255.255.25
 no ip route-cache
!
interface FastEthernet0/1
 port group 2
 spanning-tree portfast
!
interface FastEthernet0/2
 port group 2
 spanning-tree portfast
!
interface FastEthernet0/3
!
interface FastEthernet0/4
!
interface FastEthernet0/5
!
interface FastEthernet0/6
!
interface FastEthernet0/7
!
interface FastEthernet0/8
!
interface FastEthernet0/9
!
interface FastEthernet0/10
!
interface FastEthernet0/11
 switchport access vlan 2
 port block unicast
 port block multicast
 spanning-tree portfast
!
interface FastEthernet0/12
 switchport multi vlan  1 2
 switchport mode multi
!
interface FastEthernet0/13
!
interface FastEthernet0/14
 switchport access vlan 2
 port block unicast
 port block multicast
 spanning-tree portfast
!
interface FastEthernet0/15
 port block unicast
 port block multicast
 spanning-tree portfast

interface FastEthernet0/16

ip default-gateway 200.200.25.223
snmp-server community 99bottles RO
snmp-server community 99party RW

line con 0
 stopbits 1
line vty 0 4
 password 7 120D000406
 login

end

Switch#
```

used to connect to users that only require occasional access to this server, be they direct connect or via hubs. There is a dedicated connection to a router that routes between these two VLANs and the rest of the corporate network.

The special configurations in this setup are as follows:

- The ports directly attached to PCs have the `portfast` command for spanning tree.
- The switch has its priority lowered to ensure it is selected as the root bridge.
- The server is connected via a port group containing two ports.
- CGMP is enabled.
- The singly attached workstations have blocking set up for unicast and multicast addresses.
- The port connecting to the router port belongs to both VLAN 1 and VLAN 2.
- The only crossover RJ-45 cable in use is the one connecting port 0/13 to the hub.

This configuration gives us the benefit of two full-duplex 100-Mbit/sec Fast Ethernet links, providing an aggregate bandwidth of 200 Mbit/sec in each direction simultaneously between the switch and the server. Also, we are creating two separate broadcast domains with the two VLANs and giving each of the power users PCs their own collision domain. These directly connected workstations (with appropriate NICs) will negotiate full-duplex 100-Mbit/sec operation automatically. The directly connected PCs have connections untroubled by spurious searches for either unicast or multicast addresses by the `port block` commands. These ports are always brought up in the STP forwarding state as quickly as possible via the `portfast` command.

This base configuration can be expanded upon by a crossover cable to connect a port associated in one VLAN to another switch, which has ports configured for the same VLAN, thus extending the number of ports available for that VLAN. The generic configurations made were to add a password for telnet access, provide a default gateway for IP routing, and set nonstandard strings for SNMP access. When the nonstandard community strings for SNMP were added, the default values had to be removed with the `no snmp-server community` command; otherwise, the switch will accept both the old and new community string values for read-only and read-write SNMP access.

We have also added the `service password` global configuration command, which shows itself in the configuration file as `service password-encryption`. This hides the enable password from anyone that can see the configuration file.

Password Recovery

There may well come a time when the password is lost, and even if the last configuration file is stored on a TFTP server, with the `service password-encryption` configuration option set, you cannot determine the enable password. As we did with routers in the *Cisco TCP/IP Routing Professional Reference,* you can follow a password recovery procedure to change the enable password should it be lost, as long as you have physical access to the device.

The first stage is to power-cycle the device while holding down the Mode button on the switch's front panel. The Mode button only needs to be held down for 2 seconds and can be released after the LED above the first Ethernet port goes out. This should generate a screen display as shown below. If this is not displayed, it means the Mode button was not held down properly or was not held down long enough.

```
The system has been interrupted prior to initializing the flash filesystem.
The following commands will initialize
the flash filesystem, and finish loading the operating
system software:
    flash_init
    load_helper
    boot
switch:
```

At this prompt, enter the `flash_init` command. The only trick to be wary of is that if you happen to have set the console and terminal connected to it to anything other than 9600 baud, the console connection will stop working, as this command resets the console port to the 9600 default. The process we are about to follow is to rename the configuration file and boot with a blank configuration, allowing us to enter into enable mode without having to supply a password. Once in enable mode, we need to then get the old configuration file with the unknown enable password into memory so that it can be edited. All this is done without leaving enable mode, so that once the old configuration file is in running memory, we can change the enable password to whatever we like and save the configuration, and we have access restored. So from the `switch:` prompt, enter the following:

```
switch: flash_init
Initializing Flash...
flashfs[0]: 63 files, 2 directories
flashfs[0]: 0 orphaned files, 0 orphaned directories
flashfs[0]: Total bytes: 1728000
flashfs[0]: Bytes used: 1323520
flashfs[0]: Bytes available: 404480
flashfs[0]: flashfs fsck took 3 seconds.
...done Initializing Flash.
```

Now that the flash memory has been initialized, we can issue the `load_helper` command and review the contents of the flash memory as a reminder of the name of the configuration file to rename:

```
switch: load_helper
switch: dir flash:
Directory of flash:/
2    -rwx  913008    <date>          c2900XL-h-mz-112_8-sa3
3    -rwx   59633    <date>          c2900XL-diag-mz-112.8-SA
4    drwx    3776    <date>          html
64   -rwx    1358    <date>          config.text
65   -rwx     177    <date>          env_vars
404480 bytes available (1323520 bytes used)
switch: rename flash:config.text flash:config.old
```

Having renamed the configuration file, a switch reboot will cause the switch to start with a blank configuration, accomplished as follows:

```
switch: boot
Loading "flash:c2900XL-h-mz-112_8-
3"...########################################
```

Once the boot has completed, answer *no* to entering setup or the configuration dialog, as follows:

```
Continue with configuration dialog? [yes/no]: n
C2900XL INIT: Complete
%SYS-5-RESTART: System restarted –

Press RETURN to get started.
```

At this stage the switch has a blank configuration, so we can enter enable mode without a password, then copy the old configuration file into the running memory without leaving enable mode, as follows:

```
Switch>en
Switch#copy flash:config.old system:running-config
```

```
Source filename [config.old]?
Destination filename [running-config]?
1358 bytes copied in 3.497 secs (452 bytes/sec)
```

From here we can enter configuration mode and supply a new enable password:

```
Switch#conf t
Enter configuration commands, one per line. End with CNTL/Z.
Switch(config)#enable password manhattan
Switch(config)#end
```

The final job is to save the configuration to memory with the new enable password, so that password takes effect the next time the switch is rebooted, which is accomplished with the following command:

```
Switch#wri mem
```

Workgroup Voice over IP

In earlier chapters we have discussed ATM as a technology to integrate voice and data traffic on the same physical network cables. It is, however, not essential to go whole hog and replace your existing networks with ATM to reap the benefits of voice and data integration. With Cisco devices, like the MC3810, there are options to incorporate voice traffic on existing Frame Relay or HDLC encapsulated links. These devices transport voice traffic over existing IP network connections by combining voice and data traffic on the same physical cables. As we mentioned in the analysis of ATM as a means of transporting voice traffic, one of the enablers for ATM to effectively transport voice traffic over a packetized network is the small size of the cell. It is, in fact, the same with many voice over IP implementations—the voice traffic is carried within small frames, which helps reduce variable delays in packet delivery.

It should be noted that the MC3810 is not strictly a switch, even though it will support bridging functions; it is really a router with voice capability. However, the 3810 does not route the voice traffic that is switched over a WAN link from a voice module on one 3810 to a voice module on the directly connected 3810. Voice data is encapsulated within the frame format of the WAN protocol and sent directly from one 3810 to another.

In this section we'll look at the MC3810 (the *MC* stands for Multiservice Concentrator) hardware, modules, configuration, and deployment in various applications.

MC3810 Connectors

The first point to cover is that the 3810 has a very slim base configuration. The chassis only comes with one Ethernet port, two serial ports, and the usual console port for terminal access and aux port for remote access via modem. This means you have to order the specific modules for voice connectivity that match your requirements. These voice modules support connections to either analog or digital voice services. This concept requires further explanation before we continue.

Even though the vast majority of the voice networks deployed by telephone companies today use digital transmission, still what is termed "the last mile" from the telco central office to the customer premises equipment is often using old-style analog communications for voice transmission. (This and what follows is a gross oversimplification, but it serves its purpose at this stage.) Analog transmission uses the shape of the electromagnetic wave to infer information about the contents of its transmission. Analog is therefore quite susceptible to interference; if anything interferes with the shape of the waves being transmitted, the information that wave is carrying is altered (as perceived by the device receiving the wave).

By contrast, digital communications systems encode the information to be transmitted in to binary 1's and 0's and is less prone to interference; the receiving device only has to determine if the incoming signal represents a 1 or 0. However, if you look at analog and digital communications on an oscilloscope, they look remarkably similar. The difference is not in what goes down the wire; it is in how the sending station encodes the information and how the receiving station decodes it. In many technical books, digital waveforms are represented as square waves. This is not accurate. Things like the natural capacitance and impedance of data cables round off the edges of a square wave, so that a transmitted digital wave looks like a well-rounded analog waveform on the oscilloscope.

The 3810 supports both analog and digital voice connections and either can be used on any of several connector types. Although, justifiably, there is often confusion regarding what is an RJ-11, an RJ-45 cable, and an RJ-48 connector, the basics are quite simple, and we will look at each case next before continuing with examining the 3810 hardware. Internal wiring schemes these days are mostly based around unshielded twisted pair (UTP) cabling plant, which is suitable to carry analog or digital traffic. The cable terminators of choice tend to be RJ-45; however, RJ-11 and RJ-48c connectors are still used in specific instances.

Figure 4-18 RJ-11 connector pinouts for use with FXS and FX0 ports in analog communication.

RJ-11 pins	Signal
3	Ring
4	Tip

The RJ-11 connector is visibly the smallest of these three types of connector and is based around a two-wire connection, as shown in Figure 4-18. The RJ-11 cable is used when connecting 3810 FXS voice module ports to analog phones or fax machines, or connecting voice module FXO ports to a telco analog phone line or PBX analog port. This may be a little confusing, as the FXS and FXO modules are supplied with RJ-45 sockets; however, the RJ-11 connector fits in these sockets quite happily and there is an adapter available should you desire.

The simple way to look at it is that FXS ports go to the user equipment (phone, fax, etc.) and the FXO ports go to the line equipment. *FXS* stands for Foreign eXchange Station, and *FXO* stands for Foreign eXchange Office. E&M ports on the voice module require an eight-conductor straight-through cable with RJ-1CX connectors. The E&M ports are used to connect the 3810 to an analog PBX. These connections are typically used when you define a tie line on the PBX and are using a pair of 3810 concentrators to emulate a leased-line connection between two PBXs. E&M is a signaling standard and can be of type 1 through 5. In the United States, the standard is for type 1 (the 3810 default); however, that does change internationally. In the United Kingdom for example, E&M signaling is known as DC-5 and equates to E&M type 5 signaling.

Digital voice connections are supported by a separate interface, the Digital Voice Module (DVM), which uses a straight-through eight-connector RJ-48 cable that can be inserted in place of the analog voice module. A 3810 cannot support both at the same time; there is only one physical slot available for these modules. The DVM can support different types of channel associated signaling methods to communicate with either a PBX or voice channel bank. The only point of concern is that the method configured matches between the concentrator and the PBX/channel bank. The DVM can multiplex up to 24 voice channels over the one physical connector. Cable pinouts for the RJ-48 cable are given in Figure 4-19.

There is also the option to connect the 3810 to a T-1/E-1 trunk via an RJ-48 connector and RJ-45 straight-through cable, which is supplied via

Figure 4-19 Connectors in an RJ-48 straight-through cable.

RJ-48 pins	Signal
1	Receive
2	Receive
3	Transmit
4	Transmit

the Multiflex Trunk module (MFT). This is not a connector that is used to connect directly to voice equipment (such as PBX, channel bank, etc.); it is a built-in CSU/DSU that can be used as an alternative to the serial interfaces for connecting the 3810 to the leased lines that form part of your WAN.

Typical MC3810 Applications

Having reviewed the connector types available on the 3810, let's take an overview of some typical applications before we delve into the specifics of how the device should be configured. Figure 4-20 shows how a 3810 could

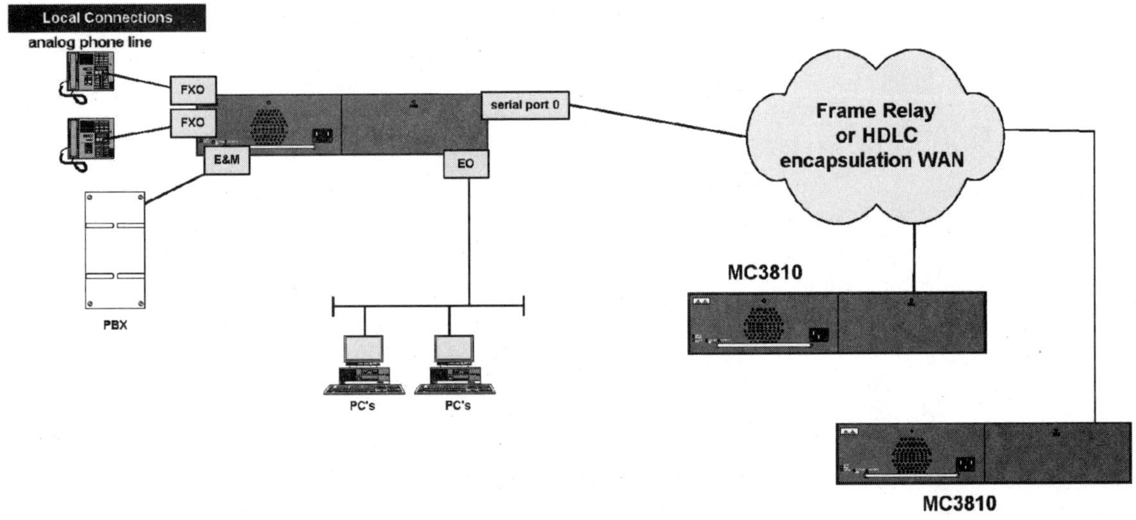

Figure 4-20 MC3810 using analog voice and serial port modules.

be connected using the analog voice modules and serial ports to transport voice traffic over WAN connections. Figure 4-21 shows the digital voice module being used for voice connections and the T-1/E-1 trunk module being used for the WAN. These are for illustration only. The analog voice modules could be used in conjunction with the T-1/E-1 trunk module just as well as the digital voice module could be used with the serial ports to connect to the WAN.

The key issue here is that the 3810-to-3810 communication needs to be via either the serial ports or the T-1/E-1 trunk module for voice traffic; the Ethernet interface does not support the transmission of voice traffic. The 3810 can route between all its data interfaces and use IEEE 802.1d bridging for data traffic; however, voice traffic is addressed and switched using peer information rather than destination IP addresses and, therefore, cannot be routed through interfaces. We'll cover voice peers in the next section.

For the WAN links shown in the above figures, the 3810 uses AAL5 when communicating over ATM networks. As such, the 3810 is making use of ATM's circuit emulation service. In Frame Relay environments, the 3810 uses a DLCI to identify each remote 3810 it will communicate with, thereby enabling you to contact multiple remote 3810s, forming what can be quite complex voice networks.

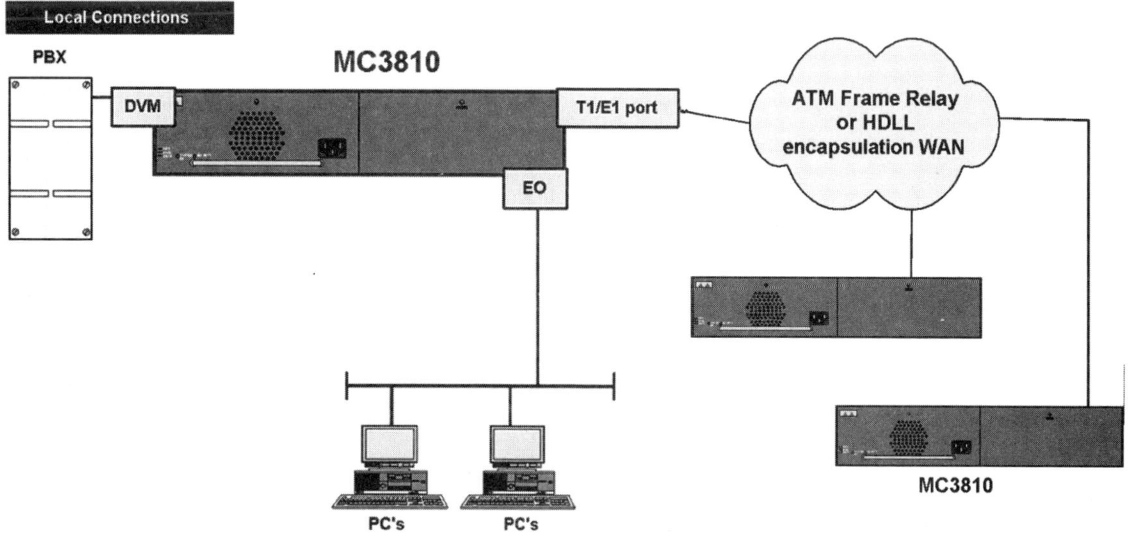

Figure 4-21 MC3810 using digital voice and T-1/E-1 port modules.

Using the HDLC encapsulation restricts the 3810 to supporting point-to-point voice communication, rather than having a 3810 able to address multiple remote devices. For planning purposes, you should allocate 8 Kbit/sec for each voice channel you plan to transmit over the WAN.

Voice Dial Peer Concepts

The basic function of the `dial-peer` commands is to configure the phone number for 3810 voice ports and determine which interface to use for contacting another 3810. The first variant of the `dial-peer` command is `dial-peer voice 1 vohdlc`, which will have two or more subcommands associated with it. The `1` in this command is a tag and can have a value of between 1 and 2147483647. It does not matter what tag value you apply. It merely serves to differentiate one dial-peer entry from another. You can reuse these tag numbers on different 3810s within your network, but each `dial-peer voice` entry should have its own unique tag within the same concentrator.

To understand this command, it is necessary to know the `destination-pattern` and `session-target` commands. Put simply, the session target is used to identify which interface the voice connection will be sent out. The destination pattern is used to match an incoming call destination with a specific session target. It's best to look at a specific example. A sample configuration to call a remote port on another 3810 might be as follows:

```
Dial-peer voice 100 vohdlc
      Destination-pattern 1234
      Session target serial 1
```

Here, the arbitrary tag of 100 was used. The destination pattern of 1234 defines the number that is being called, with the session target defining that local voice traffic will travel over the WAN via the serial 1 link. Say, for instance, an attached phone is taken off the hook and 1234 is dialed; the 3810 will match that destination with the entry here and place the call over serial 1. If any other combination of numbers are dialed on the handset, no action is taken by the 3810. This, of course, is of limited functionality.

A more useful configuration would be if we were able to define a dial-peer that would take a 1 followed by any three following digits as a match, resulting in a dialed connection. This would be achieved as follows:

```
Dial-peer voice 101 vohdlc
     Destination-pattern 1...
     Session target serial 1
```

The period acts as a wildcard. The benefit here is that with one `dial-peer` command, we have defined an action the 3810 will take if it receives a call destined for a four-digit extension number starting with a 1. In a configuration of a 3810, you can see as many of these dial-peer entries as is suitable, so that all the desired dialing strings entered on the handset are matched and acted upon.

The concept is that the dial-peer entries tell the 3810 what to do with an incoming call, if its destination matches one of the dial-peer patterns. There are additional voice port configurations that identify how the individual voice ports should be configured to interact appropriately with the attached equipment. We will examine those when we generate a complete configuration for a sample application.

As with most router and switch configurations, generating the config is much easier if you have a written plan for what you want to achieve. This can be termed the *dial plan.* The dial plan lists for each 3810, the dial-peer tag used, any extension number that should be associated with that peer, the voice port in use, the destination pattern, and the appropriate session target.

The next option in the `dial-peer` command set to look at is the `dial-peer voice pots` command, which is quite different from the previous HDLC command. A typical configuration using this command is as follows:

```
Dial-peer voice 200 pots
     Destination-pattern 1010
     Port 1/1
```

This configuration string uses the same syntax but has quite a different meaning than the `dial-peer voice 1 vohdlc` command we looked at previously. What this configuration does is identify the extension number of the phone connected to voice port 1/1. Previously, the `dial-peer voice 100 vohdlc` command was used in conjunction with the `session target` command to identify an interface to send the voice traffic out over when an incoming call reached the 3810 that matched the destination pattern string. The `pots` keyword however, is used to associate extension numbers with the voice ports they are connected to.

The other two variants of the `dial-peer voice` command are for Frame Relay and ATM WAN communications, respectively, and are quite similar to the command when used for HDLC encapsulation. An example of the Frame Relay command is as follows:

```
Dial-peer voice 200 vofr
      Destination-pattern 8...
      Session target serial 0 120
```

This configuration tells the 3810 that if the number 8 followed by any three digits is incoming to the concentrator, a call is to be set up through serial 0 using DLCI 120.

The ATM configuration is quite similar:

```
Dial-peer voice 320
      Destination-pattern 7...
      Session target serial 2 30
```

There are a couple of differences here, however. This command tells the 3810 that if there is an incoming call being made to the number 7, followed by any three digits, it should be switched out serial 2 (the T-1/E-1 interface) using ATM VCD 30. ATM can only be used on the serial 2 interface, not the serial 0 or 1.

A Sample MC3810 Application of Dial-Peers

Having covered the basics, it is simpler to get a full understanding of dial-peer arrangements when they are examined in the context of a real-world example. The most common first application for a 3810 is to transport voice connections from a remote branch to the head office over an existing leased line. The leased line is probably there, justified on the basis of the remote branch accessing centrally managed databases, exchanging e-mail, and possibly making use of the head office Internet connection. The benefit of using the MC3810 to connect the remote branch is that voice communications can also make use of the leased-line connection, thus reducing call charges.

In this configuration, IP data traffic is routed in the normal way between the WAN and LAN interfaces, and dial-peers are set up to switch traffic from the voice ports on the 3810 at the remote branch to the voice ports on the 3810 at the head office. If the central office had been using channelized T-1/E-1 connections with separately groomed-out DS0 channels to the remote branches, some network reconfiguration will be necessary. If your network is configured like this, the head office router that is connecting to branch offices via groomed-out DS0 connections needs voice ports that the incoming voice encapsulated traffic can be switched to.

Generally, if two 3810s are to be used to transport voice and data traffic, you always have to configure the WAN link to be directly between two 3810 concentrators. This is because the voice traffic is not transported within IP datagrams and therefore not routable; it is encapsulated directly within the frame type appropriate for the WAN link and transported between the voice ports on the 3810.

The real-world scenario we will examine here is a 3810 that is configured to connect a remote handset to a PBX over an HDLC encapsulated leased line connected to serial 1. In addition, the remote 3810 will have one analog phone line connected, so that the remote branch can call outside the organization. The analog handset at the remote branch can be dialed by all head office extension users via a tie line configuration. The physical connections are shown in Figure 4-22A and the dial plan is illustrated in Figure 4-22B.

What we want to achieve is a configuration that will perform the following:

- Identify the branch office handset as an extension of the head office PBX to other PBX users, accessible by dialing a tie line code. The traffic for these calls will traverse the 3810 serial port-to-serial port link.
- Identify the branch handset as the device to receive any incoming calls from the analog phone line attached to the branch office 3810.
- Enable the branch phone to use the analog line attached to the 3810 if the number 9 is dialed first.
- Enable the handset to use the WAN link to call any PBX extension at the head office.

What we will have to do is configure the dial-peer arrangements, along with the voice ports used on both 3810 concentrators. Let's take this one facility at a time for each 3810. The first peer sctup will be to tell the head office 3810 to send any voice connections destined for an extension starting with the number 4 to the branch 3810 over the serial 1 connection using HDLC encapsulation. The remote office 3810 also has to be told that if it gets a call for extension 4789, it is to be routed to the handset on voice port 1/1. This presupposes that we have some order to our extension numbering scheme. For illustration purposes, we will have the head office PBX use extensions starting with the number 3 and the remote office have an extension starting with the number 4. This makes the dial-peer configurations simpler.

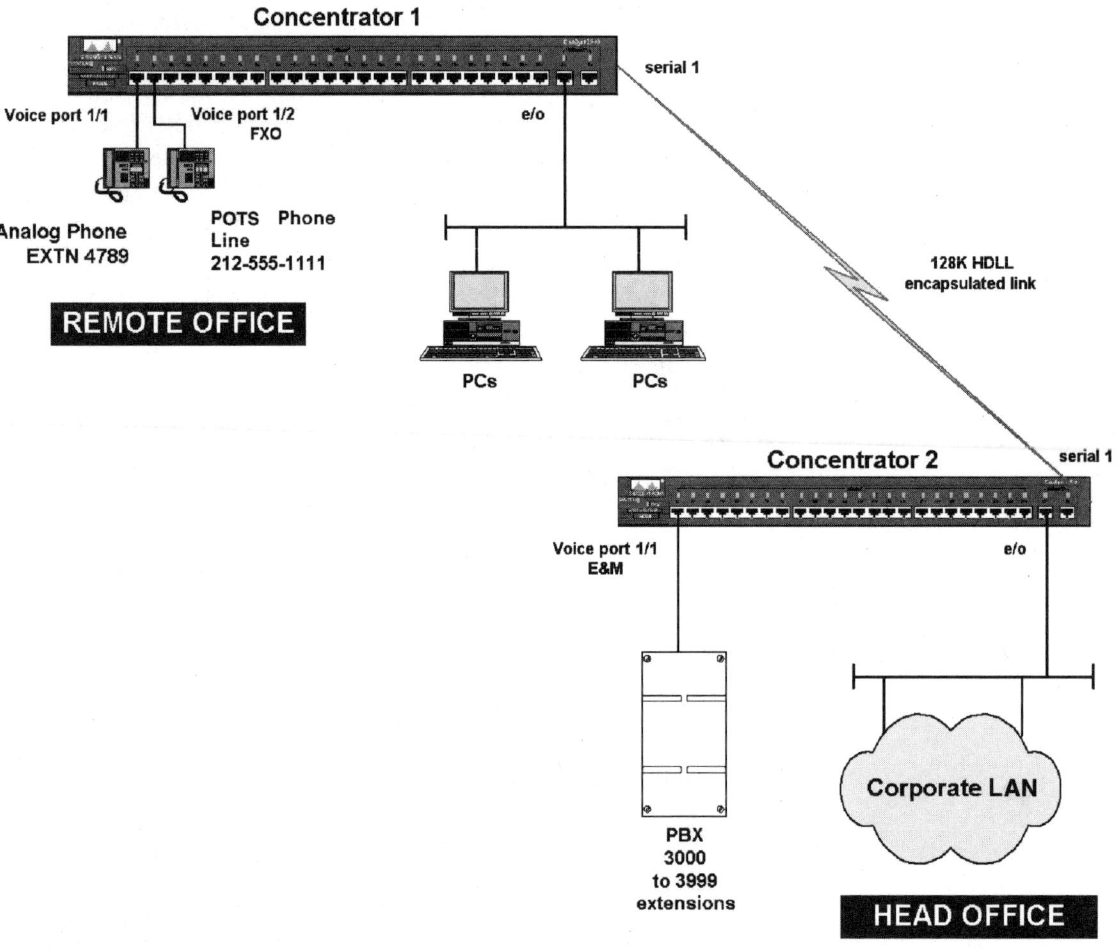

Figure 4-22A *Single connectivity to illustrate* `dial-peer` *commands.*

So, the first facility requires a dial-peer configuration to be set on both 3810 concentrators, as follows:

Concentrator 2

```
dial-peer voice 200 vohdlc
     Destination-pattern 4...
     Session target serial 1
```

Concentrator 1

Figure 4-22B
The dial plan.

Dial Peer	Phone Number	Destination Pattern	Type	Port	Session-Target
Concentrator 1 100 300 500 700		4789 3... 9 4970	POTS VOHDLC POTS POTS	1/1 1/2 1/2	serial 1
Concentrator 2 200 400		4... 3	VOHDLC	1/1	serial 1

```
Dial-peer voice 100 pots
      Destination-pattern 4789
      Port 1/1
```

This requires a tie line to be set up within the head office PBX. Typically, the PBX will assign a tie line number, say, 65, and when PBX extension users key the code for this tie line, they will be presented with a dial tone that is generated by the 3810. At this point they dial 4789, which the head office 3810 switches out the serial 1 interface. When the remote branch 3810 receives the call destined for 4789, it will send the call on to the extension on voice port 1/1.

The following is the output of a `debug` command (`debug voice eecm`) that shows how a 3810 can report the information it receives from a PBX operating in this mode:

```
1/1: EECM(out), ST_NULL      EV_ALLOC_DSP
1/1: EECM(in), ST_DIGIT_COLLECT EV_PARSE_DIGIT  4
1/1: EECM(in), ST_DIGIT_COLLECT EV_PARSE_DIGIT  7
1/1: EECM(in), ST_DIGIT_COLLECT EV_PARSE_DIGIT  8
1/1: EECM(in), ST_DIGIT_COLLECT EV_PARSE_DIGIT  9
```

This does, of course, require the voice port 1/1 on concentrator 2 to be appropriately set up, and for a Northern Telecom PBX, this could be as follows:

```
voice-port 1/1
 connection Tie-line 4789
 operation 4-wire
```

The string that follows the `tie-line` command is quite important; the command cannot be completed without a valid phone number being entered. In this case we have chosen the number of the remote extension. All we had to do to configure the voice port 1/1 to receive information from the PBX was to put the port in four-wire mode and configure it for tie line operation. The `connection tie-line` command is used in conjunction with the dial-peer configuration for the phone number 4789, to decide where to route the call once it has been received on this port.

Therefore, to configure the 3810s to make a connection based on someone at the head office PBX dialing the tie line followed by 4789, we need three configuration pieces. In the head office 3810, there needs to be a dial-peer to set up calls over the serial 1 interface if the destination is 4, followed by any three digits, and the voice port connecting to the PBX for that tie line needs to be told the destination phone number to route calls from the PBX connection on to. At the remote end, the 3810 needs to be told which voice port to route calls for 4789 to.

The next configuration to look at is getting the analog phone on voice port 1/1 of concentrator 1 to be able to dial the head office PBX extensions via the WAN link. Again this requires a dial-peer configuration on both concentrators. On concentrator 1 we want to set up a dial-peer to tell the 3810 to send any calls destined for the number 3, followed by any four digits out of the serial 1 interface. Once that call reaches concentrator 2, we need a dial-peer set up there to pass the four-digit extension number to voice port 1/1. This can be achieved as follows:

Concentrator 1

```
Dial-peer voice 300 vohdlc
      Destination-pattern 3....
      Session target serial 1
```

Concentrator 2

```
Dial-peer voice 400 pots
      Destination-pattern 3
      Port 1/1
```

This highlights the difference in the way that destination patterns are played out through their target interfaces for dial-peer types `pots` and `vohdlc`. Supposing the user of the phone on concentrator 1 wants to ring extension 3067 on the head office PBX. He will have to dial 33067. As this pattern matches the destination pattern in dial-peer voice 300, all five digits will be sent out of serial 1. When those five digits reach concentrator 2, 33067, that string again matches the destination pattern for dial-peer voice 400. Here is where the difference occurs, with a `pots` peer, the first 3 is used for matching and, hence, making the direction to port 1/1, then the remaining four digits are played out to the PBX. Previously, we used 4789 as the complete matching string to place a call to the analog phone on concentrator 1.

This difference in behavior is beneficial when you want to enable the phone on concentrator 1 to dial 9 and get connected to the analog phone line, so that it can make calls outside the organization. This can be accomplished with the following configuration:

Concentrator 1

```
Dial-peer voice 500 pots
      Destination-target 9
      Port 1/2
```

In this instance, having the handset dial a 9 initiates a connection to the analog phone line on port 1/2. When that connection is made, a dial tone is sent back to the 3810, at which point the rest of the digits are played out port 1/2. The configuration above will allow the handset user to dial 95324434 and get connected to the local phone number 5324434.

Now it may be desirable to enable the head office PBX extension users to make use of this remote phone line. The way to do that is to identify that phone line as another extension starting with 4, let's say 4970. Dial-peer 200 on concentrator 2 already directs calls made on the tie line from the PBX down serial 1 towards concentrator 1, so no new peer configuration is necessary there. What we have to do is tell concentrator 1 that if it gets a call destined for 4970, it is to be directed to port 1/2. We can achieve this with the following configuration:

```
Dial-peer voice 700 pots
      Destination-target 4970
      Port 1/2
```

The result here is that users of the PBX will dial the code for the tie line, followed by 4970. The 4970 will be passed over the HDLC link to concentrator 1, which will match 4970, initiating a connection to port 1/2. Once that connection is made, no digits are passed to the phone line until the PBX extension user inputs a phone number to dial out this phone line. The dialing sequence for the PBX user would be something like *65 (if that is the code for the tie line), followed by 4970, which returns a dial tone, followed by the phone number to dial.

The last configuration is to identify the branch handset as the device to receive any incoming calls from the analog phone line attached to the branch office (concentrator 1). If, for example, the analog phone line attached to concentrator 1 has been assigned a phone number of 555-1111 by the local telephone company, the user in that remote branch could give that phone number out on business cards. With the following configuration, when a call comes in on 555-1111, it will cause the analog handset on concentrator 1 to ring:

Concentrator 1

```
Voice-port 1/2
       connection plar 4789
```

This command uses the Private Line Auto Ringdown feature (PLAR). With this command, when a call comes in on voice port 1/2, it is directed toward extension 4789, as there is a dial-peer configuration directing 4789 to voice-port 1/1 (dial-peer voice 100), the handset on that port rings.

The concentrator we have been issuing these commands on was shipped by Cisco with IOS 11.3 (1) MA3, which, if upgraded to 11.3(1)MA5, will support some additional features for this command. Note that the 2916XL used IOS revisions that were identified as all on 11.2(8), but had a different SA number following the IOS revision. It is the same with MC3810s. All the software for them is 11.3(1); it is the MA number that follows that is important. The enhancements for the `plar` command have to do with how an incoming call is handled if the extension is busy. With early IOS releases, the call was just not completed, with MA4 and above, a busy signal was generated. It is conceivable with later releases, features like call waiting could be available for this condition.

After all these configurations have been made, the `show dial-peer voice summary` command shows the voice equivalent of a routing table. It tells you in tabular form, for each destination pattern, the interface the voice communication will be switched out of. To equate this to an IP routing table, the destination pattern can be thought of as the destination network number, and the session target (or port, whichever is appropriate for that dial-peer) equates to the interface to switch packets out of, in order to reach the next hop on the path to the destination. The following is the summary for concentrator 1 in Figure 4-22A:

```
RTR-NY#sho dial-peer voice sum
TAG TYPE   ADMIN  OPER  PREFIX DEST-PATTERN  PREF SESS-TARGET PORT
100 pots    up     up               4789        0               1/1
300 vohdlc up      up               3...        0    Serial0      1
500 pots    up     up               9           0               1/2
700 pots    up     up               4970        0               1/2
```

PBX-to-MC3810 Communications

In the previous example, we discussed why it was necessary to dial five digits from a 3810 to ring a four-digit extension on a PBX that is connected to the other side of a remote 3810. That is somewhat inconvenient and does not make much sense from a user's point of view. Although discussing that example was useful from the point of view of understanding pattern matching and the difference between how the `pots` and `vohdlc` (and `voatm` and `vofr`, for that matter) dial-peers pass digits on to interfaces, we should look at how to make operation more intuitive.

If we take the configuration in Figure 4-22A, our goal will be to enable a PBX attached phone on concentrator 2 to dial a four-digit extension to reach a phone on concentrator 1 instead of a five-digit one. This can be accomplished in one of two ways. The configuration for concentrator 1 does not change; it is at concentrator 2 where we can introduce some more commands.

The first option is to use the `forward-digits all` command that was first available on IOS release MA4. When applied to a dial-peer configuration like that below, the 3810 sends all four digits out voice port 1/1, not just the last three as before (to send just the excess digits is the default).

Concentrator 2

```
Dial-peer voice 1000 pots
       Destination-pattern 3...
       Forward-digits all
       Port 1/1
```

So, in this solution, concentrator 1 still sends four digits, but concentrator 2 now forwards all those out port 1/1.

An alternate solution is to use the `prefix` command that will add a prefix to every call placed out of the port identified in the dial-peer configuration, as follows:

Concentrator 2

```
Dial-peer voice 2000 pots
       Destination-pattern 3
       Prefix 3
       Port 1/1
```

Operation of the 3810 is similar to the case discussed in the previous section in that we are relying on excess digit playout to send all the digits that follow the 3 to be sent out to the PBX. The difference here is that the concentrator prefixes a 3 to all calls placed out voice port 1/1. Note that in the configuration with the `forward-digits all` command the `destination-pattern` was a `3` followed by three periods. This makes the 3810 wait for four digits before it will place a call. If the `forward-digits all` command were not there, no digits would be passed to the PBX. As with the `pots peer` command, the 3810 waits for a pattern match to place the call.

The `prefix` command also has one other use. There can be some PBXs that require a slight pause in what the 3810 is sending them, and a slight pause can be introduced by using the `prefix` command followed by a blank in the 3810 configuration.

When connecting a 3810 to a PBX, another configuration to consider is that of hunt groups. So far we have configured individual dial-peer destination patterns with a single port or session target. The question arises of what happens if that single port is busy when another call comes in. A typical configuration may be that at the central location, a 3810 has four E&M ports connected to the PBX. What we want is for incoming calls to be able to use any of those available lines, rather than be restricted to just one port. So, we configure the same destination pattern multiple times for different ports and assign a preference level to each port. A dial-peer configuration for the first two E&M ports is as follows:

```
dial-peer voice 10 pots
 destination pattern 8...
 port 1/1
 preference 0
dial-peer voice 20 pots
 destination pattern 8...
 port 1/2
 preference 1
```

This configuration will, for incoming calls, match the number 8, then pass on the following three digits, initially to voice port 1/1. If a second call comes in while the first is still established, the preference settings will direct that call to port 1/2. Clearly, the lower the preference, the more likely the port is to receive a call. Of course, if the 8 is part of the extension, we could use the `forward digit all` or `prefix` commands to pass the 8 as well.

So far we have considered two types of matching as regards the destination pattern. The first we use mainly in the `vofr`, `vohdlc`, and `voatm` dial-peers, whereby we specify the number of characters that will be matched and passed on to the session target destination. The second use is in the `pots` dial-peer, where we rely on excess digit playout to forward all digits after the matching destination pattern to the session target destination. This method does allow us to accommodate variable-length dial plans, albeit in a simple fashion.

There is another option for supporting variable-length dial plans, which is to use the `T` character in the destination pattern. The advantage in accommodating variable-length dial patterns with this option is that digits are played out evenly to the PBX. With the excess digit playout option, the rate at which digits are forwarded to the PBX is determined by the rate at which they are dialed in. Variable-length dial plans are particularly useful in inter 3810 connections across national boundaries. The way this `T` character is used is as follows:

```
dial peer voice 15 pots
destination-pattern 8T
port 1/1
```

In this example, the 3810 will see the 8 as a trigger to place a call out of port 1/1. It will wait for the interdigit timeout to expire before forwarding however many digits were dialed in after the 8 out of port 1/1. The interdigit timeout is set to 10 seconds by default. A maximum of 31 digits will be collected as long as no more than 10 seconds elapse between the input of each digit. Of course, this does extend the amount of time it takes to place a call, as the 3810 will wait 10 seconds after the final digit before placing a call. There are two options for speeding this up. You can either have the users dial the # character after the number has been dialed in, which tells the 3810 to dial immediately, or you can reduce the interdigit timeout by the `timeout inter-digit` voice port command.

We will look at specific configuration commands for voice ports in more depth, such as setting signal types, compression, and dial types, when we look at voice port configuration next.

Voice Port Configurations

In this subsection we'll look at the configuration options for both the analog voice ports (type FXO, FXS, and E&M) and the Digital Voice Module (DVM). In general, the default values for FXO and FXS ports are fine; however, we will look at when you may want to customize them and how to do so. The only real difference between configuring the digital port is that the timeslots in use by that interface must be defined. The only generic issue to be aware of is that for either the DVM (which can be used to connect to a local PBX) or the Multiflex Trunk Module (used for connection to a WAN), channel number 16 is not available for use on E-1 lines. This is a restriction that is imposed by the telephone companies; channel 16 is used for signaling.

We'll now look at general voice port configuration options, followed by specific configurations for each type of port.

General Voice Port Configuration Just to keep you on your toes, Cisco will change when the first interface is numbered 0 or 1. For most interfaces, like a serial or Ethernet interface, the numbering starts at 0, whereas with voice ports, the numbering starts at 1. For the MC3810, the first numbered slot is where analog voice ports go, so the first port (leftmost port when viewed from the rear of the chassis) is numbered 1/1 (the convention is *slot/port*).

The most common voice port configuration options are to select the compression mode as defined by the `codec` command, configure any tie line or auto-ringdown facilities, set the operation to two or four wire, and select the E&M signaling type. It is recommended that you use the default codec setting for voice compression, unless you are interfacing with equipment that demands some other specific type. The default is the g729ar8, which requires roughly 8 Kbit/sec per voice channel, which is significantly down from the old g711alaw and g711ulaw that used 64 Kbit/sec for a voice channel. As far as the `connection` command, we have covered the useful options in earlier sections. Essentially, you set the connection to `tie-line` for connecting to a PBX, and `plar` if you want incoming calls on an FXO connected phone line to be routed to a specific phone number.

The most options you are likely to configure for a voice port are with the E&M ports, so we'll consider those settings first. It is not necessary to have a deep, theoretical understanding of what these settings mean; it is enough to know that these options exist and that they must match the settings on the PBX you are connecting the E&M port to. A sample configuration for an E&M port being connected to a PBX is as follows:

```
Voice port 1/1
      Connection tie-line 45
      Operation 4-wire
      Type 1
      Signal wink-start
      Dial-type dtmf
      Cptone northamerica
```

This configuration uses default settings that would not appear in the configuration but are shown here for convenience. The connection command may be omitted. If it is, the voice port will emit a dial tone when it is taken off the hook, until enough digits are connected that match a dial-peer destination, at which point a call is placed.

The operation 4-wire is the most likely option when connecting to a PBX; however, a two-wire option is also available. The type command defines the E&M signal level, which in the United States is the default value of 1; in the United Kingdom, the correct setting is type 5 to match the PBX setting of DC-5. The signal value must match that of the PBX also. The default and most common setting is wink-start, although there are options for immediate and delay-dial. The dial-type is practically always set to DTMF (dual-tone multifrequency); it would be a very old connection indeed that required pulse dialing. The call progress tone, set in the cptone command, sets the tones used for dial tone, busy signal, and so on for the region you are in. The 3810 IOS has options for all major regions in the world.

Provided the settings you choose match those of the PBX to which you are attaching, this completes all the settings you will probably need to make for any E&M port. One point to note is that unlike other interfaces, it is a good idea to shut down, then unshut a voice port when a change in configuration occurs. With Ethernet, serial, and other standard data interfaces, changes in configuration take place immediately, but this is not so for voice ports.

Beyond these configuration commands, there are options that may be useful in certain circumstances. The most common of these are as follows:

```
3810_A(config-voiceport)#timeouts initial
3810_A(config-voiceport)#timeouts interdigit
3810_A(config-voiceport)#timing wink-wait 1000
```

The timeouts initial has a default value of 10 seconds and defines the amount of time the 3810 will give the user to dial the first digit before terminating the call. The timeouts interdigit does the same for subsequently dialed digits and was discussed along with variable-length dial plans earlier. If you suspect there are timing problems with the 3810 communicating to the PBX, you may want to alter the timing wink-wait parameter. This command sets the wink-wait duration for a wink-start signal; the default is 200 milliseconds and can be increased to 5000 milliseconds if you suspect that signal is being missed. If you had to configure your 3810 for immediate or delay-dial, there are timing values that can be set. The simplest way to view the available options is to type in the following:

```
3810_A(config-voiceport)#timing ?
```

This will generate a list of timing commands available to you.

The additional configurations for FXO and FXS ports are used very rarely. For FXO, the `ring number` and `timing guard-out` options can be used to set the number of rings allowed before a connection on the FXO port is terminated by the 3810 and the time that must pass between one call being terminated and another being allowed, respectively. With FXS ports, there are no options that I recommend you change; the only available options refer to the ring frequency and cadence, which merely affects the sound of ring and not the operation of the device.

Configuring the MC3810 for ATM

Having looked at dial-peer arrangements in a simple case using a point-to-point communication with HDLC encapsulation between two 3810 concentrators, we can now look at some other possibilities for inter-3810 connections, starting with ATM. Using a 3810 to transport voice traffic over an ATM backbone will probably be used in a transition mode. If a backbone ATM network is cost-justified, it makes more sense to move to a native ATM environment end to end. However, it is unlikely that a big bang swapout from existing routers/switches and PBXs to ATM switches will happen overnight at many installations. The sensible approach is to deploy the ATM backbone and gradually migrate services to native ATM when appropriate. In such conditions, using a 3810-type device to send voice traffic over ATM is useful.

The first point to note is that a 3810 does not support the SVC capability of ATM; it requires PVCs to be established. Therefore, the configuration of thc 3810 will look similar to that when using Frame Relay, which also only provides PVC capability via DLCI connections. In addition, to support ATM, you must have an appropriate version of IOS for the 3810, which will have an "a" notation. The latest release of ATM-capable IOS is mc3810-a2binr3v2-mz_113-1_MA5a.bin, which is available at www.cisco.com in the software image section.

Loading a new version of IOS on a 3810 is similar to loading new IOS on a 2x00 series router, in that you use the `copy tftp flash` command. This prompts you for the IP address of the TFTP server holding the new IOS and its filename. Once the file has been copied, it is a good idea to use the show flash command, which will show you something like the following:

```
Directory of flash:
2 -rwx 3482320 Mar 01 1993 00:24:17  mc3810-binr3v2-mz_113-1_ma6.bin
3 -rwx    1071 Mar 05 1993 22:58:30  current
4 -rwx    1071 Mar 05 1993 23:00:07  voice-ip1-confg
5 -rwx 4234563 Mar 04 1993 21:54:21  is mc3810-a2binr3v2-mz_113-1_MA5a.bin
8128000 bytes total (4641280 bytes free)
```

This example is showing that we are using 3810 software release MA6 and have just loaded the ATM code as the fifth image in flash. The other two files in flash are the ASCII configuration files. To have the new IOS take effect, we need to either rename the MA6 file with an .old extension or delete it entirely, then issue a reload command.

Thought must also be put into the physical connections that will be made between the 3810 and the ATM network. Assuming a LightStream 1010 is the switch that the 3810 will be connected to, careful selection of the interface module that is to be used for this connection is needed. The 1010 has Port Adapter Modules (PAMs) for various types of SONET, along with T-3/E-3 and T-1/E-1 Channel Emulation Service connections, all of which are not appropriate. The right module to use is the PAM with four T-1/E-1 trunk connectors (this module uses RJ-48 connectors). With this module it is possible to define multiple PVCs that will be seen by the 3810, in much the same way that a 3810 Frame Relay encapsulated interface will see multiple DLCIs presented by an attached Frame Relay network.

The primary tasks are to configure the T-1/E-1 controller and serial interface 2 to support ATM. Dial-peer configurations will not be discussed in detail here or in the section on Frame Relay configuration, as we have already discussed enough detail in the section on HDLC. The dial-peer voice 1 voatm and dial-peer voice 2 vofr commands behave in a similar way to the dial-peer voice 3 vohdlc command discussed earlier in that when the destination pattern is matched, all digits that matched that pattern are sent out over the interface (and PVC) identified in the session target.

As discussed previously, to interface a 3810 to an ATM network, a connection needs to be made to an ATM switch, something like a LightStream 1010 interface. The only supported connection for ATM is the serial 2 interface, which connects to T-1 or E-1 lines. The 3810 sends cells to the LS1010 interface at T-1/E-1 speeds. Let's look at the first stage, which is configuring the controller to run ATM over a T-1/E-1 connection:

```
3810_A#conf t
3810_A(config)#controller T1 0
3810_A(config-controller)#framing ESF
3810_A(config-controller)#linecode b8zs
```

Note that the only real difference when using E-1 services is to set the linecode to `hdb3` and the framing is set to `CRC4`. The *Cisco TCP/IP Routing Professional Reference* covers the similarities and differences between E-1 and T-1 lines in much more detail.

The next configuration to make is for the serial 2 interface. On the serial 2 interface we will set the encapsulation to ATM (telling the concentrator to use ATM AL5 cells for communication on this interface) and setting up the ATM PVCs that will be in use. The key tasks in setting up the PVC to be used are as follows:

- Identify the VCD, VPI, and VCI of the PVC in question.
- Define the AAL5 type to be transported over this PVC. Multiple types can be defined, although voice and data traffic will travel over different PVCs.
- Set the peak, average, and burst size for voice traffic.

Once this has been done, the `show atm pvc` command can be used to verify the configuration. The peak, average, and burst sizes for voice traffic are there so that the PVC can effectively handle the number of calls being made. If we have six voice channels enabled, the peak average and burst values would be calculated as follows:

- The peak value is the peak Kbit/sec the virtual circuit can transmit at; it is calculated as 32 times the number of calls. For six calls, this is 192.
- The average value is the Kbit/sec that the virtual circuit will normally transmit at and is calculated as 16 times the number of calls, giving a value of 96.
- The burst size does not relate to a Kbit/sec rate; it refers to the peak number of cells that can be transmitted over the virtual circuit. It is calculated as four times the number of calls, and for six voice channels, this comes to 24.

A typical configuration for serial 2 would therefore be as follows:

```
3810_A#conf t
3810_A(config)#interface serial 2
3810_A(config-int)#encapsulation atm
3810_A(config-int)#atm pvc 30 2 12 aal5voice 192 96 24
```

Here, the `atm pvc` command defines communication for the Virtual Circuit Descriptor 30 (which behaves in much the same way as a DLCI 30 would). This command further goes on to associate VCD 30 with VPI 2, VCI 12. There is no relationship between the specific value of the VCD command and the VPI/VCI pair it uses; any value can be assigned. As its name suggests, it is a descriptor. The encapsulation used here is the `aal5voice` encapsulation, which is the appropriate one for voice over ATM. There are other options for encapsulation types, as follows:

`aal5snap`—Used for transporting LAN data traffic over ATM

`aal1`—Used for carrying streaming video packets over ATM

`aal5fratm`—Used for the Frame Relay-ATM interworking function (discussed in a later section)

`aal5nlpid`—Used for High-Speed Serial Interfaces (HSSIs) that are using an ATM data service unit (ADSU) and running ATM-Data Exchange Interface (DXI)

`ilmi`—Used for PVCs set up for ILMI communications

There are other options for this command. You can enable `oam`, `inarp`, and `compress` options. The `oam` option enables the interface to send Management F5 loopback cells. It is not essential to enable OAM cell generation. If it is enabled, an OAM cell is periodically generated, which must be responded to by the remote end of the virtual circuit. It is similar in concept to a TCP keep-alive. The `inarp` option requires the `aal5snap` encapsulation and is used to customize the amount of time between inverse ARP requests that are sent down each PVC. In the *Cisco TCP/IP Routing Professional Reference* we covered how Frame Relay inverse ARP was used to discover the protocol addresses available down each DLCI. In ATM communications, this inverse ARP process performs a similar function.

The `compress` option is only available on the MC3810 and will either use hardware compression (we will cover compression more fully in the section on voice ports) if that is available; otherwise, software compression is used. The compression is of the cell contents, rather than of any header.

It must be noted that the syntax for ATM implementation is changing as the releases of MC3810 IOS change. When release 12 is widely deployed, the serial 2 interface will no longer be valid for ATM. A new ATM 0 interface will have to be specified, and the controller set to ATM mode. The other key differences are that the encapsulation type is now `aal5mux voice` for voice communication over a PVC and the peak average and burst rates are now set by the `vbr-rt` PVC configuration command.

Clearly, with IOS release 12 using a different interface ID for ATM communications, there are some differences when establishing dial-peer configurations when compared to IOS 11. With release 12, the `session target` has to identify the ATM 0 interface, along with a PVC name or VPI/VCI pair.

Configuring the MC3810 for Frame Relay

We have covered the basics for establishing a Frame Relay connection using the `vofr` keyword in the dial-peer configuration. The only other necessary configuration is to set Frame Relay encapsulation on the serial interface connecting to the frame network. There are, however, a number of additional configurations that are desirable when sending voice over Frame Relay DLCI connections. The *Cisco TCP/IP Routing Professional Reference* covered configuring Frame Relay interfaces and Frame Relay concepts in adequate detail, and it is assumed the reader has familiarity with that level of detail in configuring Frame Relay connections.

We will now examine assigning map-classes, traffic shaping properties, and setting data segmentation sizes.

Frame Relay Map Classes The `map-class` command comes into its own if you have a network that has many DLCI connections into the one central 3810 and you want to assign the same traffic shaping properties to all of them without configuring each DLCI separately. A network where this would be appropriate is shown in Figure 4-23. Note that for 3810 E, there will be dial-peer configurations identifying a phone number range with each DLCI link. We'll examine a full configuration for this setup a little later.

Before we start the configuration of a Frame Relay map-class, it is worth noting that traffic shaping should only be enabled when sending voice and data traffic over a public Frame Relay network. When using Frame Relay encapsulation on a private network, or 3810s in a back-to-back configuration, it is not necessary to enable traffic shaping. By implication, it is therefore not necessary to configure a map-class. The reason is that traffic shaping parameters prevent the carrier network from discarding frames unnecessarily. The traffic shaping configuration should make your device match the parameters of the public Frame Relay network operation.

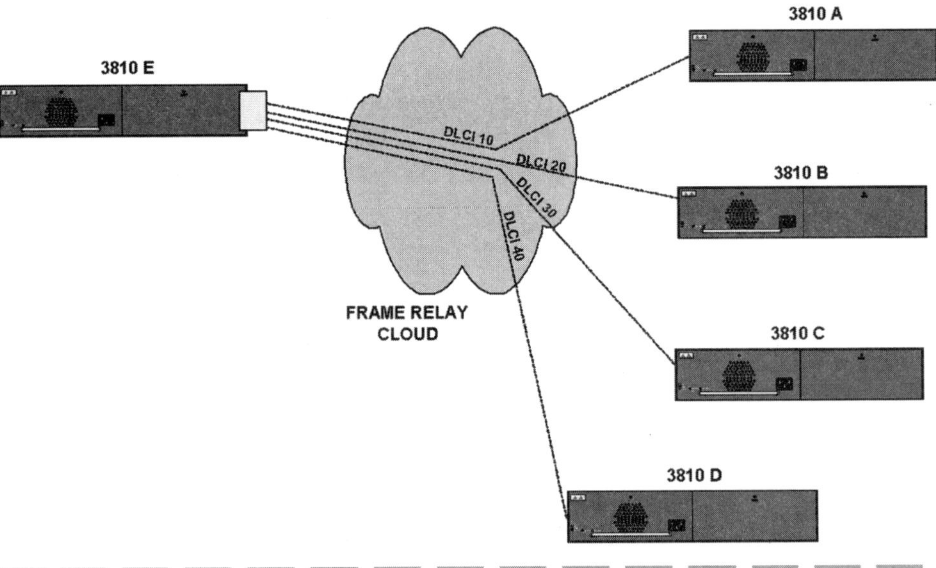

Figure 4-23 Network that has many DLCI connections into one central 3810.

The key information required in the map-class is excess burst size, related to the CIR (discussed more fully in Chapter 2). The goal is to match the burst size and CIR on the 3810 with that contracted by the Frame Relay network provider. Creation of a typical map-class is as follows:

```
3810_A(config)#map-class frame-relay test
3810_A(config-map-class)#frame-relay be in 64000
3810_A(config-map-class)#frame-relay be out 64000
3810_A(config-map-class)#frame-relay adaptive-shaping becn
3810_A(config-map-class)#frame-relay cir 64000
```

These commands create a map-class called `test`, with a CIR and excess burst size both inbound and outbound of 64000, and enable the traffic rate to adapt to Backward Explicit Congestion Notifications (BECN). These settings show up in the configuration under a `map-class frame-relay test` section, as follows:

```
map-class frame-relay test
 frame-relay adaptive-shaping becn
 frame-relay cir 64000
```

Traffic shaping is particularly beneficial when transmitting voice traffic over Frame Relay networks. The goal with transmitting voice traffic is to minimize dropped packets and variable delays in the delivery of packets carrying voice information. Remember, voice traffic is simply encapsulated in Frame Relay format; there is no TCP-style rerequest and error recovery or sequencing of packets. This concern with traffic shaping ensures that the carrier can properly support the traffic you are sending. Without traffic shaping, the carrier will more likely discard frames, or queue them up to even out the flow of traffic, both of which are particularly detrimental to good voice transmission.

Having configured the map-class, we move on to configuring the interface used to connect to the frame network. The example here uses the serial 0 interface. The serial 2 interface to a T-1 or E-1 could equally well be used; the only extra configuration needed is to assign a channel group number to the timeslots used for this DLCI.

```
3810_A(config)#int serial 0
3810_A(config-if)#encapsulation frame-relay
3810_A(config-if)#frame-relay interface-dlci 200 voice-encap 160
3810_A(config-fr-dlci)#class test
```

Here, we configured the serial 0 interface for Frame Relay encapsulation and identified DLCI 200 to use a data segmentation size of 160 bytes (this is based on the interface access rate being 128 Kbits/sec), which also identifies this interface to use FRF.12 data segmentation for voice encapsulation. Additionally, we assigned the traffic shaping properties specified in the test map-class. Note that the class designation has to come after the DLCI identification. The rule of thumb is to give a data segmentation size of 80 bytes for every 64K of the slower PVC rate at each end of the DLCI. For example, if the central 3810 has an access circuit rate of 256 Kbit/sec, you may be tempted to set the data segmentation size to 320 bytes. However, if the remote end has a 64-Kbit/sec access rate, better results will be achieved with an 80-byte data segmentation size.

There are other configuration parameters appropriate when using 3810 concentrators in a back-to-back configuration with Frame Relay encapsulation. But I prefer to keep back-to-back configurations using the Cisco HDLC encapsulation. It is far simpler and there are no real advantages to using the Frame Relay encapsulation in this instance.

Configuration for Multiple Destinations over Frame Relay So far we have shown how to configure a 3810 to communicate over a single DLCI. A more typical configuration for a Frame Relay network was illustrated in Figure 4-23. It is a fairly simple matter to extend the capability of a central 3810 to communicate over multiple DLCI connections. Simple, that is, as long as the dial plan makes sense. As previously stated, it is sensible to associate ranges of extension numbers with a destination. For example, we may wish to direct all extensions starting with 5 to 3810 A in Figure 4-23, all extensions starting with 6 to 3810 B, and so on. If you have more than 10 destinations, you can be more specific, such as all extensions starting with 71 to 3810 C and all extensions starting with 72 to 3810 D.

To enable 3810 E in Figure 4-23 to address these remote locations, simply enter multiple voice over Frame Relay dial-peer configurations:

```
Dial-peer voice 100 vofr
      Destination-pattern 5...
      Session target serial 2 10
Dial-peer voice 200 vofr
      Destination-pattern 6...
      Session target serial 2 20
```

And so on for as many DLCI connections as you wish to configure.

At the remote end, you can simplify the configuration by making use of the voice default route concept. So far we have always specified a destination pattern that starts with a digit. If, however, we have a destination pattern consisting of .... we match any four digits and send those out the interface specified in the `session target` command. This is a similar concept to a 0.0.0.0 destination route in an IP routing table. Both are used in similar circumstances, typically, when a remote branch is being connected into the corporate network by one physical circuit. This means that to get anywhere else on the network, the remote device will have to traverse that one link first. The obvious benefit is that you do not have to add dial-peer configurations for each location you wish to route calls to. In the example shown in Figure 4-23, the default route will be set up on all the remote 3810s to send all calls to the central 3810, which will forward calls on from there.

The MC3810 Interworking Function

As we discussed in Chapter 3, there is a Frame Relay-to-ATM interworking function, which is also supported in the 3810 concentrator. Essentially, what occurs is that Frame Relay traffic is encapsulated within ATM cells. This encapsulation is achieved by use of a virtual interface within the 3810, which takes input from either Frame Relay traffic coming in on a standard serial interface (or data traffic on an Ethernet interface). This virtual interface is then responsible for taking the input and encapsulating the data within ATM cells (à la RFC 1483) and sending those cells out the T-1/E-1 controller. These concepts are illustrated in Figure 4-24.

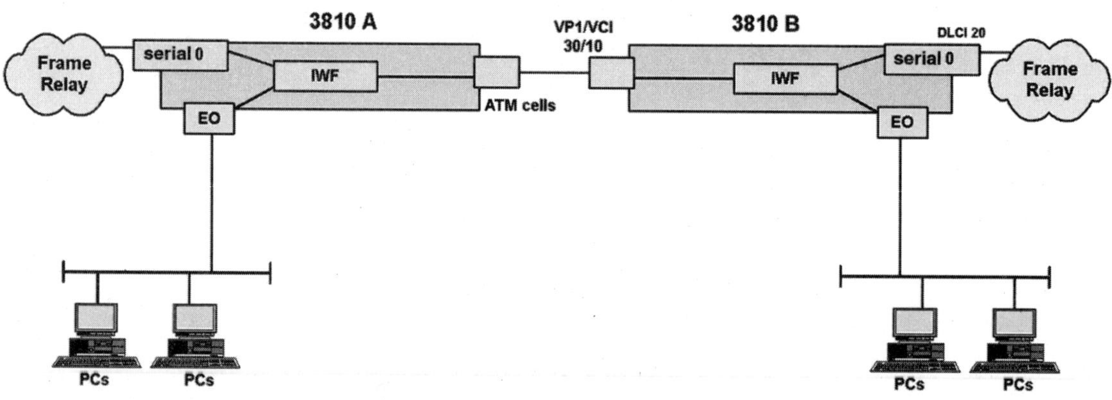

Figure 4-24 3810 A encapsulates Frame Relay and Ethernet packets within ATM cells. 3810 B strips off cell headers to pass Frame Relay and Ethernet traffic out the appropriate interfaces.

The key to configuring the interworking function is to generate the virtual Frame Relay-to-ATM interface. The key tasks to define a configuration of this kind are as follows:

- Create the Frame Relay-to-ATM interworking interface and number it. Valid numbers are between 0 and 20.
- Continue to configure this virtual interface as if it were a regular Frame Relay interface by setting Frame Relay encapsulation. Set the DLCI with data segmentation size and map a Frame Relay DLCI to an ATM VCD.
- Configure serial 2 for ATM and the VCD that will be used for the encapsulated Frame Relay traffic to `aal5fratm`.

These configurations can be input on a release 12 version of IOS by the following commands:

```
3810_A(config)#interface fr-atm 1
3810_A(config-if)#encapsulation frame-relay
3810_A(config-if)#frame-relay interface-dlci 20 voice encap 160
3810_A(config-if)#fr-atm connect dlci 20 atm0 pvc 30/10
```

Here we have configured the 3810 to perform interworking between a Frame Relay DLCI numbered 20 (a data segmentation size of 160 bytes was chosen, implying a DLCI access rate of 128 Kbit/sec) and an ATM PVC on interface ATM0, identified with VPI/VCI 30 and 10, respectively. This completes all that is needed for data interworking. All that is necessary to add voice capability is to define the appropriate dial-peer configurations to direct voice traffic from voice ports over the Frame Relay or ATM connections as desired.

Clock Synchronization Issues

In data networking, clock sources generally are taken for granted. On Ethernet interfaces, the preamble at the beginning of each frame transmitted on the network synchronizes all devices to read the packet contents. In serial interfaces, the attached CSU/DSU supplies the clock source from the telco, setting the clock to whatever the line rate is (64K, 128K, and so on). For voice communications, there are more considerations for clocking. The reason is that for voice to be properly transmitted and decoded, a single clock source must be used end to end due to the real time and continuous nature of voice communication. The per-hop clocking used in data networking can be inadequate and lead to distortion of the voice signal.

The obvious alternative to using a different clock source on each link (the per-hop data networking clock model) is to use a single master clock source that is used by all devices on the network. Telcos have to take these clocking issues very seriously for their voice networks, and as we are building a mini voice network by interconnecting 3810 devices with PBXs, we have the same issues to consider. At its worst, a 3810 can cause an interface to be reported as down due to clock mismatches.

This is illustrated in Figure 4-25, where a 3810 is configured with both a Digital Voice Module and a Multiflex Trunk Module. In this instance, there is a delta between the clock waveforms submitted to the two digital interfaces. For convenience, the delta is illustrated as the difference

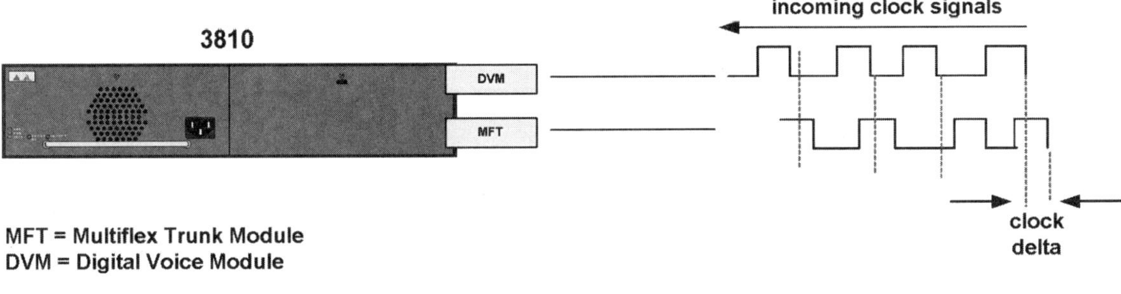

Figure 4-25 Clock source variance.

between the trailing edge of the two clock signals. To maintain synchronization and continuous throughput of voice traffic, the 3810 is forced to try to resolve the difference between these two clock sources. When attempting to do so, the 3810 can take an excessive amount of time to pass data from the frames on one connection to the other, resulting in one or more of the interfaces being reported as down.

So, having made the decision to drive the network from a single master clock, we must decide how to distribute, recover, and have fallback for this signal throughout the voice network. You really have a choice of configuring the 3810 to take its clock from an externally attached device (which is the norm for data networking also) or generating it internally. In the example shown in Figure 4-25, the right thing to do is configure one of the digital interfaces to take its clock from the network (say, the MFT for argument's sake) and configure the other (the DVM) to take its clock from an internal source. This internal source will end up being the MFT clock, which means both interfaces have been configured to use the same clock source. As Figure 4-25 shows, with a difference in the clock source, shown as the clock delta, voice traffic is not transported in synchronization.

It should be noted that in this discussion we are only concerned about configuring a single clock source across interfaces that are carrying digital voice traffic. When taking a clock source from an external device, the clock source can come from a device attached to a T-1/E-1 controller or a device attached to a serial interface. We'll look at each in turn.

Taking a Clock Source from a Device Attached to the T-1/E-1 Controller When we configure a 3810 to take its clock source from a device attached to the T-1/E-1 controller, we are telling the 3810 to take this clock and use it for clocking all the other synchronous interfaces. The mechanics of this involve the use of an internal clock generator that uses a phase locked loop (PLL) circuit. PLLs are special circuits that are guaranteed to produce a steady and reliable clock source. As such, we are not directly configuring all the other interfaces to take their clock from the chosen T-1/E-1 controller. We are actually telling the other interfaces to take their clock from the PLL, which has derived its clock from input to the T-1/E-1 controller.

In this first example we'll take the clock source from the T-1/E-1 controller 0 and use it to drive the PLL, which then feeds all other interfaces. In the example T-1/E-1 controller 0 is the MFT and T-1/E-1 1 is the DVM.

```
3810(config)#controller T1 0
3810(config-controller)#clock source line
```

```
3810(config-controller)#controller T1 1
3810(config-controller)#clock source internal
3810(config)#network-clock base-rate 64
3810(config)#interface serial 0
3810(config-if)#clock rate network 128000
```

So, with this configuration we take the clock from the device attached to the MFT and feed it into the internal PLL. The output of the PLL feeds both the DVM and the serial 0 interface. There are, however, a couple of additional commands that need explaining when we configure the serial interface to take its clock from the external rather than internal source (this would be unnecessary if no voice traffic were being transported over the serial interfaces). The default base rate for the 3810 is still set at 56 Kbit/sec even though the most common channel rate is 64 Kbit/sec. We therefore change the default to 64K. The clock rate command also assumes that the cable connected to the serial interface will configure it as a DCE (the *Cisco TCP/IP Routing Professional Reference* covered the effects of Cisco cables on interface configuration in depth). Once the device is set as a DCE (data circuit-terminating equipment), it will supply a clock at whatever rate is set by the rate command (it must be a multiple of the base rate figure). Of course, the device attached to the serial 0 interface must be configured to receive its clock source from the 3810, implying that device is in DTE (data terminal equipment) mode. The serial interfaces on a 3810 that is using its PLL as the network clock source must be in DCE mode. Remember, DCEs generate clock signals; DTEs take their clock from an attached device.

Taking a Clock Source from Serial 0 It must be noted that if you choose to configure your 3810 to take its clock source from a serial interface, that serial interface must be serial 0, which, of course, must have an attached cable that configures it in DTE mode. Consequently, serial 1 must still be in DCE mode to pass that clock on to other network devices.

There is one additional step when setting the clock source to be driven from serial 0: setting up the clock multiplier. This is necessary because the internal PLL circuit requires a 2048-Kbit/sec clock input. The T-1/E-1 controller has a 2048-Kbit/sec clock to feed the internal PLL, but to use the serial 0 interface as a clock source, the 3810 configuration needs to be told what rate the clock incoming to serial 0 is, so that it can be multiplied up prior to being fed to the internal PLL. We can configure the 3810 to take its clock from the serial 0 interface with the following configuration commands (it is assumed the serial 0 interface is connected to a 128-Kbit/sec line):

```
3810(config)#network-clock base-rate 64
3810(config)#network-clock-select 1 serial 0
3810(config)#interface s 0
3810(config-if)#clock rate line 128000
```

Then we set serial 1 and the T-1/E-1 controller to take their clock from the internal PLL with the `clock source internal` command.

Configuring Clock Source Redundancy So far we have shown how to select a single source of clocking for a 3810 and how to distribute that to other interfaces on the same 3810. Other devices on the network need to be configured to take their clock from this selected source. Of course, this does present a single point of failure, so some form of backup should be implemented.

The `network-clock-select` command allows you to define a list of clock sources that can be assigned a priority order, such that in the event of the clock source with the best priority failing, the next-most-favored clock takes over. As usual, the source with the lowest numeric value assigned to its priority is the one with the highest priority (priority 1 is higher priority than priority 2). The steps in configuring this functionality are as follows:

- In global configuration, define the priority of each clock source on the system.
- Define the amount of time the 3810 will wait after detecting a failure in the clock source before it swaps to the next-highest-priority source.
- Define the time that the 3810 will wait before switching back to the higher-priority clock source after that clock source has come back up.
- Configure the clock sources for all active interfaces, including the one that will be used as the primary clock source.

When we complete this configuration, each T-1/E-1 controller will have a configuration of `clock source line` and the serial 0 interface will have a clock source set by `clock rate line`. The status of these clock sources, however, will be different from the configuration in normal operation. This is necessary, as the configuration commands actually configure each source that may be used in the list of backup clocks as active, and the 3810 temporarily overrides its configuration as part of the process of selecting the available clock source with the highest priority.

The actual setting of the clock sources not being used by the 3810 is that of `loop-timed`. This setting is changed to be active (i.e., reset to `line` to agree with the configuration setting) if the clock source in question is selected as the active clock. So let's configure a simple setting that defines the T-1/E-1 0 controller as the most preferred clock source, backed up by the clock from the serial 0 interface:

```
3810(config)#network-clock-select 1 t1 0
3810(config)#network-clock-select 2 serial 0
3810(config)#network-clock-switch 15 15
3810(config)#controller t1 0
3810(config-controller)#clock source line
3810(config)#interface serial 0
3810(config-if)#clock rate line 128000
```

This configuration sets the clock feeding the T-1 controller 0 to be the preferred clock source, backed up by the clock source feeding the serial 0 interface. The amount of time the 3810 will wait for a clock source to either appear or disappear before a clock source switch is made is 15 seconds (it is assumed the serial 0 interface is connected to a 128-Kbit/sec line). For this configuration, it is assumed that the `network-clock base-rate` command has been appropriately entered, as discussed previously.

Now, suppose this 3810 is connected via the 128-Kbit/sec line to a second 3810. That second 3810 must be configured to have its primary clock driven from this 128K line. This will then set both 3810s to be running from the one clock source. A sample 3810 network that shows how you may wish to identify a primary and backup clock scheme is shown in Figure 4-26.

In this network, if the clock derived from the PBX fails when connected to 3810A, a completely different 3810 (3810 B) takes over as the master clock source for the network. There are, of course, many other variations on this scheme that could have the internal clock on 3810 A take over in the event of the clock from the PBX failing. This, however, would introduce a single source of failure for the whole network in the event that one 3810 goes down.

A Complete MC3810 Configuration

In this section we'll look at complete configurations for two 3810s that provide direct access between two PBXs over an IP connection that acts as a tie line. Planning forms for connectivity and dial-peers prior to implementation should be completed as illustrated in Figure 4-27.

These planning forms mirror the two-stage process you have to follow to get a 3810 operational. The first stage is getting the PBX and the 3810 to communicate, and the second is to configure appropriate dial-peer configurations to have the voice traffic switched to the proper destination.

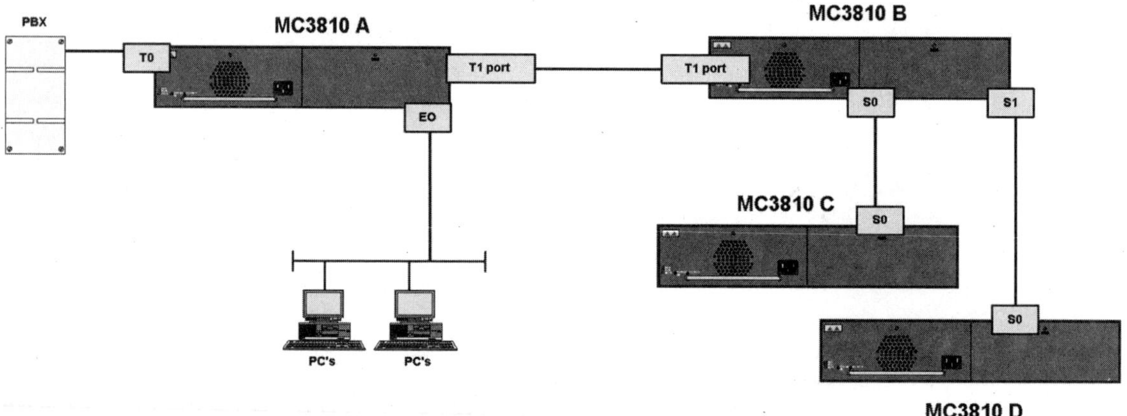

Clock Source Summary

	Primary	Backups
3810A	T0	T1
3810B	T1	system
3810C	S0	S0
3810D	S0	S0

Figure 4-26 Master clock distribution in a 3810 network.

Considering the first stage, the tricky stuff is when you come to connect E&M ports to a PBX. For each E&M port identified by slot/port number, the planning form for E&M ports identifies:

- The E&M type (generally, the default of 1 is used in the United States, and type 5 for DC5 is used in Europe)
- The signal setting (normally, wink-start or immediate)
- The default two-wire or four-wire operation
- Any connection command (setting the port-to-trunk operation for a tie line)

In addition to these configurations, the other critical area in getting a working connection is the cabling. Figure 4-28 shows the wiring between a 3810 E&M port and, as an example, a Toshiba PBX. The important thing is to get a pinout diagram of your PBX port and match that the same way.

The first command to use on the Cisco when establishing communication with a PBX is the `show voice port summary` command, a sample output of which is here:

```
                                                            IN   OUT   ECHO
PORT   SIG-TYPE   ADMIN  OPER IN-STAT OUT-STAT  CODEC   VAD  GAIN ATTN CANCEL
1/1    e&m-imd    up     up   idle       idle   g729ar8  n     0    0     y
1/2    e&m-imd    up     up   idle       idle   g729ar8  n     0    0     y
1/3    e&m-imd    up     up   idle       idle   g729ar8  n     0    0     y
1/4    e&m-imd    up     up   idle       idle   g729ar8  n     0    0     y
```

The interesting part of this display shows you for each port the signal type it is set to, the admin and operational state, plus the in-status, which is the status of incoming calls. Your first goal is to get the 3810 to send a dial tone to the PBX. The way you test this is to dial the tie line number on the PBX that is set up to connect to one of these ports and listen for a dial tone. If you get a busy signal, it is probably an incorrect E&M signal type set (that is, you are using type 1 when it should be type

Figure 4-27 Planning forms for voice port and dial-peer configurations.

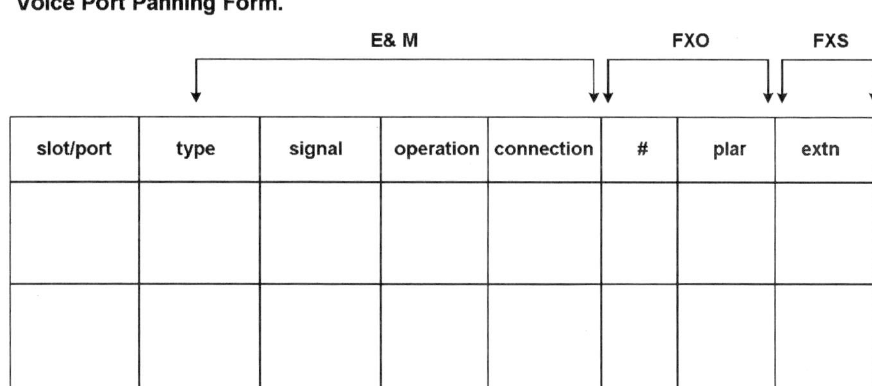

Voice Port Panning Form.

slot/port	type	signal	operation	connection	#	plar	extn

Dial-peer planning form.

tag	type	pattern	target	preference

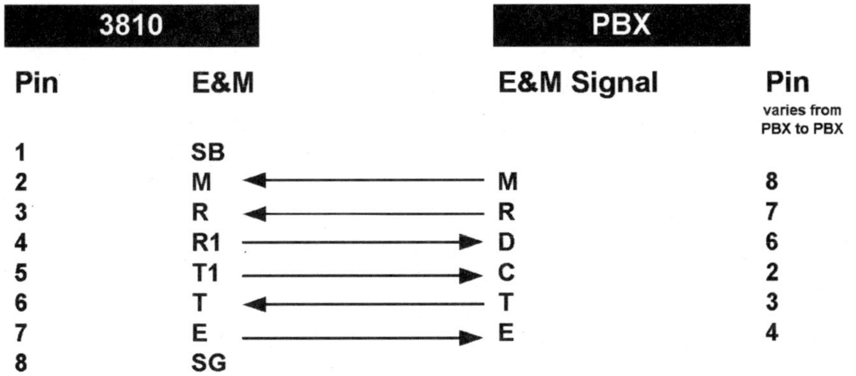

3810		PBX	
Pin	E&M	E&M Signal	Pin (varies from PBX to PBX)
1	SB		
2	M ←	M	8
3	R ←	R	7
4	R1 →	D	6
5	T1 →	C	2
6	T ←	T	3
7	E →	E	4
8	SG		

On the PBX, T&R are used for transmit, C&P are for receive. On the 3810, T1 and R are for transmit, T and R for receive.

Figure 4-28 Full configurations for PBX-to-PBX communication via two 3810 concentrators using four-wire operation.

5, for example). If you get no tone, the cabling is probably incorrect or the signal condition is set to wink-start when it should be immediate.

Unfortunately, the method with the highest success rating in getting past this first hurdle is trial and error, varying each setting one at a time to record its effect. I have been involved in implementing 3810 networks that required the PBX to be set for wink-start, but communication would not start until the 3810 was set to immediate. My best advice here is to go with four-wire operation and just vary the E&M type between 1 and 5, then vary the signal between wink-start and immediate.

Once the compatible settings are made, you will see the following change in the `show voice port summary` command output:

```
                                                              IN    OUT     ECHO
PORT  SIG-TYPE  ADMIN OPER  IN-STAT OUT-STAT  CODEC   VAD   GAIN  ATTN   CANCEL
1/1   e&m-imd   up    up    idle       idle   g729ar8  n      0     0        y
1/2   e&m-imd   up    up    idle       idle   g729ar8  n      0     0        y
1/3   e&m-imd   up    up    idle       idle   g729ar8  n      0     0        y
1/4   e&m-imd   up    up    seized     idle   g729ar8  n      0     0        y
```

Here, as a result of a PBX handset dialing the tie line ID associated with the PBX connection to 3810 voice port 1/4, the PBX has made a successful connection with that voice port, and we see that via the seized command in the in-stat column.

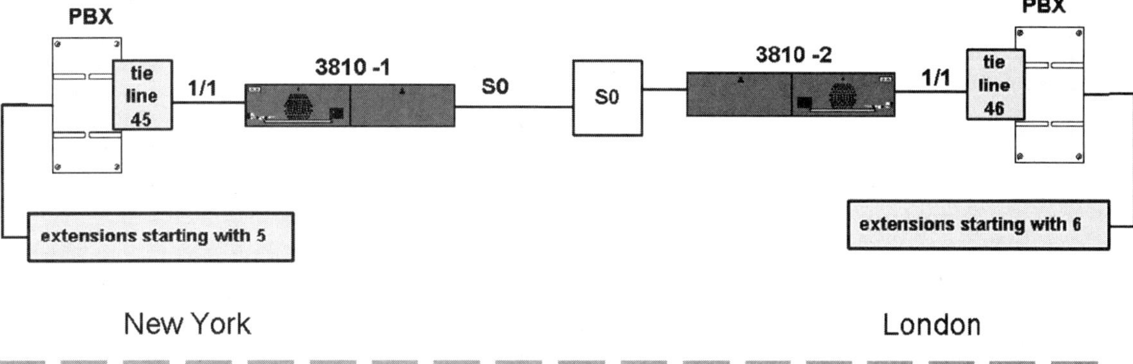

Figure 4-29 Network configuration for `connection tie-line` command.

With this first stage accomplished, we can now look at the dial-peers. The first decision is whether to use the `connection tie-line` command. At first, it may seem that as we are configuring the 3810 to connect to a tie line defined on the PBX, it is necessary to select the 3810 tie line setting. This is not the case. The `connection tie-line` setting tells the 3810 to establish a connection to the remote end as soon as the PBX signals a seized condition to the port in-status. The remote end is defined by the string entered after the `connection tie-line` command and the corresponding dial-peer entry for that string. This is best understood by way of an example.

In Figure 4-29 we have a PBX in New York that has tie line 45 configured for the ports that connect to the 3810. In London the PBX has a tie line 46 defined that identifies the ports connected to the 3810 there. Assuming all the signaling has been configured correctly, when a PBX handset at either end dials the appropriate tie line code, he will hear a dial tone generated by the 3810. At that point, an extension number at the remote end can be dialed and the remote extension should ring.

Looking at the New York end first, the following configuration will make this so:

```
voice-port 1/1
 connection tie-line 46
dial-peer voice 1 vohdlc
 destination-pattern 46....
 session target Serial 0
dial-peer voice 2 pots
 destination-pattern 5
 port 1/1
```

The first section defines voice port 1/1 to act as a tie line. The 46 is a descriptor that is only used within this 3810. What happens is that internally, the 46 is prepended to any digits that are dialed by the New York PBX when a call is made into this 3810. This 46 is then matched by the associated `dial-peer` command to enable the 3810 to switch these calls out the serial 0 interface. *Note:* The 46 is not sent out of the 3810 on serial 0, only the digits dialed by the PBX user, after the connection to the voice port 1/1 has been made. We chose 46 here, as it gives us a good idea of where we are directing calls to—that is, tie line 46 in London.

The second `dial-peer` command directs incoming calls that start with the digit 5 towards the PBX. Note that I have left out the additional configurations that are necessary to make this work, like forward-digits, all to focus attention on the configuration being discussed.

A configuration for the London end would be something like this:

```
voice-port 1/1
 connection tie-line 45
dial-peer voice 3 vohdlc
 destination-pattern 45....
 session target Serial 0
dial-peer voice 4 pots
 destination-pattern 6
 port 1/1
```

This network could be equally well configured without the `connection tie-line` commands. In that instance, we rely on the `dial-peer` commands to look at the content of the digits being dialed when deciding where to switch calls to. The dial-peer planning form will help in keeping track of the following for each tag number you assign to a `dial-peer voice` command:

- The type—either POTS, VOFR, VOHDLC, or VOATM
- The pattern being matched to trigger a call initiation
- The target port or interface that calls for this pattern will be switched out of
- The preference assigned to this `dial-peer` command with respect to others that match the same destination pattern

We'll finish the chapter with a full configuration for a network that is similar to the one shown in Figure 4-29. The only difference is that there are four ports connecting each 3810 to its PBX. In this configuration we will not use the `connection tie-line` command. We will rely solely on matching `dial-peer` commands to initiate a call. The configuration for both 3810s is given in Figure 4-30, starting with the configuration for the 3810 in the London end.

Figure 4-30
Configurations for both 3810s.

```
interface Ethernet0

 ip address 250.250.25.1 255.255.255.0
!
interface Serial0
 description 128k Link to New York
 ip address 201.201.10.2 255.255.255.0
  load-interval 30
 no fair-queue
 voice-encap 160
 hold-queue 1024 out
!
router rip
 redistribute static metric 1
 network 250.250.25.0
 network 201.201.10.0
 !
ip classless
logging buffered 4096 debugging
!
line con 0
 password 7 115A1C021001
 login
line aux 0
line vty 0 4
 password 7 005716010348
 login
!
!
voice-port 1/1
 cptone united kingdom
 description voice over ip 1
 operation 4-wire
 type 5
 signal immediate
!
voice-port 1/2
 cptone united kingdom
 operation 4-wire
 type 5
 signal immediate
!
voice-port 1/3
 cptone united kingdom
 operation 4-wire
 type 5
 signal immediate
!
voice-port 1/4
 cptone united kingdom
 operation 4-wire
 type 5
 signal immediate
!
dial-peer voice 1 vohdlc
 destination-pattern 3...
 session target Serial0
!
dial-peer voice 2 pots
 forward-digits all
 destination-pattern 5...
 port 1/1
!
dial-peer voice 3 pots
 forward-digits all
 preference 1
 destination-pattern 5...
 port 1/2
!
dial-peer voice 4 pots
```

Figure 4-30
Configurations for both 3810s.

```
 forward-digits all
 preference 2
 destination-pattern 5...
 port 1/3
!
dial-peer voice 5 pots
 forward-digits all
 preference 3
 destination-pattern 5...
 port 1/4
!

Configuration for New York Router

interface Ethernet0
 description voice over ip
 ip address 220.220.5.4 255.255.255.0
!
interface Serial0
 no ip address
 shutdown
!
interface Serial1
 description Voice-IP port to London
 ip address 201.201.10.1 255.255.255.0
 bandwidth 128
 no fair-queue
 voice-encap 160
 hold-queue 1024 out
!
interface Serial2
 no ip address
 shutdown
!
router rip
 network 220.220.5.0
 network 201.201.10.0
!
ip classless
logging buffered 4096 debugging
!
line con 0
password 7 06550A264B5D
 login
line aux 0
line vty 0 4
 password 7 15410E0B0339
 login
!
!
voice-port 1/1
 description voice over ip
 operation 4-wire
!
voice-port 1/2
 operation 4-wire
!
voice-port 1/3
 operation 4-wire
!
voice-port 1/4
 operation 4-wire
!
dial-peer voice 11 vohdlc
 destination-pattern 5...
session target Serial1
!
dial-peer voice 12 pots
 forward-digits all
 destination-pattern 3...
```

```
 port 1/1
!
dial-peer voice 13 pots
 forward-digits all
 preference 1
 destination-pattern 3...
 port 1/2
!
dial-peer voice 14 pots
 forward-digits all
 preference 2
 destination-pattern 3...
 port 1/3
!
dial-peer voice 15 pots
 forward-digits all
 preference 3
 destination-pattern 3...
 port 1/4
!
end
```

Figure 4-30 Configurations for both 3810s.

The first essential configuration to note is in the configuration of the serial 0 interface that will carry both voice and data traffic over the WAN between London and New York. The simple entry of `no fair-queue` has a dramatic impact on the operation of this interface. Leaving fair queueing can let voice traffic take control of the interface, to the exclusion of data traffic. What happens is that once a dial-peer destination pattern has been matched and the 3810 places a call over its serial 0 interface, if that call cannot be completed for any reason, all data traffic is prevented from traversing this link, including even `ping` commands. The interface will still show a status of line and protocol up in the `show interface serial 0` command output, but it will be unavailable until the system is reloaded. The `no fair-queue` is really an essential entry for the serial interface configuration.

An equally essential configuration entry for the serial interface is the `voice-encap 160` command. This does more than just that described in the section on Frame Relay operation. In that section, we discussed the `voice-encap` command as setting the operation to FRF.12 data segmentation. In reality, this command is necessary for all interfaces that will carry both voice and data traffic. Without this command in the configuration, no voice packets will be sent out.

Next we see that the first four voice ports in use are of type E&M and connected to a PBX using E&M signal type 5, immediate signaling, and four-wire operation. The dial-peer configurations direct all calls to extensions starting with a 3 out the serial 0 interface and calls made to extensions starting with 5 towards the E&M ports. The preference ranks ports in order from 1/1 through to 1/4. Of course, with the `dial-peer voice x pots` command, the first digit used to match the destination pattern would not normally be passed on, but since the PBX will need that digit to complete the call, we use the `forward-digits all` command.

The New York concentrator configuration is also shown in Figure 4-30, and it utilizes a similar configuration. The notable differences are the signal and type commands in the E&M ports, which use the U.S.-style defaults.

Once these concentrators are configured and interconnected and we have verified signaling via the `show voice port summary` command and seen that the PBX can send digits to the 3810 via the `debug voice eecm` command, we can look at some other command outputs to verify operation. One of the most useful is the `debug voice all 64000` command. This is the `debug` command to see all information regarding the initiation and setup of voice calls. The 64000 is the length the trace will remain active for (and is the maximum value). If this command is entered without the length of trace, no output will be seen on the console or in the log (if the `logging buffered` is entered in the configuration).

The first thing to do when troubleshooting an end-to-end connection is to see if the local 3810 is sending the voice call over its WAN connection to a remote 3810. That can be done by setting the `debug voice all 640000` command on the remote 3810 and initiating a call from the PBX to the local 3810. The remote 3810 should then see a voice call coming in its serial interface, match the destination pattern, and switch the call out one of the voice ports. All this activity should be seen on the debug output.

Once you can get this level of communication operational by correct cabling, voice port settings, fair queuing, and voice-encap settings, it is a simple matter to troubleshoot the dial-peer configuration to be sure calls are being switched correctly by using the `show dial-peer voice` command, a sample output of which follows:

```
VoiceOverHDLCPeer1
        tag = 1, destination-pattern = '3...', preference = 0,
        Admin state is up, Operation state is up
        type = vohdlc, session-target = `Serial0',
VoiceEncapPeer2
        tag = 2, destination-pattern = '5...', preference = 0,
        Admin state is up, Operation state is up
        type = pots, prefix = '',       fwd-digits = 33,
```

This output gives a convenient summary of all the dial-peers configured on the 3810, and you can see how different patterns will be switched.

Once active calls can be placed, it can be interesting to use the `show voice call` command to view which ports are in use. Following is a sample output for the first two voice ports when they are idle:

```
1/1 (   ): eecm = IDLE
LEM = idle,  CPD = idle
lss_voice = BLOCK, cps_voice = BLOCK, digit = BLOCK
1/2 (   ): eecm = IDLE
LEM = idle,  CPD = idle
lss_voice = BLOCK, cps_voice = BLOCK, digit = BLOCK
```

Summary

This chapter focused on workgroup switch deployment and introducing voice integration into existing data networks. We started by exploring how a 2916XL switch could be introduced to an existing network that currently uses shared media hubs. We then looked at how to extend that switch's capabilities by using a second switch to increase the number of ports available within a VLAN. Additionally, we explored the creation of multiple VLANs on the one switch, using a one-armed router to route between them. We also covered the basics of the user interface and the most common commands that will be used to get the switch operating in an efficient manner in simple installations. Within the configuration of the switch, we noted that VLAN 1 is the default VLAN to which all ports are automatically assigned, and it is the only VLAN on the switch that has any IP address information configured for it. The IP address of VLAN 1 is used by remote devices wishing to establish IP connectivity with the switch; it defines the default router for the switch. Subsequent VLANs on the switch have no knowledge of the IP network layer.

We covered hardware features of the 2916XL, including the LED and front-panel operation. We also took a step-by-step look at upgrading the IOS and storing and retrieving configuration files with the use of a TFTP server. This gave us the opportunity to examine files held in flash memory, such as the config.text configuration file and the IOS itself.

We examined the commands that are pertinent to single workstation attachment, like the unknown address blocking and portfast features. We also created a port group to provide increased throughput to a server, by having the switch treat two ports as one for the purposes of data transfer. Additionally, we used the commands available to manage the MAC address table and implement port security and learned how to utilize broadcast storm control. Finally, for the 2916XL we looked at the SPAN port operation for network troubleshooting and the 2916XL password recovery procedures.

From the 2916XL we moved on to look at the MC3810 multiservice concentrator as an entry into voice and data integration. We overviewed the modules available: the MFT for connection to T-1/E-1 lines, the DVM for digital connectivity to a PBX, and the AVM for analog voice connections. The AVM is populated by submodules, called *personality modules,* that are of types E&M, FXO, and FXS. E&M is the type used for tie line connectivity to PBXs. The key to setting up E&M ports is to match the configuration between this port setup and the PBX it is connecting to. The most important configurations to match are E&M type (1 in the United States, 5 in Europe), four-wire or two-wire operation, and setting of wink-start signaling (other signaling types, like immediate or delayed, are available and are more common in Europe). The FXO ports are used to connect analog phone lines to the 3810, and the FXS ports are used for analog handsets.

That covered the first stage of getting the 3810 operational, by enabling the 3810 to communicate with the voice devices it will be switching traffic for. The second stage of making the 3810 operational is to enter the dial-peer configurations to direct voice traffic through a 3810 network. Verification of this first stage is by use of the `show voice port summary` command to see ports getting seized when a PBX initiates a call to the 3810 and the `debug voice eecm` to see digits being passed from the PBX to the 3810.

The `dial-peer voice` command comes in four flavors: `vohdlc`, `vofr`, `voatm`, and `pots`. Each relates to transporting voice traffic over the medium of the interface in question, specifically HDLC encapsulated serial interfaces, Frame Relay encapsulated serial interfaces, ATM interfaces generating cells, and Plain Old Telephone Service, respectively. The operation of the `dial-peer voice` command when used with any of the `vohdlc`, `voatm`, or `vofr` options is similar. The 3810 waits until a set of digits that match a destination pattern have been entered, then it forwards all these out the interface (and, if appropriate, the PVC) specified in the `session target` command. The `dial-peer voice pots` command behaves differently in that the string entered in the destination pattern is used to initiate a call and not necessarily passed on by the 3810. Once a pattern is matched under this command, any excess digits entered are passed out through the POTS port.

The `dial-peer voice` commands set up the voice call switching within the 3810. Each command of this type tells the 3810 where to send a call whose digits match those defined in the command.

We also covered some of the specifics for sending voice packets over each encapsulation type, like traffic shaping for Frame Relay and the associated time-saving configuration of map-classes. The ATM option was noted as requiring a special IOS version. The interworking function for passing traffic between ATM and Frame Relay networks also received an overview.

Finally, we illustrated a real-world configuration and highlighted the essential nature of the `no fair-queue` command for proper operation of voice and data over the same link, as well as suggested ways of determining the correct signal and type configurations for various PBXs. As is always the case with using equipment from multiple suppliers, the most difficult part is finding a configuration that the two devices agree to talk to each other with. To assist, we also gave some suggestions for cabling configurations.

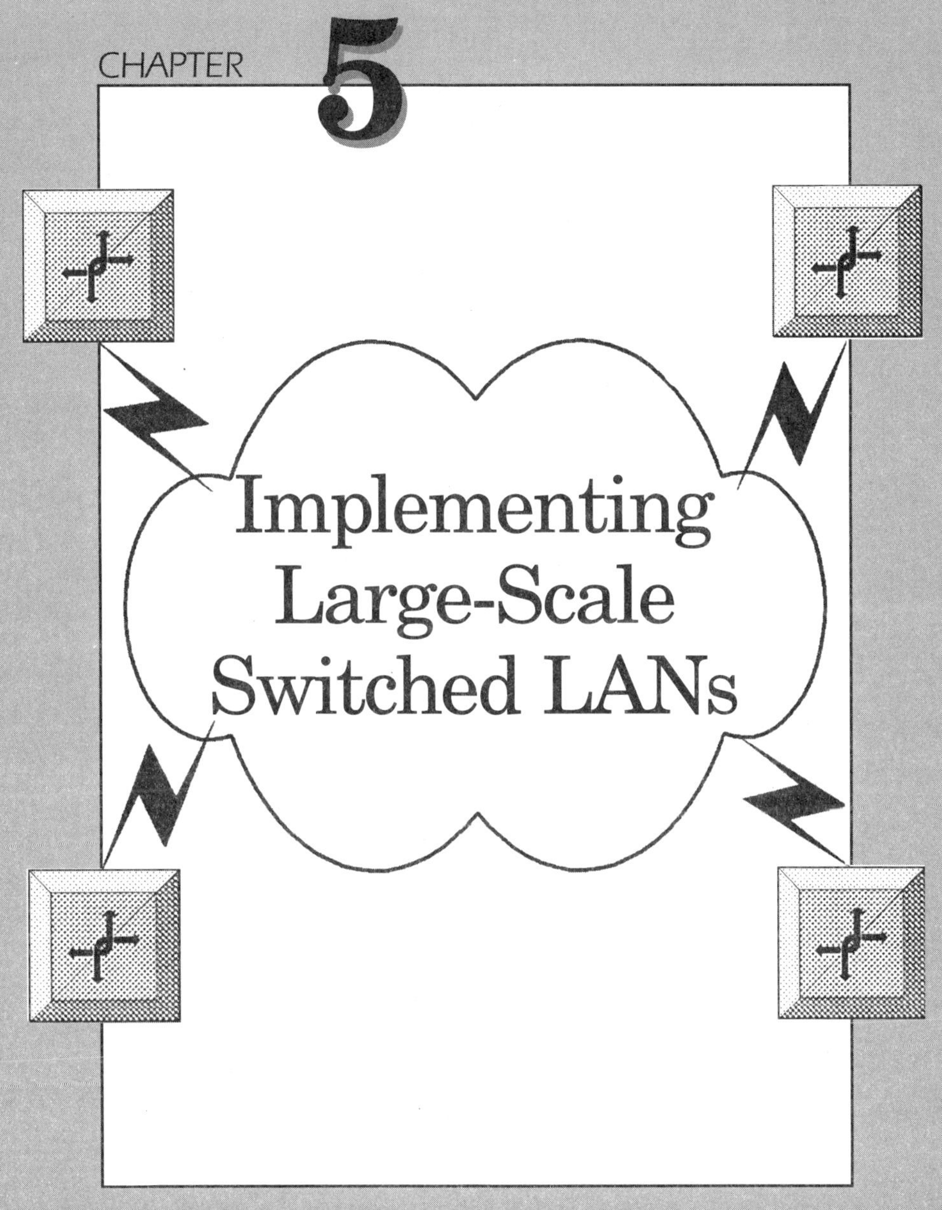
CHAPTER 5
Implementing
Large-Scale
Switched LANs

Introduction

In this chapter, we'll examine the configuration of Catalyst 5000 series switches for deployment in large-scale LANs. This class of switches from Cisco fully supports trunking, routing between VLANs, and ATM LEC operation. First, we'll examine the 5000 and 5500 series hardware, with particular attention to LEDs, module capability, and supervisor processor operation. Starting from a blank configuration, we will then add features such as ISL trunking, inter-VLAN routing, connection to FDDI LANs, and VTP. We will also look at optimizing VLAN traffic, as well as setting up the LANE LEC function and inter-VLAN communication over ATM emulated LANs.

Catalyst 5000 and 5500 Hardware

The Catalyst 5000 range, referred to as the 5K range, includes the 5500, 5509, 5505, 5000, and 5002. The 550x switches are the top-of-the-line chassis devices, with the 5500 having 13 slots; the 5509, 9 slots; and the 5505, 5 slots. An entry-level device in this class is the 5002, which has two slots available, one of which must be taken by the supervisor module (we'll cover the modules next). The 5000 (a five-slot chassis) is being phased out, leaving the 550x as the chassis that most will purchase, depending on their requirements for the number of modules.

The whole 5K range shares the following features:

- A supervisor module that supports a maximum of 16,000 MAC addresses in its address table
- Dual power-supply options
- Hot swapping of all modules
- Netflow switching and a dedicated Route Switch Processor for inter-VLAN and general IP routing
- Three levels of priority for traffic on the backplane, supporting ATM, token ring, and user-defined priority settings
- Software features of Fast EtherChannel, CGMP, spanning tree, broadcast suppression, ISL, VTP, SPAN, and for the RSM, TACACS, and IP access lists

The media supported by the 5K range covers all the expected options, such as 10/100 Ethernet, token ring, ATM LANE, CDDI/FDDI, T-1/E-1, and ATM at speeds from 25 Mbit/sec through to OC-12 (622 Mbit/sec) on fiber.

Catalyst 5K Modules

This section will look at the individual modules that can be used to populate a 5K chassis. The next section on 5K internals will discuss the backplane itself and the process of frame switching through the backplane. The 5000 and 5002 have a single 1.2-Gbit/sec backplane, whereas the Catalyst 5500 has three switching backplanes, each of 1.2-Gbit/sec throughput. With the Supervisor III card, a full 3.6-Gbit/sec throughput can be realized. Additionally, the larger 5500s incorporate a LightStream 1010 switch chassis, which has its own 5-Gbit/sec backplane, giving the 5500 a theoretical throughput of 8.6 Gbit/sec. Currently the 3.6-Gbit/sec and 5-Gbit/sec backplane do not communicate internally; external cabling is necessary for the LightStream modules to communicate with the Catalyst modules. By mid-1999 internal communication between these two backplanes is expected.

Supervisor Modules As its name might suggest, the supervisor module is the brains of the box and provides the 5K with its switching functionality. The supervisor also controls access to the backplane, packet destination within the switch, the network management processor, and LED displays for status. The supervisor contains NVRAM, which is used to store all interface configurations.

The supervisor comes in three flavors: the Supervisor Engine I, the Supervisor Engine II, and the Supervisor Engine III. The Supervisor I is only shipped with the five-slot 5000 and the two-slot 5002, both of which are being phased out and not expected to be available for long. The Supervisor II can be placed in any of the 5000, 5002, or 5500 range and offers improved Network Management Processor (NMP) performance (by a factor of between two and three times) and support for Fast EtherChannel. The Supervisor III only fits in the 5500 range; it offers up to 10 times NMP performance, plus the full 3.6-Gbit/sec switching fabric performance by connecting to all three backplanes in the 5500. It will also support Gigabit Fast EtherChannel.

The LEDs on the supervisor provide status for the following:

- System status; colored green if all tests pass, red if any tests fail, and red also if a redundant power supply is installed but not turned on.

- Both left and right power bays have their own LEDs to indicate the status of the respective power supplies, again using green for OK and red for a failure. In the event that one of the power supplies is off or not installed, the respective LED is off.
- The fan has its own LED, using green for good and red for bad.
- The 100-Mbit/sec Ethernet port on the supervisor uses a green LED to indicate 100-Mbit/sec operation and a separate link light that colors green for operational, off for no device attached, orange for software disabled, and blinking orange for a bad link.

The supervisor module can also be ordered with fiber connectors. In this case, the RJ-45 connectors are replaced with fiber connectors of varying types. These fiber-friendly supervisors use the familiar SC connectors for either multimode or single-mode fiber. For the 5500, a redundant supervisor can be installed to take over from the primary in the event of a hardware failure. The primary supervisor must always be placed in slot 1, with the backup, if present, in slot 2.

Ethernet and Fast Ethernet Modules The Ethernet modules come in 12- or 24-port varieties for switched 10, 100, or 10/100 autosensing types. There is also the option for a 48 switched-port 10-Mbit/sec card. The 12-port devices use standard RJ-45-type connectors for UTP cabling and either ST or SC connectors for fiber. The 24- and 48-port devices use telco connectors to achieve the higher port density. Typically the telco connectors are cabled to a patch panel that connects to the internal cabling plant; each telco connector supports 12 individual switched Ethernet ports. It should be noted, however, that there is a 24-port RJ-45 card, but that is limited to 10-Mbit/sec operation. No matter what the physical options chosen are, each port can be assigned to a different VLAN, and the 100-Mbit/sec ports can be used for ISL trunking.

Every module has a status LED, and every Ethernet port on a card has its own link LED; those that support both 10- and 100-Mbit/sec operation have LEDs to report that operation also. In general, the 10BaseT and 100BaseTX ports are limited to 100-meter cabling runs, whether running full or half duplex. Single-mode fiber can run to 6 miles, whereas multimode fiber can cover 1.5 miles for 10BaseFL operation on either half- or full-duplex. 100BaseFX, however, is limited to 440 yards, with 100BaseFX for half-duplex operation.

There are also what are known as *group switching modules,* which are like a low number of switched ports with built-in hubs. An example is the 10BaseT 48-port telco module. This has four telco connectors, each of which supports 12 RJ-45 cables. Each of the telco connectors can be thought of as 12 hub ports connected to a single switchable interface on the module. The 100BaseTX 24-port group switching module clearly does not support trunking like other 100-Mbit/sec modules, as each port on this module is not dedicated; rather, the available bandwidth is shared between all the ports in the group.

Miscellaneous Modules The miscellaneous modules include the token ring switching module, the FDDI/CDDI module, and the ATM LANE module. The token ring switching modules offer 16 ports, with either RJ-45 or fiber connectors, and offer support for SRS, SRT, and SRB switching, as well as DTR (data terminal ready) for direct device attachment. It is also possible to use these modules for ISL encapsulation of token ring VLAN packets, and, likewise, transporting of token ring VLANs over LANE is also supported.

The FDDI/CDDI modules each offer two connectors per module: RJ-45 for copper UTP, MIC connectors for multimode fiber, and ST connectors for single-mode fiber. This is the same physical connector layout as for the ATM LANE module, except that the fiber connectors are of the SC type. This module supports the ATM LEC functions on both the copper and fiber ports, but requires the fiber ports to fully support LANE 1.0 in terms of LES/BUS and LECS features.

Route Switch Module As we discussed in Chapter 4, to enable inter-VLAN communication, a router of some kind is necessary, as each VLAN uses its own subnet for IP addressing. With the 2900XL range we were forced to use an external router and have packets traverse wiring external to the switch to get from VLAN to VLAN. With the 5K range, there is a Route Switch Module (RSM) that performs IP, IPX, and AppleTalk routing within the switch. The RSM runs regular versions of Cisco IOS routing software, which can be stored on the PCMCIA memory slot. As we will see later, configuring modules within the 5K range requires an active mind, as each class of module utilizes a different command-line interface. The switching modules do not have different modes for `show` and configuration commands, whereas that is what is done on the RSM. The LightStream modules are different again. The RSM offers the standard console and auxiliary ports, along with status, CPU, and PCMCIA slot LEDs.

The RSM also contains a MAC address PROM, which is used to assign MAC addresses for use by VLANs. In the case of VLAN 0, the MAC address is used for diagnostics and identification of the RSM within the switch. Subsequent VLANs use the MAC address when accessing the RSM to route between VLANs; essentially, this identifies the MAC address of the router interface each VLAN is sending its data to when needing to route packets. It is possible to override these default values for the MAC address assignment of VLANs, but it is not recommended.

The Backplane The key thing to note about the backplanes used on the 5K range switches are that online insertion and removal is supported and the connector pins to the modules are on the backplane itself, rather than on the card. Having the pins within the chassis of the 5K and the socket part of the connector on the board makes it less likely that the module pins will be bent and kept from making a connection when inserted in the chassis. The 5K uses a 25-MHz clock to control a 48-bit-wide data bus for frame and packet switching. This is where the 1.2-Gbit/sec throughput on each backplane comes from—the potential of 48 bits of data being switched 25 million times a second.

A significant difference between the chassis of the 5000 and the 5500 is that for the 5000, the clock is generated onboard the supervisor, whereas on the 5500 the supervisor uses a clock generated by the backplane. It is also worth noting that for both the Ethernet and token ring card, the run-time code and configuration are downloaded from the supervisor, which makes both modules hot swappable, as they will retain their configuration.

The only tricky thing to look out for with backplane use on the 5500 is slot utilization. By this I mean what each slot is used for. The 5000 is not so fussy in this area. Keep in mind that not every slot has access to all the three buses (four buses if you include the 5-Gbit/sec ATM cell switching bus). Clearly, if you are looking to insert an RSM module to route between VLANs that may be online modules attached to different buses, you want to insert the RSM in a slot with access to all buses. The bus slot usage is given below:

- The supervisor module has to go in slot 1.
- Slots 2 through 5 have access to all three buses; however, if there is a backup supervisor to be installed, it must go into slot 2.
- Slots 6 through 8 have access to bus number 2 only.
- Slot 9 has access to bus B and the LS1010 bus.
- Slots 10 through 12 have access to bus C and the LS1010 bus.
- Slot 13 is reserved for use by the LS1010 ATM Switch Processor (ASP).

Even though the 5500 is really a tri-bus 5000 plus an LS1010 in the same box, the ASP used in a 5500 is different than that used in the LS1010. The key operational difference is that the 5500 ASP is hot swappable, whereas the LS1010 ASP is not. When the 5500 version of the ASP is placed in a 5500 chassis, it recognizes that fact and adjusts its understanding of module arrangement accordingly. The slot map—i.e., which LS1010 slot corresponds to which 5500 slot—is illustrated in Figure 5-1.

Catalyst 5K Internals

In this section we'll take a closer look at the internal operation of the 5K series switches and see how the switch handles packet switching through its various components. The 5K range use a store-and-forward mechanism to accept incoming frames and place them on the 1.2-Gbit/sec backplane bus. Each port has its own buffer for holding inbound frames. Each time a port wants to send its stored packets on to the backplane bus, it must get permission from the central bus arbiter. Once on the backplane bus, recognition logic built into ASIC hardware determines which ports need to transmit the frame. Interestingly, each port does get the frame; it is the recognition logic that tells the port either to flush the frame (drop it) or keep it. This mode of operation is quite efficient and contributes to the 5K range keeping its latency down to 10 microseconds to switch a frame. The exception to this is when switching between Ethernet and FDDI, which has 100-microseconds latency due to the frame conversion process necessary between those two media.

Figure 5-1 Map of 5500-to-LS1010 slots.

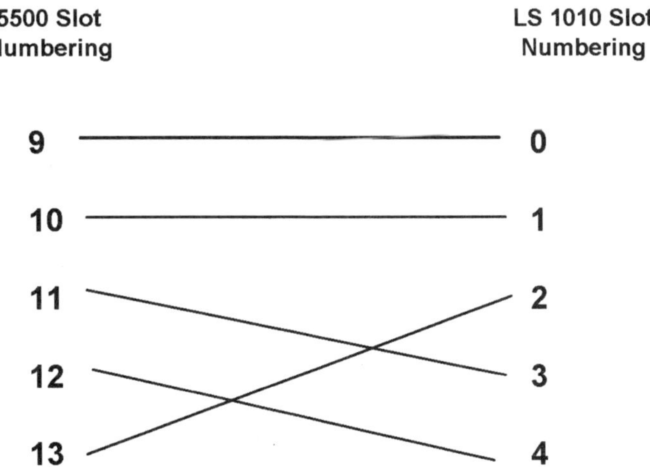

Within the switch there are three processors: a Network Management Processor (NMP), Master Control Processor (MCP), and Line-module Control Processor (LCP). Logical functions are supported via the bus arbiter (known as the SAMBA), recognition logic (referred to as the EARL), color blocking logic (CBL), and local target logic (LTL).

In addition to the frame and cell switching buses already discussed, there is a management and index bus. Let's now look at the major components in a bit more detail. The NMP contains the switch system software and configuration, along with diagnostic capabilities. It performs system control and provides the command-line interface and SNMP features, as well as running a copy of the Spanning Tree Protocol for each VLAN. The NMP connects to both the switching and the management bus.

The MCP, however, only connects to the 761-Kbit/sec management bus, which it uses to communicate information between the NMP and each LCP. The MCP uses LTL and CBL to control port operation for things such as stopping frames belonging to one VLAN appearing on another VLAN's port.

Each module has an LCP on board that processes the information the MCP sends to the module over the management bus. The LCP is responsible for performing power-up self-tests on each module and reporting operational status back to the MCP, so that the MCP can start using that module.

On the Ethernet modules, each port has a dedicated ASIC (application-specific integrated circuit) plus 192 KB of memory used to encapsulate incoming Ethernet frames in preparation for transmission across the switching bus. The 192 KB of memory is split between input and output. Frames going to the switching bus use the input buffer, which is 24 KB in size, and frames leaving the switch use the output buffer, which is 168 KB in size. Frames need to be encapsulated with VLAN and port information for the switching logic to determine the correct destination for the frame. This encapsulation is 12 bytes in size and notes the source port, VLAN ID of the frame, and a frame check sequence. This encapsulation is different from the 30-byte encapsulation used by ISL and never leaves the switch. Each port, whether a regular or ISL port, will strip off the encapsulation header and trailer that was used to transmit the frame across the switching bus prior to transmitting the frame on to external media.

ATM and FDDI ports do not understand 802.3 and therefore use a different ASIC and additional (up to 2 MB) buffering memory. For outgoing packets, the Ethernet ASIC on each port can perform ISL encapsulation when the port is configured for trunking. The only module that does not provide a dedicated ASIC per port is the group switching module; that provides an ASIC per group of ports.

A simplified illustration of the bus connections for each major device is shown in Figure 5-2. The module ports are the only devices that communicate over all three buses in the 5K switch. The switching bus is clearly the bus used to transmit frames that are received by, or about to be sent out by, the switch. The management bus carries configuration information from the NMP to each module and returns performance information back from the modules to the NMP. The index bus is used solely for module port-to-recognition logic communication. It is this communication that informs each port whether to flush or retain the frame currently in the port's buffer. Interestingly, the default operation is for all packets to go to all ports, and the decision is then made as to whether each port should forward the packet. If the port decides not to forward the frame, it drops the packet, which is referred to as "flushing" the packet.

So far, we have only talked about "the arbiter" as if it were one device that controlled the switching of frames on to the switching bus. This is, in fact, not the case, and there are arbiter ASICs (referred to as SAMBAs) on both line modules (such as Fast Ethernet modules) and the supervisor. This facilitates two levels of arbitration. First is arbitration between individual ports on the module to access the switching bus, and second, arbitration between different modules in the switch. The arbiter on the supervisor is strapped as a master and can support arbitration between 13 module cards. The arbiter on each line module is strapped as a slave and can support arbitration between up to 48 module ports. When a port wants to send a frame on to the switching bus, it will first

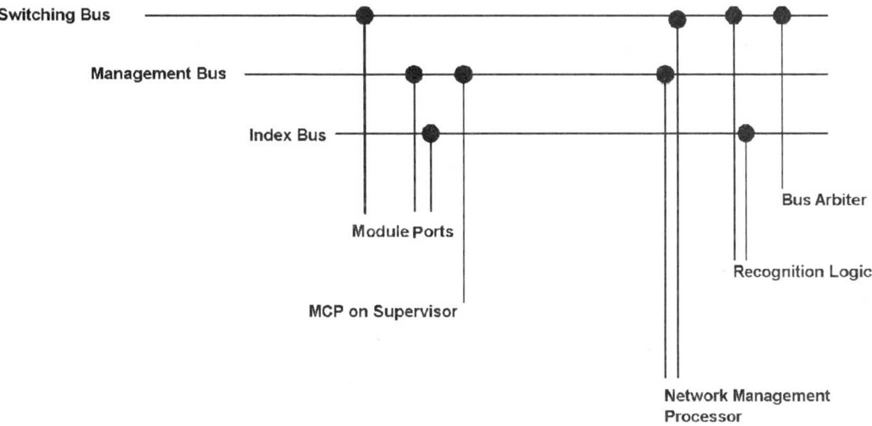

Figure 5-2 Device/bus connectivity in the 5K range. Note the module ports are the only devices connected to all buses.

seek permission from its module slave arbiter, then the slave arbiter requests access of the master arbiter. Once the slave has received permission, the slave will grant access for the port to the switching bus.

It is this two-tier arbitration process that enables the 5K range to support time-sensitive traffic and provide higher priority to server devices on the network. Each line module arbiter (operating in slave mode) will populate two queues: the normal- and high-priority levels that are configurable by the user (we will see how to set this in a later section). A third priority, critical, can be assigned by the system itself to avoid things like buffer overflow. The second tier of arbitration, performed by the master arbiter, uses a round-robin technique for both normal- and high-priority requests. Critical priority requests are always serviced before any other type of priority. Normal- and high-priority requests are not serviced until all the critical requests are completed. Once the master arbiter gets to deal with normal- and high-priority requests, it deals with high priority over normal priority with a factor of 5 to 1. That is to say, if there are 15 high-priority requests and 30 normal-priority requests, the master arbiter will deal with 5 high-priority requests followed by 1 normal-priority request three times. When all the high-priority requests have been dealt with, the remaining normal-priority requests are processed.

The recognition logic ASIC we have referred to is known as an *EARL chip,* and it maintains the MAC address-to-VLAN and port table that is used to switch frames within the 5K. This is similar in operation to the content addressable memory we discussed in earlier chapters and is generated in the same way that simple learning bridges generated their MAC address bridge table. The EARL enters MAC addresses into its table by learning the port that originates frames with that MAC address in the source address field and sets the VLAN membership according to the configuration set on the port. This EARL chip can store up to 128,000 addresses.

The EARL then makes decisions on which port will keep the frames it receives from the switching bus and which port will flush the frames based on lookups performed on this table. The EARL is assisted in its tasks by two specialized pieces of logic hardware. The first is the local target logic (LTL), which speeds up the search process to determine the ports that will receive a frame. The EARL generates index values that are stored by the LTL, which speed up the selection of destinations as unicast, multicast, or broadcast. The color blocking logic (CBL) stops frames from passing into ports that are not on the same VLAN as the frame originator and helps the Spanning Tree Protocol block ports when preventing loops.

To conclude this section, let's examine in a bit more detail how a frame is handled from when it comes into an Ethernet port, is switched across the switching bus, and is sent out another port. When a frame first arrives at a switch port, it is stored in the port input buffer, and a full frame check is performed to make sure that there is no corruption in the frame. This is part of the normal mode for a store-and-forward system; cut-through and frag-free operation will not perform complete frame check sequences (FCSs) prior to accepting and switching the frame. The trade-off is that the 5K range does introduce a very small amount of latency into the network, but it does not propagate damaged or corrupt frames, which is the danger with cut-through and frag-free operation.

Once the frame has passed the FCS, it is encapsulated with a 12-byte header that includes VLAN membership and source port in the header. At this stage, the previously described two-tier arbitration process kicks in, and the encapsulated packet is sent toward the switching bus. The switching bus will deliver the encapsulated frame to all ports on the switch; the ports store the frame in their input buffers. The switching bus operation is similar in concept to a 10Base2 coaxial cabling system that delivers each frame to each node. The benefit of this type of operation is that there is only one copy of each multicast and broadcast frame sent on the bus.

At this point the process varies depending on the nature of the encapsulated frame. For unicast and multicast frames the process is the same. The switching logic in the form of the EARL, LTL, and CBL determines the list of ports that need to forward the packet on to their attached media, then it signals over the index bus to each port, telling it what to do with the frame. This, of course, presupposes that multicast addresses and the ports that are associated with them are known to the 5K, either by manual configuration or by CGMP notifications from an attached router. In the case of a frame addressed to a broadcast or unknown address, it is forwarded out all ports. If the 5K does not know which ports are to receive specific multicast traffic, it will treat the multicast frames as broadcast frames and send them out all ports. In the event that the recognition logic determines that the frame does not need to go to any other port—i.e., that it is a frame destined for another device on the same segment—the EARL tells all ports to flush their buffers and terminate the transmission of this frame.

The only other potential outcome is if the destination port has no buffer space available. In this instance, the destination port issues a retry to the source, which terminates the frame transfer and retries later. This process is summarized in Figure 5-3.

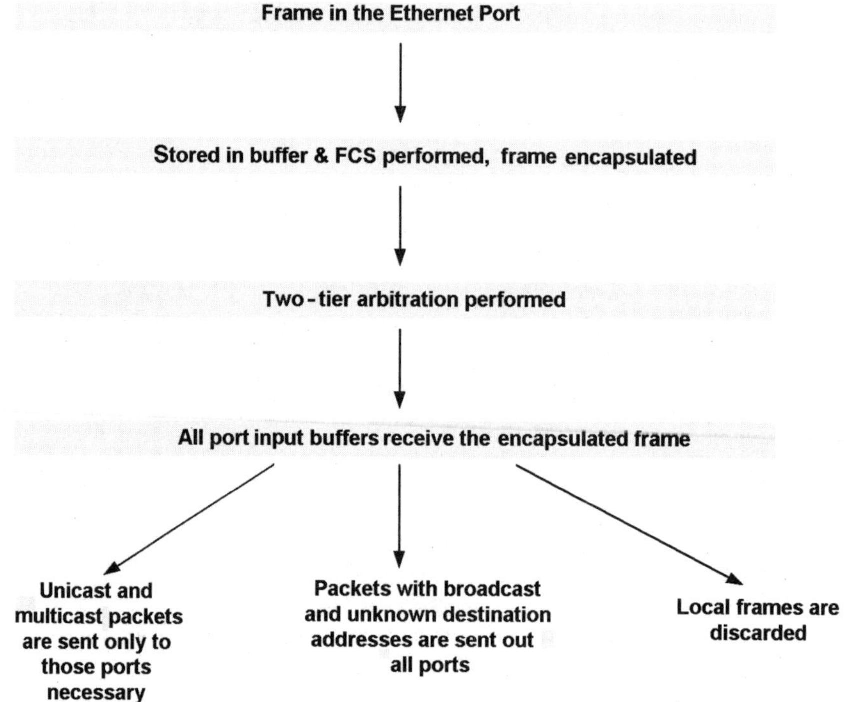
Frame in the Ethernet Port
Stored in buffer & FCS performed, frame encapsulated
Two - tier arbitration performed
All port input buffers receive the encapsulated frame
Unicast and multicast packets are sent only to those ports necessary
Packets with broadcast and unknown destination addresses are sent out all ports
Local frames are discarded

Figure 5-3 Summary of frame switching within the 5K.

Catalyst 5K Initial Configuration

Once you get your Catalyst 5K, the first thing that requires attention is the user interface, which is a little different from what is encountered on Cisco routers, or indeed the 2900XL range we looked at earlier. Additionally, it is almost a given that you will need to upgrade the software on the supervisor module. With new line modules consistently being made available by Cisco, each requiring the latest supervisor software, it is a good idea to have a well-honed software upgrade procedure at hand. To start this section we'll look at the 5K user command-line interface (CLI) and software upgrade procedures.

Using the 5K CLI for Software Upgrades

Connecting a terminal to the 5K is much like connecting to a 7500 series router. The 5K has a female DB-25 connector on the supervisor module marked "console." To this you connect the DB-25 male connector supplied with the Catalyst that is marked "modem." You can then use the RJ-45 cable supplied to connect to your terminal (if required, the DB-25 or DB-9 connector marked "terminal" can be used to connect to the terminal). Clearly, the console port on the supervisor is configured for DCE, and as terminals are DTE devices, the RJ-45 cable needs to be a straight-through.

Once you are physically connected to the supervisor, the first thing to notice is that there is no longer separate CLI modes for view access and configuration. The two forms of access are via `set` or `show` commands. The `set` commands replace the functionality provided by `configure terminal` mode in routers. There is still an `enable` mode that is used to distinguish privileged users with write access from regular users with view access. The difference here is that `enable` mode is identified by the word "enable" appearing in parenthesis after the hostname prompt, rather than a change of the prompt delimiter from > to #. The "?" followed by a return will give you all the options for commands that can be entered at that point, just as can be done on a regular router.

The 5K CLI has some slightly more advanced key commands also. For example, if you enter a lengthy command line and realize that it has an error at the beginning, you can delete the whole line by pressing Ctrl-U. To delete just one word, press Ctrl-W. The CLI also shows some similarity to the UNIX vi editor in its use of the "!" symbol. By entering `!!` it is possible to retrieve the last command and save having to type it again. This is equivalent to the router Ctrl-P or up-arrow sequence. `!-10` retrieves the command you entered 10 commands ago and `!abc` retrieves the last command that started with "abc." This can be useful if you don't remember how many commands ago a specific command that you wish to reenter was executed. To view the command history typed in, enter `history` at the switch prompt.

The last thing of interest with the CLI is that to configure modules individually, you use the `session` command. The command string below illustrates this use to access the Route Switch Module in slot 4.

```
Console> session 4
Trying Router-4...
Connected to Router-4.
Escape character is '^]'.
Router>
```

Now that you have logged in to the RSM, you configure it using the standard router CLI and router IOS commands. To configure a specific port on a module, it is possible to specify the module and port number; we'll look at an example of that later when we configure the Ethernet card in the next section.

So, having covered the basics, let's upgrade the software. To see the current version of software, enter the following command:

```
Console> show ver
WS-C5000 Software, Version McpSW: 3.1(1) NmpSW: 3.1(1)
Copyright (c) 1995-1997 by Cisco Systems
NMP S/W compiled on Dec 31 1997, 18:04:22
MCP S/W compiled on Dec 31 1997, 18:12:31
System Bootstrap Version: 3.1(2)
Hardware Version: 2.4 Model: WS-C5000 Serial #: 009615555
```

After this, the display shows the hardware, firmware, and software revisions of all the modules active in the 5K. The important part of this display tells us that the supervisor module is running software version 3.1(1). Now, because the rest of our configuration examples in this section use the 48-port Ethernet module, which requires software version 4.2 (2) or higher, we have to upgrade. A simple giveaway that this is necessary is the following console display message:

```
Module 3 has invalid Feature Index: 41
12/14/1998,11:09:08:SYS-5:Module 3 not responding...resetting module
```

The usual method of upgrading software is to use TFTP, which assumes IP connectivity. Given that the module we have to upgrade for is the Ethernet module, we connect the 10/100 interface on the supervisor to the network with the TFTP server on it. Of course, the first thing to do here is to assign an appropriate IP address to the supervisor to enable IP connectivity. To do this, we need to introduce the sc0 interface that is used on 5K switches.

The sc0 interface can be thought of as performing two roles. The first is as the console that enables access via telnet to the switch, and the other is to be a thin IP stack to define things like the default gateway for a VLAN. We will examine this further when we look at setting up multiple VLANs and routing between them. So, to give the supervisor an IP address that we can telnet to, the following needs to be entered:

```
Console> (enable) set interface ?
Usage: set interface <sc0|sl0> <up|down>
       set interface sc0 [vlan] [ip_addr [netmask [broadcast]]]
       set interface sl0 <slip_addr> <dest_addr>
Console> (enable) set interface sc0 200.200.25.111 255.255.255.0
Interface sc0 IP address and netmask set.
```

In this case we have set the sc0 interface to use IP address 200.200.25.111 with netmask 255.255.255.0. The sc0 interface is up by default, so it does not need to have a `set int sc0 up` command issued, unless it has already been turned down. Once the sc0 interface has been addressed, that port can be connected either directly to a NIC in a PC via a straight-through cable, or to a switch or hub via a crossover cable.

With IP connectivity to a TFTP server available, we can use the `download` command. The `download` command is used to copy a software image from a specified host to a module's flash memory, whereas the `upload` command does the reverse. Following is an example of how the `download` command is used:

```
Console> (enable) download 200.200.25.13 cat5000-sup_4-2-2.bin
Download image cat5000-sup_4-2-2.bin from 200.200.25.13 to Module 1
FLASH (y/n)[n]? y
Finished network single module download. (2677392 bytes)
FLASH on Catalyst:
Type            Address              Location
AMD 29F016      20000000             NMP (P3) 8MB SIM
Erasing flash sector...done.
Programming flash sector...done.
Erasing flash sector...done.
Programming flash sector...done.
Erasing flash sector...done.
Programming flash sector...done.
The system needs to be reset to run the new image.
```

This copies the file cat5000-sup_4-2-2.bin from the host 200.200.25.13 to the supervisor module. For this upgrade to then take effect, you must issue the `reset` command, which is similar to the `reload` command used on Cisco routers. If you reset the switch and are presented with a "boot" prompt, you can run the `execflash` command to make the new software operational.

With the correct software, we can use the `show module` command to see the switch recognize the Ethernet module in slot 3:

```
Console> sho mod
Mod Module-Name  Ports Module-Type           Model    Serial-Num Status
--- -----------  ----- -----------           -----    ---------- ------
1                2     100BaseTX Supervisor  WS-X5509 009615555  ok
2                      10BaseT Ethernet Ext
3                48    10BaseT Ethernet      WS-X5014 010294029  ok
4                1     Route Switch          WS-X5302 010909362  ok

Mod MAC-Address(es)                        Hw   Fw      Sw
--- -------------------------------------  ---  ------  -------------
1   00-90-d9-17-ac-00 to 00-90-d9-17-af-ff 2.4  3.1(2)  4.2(2)
3   00-90-6f-68-f8-40 to 00-90-6f-68-f8-6f 1.0  4.2(1)  4.2(2)
4   00-e0-1e-92-3b-7c to 00-e0-1e-92-3b-7d 7.0  20.7    11.2(12a.P1)P1
```

The first half of the display shows the slots that are populated, the model number of the module in that slot, and its status. As we have a 48-port module in slot 3, which is a double-height module, slot 2 shows up as populated by the Ethernet extension of the card in slot 3. The second half of the display lists the available MAC addresses that can be used by each module. If you want the switch to automatically retrieve its IP address configuration from a BOOTP server on the network when it is first powered up, you need to set the sc0 IP address to 0.0.0.0 and use the first MAC address for module 1 for the BOOTP server entry.

Interestingly, the 5K switch allows you to configure multiple IP default gateways. The benefit here is that if the primary default gateway fails, up to two other routers can be contacted to provide access to remote networks. Typically, multiple default gateways are supported by HSRP, as it is assumed that hosts do not have the ability to select multiple default gateways. HSRP is fully covered in the *Cisco TCP/IP Routing Professional Reference.* The primary default gateway is defined as follows:

```
Console> (enable) set ip route default 200.200.25.1 primary
Route added.
```

It is possible to specify a metric for the default gateway, but this should not be necessary. We can check what this has done to the configuration by using the following command:

```
Console> (enable) sho ip rout
Fragmentation  Redirect  Unreachable
-------------  --------  -----------
enabled        enabled   enabled
The primary gateway: 200.200.25.1
Destination          Gateway            Flags     Use     Interface
-----------          -------------      -----     ---     ---------
default              200.200.25.1       UG          0        sc0
200.200.25.0         200.200.25.111     U           0        sc0
```

Up to two more default gateways can be entered this way (obviously without the `primary` option entered). Without the `primary` option entered, the switch selects the next default gateway based on the order in which they were entered into the configuration.

Supervisor Configuration

If you are planning to use the 5K range in mission-critical applications, use of a redundant supervisor is prudent. Establishing a redundant supervisor is pretty much an automatic event for a 5K; you just need to plug identical supervisor cards into slot 1 and slot 2. The supervisor in slot 1 will be the primary, leaving the supervisor in slot 2 as the backup. As the configuration in NVRAM or system image changes in the primary supervisor, it will automatically update the secondary.

With a redundant supervisor installed in slot 2, the `show module` command displays an output similar to the following, indicating that the supervisor in slot 2 is in standby mode:

```
Console> sho mod
Mod Module-Name Ports  Module-Type          Model     Serial-Num Status
--- ----------- -----  -------------------- --------  -----------------
1               2      100BaseTX Supervisor WS-X5509  009615555 ok
2               2      100BaseTX Supervisor WS-X5509  009614444 standby
3                      10BaseT Ethernet Ext
4               48     10BaseT Ethernet     WS-X5014  010294029 ok
5               1      Route Switch         WS-X5302  010909362 ok
```

So, having set the IP information for the sc0 interface, loaded new software, and defined the default gateways, there is little else in the way of configuration available for the Supervisor II Engine. The only additional commands that show much of interest are the `show port` and `show test` commands. The `show port` command, when followed by the slot number the supervisor module is in, produces a simple display, as shown here:

```
Console> sho port 1
Port  Name              Status      VLAN    Level   Duplex  Speed Type
----  ----------------  ----------  ----    ------- ------  ----- --------
1/1                     connected   1       normal  half     100   100BaseTX
1/2                     notconnect  1       normal  half     100   100BaseTX
Port  Security Secure-Src-Addr Last-Src-Addr Shutdown  Trap IfIndex
----  -------- --------------- ------------- --------  -------------
1/1   disabled                                  No       disabled 3
1/2   disabled                                  No       disabled 4
```

This shows us the connect status of the ports, along with their speed and duplex, then goes on to show that port security (as discussed in Chapter 4) is not configured. Subsequent tables in this display show the status of broadcast control and Ethernet errors.

The `show test` command is useful for troubleshooting the status of all the internal workings of the supervisor. A period indicates a properly operating subsystem. Following is a sample display of this command:

```
Console> show test 1
Module 1 : 2-port 100BaseTX Supervisor
Network Management Processor (NMP) Status:(. = Pass, F = Fail, U = Unknown)
  ROM: .     Flash-EEPROM: .   Ser-EEPROM: .     NVRAM: .    MCP Comm: .
  EARL Status :
        NewLearnTest:
```

```
IndexLearnTest:          .
DontForwardTest:         .
MonitorTest              .
DontLearn:               .
FlushPacket:             .
ConditionalLearn:        .
EarlLearnDiscard:        .
EarlTrapTest:            .
```

The Supervisor III has more available for configuration, as its flash contains a file system that is not unlike a cut-down version of UNIX. Common UNIX commands like `cd`, `pwd`, `delete`, and so forth can be used on a Supervisor III to manage the file system. This gives you the opportunity to store several different images and control which one the Supervisor III will boot and run with. Within the Supervisor III there are three addressable devices: the bootflash, and PCMCIA slots 1 and 2. (*Note:* PCMCIA memory needs to be formatted with the `format` command before it can be used.)

The command to specify which system image will be used is `set boot system flash`. Just as with Cisco routers, there is a low-functionality ROM version of the operating system that the switch will boot into if it cannot find a suitable operating image to load. This ROM image supports just enough functionality for you to load full images of the system code, should there be a problem with what it was configured to do. It is also possible to enter ROM monitor mode by pressing the Break key during the first 60 seconds of the 5K power-up sequence. This option can be useful if you want to load a new version of operating software or otherwise manage the files in flash.

A typical use of the `set boot` command is given below:

```
Switch(enable)set boot system flash slot1:cat5K-r45.cbi
```

This is effectively setting the `boot` environment variable to cat5K-r45.cbi. Subsequent `set boot` commands will list in sequence order the images the system will try to load, if an image is not available. This provides a means of prioritized backup of image files. Should you wish to re-order the sequence in which images will be loaded, it is safest to use the `clear boot system all` command and then redefine the list order.

Those familiar with upgrading IOS remotely on routers will know about changing configuration registers to control how a router boots next time it is reloaded. The same exists in the 5K. The Catalyst Supervisor III configuration register can be set to boot the system into the ROM monitor, onboard flash, or the system as specified by the set boot system command, by the following commands, respectively:

```
Console (enable)setboot config-register rommon
Console (enable)setboot config-register bootflash
Console (enable)setboot config-register system
```

Navigating your way around the Supervisor III file system is fairly straightforward. The show boot command shows you what the current contents of the boot environment variable is, and the show flash command lists the files in flash. In addition, copying flash files is available via the copy command. There are options to copy files from a TFTP server to a flash file location or to the running configuration. There is also the option to copy files from a flash file location or the running configuration to a TFTP server. Note that the switch configuration can be copied to and from a TFTP server using the usual write net and conf net commands.

The first argument to follow the copy word is the source of the transfer, while the second is the destination. As an example, the following command copies the current flash configuration to a TFTP server:

```
Console> (enable) copy config tftp:switch.cfg
IP address or name of remote host [200.200.25.13]? y
Upload configuration to tftp:switch.cfg (y/n) [n]? y
............
.............
...
Configuration has been copied successfully. (9278 bytes).
```

The available arguments to this command are TFTP to identify a TFTP server, config to identify the running configuration (of flash, not the switch), a file-id to identify a flash device, or flash for flash memory.

The Default Configuration Explained

Unlike other Cisco devices, the 5K range comes with a substantial initial configuration file. We will progress through this chapter to configure the 5K to use multiple VLANs, then we will route between them, use several different types of media, and optimize its operation. However, it is beneficial to have a clear understanding of the device configuration as it comes out of the box before we start to modify it. Unlike routers that use write erase to clear the configuration, the 5K range uses the clear conf command as follows:

```
Console> (enable) clear conf
Usage: clear config all
       clear config <mod_num>
       clear config rmon
Console> (enable) clear config all
This command will clear all configuration in NVRAM.
This command will cause ifIndex to be reassigned on the next system
  startup.
Do you want to continue (y/n) [n]? y
```

Of course, to clear the configuration of the router or ATM module, you will have to use the `session` command to access them and use the appropriate command for that module. The initial configuration of the switch after a `clear config all` command has been executed is shown in Figure 5-4. As you can see, this is a lengthy default configuration with many sections and commands to explore. We'll now discuss each section in turn.

The `begin` Section. This section has entries for the telnet and enable mode password, both of which are encrypted. It then sets the switch prompt, number of lines printed per screen, the time in minutes after which no keyboard activity will force a logout, and the contents of the message of the day, displayed after each successful login.

The `system` Section. This section sets the baud rate for the console port to 9600 and disables the modem control signals on the console port (like DTR and RTS, or Request to Send), since they are generally not necessary when connecting a terminal to the console port and can cause disruption with a terminal connected. The system, name location, and contact are blank and may be set for administrative purposes.

The `snmp` Section. This section first sets the access level for given SNMP community strings. There are three levels: read-only, read-write, and read-write-all. In essence, the read-write-all can be considered the same as read-write. A community string must be supplied by any remote device that is querying the switch via the SNMP protocol. In addition, this section sets RMON (remote monitoring) support to enable or disable. To enable RMON, you will most likely require an additional software license from Cisco. RMON allows statistics to be remotely collected for alarms and events as listed in RFC 1757, but only for Ethernet ports.

The last part of this section disables all the SNMP traps that can be set on the switch. SNMP traps are generated by MIBs on devices when prespecified conditions are met. For a fuller discussion on SNMP in a

Figure 5-4 Initial configuration of the switch after a `clear config all` command has been executed.

```
Console (enable) wr t
...
..........

..........
.........

..

begin
set password $1$FMFQ$HfZR5DUszVHIRhrz4h6V70
set enablepass $1$FMFQ$HfZR5DUszVHIRhrz4h6V70
set prompt Console>
set length 24 default
set logout 20
set banner motd ^C^C
!
#system
set system baud  9600
set system modem disable
set system name
set system location
set system contact
!
snmp
set snmp community read-only      public
set snmp community read-write     private
set snmp community read-write-all secret
set snmp rmon disable
set snmp trap disable module
set snmp trap disable chassis
set snmp trap disable bridge
set snmp trap disable repeater
set snmp trap disable vtp
set snmp trap disable auth
set snmp trap disable ippermit
set snmp trap disable vmps
set snmp trap disable entity
set snmp trap disable config
set snmp trap disable stpx
!
#ip
set interface sc0 1 0.0.0.0 0.0.0.0 0.0.0.0

set interface sc0 up
set interface sl0 210.210.5.5 210.210.5.6
set interface sl0 up
set arp agingtime 1200
set ip redirect   enable
set ip unreachable   enable
set ip fragmentation enable
set ip alias default         0.0.0.0
!
#Command alias
!
#vmps
set vmps server retry 3
set vmps server reconfirminterval 60
set vmps tftpserver 0.0.0.0 vmps-config-database.1
set vmps state disable

!
#dns
set ip dns disable
!
#tacacs+
set tacacs attempts 3
set tacacs directedrequest disable
set tacacs timeout 5
set authentication login tacacs disable
```

Figure 5-4
(Cont.)

```
set authentication login local enable
set authentication enable tacacs disable
set authentication enable local enable
!
#bridge
set bridge ipx snaptoether   8023raw
set bridge ipx 8022toether   8023
set bridge ipx 8023rawtofddi snap
!
#vtp
set vtp mode server
set vtp v2 disable
set vtp pruning disable
set vtp pruneeligible 2-1000
clear vtp pruneeligible 1001-1005
!
#spantree
#uplinkfast groups
set spantree uplinkfast disable
#backbonefast
set spantree backbonefast disable
#vlan 1
set spantree enable     1
set spantree fwddelay 15    1
set spantree hello    2    1
set spantree maxage   20    1
set spantree priority 32768 1
#vlan 1003
set spantree enable     1003
set spantree fwddelay 15    1003
set spantree hello    2    1003
set spantree maxage   20    1003
set spantree priority 32768 1003
set spantree portstate 1003 auto 0
set spantree portcost 1003 80
set spantree portpri  1003 32
set spantree portfast 1003 disable
#vlan 1005
set spantree enable     1005
set spantree fwddelay 15    1005
set spantree hello    2    1005
set spantree maxage   20    1005
set spantree priority 32768 1005
set spantree multicast-address 1005 ieee
!
#cgmp
set cgmp disable
set cgmp leave disable
!
#syslog
set logging console enable
set logging server disable
set logging level cdp 2 default
set logging level mcast 2 default
set logging level dtp 5 default
set logging level dvlan 2 default
set logging level earl 2 default
set logging level fddi 2 default
set logging level ip 2 default
set logging level pruning 2 default
set logging level snmp 2 default
set logging level spantree 2 default
set logging level sys 5 default
set logging level tac 2 default
set logging level tcp 2 default
set logging level telnet 2 default
set logging level tftp 2 default
set logging level vtp 2 default
set logging level vmps 2 default
set logging level kernel 2 default
```

Figure 5-4
(Cont.)

```
set logging level filesys 2 default
set logging level drip 2 default
set logging level pagp 5 default
set logging level mgmt 5 default
set logging level mls 5 default
set logging level protfilt 2 default
set logging level security 2 default
!
#ntp
set ntp broadcastclient disable
set ntp broadcastdelay 3000
set ntp client disable
clear timezone
set summertime disable
!
#permit list
set ip permit disable
!
#drip
set tokenring reduction enable
set tokenring distrib-crf disable
!
#igmp
set igmp disable
!
#module 1 : 2-port 100BaseTX Supervisor
set module name    1
set vlan 1    1/1-2
set port channel 1/1-2 off
set port channel 1/1-2 auto
set port enable     1/1-2
set port level      1/1-2  normal
set port duplex     1/1-2  half
set port trap       1/1-2  disable
set port name       1/1-2
set port security   1/1-2  disable
set port broadcast  1/1-2  100%
set port membership 1/1-2  static
set cdp enable   1/1-2
set cdp interval 1/1-2 60
set trunk 1/1  auto isl 1-1005
set trunk 1/2  auto isl 1-1005
set spantree portfast    1/1-2 disable
set spantree portcost    1/1-2  19
set spantree portpri     1/1-2  32
spantree portvlanpri 1/1  0
set spantree portvlanpri 1/2  0
set spantree portvlancost 1/1  cost 18
set spantree portvlancost 1/2  cost 18
!
#module 2 empty
!
#module 3 : 48-port 10BaseT Ethernet
set module name    3
set module enable  3
set vlan 1    3/1-48
set port enable     3/1-48
set port level      3/1-48  normal
set port duplex     3/1-48  half
set port trap       3/1-48  disable
set port name       3/1-48
set port security   3/1-48  disable
set port broadcast  3/1-48  100%
set port membership 3/1-48  static
set cdp enable   3/1-48
set cdp interval 3/1-48 60
set spantree portfast    3/1-48 disable
set spantree portcost    3/1-48  100
set spantree portpri     3/1-48  32
!
```

Figure 5-4
(Cont.)

```
#module 4 : 1-port Route Switch
set module name    4
set port level     4/1  normal
set port trap      4/1  disable
set port name      4/1
set cdp enable  4/1
set cdp interval 4/1 60
set trunk 4/1  on isl 1-1005
set spantree portcost   4/1  5
set spantree portpri    4/1  32
set spantree portvlanpri 4/1  0
set spantree portvlancost 4/1  cost 4
!
#module 5 empty
!
#switch port analyzer
!set span 1 1/1 both inpkts disable
set span disable
!
#cam
set cam agingtime 1,1003,1005 300
end
Console> (enable)
```

Cisco environment, refer to the *Cisco TCP/IP Routing Professional Reference*. The `set snmp trap` command can also be used to add an entry to the trap receiver table. This is accomplished by adding the IP address and community string to be used when sending the trap to the machine at the IP address specified. The traps disabled in this section are defined as follows:

Module—When enabled will generate a trap for each module up and module down event.

Chassis—Generates a trap for each chassis-on and chassis-off event.

Bridge—Generates a trap when a new root bridge has been selected, or for any other topology change.

Repeater—Generates a trap for reset events.

VTP—Generates traps for Cisco Virtual Trunk Protocol events.

Auth—Generates a trap if an authentication failure event occurs.

Ippermit—Generates a trap if an IP permit denied event occurs.

VMPS—Generates a trap when a VMPS change event occurs.

Config—Generates a trap when the configuration of a switch has been changed.

Entity and STPX are not commonly used.

The `IP` Section. This section sets the sc0 and sl0 interfaces up and assigns them default IP addresses. The sc0 interface has 0.0.0.0 address, which means the switch will try to use BOOTP to obtain its IP configuration upon startup. This will manifest itself as the switch sending out 10 each of BOOTP and RARP broadcast requests for its IP configuration. If the sc0 interface has been given an IP address manually, it will not go through this BOOTP and RARP procedure. The sl0 IP address is left over from when we were examining that command earlier, even though a `clear config` command has been executed. The `set arp agingtime` is set to 1200 seconds. If the switch has not heard from a MAC address within the time set by this command, the MAC address will be removed from the switch's MAC address table.

In addition, this section enables IP redirect message processing, generation of destination host unreachable messages, and fragmentation of IP packets that are bridged between FDDI and Ethernet networks. This is necessary, as Ethernet and FDDI have incompatible MTUs (maximum transmission units). If fragmentation is disabled at any stage, packets coming from an FDDI segment that are longer than the Ethernet MTU will be dropped by the switch. The `set ip alias` command links names to IP addresses, like entries in a host's file. The entry here links the IP address 0.0.0.0 to the name default.

The VMPS Section. The `set vmps server` command is usually there to set the IP address of the VMPS server to be queried. The commands in this section identify the number of retries (3) that will be executed before a secondary VMPS server will be tried. The switch will check the primary VMPS every 5 minutes to see if it has come back up, and the `reconfirminterval` setting configures the switch to wait for the specified time before it points back to the primary. The `set vmps tftpserver` command tells the switch the location and filename of the VMPS database to download. By default, VMPS is disabled by the `set vmps state disable` command.

The dns Section. The Domain Name Service is disabled by default.

The tacacs+ Section. The tacacs+ command disables all the TACACS+ functionality. One of the main differences between TACACS and TACACS+ is that TACACS used UDP, whereas TACACS+ is based on TCP connections for information exchange. TACACS was discussed more fully in the *Cisco TCP/IP Routing Professional Reference.* The default TACACS+ setup here allows three tries to log in to the TACACS+ server, disables the ability to direct requests to multiple TACACS+ servers, and requires a TACACS+ server to respond within 5 seconds. The `set authentication` command has several options. TACACS+ is used to determine the access rights of users trying to gain access to the switch; it references a central database, thus simplifying management of multiple devices. The `login tacacs disable` command disables TACACS+ from operation, whereas the `login local enable` entry uses the local password to authenticate access permission to the switch.

The `bridge` Section. This section sets the translation types used when translating packets between the different network types listed. The `set bridge ipx snaptoether 8023raw` command sets the default method for translating IPX FDDI SNAP frames to Ethernet frames as the Novell 802.3 raw format. The remaining entries specify that 802.3 and 802.3 raw frames on FDDI will be translated into 802.3 and SNAP frames on Ethernet, respectively.

The `spantree` Section. This section sets the default operation of the Spanning Tree Protocol. Here, Uplink Fast and Backbone Fast are disabled, and spanning tree itself is enabled for the default VLANs 1 for Ethernet and 1003/1005 for token ring. Backbone Fast is a relatively new feature that speeds up the detection of link failures under certain conditions. Enabling Backbone Fast allows a blocked port to move immediately into listening mode after a link failure occurs. Without this enabled, the port needs to wait for the maximum age time to expire. The rest of the settings are as follows:

`set spantree hello 2 1`—Sets the time between hello packets to 2 seconds for VLAN 1.

`set spantree maxage 20 1`—Sets the amount of time the bridge will hold information learned via the Spanning Tree Protocol to 20 seconds for VLAN 1.

`set spantree priority 32768 1`—Sets the default spanning tree priority for VLAN 1; this is the value that is used to select the root bridge for each instance of the spanning tree.

`set spantree fwddelay 15 1003`—Sets the bridge forward delay for spanning tree packets to 15 seconds for VLAN 1003.

`set spantree portstate to auto`—Lets the port follow the previously discussed five states, rather than force a particular state. To recap, the five states are blocking, listening, learning, forwarding, and disabled. The command `set spantree portstate 1003 auto 0` sets the portstate for VLAN 1003.

`set spantree portcost 1003 80`—Sets the cost associated with a port (or TR-CRF if operating in a token ring environment) to 80 for

VLAN 1003. The lower the cost, the more attractive the port seems in the spanning tree calculations that select routes through a bridged network. The number 80 relates to 16 Mbits/sec, as we are setting it for a token ring. As a contrast, 4 Mbit/sec is identified with cost 250, and 1 Gbit/sec has cost 4.

`set spantree portpri 1003 32`—Sets the spanning tree priority for a port or TR-CRF (in this case, TR-CRF 1003) to 32. The lower the value assigned, the higher priority that is associated with that TR-CRF.

`set spantree multicast-address 1005 ieee`—Sets this switch to use the IEEE rather than IBM registered multicast address and only applies to a Trbrf.

The `cgmp` Section. This section disables CGMP and CGMP leave processing. This is something we will want to revisit, as CGMP is one of the enablers that make multicast feasible in switched internetworks.

The `syslog` Section. This section enables the sending of system logging messages to the console and disables the sending of these messages to a syslog server. The rest of this section sets the logging severity level (0 through 7) for the various protocols that can generate system messages. The default keyword sets the level to that specified in the command for all sessions, not just the one currently running: 0 is system unstable, 1 is an alert that requires immediate action, 2 is a critical condition, 3 is an error condition, 4 is a warning, 5 is a normal bug condition, 6 is an informational message, and 7 are debugging messages.

The `ntp` Section. This section configures the Network Time Protocol operation of the switch. If you choose to enable the command `set ntp broadcastclient`, it assumes that some device such as a router will be regularly sending broadcasts that contain NTP information on the current network time. If you do enable NTP, it is reasonable to assume that there is some propagation delay for the broadcast packet to get from the NTP server to the switch. To account for this difference, the command `set broadcastdelay` can be used to compensate. By default, the configuration sets 3000 microseconds as the propagation delay. The next command, `set ntp client disable`, disables the switch as an NTP client. The difference between this and the `broadcastclient` mode is that the `broadcastclient` mode assumes the switch will receive NTP broadcasts; the `ntp client` mode configures the switch to make regular requests for time. The `set summertime` command makes automatic adjustments for the 1-hour clock change in spring and fall, based on the American dates for time changes.

The `drip` Section. This section sets secondary parameters for token ring operation. The `set tokenring distrib-crf` command can be used to enable distribution of CRF VLANs across the switch, which is infrequently used. The `set tokenring reduction` command has the effect of reducing broadcast storms that can occur in a token ring environment.

The `igmp` Section. This section disables IGMP processing by the switch. It is unlikely that the switch itself will want to join any multicast groups (currently, endstations are the ones that most commonly request IGMP groups membership); however, future features may warrant giving the switch the ability to join IGMP groups.

The next sections carry module-specific configuration and are obviously dependent on the modules installed in the switch. The first section here carries the configuration for the supervisor card. The first command, `set module name 1`, defines the number 1 as the supervisor card for the `session 1` command. All the subsequent configurations set the parameters for the two Fast Ethernet ports on the card. Essentially, these settings are identical to those made for the 48-port Ethernet module in slot 3.

All ports are set to membership of VLAN 1 by default, and the ports on the supervisor are no different. The `set port channel` commands are configured to have the two Ethernet interfaces operating independently, rather than in Fast EtherChannel mode:

`set port enable 1/1-2`—Enables both Fast Ethernet ports on the supervisor. These ports can be shut down with the `disable` option of this command.

`set port level 1/1-2 normal`—Sets the packets that travel through the specified ports on to the switching backplane to normal priority. There is an option to set the priority to high, which gives preference to those packets over normal-priority packets being sent to the backplane.

`set port duplex 1/1-2 half`—Sets the ports to half-duplex mode.

`set port trap 1/1-2 disable`—Disables the port from being able to send a link-up or link-down SNMP trap message should the port state change.

`set port name`—Does not associate any name with the port. This command can be used to make it easier to manage the switch. When using the `show port` command, it can be simpler to reference a name rather than a module and port number, particularly if the ports are named after the user for directly connected workstations, or are the name of a connected router or hub.

`set port security 1/1-2 disable`—Disables the use of port security (which, as previously discussed, restricts the MAC addresses that may use the port).

`set port broadcast 1/1-2 100%`—Allows broadcast or multicast to use potentially 100 percent of the available bandwidth on both these ports. This is the safest option to start with, as the configuration will not force the dropping of any packets when bandwidth is still available.

`set port membership 1/1-2 static`—Configures the ports to be statically assigned to a VLAN, rather than to dynamically take their VLAN membership from a VLAN Membership Policy Server.

`set cdp enable 1/1-2`—Enables the Cisco Discovery Protocol on both supervisor ports. This allows the switch to exchange configuration information with attached Cisco devices and can be a security concern in some installations.

`set cdp interval 1/1-2 60`—Sets the interval for the distribution of cdp updates to 60 seconds.

`set trunk 1/1 auto isl 1-1005`—Sets the port to become a trunk, if the Ethernet port it is connected to is configured as a trunk.

`set spantree portfast 1/1-2 disable`—Disables the port from moving straight into forwarding mode when the switch is powered up or from recalculating the spanning tree due to a link failure. As previously discussed, it is beneficial to enable this command for all ports that have directly connected workstations.

`set spantree portcost 1/1-2 19`—The STP algorithm selects the port with the lowest cost to become the port that forwards traffic during normal conditions (i.e., nonfault conditions). The higher the bandwidth of the link, the lower its cost (19 equates to a 100-Mbit/sec port).

`set spantree portpri 1/1-2 32`—Sets the bridge priority for both ports to 32. The highest priority that can be set is 0, and the lowest is 63. This value will be used when calculating which port will be used for forwarding packets in the spanning tree. This command sets the priority for all VLANs using the bridge.

`set spantree portvlanpri 1/2 0`—This is a more useful command, as we will see later, that can be used to direct different VLANs to prefer different ports on the one switch to get to the same destination; it is only available for trunk ports. Again, the priority itself can be between 0 and 63, with 0 being the highest.

`set spantree portvlancost 1/1 cost 18`—Sets the path cost for the specified port to 18 for the VLANs listed. Other VLANs will take the cost defined in the `set spantree portcost` command. As no VLAN is listed, VLAN 1 is assumed in this case.

The `module 3` Section. This section lists the same configuration options, but for the 48-port Ethernet module.

The `switch port analyzer` Section. This section disables the port monitor that is referred to as the *span* port on a 5K switch. This is similar to the `port monitor` command used on 2916XL switches. You may elect to monitor a port, a list of ports (provided they are on the same VLAN), or traffic for a complete VLAN, for transmit or receive, or for both directions. Clearly, you must define which port will be used to attach the LAN analyzer to and the traffic it will monitor. For example, the command `set span 3/1-5 3/6` will send both transmitted and received packets from ports 3/1 through 3/5 to port 3/6.

The `cam` Section. This section sets the aging time for the default VLANs 1, 1003, and 1005 to 300 seconds, which means MAC addresses not heard from within 5 minutes are deleted from the CAM table. Setting the value to 0 disables aging. This command may also be used to manually add entries to the CAM table. The most useful part of this is to define the MAC address for multicasts, so that they are forwarded to the relevant ports, rather than to all ports. An example of this configuration is `set cam permanent 01-40-0c-12-34-ff 3/1-15`, which adds a permanent entry to the CAM table for the first 15 ports on module 3, meaning that multicast packets sent to that MAC address will be sent out the specified ports.

This rather lengthy discussion completes the description of the default configuration. As we progress through the chapter, we'll only illustrate the changes made to this default, rather than display the complete configuration again.

Ethernet Module Configuration

With a 48-port Ethernet module installed in the switch, along with a default configuration, we have in effect created a single VLAN, with all 48 ports as members of VLAN 1. Although this configuration will allow us to use the switch, getting a Catalyst 5K just for this level of functionality is a very expensive proposition. Clearly, if we have gone to the expense of such a full-featured switch, we will want to expand upon this configuration. The first step in doing so is to set up multiple VLANs and configure routing between them. In this section, we'll look at the Route Switch Module (RSM) configurations necessary to support inter-VLAN routing; however, we will cover RSM operation in much more depth later on in its own section.

Creating Multiple VLANs

Merely creating multiple VLANs by hand is a simple task and is executed by the `set vlan` command. To illustrate, we'll create two additional VLANs—VLAN 2 and VLAN 3—and assign some ports to each. Note that with the 5K we are actually adding VLANs to the configuration with these commands. With the 2916XL range, all the VLANs were already in existence in the configuration; we merely added ports to the VLANs as needed. This can be verified by looking at the output of the `show vlan` command both before and after a new VLAN is created. The `show vlan` command is as follows for the default configuration:

```
Console> (enable) sho vlan
VLAN  Name                        Status    IfIndex    Mod/Ports, Vlans
----  ------------------------    ------    -------   -------------------
1     default                     active     5        1/1-2
                                                      3/1-48
1002  fddi-default                active     6
1003  token-ring-default          active     9
1004  fddinet-default             active     7
1005  trnet-default               active     8
```

There are some further parts to the display generated by this command, but this is all we are concerned with at the moment. This display shows the default VLANs that are created, their name, their status, their SNMP ifIndex, and the module and numbers of the ports associated with that VLAN.

There are many options to the `set vlan` command. The most common are as follows:

- VLAN number and VLAN name.
- VLAN type. The default is Ethernet, but it can be FDDI, token ring, or FDDI/token ring net (the BRF as opposed to the CRF function).
- The MTU for the VLAN.
- A SAID used for each FDDI VLAN.
- The FDDI and token ring number.
- A token ring bridge identification number.
- If source routing, a parent ring number.

Most of these are optional; the simplest example is just defining a VLAN number and the ports that will be in that VLAN. Here, however, is the first real difference in 5K configuration compared to what we did for the 2916XL: To use the `set vlan` command, the switch must either be in VTP transparent mode, or a VTP domain name must be set.

We'll cover VTP in more depth in the next section. For now we'll set the switch to VTP transparent and add the first of the two VLANs discussed:

```
Console> (enable) set vtp mode transparent
VTP domain modified
```

Now we can create the new VLAN and add ports to it.

```
Console> (enable) set vlan 2 3/1-10
Vlan 2 configuration successful
VLAN 2 modified.
VLAN 1 modified.
VLAN Mod/Ports
---- ------------------------
2 3/1-10
```

Now we can have a look at the new output of the `show vlan` command:

```
Console> (enable) sho vlan
VLAN Name                         Status    IfIndex Mod/Ports, Vlans
---- ---------------------------- ------    ------- ----------------
1    default                      active     5      1/1-2
                                                    3/11-48
2    VLAN0002                     active     59     3/1-10
1002 fddi-default                 active     6
1003 token-ring-default           active     9
1004 fddinet-default              active     7
1005 trnet-default                active     8
```

Deleting a VLAN from the configuration can be accomplished as follows:

```
Console> (enable) clear vlan 10
This command will deactivate all ports on vlan 10
in the entire management domain
Do you want to continue(y/n) [n]? y
Vlan 10 deleted
```

It is worth noting that we do not have to write these configuration commands to nonvolatile memory for the switch to retain them. As soon as any `set` command is entered, it is written to memory and remains in the configuration for when the switch boots up next time. This is, of course, in contrast to routers and the 2916XL range, which have a startup and running configuration, requiring the `wrt` command to write the running configuration to startup configuration for commands to be retained by the switch after the next boot sequence.

As we can see, the switch has designated the name VLAN0002 to the newly created VLAN, since we had not specified a name in the command. The ports that were in VLAN 1 have now been assigned to VLAN 2, and the switch tells us that VLANs 1 and 2 have been modified, which is confirmed by the `show vlan` command.

So far, we have not added any functionality that could not be satisfied by the 2916XL switch at far lower cost. The first feature that we will examine that starts to justify the 5K price tag is the ability to route packets between these VLANs internally, without recourse to an external routing device. There is actually quite a lot to understand about the RSM, but for this simple case, we'll start with just setting up a couple of VLANs and configure the RSM to route between them. To do this, we'll configure VLAN 10 to be on port 3/20 and VLAN 4 to be on port 3/21 as follows:

```
Console> (enable) set port enable 3/20
Port 3/20 enabled.
Console> (enable) set vlan 10 3/20
Vlan 10 configuration successful
VLAN 10 modified.
VLAN 1 modified.
VLAN Mod/Ports
10 3/20
Console> (enable) set port enable 3/21
Port 3/21 enabled.
Console> (enable) set vlan 11 3/21
Vlan 11 configuration successful
VLAN 11 modified.
VLAN 1 modified.
VLAN Mod/Ports
11 3/21
```

We next use the `session` command to log in to the RSM and configure an IP address subnet to be associated with each VLAN, as follows:

```
Console> (enable) session 4
Router>en
Router#conf t
Router(config)#interface vlan 10
Router(config-if)# ip address 172.8.5.1 255.255.255.0
Router(config-if)#no shut
Router(config-if)#interface vlan 11
Router(config-if)#ip address 172.8.6.1 255.255.255.0
Router(config-if)#no shut
```

At this point, if there is no device connected to ports 3/20 or 3/21, the routing table of the RSM will not contain the subnets 172.8.5.0 and 172.8.6.0. As soon as a device is connected and the line protocol on that port comes up, the subnet is added to the routing table, as follows:

```
Router>sho ip rout
Gateway of last resort is not set
C     127.0.0.0/8 is directly connected, Vlan0
      172.8.0.0/24 is subnetted, 1 subnets
C        172.8.5.0 is directly connected, Vlan10
C        172.8.6.0 is directly connected, Vlan11
```

We have now enabled the 5K to route packets between different VLANs internally, without having to send the packet to an external router. We'll now go on to look at VTP and VLAN configuration in more depth.

VTP and VLAN Configuration

VTP, the VLAN Trunking Protocol, is like a layer 2 equivalent of a layer 3 routing protocol such as IGRP. What VTP enables you to do is make central changes to VLAN configurations and have them distributed throughout the network via VTP updates. This is a useful feature and simplifies the job of maintaining VLAN consistency throughout the network. The only issue to be concerned with is which version of VTP to use, as all devices on the network must use the same version. There is currently a version 1 and version 2. If you are using token ring, you must select version 2. The only reason not to select version 2 is if you have a device in the network that cannot support it.

In the previous section we configured the switch for VTP transparent mode, which is effectively disabling VTP. When we come to enable VTP, we must select a VTP domain within which the VTP advertisements are valid. The VTP domain is at times referred to as a *VTP management domain*. This is a similar concept to the autonomous system number that needed to be specified when enabling IGRP as a routing protocol on a collection of routers.

Given that we have now chosen to use VTP, the first choice is to configure the switch as a VTP server or client. Both clients and servers can update their configuration based on the VTP advertisements they receive on their trunk links; however, a server is needed to add, delete, or change an existing VLAN in a domain. This is an important point. VTP advertisements do not get sent out all interfaces like a routing protocol or Spanning Tree Protocol; the VTP advertisements are restricted to the trunk links and therefore have less of an impact on the network bandwidth that is available to endstations.

As a general note, it is best to create the VTP domain first, then create the VLANs within that domain. Currently, my preference is to configure all switches within a domain as servers. The recommendation from Cisco on this has changed from one software release to another. Making all switches servers does mean that each switch will need its own VTP configuration on bootup, but there have been instances where configuring switches as VTP clients has led to the client switches losing their configuration and needing manual intervention to make them part of the network again.

So let's review the first steps in creating a VTP domain. Assuming all switches in the network are capable of supporting VTP version 2, we need to tell the switch to use this version, or it will default to version 1. Next, we will set the VTP domain name, enable VTP pruning to reduce unnecessary use of bandwidth, and set a password for the VTP domain. VTP pruning is useful in that it stops a switch from flooding a broadcast packet out ports that are not on the VLAN on which the broadcast packet originated. By default a switch will not send a broadcast packet out a port that is not on the same VLAN as the VLAN originating the broadcast; that is the concept of a broadcast domain. However, when trunks are used to connect switches, the trunk links will propagate broadcasts on all trunks unless VTP pruning is enabled.

```
Console> (enable) set vtp v2 enable
This command will enable the version 2 function in the entire manage-
  ment domain. All devices in the management domain should be version2-
  capable before enabling. Do you want to continue (y/n) [n]? y
VTP domain test_net modified
Console> (enable) set vtp domain test_net
VTP domain test_net modified
Console> (enable) set vtp mode server
VTP domain test_net modified
```

```
Console> (enable) set vtp pruning enable
This command will enable the pruning function in the entire management
  domain. All devices in the management domain should be pruning-capa-
  ble before enabling. Do you want to continue (y/n) [n]? y
VTP domain test_net modified
Console> (enable) set vtp passwd manhattan
Generating MD5 secret for the password ....
VTP domain test_net modified
```

The `password` command does not require you to manually enter a password to change the VTP or VLAN configuration on a server switch; rather, it requires incoming VTP packets to supply the correct password before the VTP updates are accepted. Clearly, this requires all switches in the one domain to use the same password. The password is sent in outgoing VTP packets and checked against the local configuration for incoming packets. The VTP configuration is verified by the command and display shown here:

```
Console> (enable) sho vtp domain
Domain Name                 Domain Index VTP Version Local Mode Password
-----------------------     ------------ --- ------- ---------- --------
test_net                    1             2          server configured
Vlan-count Max-vlan-storage Config Revision Notifications
---------- ---------------- --------------- -------------
10         1023              4              disabled
Last Updater     V2 Mode  Pruning  PruneEligible on Vlans
--------------   -------  -------  ----------------------
200.200.25.120   enabled  enabled  2-1000
```

Once VTP is configured as illustrated, you can use the `show vtp statistics` command to see how many advertisements have been sent, what trunks are configured, and how many advertisements have been received. This display keeps a separate count of the MD5 errors generated by incoming packets with an incorrect password. As a point of interest, VTP packets are sent to a multicast address to neighboring devices only. These multicasts go out over all trunks, whether they be configured as ISL, 802.1Q, 802.10, or LANE.

The periodic VTP multicasts include the following information for each VLAN:

- VLAN ID for ISL and 802.10 LANs
- 802.10 SAID values for FDDI LANs
- Emulated LAN names for LANE LANs
- MTU for the LAN
- Frame format of the LAN

VTP is a useful feature and should be part of any large switched LAN configuration.

Creating VLAN Trunks

Having discussed VTP and its ability to use trunk links to disseminate VLAN information throughout a switched network, let's look at how to create a trunk. A *trunk* is a point-to-point link between a switch port and another switch or router that is capable of carrying traffic belonging to multiple VLANs. The encapsulation on these trunk links is either ISL—the Cisco proprietary method for Fast Ethernet trunks—the industry standard 802.1Q, 802.10 for FDDI rings, or LANE for ATM trunks.

To create a VLAN trunk, we use the `set trunk` command. Having said that ISL is used on point-to-point links, there is actually a Dynamic ISL link negotiation protocol that is active on all ports. The job of this protocol is to decide whether the port will become a trunk, even if it is not expressly configured to be one. The arguments that follow the `set trunk` command control how the port will behave during the link negotiation procedure. The arguments and their effect are as follows:

`set trunk 1/1 on`—Puts a port permanently into trunking mode and effectively bypasses the negotiation procedure. The port becomes a trunk even if the port that it is connected to cannot become one. If this command is executed on an existing link, the port will try to renegotiate the link as a trunk with the device it is connected to.

`set trunk 1/1 off`—If executed on an existing trunk, will force a negotiation to nontrunk operation. This command will also stop a port that is newly brought into service from becoming a trunk.

`set trunk 1/1 desirable`—Forces the port to try to become a trunk, which it will successfully do if it is connected to a port configured for on, desirable, or auto mode.

`set trunk 1/1 auto`—Is the default setting for all ports and makes the port a trunk if the port it is connected to is configured for on or desirable mode.

`set trunk 1/1 nonegotiate`—Configures the port as a trunk but disables its ability to negotiate with a connected port by preventing it from sending out DISL packets.

There are a number of caveats to the use of these commands:

- All ISL ports default to auto.
- Off is the default setting for FDDI ports.
- Desirable and auto can only be used on ISL encapsulated ports.

This negotiation process can deliver a certain amount of flexibility when you are putting together a network. It simplifies configuration, as you only need to really configure one end of a trunk link to become a port. However, currently not all devices handle DISL packet forwarding correctly, and if you have any difficulty with links becoming trunks that you do not expect, or with trunk links configuring themselves to be non-trunks, it is best to forget the DISL process altogether. The recommendation currently is to set ports to `off` for all ports not being used as trunks and use `nonegotiate` when manually setting trunks to `on`.

Let's look at some configuration examples on our Ethernet ports for ISL and 802.1Q encapsulation. Note that for an Ethernet port to become a trunk, it must be a Fast Ethernet port. Therefore, the 48 ports on the module in slot 3 cannot be used, and we have to configure trunking for the Ethernet ports on the supervisor. In this example, we'll first configure the Ethernet port 1/1 to be an ISL trunk, then an 802.1Q trunk.

Clearly, for this to work we need to have two Fast Ethernet ports connected to each other. With the hardware discussed so far, the only two ports that fit this description are the two ports on the supervisor. We can connect these two ports with a crossover RJ-45 connector and start to experiment with settings. First, let's see the output of the `show trunk` command before we execute any trunk commands:

```
Console> (enable) sho trunk
Port      Mode         Encapsulation  Status        Native vlan
-------  -----------  -------------  ------------  ---------------
4/1       on           isl            trunking      1
Port      Vlans allowed on trunk
-------  ------------------------------------------------------
4/1       1-1005
Port      Vlans allowed and active in management domain
-------  ------------------------------------------------------
4/1
Port      Vlans in spanning tree forwarding state and not pruned
-------  ------------------------------------------------------
4/1
```

This is curious, since module 4 is the RSM, which has no Ethernet connector, only console and auxiliary ports. This relates to the channels that exist in the RSM and will be covered in the "RSM Basics" section later in the chapter. We'll ignore this trunk port in subsequent displays. We will now configure the port 1/1 to be a trunk for all VLANs:

```
Console> (enable) set trunk 1/1 on
Port(s) 1/1 trunk mode set to on.
```

We can view the effect this command has had on the trunk configuration of the switch by the usual `show trunk` command as follows:

```
Console> (enable) sho trunk
Port     Mode        Encapsulation Status       Native vlan
-------- ----------- ------------- ------------ ---------------
1/1      on          isl           trunking     1
1/2      auto        isl           trunking     1
Port     Vlans allowed on trunk
-------- -------------------------------------------------------
1/1      1-1005
1/2      1-1005
Port     Vlans allowed and active in management domain
-------- -------------------------------------------------------
1/1      1-3,5,11,1003,1005
1/2      1-3,5,11,1003,1005
Port     Vlans in spanning tree forwarding state and not pruned
-------- -------------------------------------------------------
1/1      1-3,5,11,1003,1005
1/2       1005
```

So, by setting port 1/1 to force a renegotiation of the trunk status, port 1/2 became a trunk, since it was in the default auto mode. If we wish to look at enabling this trunk for some of the VLANs, we can do that also. First, we clear the trunk configuration by the `clear trunk` command and then enable port 1/1 to be a trunk for VLANs 1 and 5 only, as follows:

```
Console> (enable) clear trunk 1/1 2-1005
Removing Vlan(s) 2-1005 from allowed list.
Port 1/1 allowed vlans modified to 1.
```

Because the default configuration allows all VLANs through, we have to disable all the VLANs we do not want to use the trunk first, then allow the ones we do:

```
Console> (enable) set trunk 1/1 on 5
Adding vlans 5 to allowed list.
Port(s) 1/1 allowed vlans modified to 1,5.
Port(s) 1/1 trunk mode set to on.
```

We can verify the configuration as follows:

```
Console> (enable) sho trunk
Port     Mode        Encapsulation Status       Native vlan
-------- ----------- ------------- ------------ -----------
1/1      on          isl           trunking     1
1/2      auto        isl           trunking     1
```

```
Port     Vlans allowed on trunk
-------- --------------------------------------------------
1/1      1,5
1/2      1-1005
```

As you can see, this will only allow VLANs 1 and 5 through port 1/1.

Now let's look at doing the same thing, but this time using the 802.1Q encapsulation. With 802.1Q we cannot use auto or desirable, so must configure both of the connected ports to be on. Unfortunately, 802.1Q encapsulation is not supported on the Supervisor II module. We would have to use a dedicated Fast Ethernet module for this. If a Fast Ethernet module that supports 802.1Q encapsulation is installed in slot 5, we could configure the first port to use 802.1Q encapsulation for VLANs 2 and 3 as follows:

```
Console (enable) set trunk 5/1 nonegotiate 2,3 dot1q
Port(s) 5/1 trunk mode set to nonegotiate
Port(s) 5/1 trunk type set to dot1q
```

The key differences here are that we use `nonegotiate` in preference to `on`, as 802.1Q does not support the DISL negotiation procedure, and we specify the `dot1q` keyword for the 802.1Q encapsulation. The `show trunk` command now shows an output similar to the following:

```
Console> (enable) sho trunk
Port     Mode        Encapsulation  Status       Native vlan
-------- ----------- -------------  -----------  ----------
1/1      nonegotiate     dot1q      trunking     1
Port       Vlans allowed on trunk
--------   -----------------------
1/1        1-3
```

There are a couple of commands to become familiar with prior to looking further into customizing the configuration. These two useful commands are `show` commands, namely `show spantree` and `show vlan`. Let's first look at the interesting parts of the `show spantree` command:

```
Console> (enable) sho spant
VLAN 1
Spanning tree enabled
Spanning tree type              ieee
Designated Root                 00-90-d9-17-ac-00
Designated Root Priority       32768
Designated Root Cost            0
Designated Root Port            1/0
Root Max Age    20 sec     Hello Time 2  sec  Forward Delay 15 sec
Bridge ID MAC ADDR              00-90-d9-17-ac-00
```

```
Bridge ID Priority          32768
Bridge Max Age 20 sec     Hello Time 2  sec  Forward Delay 15 sec
Port      Vlan Port-State  Cost  Priority Fast-Start Group-Method
--------- ---- ---------- ----  -------- ---------- ------------
1/1       1    forwarding 19          32 disabled
1/2       1    blocking   19          32 disabled
```

This is a fairly trivial display considering that we have just the one switch in the network at the moment, but it does give us the opportunity to examine the display output before we expand upon the configuration. Without specifying the VLAN number, the display will default to VLAN 1. Issuing the command `show spant 3` will show the same information for VLAN 3, which is pretty similar to that for VLAN 1. The difference is that VLAN 3 will use a different bridge MAC ID address from the pool of MAC addresses available to the switch. For each instance of spanning tree running (one per VLAN), a different MAC address is necessary for use in ties for root bridge calculations.

From this display we can see the bridge priority set at the usual 32768, which we can lower to make this switch more attractive as the root bridge to spanning tree. We can also see the state of the ports in VLAN 1 and whether they are in the spanning tree forwarding or blocking state. The final interesting piece of information is to know which port on the switch is designated as the root port (i.e., the one used to send packets back to the root bridge of the spanning tree). Interestingly, the port is shown as 1/0, which does not exist. This is displayed because this switch is the root bridge for VLAN 1, so no port will be used to send packets to the root bridge in the spanning tree. This value is only of interest on switches that are not the root bridge.

The other command is the `show vlan` command, which carries information for all the VLANs configured. This command is most useful for seeing which ports are assigned to a given VLAN. The command output illustrated below has the option of several arguments that can be added after the `show vlan` keywords, the most useful of which are as follows:

- A number to restrict the output to just the VLAN specified
- The word `trunk` to restrict the display to trunk ports
- The word `notrunk` to restrict the ports that are not trunks

The display itself is quite straightforward, listing the VLAN, its status as active or suspended, and the VLAN's port membership. As an example, VLAN 3 can be suspended for whatever reason by the `set vlan 3 state suspend` command:

```
Console> (enable) sho vlan
VLAN Name                  Status    IfIndex Mod/Ports, Vlans
---- --------------------- ------    ------- ----------------------
1    default               active    5       3/11-19,3/22-44,3/47-48
2    VLAN0002              active    59      3/1-10
3    VLAN0003              active    62      3/45
5    VLAN0005              active    63      3/46
11   VLAN0011              active    61      3/21
1002 fddi-default          active    6
1003 trcrf-default         active    9
1004 fddinet-default       active    7
1005 trbrf-default         active    8       1003
```

That really covers the basics of VLAN and VLAN configuration, along with VTP and trunk configuration. The last thing we will look at prior to examining the customization of a switch configuration is the setup of the VLAN Membership Policy Server.

VMPS on Catalyst 5K Switches

The VLAN Membership Policy Server (VMPS) is a facility that allows you to configure the VLAN membership of a port based on the MAC address of the device that connects to it. In theory, if you set up the membership of all the MAC addresses on a VMPS to belong to the required VLANs, you could then move the attached workstations from port to port, and the VLAN membership would move with the workstation. This does simplify office moves considerably; you do not have to change port membership when a user moves his or her PC from one location to another (implying connection to a different switch port).

In reality, though, you never reach the nirvana of no administration in a LAN environment. What happens when a NIC fails in a PC? You have to put a new one in, which means manual editing of the VMPS configuration to take into account the new MAC address. Whether you prefer to administer an ASCII file on a VMPS or edit port VLAN memberships to accommodate moves and NIC failures is up to you. Of course, the final consideration is that if your VMPS is not available and the switch is rebooted (which could happen after a power spike), your whole LAN is down.

If you decide to go the VMPS route, you need to complete the following:

- Generate an ASCII file of MAC address-to-VLAN membership, which can be done by using the `show cam` command from a PC logged in to the switch and, in Windows, cutting and pasting to Notepad. This will become the VMPS configuration file.

- Store this ASCII file on a TFTP server on the network.
- Enable VMPS on the switch.
- Configure the switch with the IP address of the TFTP server that will hold the VMPS ASCII configuration file.

So if we look at a typical `show cam` display, we see something like the following:

```
Console> (enable) sho cam dyn 1
* = Static + = Permanent # = System R = Router X = Port Security
VLAN Dest MAC/Route Des  Destination Ports or VCs / [Protocol Type]
---- -----------------  ----------------------------------------
1     00-00-c0-a4-ac-dc   3/38 [ALL]
1     00-aa-00-c2-69-27   3/38 [ALL]
Total Matching CAM Entries Displayed = 2
```

This shows two MAC addresses (implying this port is attached to a hub or switch) for port 3/38 as the only dynamic entries in the CAM table for VLAN 1. When using the `show cam` command, it is necessary to either specify `dynamic`, `static`, `permanent`, or `system` MAC addresses. `dynamic` is typically the appropriate selection with a newly installed switch using the default configuration. With the default configuration, the switch dynamically learns MAC addresses based on the source MAC address in packets that travel through the switch. With this configuration, all ports are in VLAN 1, so the 1 specified in our example above does not make any difference to the display. When other VLANs are specified, using the number of the VLAN at the end of the `show cam dynamic` command shows the MAC addresses for the VLAN named.

The construction of this ASCII VMPS configuration file is not trivial; it must contain a lot of very specific information, including the following:

- The VMPS domain name
- MAC address-to-VLAN name association
- Identification of ports in specific port groups
- VLAN grouping information
- VLAN port policies

The VMPS domain name is the same as the VTP domain name being used in the switch. The MAC address-to-VLAN association uses names, which presumes that each VLAN created with the `set vlan` command has been given a name (which is an optional configuration). The port group, VLAN group, and VLAN policies settings are not trivial. The best way to understand these settings is to first look at the VLAN port policies as defined in the vmps-port-policies section in the following ASCII file example:

```
Vmps domain test
Vmps mode open
Vmps-mac-addrs
       Address 00c0.1111.2222 vlan-name new
       Address 00c0.1111.2223 vlan-name old
vmps-port-group users
       device 172.8.6.4 port 3/1
       device 172.8.6.5 port 3/2
vmps-vlan-group bosses
       vlan-name managers
       vlan-name supervisors
vmps-port-policies vlan-name new
       device 172.8.6.6 port 3/3
       port-group "users"
```

The vmps-port-policies entry identifies the ports that are associated with the VLAN in question. In this example, we are saying that for the VLAN known as new, we are assigning port 3/3 and the ports defined in the port group users as the ones available for this VLAN. By creating a VLAN group known as bosses, we can put a port-policy entry for bosses as if it were a single VLAN and list a set of ports (or port groups) that can be used by the list of VLANs associated with that VLAN group bosses.

In this file, each entry must begin on a new line, which is understandable. The annoying thing is that port ranges are not allowed, so if you want to make 50 ports available to a given VLAN, you must make 50 individual entries in the ASCII file. I am not a great fan of VMPS, as the setup is not trivial, and depending on the VMPS server, it may add another point of failure for the network. Additionally, each time a new PC is added to the network, you have to download a new ASCII configuration file to the switch with the new MAC address configured. My preference when adding a new user is to just configure his or her port to the VLAN membership required and be done with it. As far as moves are concerned, again I prefer to change the port configuration as users move from one port to another, so that they keep the same VLAN membership on the new port. However, if VMPS is what you want to do, let's look at the configuration steps necessary once a suitable ASCII file has been loaded on your TFTP server.

First, tell the switch the IP address of the VMPS and enable VMPS as follows:

```
Console> (enable) set vmps tftpserver 200.200.25.150
IP address of the TFTP server set to 200.200.25.150
```

```
VMPS configuration filename set to vmps-config-database.1
Console> (enable) set vmps state enable
Vlan Membership Policy Server enable is in progress.
```

As you can see, because we did not specify the name of the VMPS ASCII file, the switch assumes the name `vmps-config-database.1`. The reason that we have the message telling us that the VMPS enable is in progress is that prior to this command being entered, VMPS was disabled, as it is by default. The switch is now trying to initiate a download from the VMPS IP address specified. Once that download is complete, the VMPS state is set to `active`. This raises a good point. If you ever change the ASCII configuration file, you will want to initiate a download of the new information, which is accomplished with the `download vmps` command.

The final and most important configuration to make is to set each port to dynamic VLAN membership as follows:

```
Console> (enable) set port membership 3/30-35 dynamic
```

Clearly, the ports chosen for dynamic membership can be specified individually, by comma separation, or as a range, by using a hyphen as illustrated above. Setting a port to `dynamic` does have some implications for other processes within the switch; for example, spanning tree sets dynamic ports to `portfast`, which is opposite from the normal default. Also, static ports that are currently configured to be a trunk need to have trunking turned off before they can become dynamic.

Customizing the 5K Ethernet Configuration

In this section, we'll make the Catalyst a little more friendly to use, connect two of them together, and expand the functionality by prioritizing VLAN traffic across multiple trunks. Given that you will have named the switch something like `central`, we can customize the individual ports as follows:

```
console> (enable) set system name central
System name set.
console> (enable) set prompt central>
```

Under normal conditions, if you are using Supervisor software 4.1 or later, issuing the `set system name` prompt will change the prompt to the name specified also. The only time that does not occur is if there is a separate set prompt command, which happens to have been the case here. We know this is the case, since the prompt did not change as a result of the set system name command, forcing us to set the prompt manually.

The task that provides possibly the greatest payback in customizing a Catalyst port is to name each port. This may seem onerous, but it will cut down a lot of time spent when troubleshooting in a highly pressured situation. I find it very helpful to name the port according to the user if it is a dedicated port, according to the connected switch name if the port is a trunk, or to use the name of a connected hub. The following is an example of naming a port after the user, in this case, user ChrisL.

```
Console> (enable) set port name 3/1 ChrisL
Port 3/1 name set.
```

It is not possible to use this name in the show commands to access a port; it is not like naming a host in a host file and being able to telnet to it. If you want to be able to name a host and telnet to that name, use the set ip alias as follows:

```
central> (enable) set ip alias chris 200.200.25.13
IP alias added.
central> (enable) ping chris
chris is alive
```

(Of course, setting an alias to Elvis produces a response that gives the rock and roll faithful some hope.)

The port name command is used to provide some online documentation to your switch's configuration. Suppose, for example, a group of users have reported problems and you are in a troubleshooting mode. Using the show port command is a good first step to identifying what might be the problem:

```
Console> (enable) sho port
Port  Name        Status     Vlan      Level   Duplex Speed Type
----- ----------- ---------- --------- ------- ------ --------------
1/1               notconnect 1         normal   half    100 100BaseTX
1/2               notconnect 1         normal   half    100 100BaseTX
3/1   ChrisL      connected  2         normal   half     10 10BaseT
T3/2              notconnect 2         normal   half     10 10BaseT
```

Here, we see user ChrisL is on port 3/1. If other users had reported problems and we saw in this display that they were all on the same module, it would be a powerful piece of troubleshooting information. From here, you have online documentation that tells you who is connected to which port. You can now use more specific show commands, as follows:

```
Console> (enable) sho port 3/1
Port  Name           Status     Vlan       Level  Duplex Speed Type
----- -------------- ---------- ---------- ------ ------ ----- ------
3/1   ChrisL         connected  2          normal   half    10 10BaseT
Port  Security Secure-Src-Addr Last-Src-Addr Shutdown Trap IfIndex
----- -------- ---------------------------------------------------------
3/1   disabled                                No     disabled 10
Port     Broadcast-Limit Broadcast-Drop
-----    --------------- --------------
3/1                    -              0
```

This display tells us basic troubleshooting information like VLAN membership, duplex and speed type, and the level of broadcast drops. To look at the port statistics in a bit more detail, use the following command:

```
Console> (enable) sho port counters 3/1
Port  Align-Err  FCS-Err    Xmit-Err   Rcv-Err    UnderSize
----  ---------  ---------- ---------- ---------- ---------
3/1           0          0          0          0          0
Port SingleCol MultiColl LateColl ExcessCol CarriSen  Runts Giants
---- --------- --------- -------- --------- --------  ----- ------
3/1      0          0          0         0         0      0      0
Last-Time-Cleared
-------------------------
Sun Jan 10 1999, 08:05:05
```

This gives us more information on the errors, if any.

There is, however, one piece of information that is lacking: the amount of traffic going through the port (as is shown on a router interface). Currently, the best you can do is assume that the bandwidth used is within limits if there are no errors reported on these displays. You can of course, use the `show mac` command to see the number of octets inbound and outbound on the port, as shown here:

```
central> (enable) sho mac 3/1
Port     Rcv-Unicast          Rcv-Multicast        Rcv-Broadcast
-------- -------------------- -------------------- ----------------
3/1             276                 5285              119345
Port     Xmit-Unicast         Xmit-Multicast       Xmit-Broadcast
-------- -------------------- -------------------- ----------------
3/1               0                  157                   0
Port     Rcv-Octet            Xmit-Octet
-------- -------------------- --------------------
3/1         20832204             20832204
```

This can be turned into a bandwidth utilization figure by timing the number of octets over a given period, say, 1 minute, and generating a bits-per-second figure manually. However, it is a long way short of giving you the throughput in a display.

The next piece of customization is to set chosen ports to high priority, meaning that those ports set on normal priority only get backplane service when all the high-priority ports have already been serviced. Choosing which ports to give high priority to is not always straightforward. It is tempting to give high priority to server ports, and in many ways this makes sense; however, it does not add anything to the performance for any specific workstation. As the process of packets going on to the backplane is not of the round-robin type (i.e., any port can send a packet to the backplane when it needs to, and the port is not given an opportunity to transmit even if it does not have packets to transmit), the value of this level of priority is debatable. This priority setting is most valuable if you have one workstation that must have the best performance available, or a server that is sending out broadcast media—like stock price or news information—or some type of multimedia traffic.

I recommend that, as with many things in switch configuration, you view it as more of an art than science and experiment with different settings on your network. Obviously, though, the more ports you assign to high priority, the less effect this setting has.

The other two basic configuration settings you may wish to make for some ports are forcing the duplex and speed settings for individual ports using the `set port duplex` and `set port speed` commands. This is only worth doing if you suspect the negotiation process between the port and its attached device is not obtaining the optimal setting for your network.

Now that we have the basics, let's connect two Catalyst 5000 switches together via trunks, then customize how the VLANs that exist within those switches communicate via the trunks. The physical connections we are establishing are illustrated in Figure 5-5. In this configuration, there are three VLANs defined on each switch: `mgrs` for the managers, `sups` for the supervisors, and `engrs` for the engineers. In practice, you will create these VLANs, with each VLAN name using the same VLAN number on both Catalysts, assign the necessary ports to the VLANs, and make the following configurations for individually connected workstations:

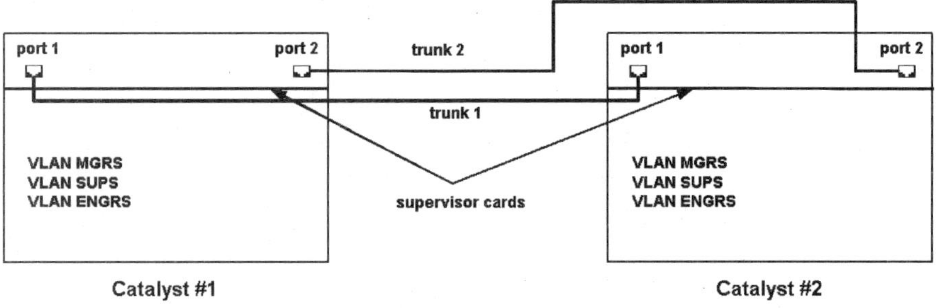

Figure 5-5 Interconnecting two Catalysts via trunk on the supervisor cards.

- Set the STP port state to `forwarding` using the `set spantree portfast` command.
- Set to full duplex (assuming the attached NICs or devices support that mode), using the command `set port duplex full`.
- Set server connections to high priority.
- Create VLAN RSM interfaces. Each VLAN is using its own subnet, and if the RSM will route between them, VLAN interfaces on the RSM must be created, with IP addresses within the VLAN subnet range. Clearly, workstations will use the value of the RSM VLAN interface IP address as its default gateway.

So, using the supervisor to connect these two catalysts, we connect port 1/1 on Cat 1 to port 1/1 on Cat 2, also port 1/2 on Cat 1 to port 1/2 on Cat 2. Before we go any further into the configuration of these machines, it is worth taking a moment to explore the behavior of the small network we have generated by these connections. Note that the interswitch connections need to be via crossover cables, and for this demonstration, we have issued the commands `set trunk 1/1 on` and `set trunk 1/2 on`.

If we issue the `ping` command from Cat 1 to an address on Cat 2, which trunk will the ping packet travel over? With routers, we could establish multiple parallel paths and if a routing protocol like IGRP was in operation, packets would be split between the two equal-cost paths. The same behavior is not seen with Catalysts, due to the operation of the Spanning Tree Protocol. A big clue to finding out which trunk will be used to transmit the packet is given by the output of the `show spantree` command, the interesting parts of which are shown here:

```
central> (enable) sho spant
VLAN 1
Spanning tree enabled
Spanning tree type          ieee
Port       Vlan Port-State   Cost  Priority  Fast-Start   Group-Method
--------- ---- ------------ ----- --------  ----------   ------------
1/1        1    forwarding     19      32     disabled
1/2        1    blocked        19      32     disabled
```

We can see that the switch has recognized that there is a potential loop condition because there are multiple paths between two switches, and the switch has disabled the second port from being able to transmit packets. With this configuration, the second trunk will only be used if the first fails, and then only after the STP has had the time necessary to recalculate. This illustrates nicely the ability of STP to allow us to have two links between the switches, for redundancy, but not to take advantage of any load sharing.

To make better use of our available resources, we need to intervene manually and change the configurations. To stop MAC addresses being used to define the root bridge, we will change the bridge ID priority to be lower than the default 32768 on Cat 1 as follows:

```
central> (enable) set spant priority 30000
Spantree 1 bridge priority set to 30000.
central> (enable) set spant prior 30000 3
Spantree 3 bridge priority set to 30000.
central> (enable) sho spant
VLAN 1
Spanning tree enabled
Spanning tree type          ieee
.
Bridge ID Priority          30000
```

The reason we wish to do this before we assign different priorities to the trunks for the VLANs configured is that port priority is calculated from the perspective of the root bridge and has an effect on outbound packets. Note that by not specifying a VLAN, the change in bridge priority is made for VLAN 1. To make the change for other VLANs, each VLAN number must be specified. Given that the other switch has default bridge priority, we have made this switch the root bridge for both VLAN 1 and 3.

We could look at setting port costs either at a port level (with the command `set spantree portcost`) or for each VLAN on a port (with `set spantree portvlancost`), but all this does is set a cost for the link when calculating which port will be the root port for a switch. Of more interest here, given our goal of using both the trunks, is to use the `set spantree portvlanpri` command. With this command we can configure the switch to use trunk 1 for VLANs `mgr` and `sups`, leaving trunk 2 for `engrs`. Of course, by using the priority setting, this is only a preference, and should one of the links fail, traffic will transfer to the good link. For information, we have set VLAN 2 as `mgrs`, VLAN 3 as `sups`, and VLAN 5 as `engrs`.

```
central> (enable) set spant portvlanpri 1/1 16 2-3
Port 1/1 vlans 1,4-1004 using portpri 32.
Port 1/1 vlans 2-3 using portpri 16.
```

This has lowered the priority for VLANs 2 and 3 on port 1/1, so they will prefer this trunk.

The following does the same thing for VLAN 5 on port 1/2, directing its traffic over this trunk:

```
central> (enable) set spant portvlanpri 1/2 16 5
Port 1/2 vlans 1-4,6-1004 using portpri 32.
Port 1/2 vlans 5 using portpri 16.
```

As an example, look at VLAN 5 spanning tree:

```
central> (enable) sho spant 5
VLAN 5
Spanning tree enabled
Bridge ID Priority        30000
Bridge Max Age 20 sec  Hello Time 2 sec Forward Delay 15 sec
Port      Vlan Port-State     Cost  Priority Fast-Start Group-Method
--------  ---- -------------  ----  -------- ---------- ------------
1/1       5    blocking         19        32  disabled
1/2       5    forwarding       19        16  disabled
3/46      5    not-connected   100        32  disabled
```

Here, it is nicely illustrated that by lowering the priority value for port 1/2 on this VLAN, we have forced the switch to use that port in preference to port 1/1.

An interesting experiment is to set up an extended ping between the two Catalysts and then break that link. It should take between 30 to 40 seconds for STP to reroute the traffic over the other trunk. You will see this as a set of periods being generated in place of the more familiar "!" symbol for successful pings.

An alternative to this is to use Fast EtherChannel for the trunk link. Fast EtherChannel enables the switch to view multiple links as if they were one and to use any of the links in the EtherChannel group to transmit packets. Because Fast EtherChannel works with trunking protocols like ISL, this alternative is potentially more efficient than using priority to split specific VLAN traffic across multiple links. Fast EtherChannel can also be used to connect servers via multiple NICs to a switch to provide greater throughput. Fast EtherChannel was discussed in Chapter 2; however, a quick review and a discussion of its configuration on Catalyst 5K switches is appropriate here.

Fast EtherChannel enables between two and four ports to be grouped together and be treated as one port by STP and the rest of the switch. With four ports grouped together, it looks like one port with four times the normal bandwidth available. This feature is not available on all Ethernet modules; it can only be enabled on Fast Ethernet port modules. As well as having to configure consecutive ports for grouping into an

EtherChannel, it is necessary to pay attention to the specific port numbers you group together. Due to the hardware used, Fast Ethernet modules are split into three groups of ports, each using its own controller. For a 12-port controller, this is obviously three groups of four, and for a 24-port controller, this is three groups of eight. What concerns us is that if you want to group four ports together, for example, with a 12-port device, these four ports must be 1-4, 5-8, or 9-12; you cannot group 2-5 together to become an EtherChannel.

In the Catalyst 5K range there is a protocol that automatically configures EtherChannel groups that is not currently available on other Catalyst products: The Port Aggregation Protocol, or PagP. The operation of PagP is to inform STP and the rest of the switch about which ports have been formed as part of the channel. As already stated, STP treats the EtherChannel as one port in terms of moving it from listening through to forwarding or blocking state (there are very few instances where one would want a four-port EtherChannel to be in the blocking state). The switch, however, also adjusts its behavior. Broadcast and multicast packets are only sent down one of the links in the EtherChannel and are prevented from being returned, and unicast packets are only sent down one of the links in the EtherChannel.

When configuring ports to be in an EtherChannel, it is best to keep all ports on both ends of the links with the same configuration as regards speed, duplex, and VLAN membership. I also recommend that the ports be enabled and statically assigned to VLANs, rather than using dynamic assignment. It should also make sense that the EtherChannel only support one VLAN if it is used to connect a single computer, or be a trunk if it is to carry multiple VLAN traffic. The last recommendation is to avoid the use of port security on an EtherChannel, which can cause unexpected results, like port disablements.

To configure EtherChannel groups on your Catalyst, use the `set port channel` command. This command is followed by the list of ports that you want to group together, followed by the mode you want those ports to be in. The mode can either be `on`, `off`, `desirable`, or `auto`. `desirable` and `auto` use the PagP negotiation protocol, with `desirable` enabling the ports to initiate PagP requests, but `auto` putting the ports into a passive listening mode for PagP packets. An example of setting the port channel state is shown below, which sets both ports on the supervisor mode to `desirable`:

```
central> (enable) set port channel 1/1-2 desirable
Port(s) 1/1-2 channel mode set to desirable.
```

This can be verified by the `show port channel` command.

Speeding Up Convergence: Uplink and Backbone Fast We discussed Uplink Fast in Chapter 2, using the sample network illustrated in Figure 2-18. We'll review the pertinent points here and show how Uplink Fast can be enabled on a Catalyst 5K switch. Uplink Fast is a way to reduce the amount of time it takes for a switched network to restore operation using the STP after an uplink failure. What do we mean by an uplink? Well, an *uplink* is defined as a link that connects a switch from one position in the switch hierarchy to the next level. An uplink is not one that connects user workstations to a switch. This is best explained here with reference to Figure 5-6.

In this figure, we have set Cat 1 to be the root bridge of the STP and Cat 2 to be its backup. To have the network cope with a failure of the root bridge, all of the switches that feed user VLANs (VLANs 1, 2, and 3) have links both to the root bridge (Cat 1) and its backup (Cat 2). Spanning tree will put the ports that connect Cat 3, Cat 4, and Cat 5 to Cat 2 in a blocked state during normal operation, as they do not provide the best connection to the root bridge. With Uplink Fast enabled, should

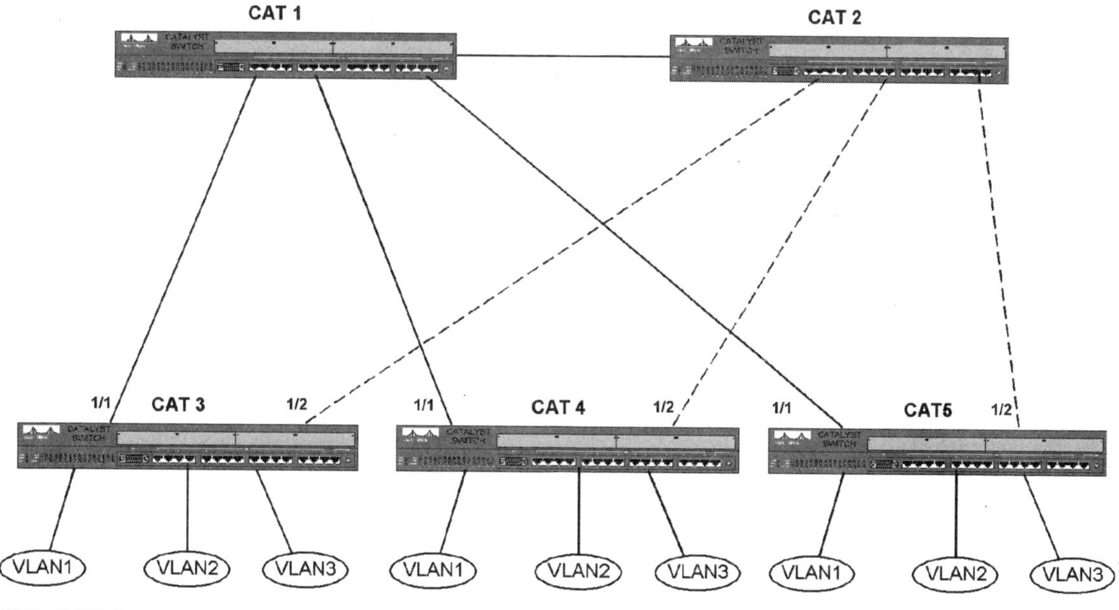

Figure 5-6 Network implemented with Uplink Fast.

the Cat 3-to-Cat 1 link fail, the Cat 3-to-Cat 2 link will be brought into the forwarding state within 5 seconds. This is a significant improvement upon standard STP, which would take several minutes to accomplish the same thing.

Let's take a look at how this is configured. The tasks we will go through are setting one of the Cat 5Ks to be root, setting another as its backup, and enabling Uplink Fast. One note before we do this. Clearly, it is advantageous to have all links carry traffic during normal operation, and in a multi-VLAN environment, like that shown in Figure 5-6, we can do it. The simplest way is to make Cat 1 the root for some VLANs and Cat 2 the root for other VLANs. As an example, we can make Cat 1 the root for VLANS 1 and 2, then Cat 2 the root for VLAN 3. Looking at Cat 3, we see that port 1/1 will be forwarding for VLANs 1 and 2, but port 1/2 will be forwarding for VLAN 3. This makes better use of the available bandwidth during normal operation.

Now, on to the necessary configurations. To make Cat 1 the root bridge for VLANs 1 and 2 and the backup for VLAN3, perform the following:

```
Cat1> (enable) set spant root 1-2 dia 5
VLANs 1-2 bridge priority set to 8192.
VLANs 1-2 bridge max aging time set to 16.
VLANs 1-2 bridge hello time set to 2.
VLANs 1-2 bridge forward delay set to 12.
Switch is now the root switch for active VLANs 1-2.
Cat1> (enable) set spant root secondary 3 dia 5
VLAN 3 bridge priority set to 16384.
VLAN 3 bridge max aging time set to 16.
LAN 3 bridge hello time set to 2.
VLAN 3 bridge forward delay set to 12.
```

So, we see that setting the switch as root lowers the priority and setting it to secondary ups the priority. We do the reverse on Cat 2, so that it is the primary for VLAN 3 and the secondary for VLANs 1 and 2. Next we have to enable Uplink Fast.

Uplink Fast is only enabled on the switches that will be selecting different ports as the way to access the root—in this case, that means Cat 3, Cat 4, and Cat 5. Uplink Fast is not enabled on the switches used as root or secondary bridges; the reason will become apparent when we execute the following command:

```
Cat3> (enable) set spant uplink enable
VLANs 1-1005 bridge priority set to 49152.
The port cost and portvlancost of all ports set to above 3000.
Station update rate set to 15 packets/100ms.
uplinkfast all-protocols field set to off.
uplinkfast enabled for bridge.
```

We see that the bridge priority has been upped, making it unlikely that a switch with Uplink Fast enabled will be chosen as the root.

That is all we really need to cover on Uplink Fast, which is a good thing if your network resembles in any way that illustrated in Figure 5-6. To sum up, Uplink Fast deals with speeding up STP convergence for direct link failures.

Another feature, called Backbone Fast, speeds up convergence when an indirect link fails. This is a little more complex to understand and warrants its own figure for explanation. Referring to Figure 5-7, suppose the link from Cat 1 to Cat 2 fails. The only route from Cat 1 to Cat 2 is now via Cat 3. This, however, is not currently possible because the Cat 3-to-Cat 2 link will be blocked until STP recalculates and moves the Cat 1 1/2 port from blocked to forwarding. As STP can take several minutes to converge, Backbone Fast was devised to bring (in this instance) Cat 1's 1/2 port into forwarding mode within 30 seconds. Unlike Uplink Fast, which is only enabled on some switches in the network, Backbone Fast must be enabled on all switches for it to be effective. The following commands show how to check the state of Backbone Fast and take it from the default disabled to the enabled state.

```
central> (enable) sho spant back
Backbonefast is not enabled.
central> (enable) set spant backbonefast enable
Backbonefast enabled for all VLANs
```

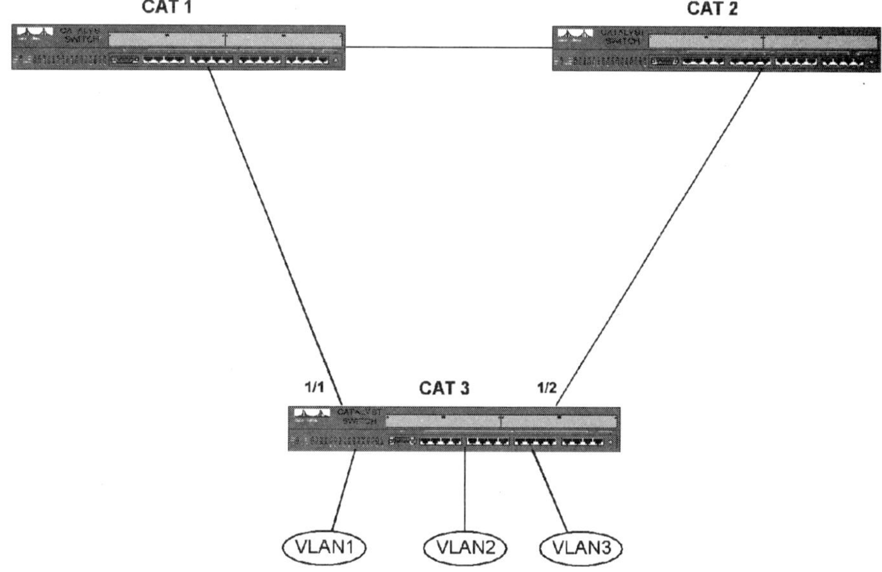

Figure 5-7 Network implemented with Backbone Fast.

The mechanism for Cat 3 to find out about the Cat 1-to-Cat 2 failure is by receiving special Bridge Protocol Data Units (*BPDUs*). These special BPDUs are called *inferior BPDUs* and inform the switch of a remote link failure. Backbone Fast takes over and brings blocked ports into forwarding without the need for the aging timer, as set by the `set spantree maxage` command, to expire.

Multicast and Broadcast Control Those that endured the pains of managing a large bridged network a decade or more ago know about the broadcast storms that can occur in bridged layer 2 networks utilizing STP. Broadcast storms occur when multiple copies of broadcast packets find their way onto the network and consume all available bandwidth. This sort of thing should not happen, but it's a fact of life. To counter this, Cisco gives us the opportunity to limit the percentage of bandwidth that broadcasts can consume. This limit should be set high enough so that during normal operation no valid broadcast packets are dropped, but low enough so that broadcast storms do not affect network operation. The best setting will vary from network to network, but starting at around 35 percent, measuring the effects, and modifying the value from there is generally a reasonable thing to do.

There is one curiosity in the command to execute broadcast control. In the command it is necessary to specify not only a module but a port also. However, once the command is executed, the setting takes effect for all ports on the module. There is one exception; the 48-port module WS-X5012 supports broadcast control on a per-port basis.

Following is an example of the command:

```
central> (enable) set port broadcast 3/16 35%
Port(s) 3/16 broadcast traffic limited to 35%.
```

Route Switch Module Support for VLANs

We covered the basics of configuring the RSM to route between multiple VLANs in the "Ethernet Module Configuration" section. In this section we'll look at the operation of the RSM in more depth.

RSM Basics

The RSM itself is much like a standalone router in that its command-line interface is the regular IOS, rather than the Catalyst interface.

Accordingly, we are back in the realm where there are two modes: A view mode, for issuing `show` commands, and a configuration mode that is accessed via `conf t`. To the rest of the Catalyst the RSM appears as a single interface that supports trunking and, therefore, has one MAC address. The key thing that binds the RSM tightly to the switch is its ability to define VLAN interfaces that are automatically connected within the switch to the ports assigned to that VLAN.

The first thing you notice when looking at an RSM is that it does not have any useful-looking interfaces to plug anything into. The only slots are for a PCMCIA card that holds the IOS, a console port, and an auxiliary port. There are, however, some interesting LEDs. The status LED shows green for everything OK, orange for booting up or a system test, and red for reset or a failed test. During normal operation the CPU Halt and Enabled LEDs are green to indicate operational status; anything else is a problem. The slot 0 and slot 1 LEDs only flash when the RSM is accessing the PCMCIA card in the respective slot.

However, the most curious LEDs are the Channel 0 and Channel 1 Transmit and Receive LEDs. The RSM uses two dedicated ASICs for packet transfer to the backplane, which relate to these two channels. These two channels can be used to support the full 256 VLANs that the switch can address. VLAN 0 is automatically mapped to channel 0, and VLAN 1 is automatically mapped to channel 1. We have not mentioned VLAN 0 before, with good reason, since it is not accessible to users. Instead, it is reserved for communication between the RSM and the switch. As additional VLANs are created, they are assigned in rotation between channel 0 and channel 1. Clearly, if every other VLAN that you create is a busy one, one of the channels will be doing more work than the other. To counter this, you can pay attention to the order in which you create VLAN interfaces on the RSM. The channel LEDs can be useful in visually gauging if one channel is working harder than the other.

We can illustrate the process where VLANs are added to one channel then the other by making use of the `show controller` command of the RSM. In the "Ethernet Module Configuration" section we showed how to create VLAN interfaces on the RSM. With no additional VLANs created on the RSM (they may be created on the switch, but that does not have any effect on the RSM configuration), the interesting part of the `show controller` command is shown below. The `c5ip` is one of three options for this command; the others show the CBUS controller that communicates with the backplane and the FDDI controller.

```
Router#show controller c5ip
DMA Channel 0 (status ok)
 Received 36 packets, 2166 bytes
   One minute rate, 225 bits/s, 1 packets/s
   Ten minute rate, 23 bits/s, 1 packets/s
   Dropped 0 packets
   Error counts, 0 crc, 0 index, 0 dmac-length, 0 dmac-synch
Transmitted 29 packets, 2217 bytes
   One minute rate, 239 bits/s, 1 packets/s
   Ten minute rate, 25 bits/s, 1 packets/s
DMA Channel 1 (status ok)
 Received 0 packets, 0 bytes
   One minute rate, 0 bits/s, 0 packets/s
   Ten minute rate, 0 bits/s, 0 packets/s
   Dropped 0 packets
   Error counts, 0 crc, 0 index, 0 dmac-length, 0 dmac-synch
Transmitted 0 packets, 0 bytes
   One minute rate, 0 bits/s, 0 packets/s
   Ten minute rate, 0 bits/s, 0 packets/s
Vla     Type        DMA Channel   Method
```

As you can see at the bottom of the display, there are no VLANs listed; however, DMA channel 1 and DMA channel 0 are shown to be OK. If we create VLAN 1 and VLAN 2 on the RSM, the VLAN listing will show something similar to the following:

```
Vlan    Type        DMA Channel   Method
1        ethernet   1              auto
2        ethernet   0              auto
```

Here we can see that the first VLAN created was assigned to channel 1, and the next to channel 0. This process of alternate assignment will carry on until we have created the maximum 256 VLANs. If we were to create a VLAN 3 (as long as VLAN 3 was created and active on the switch) that would be assigned to channel 1.

Because the RSM is a router on a card (a card is often termed a "blade" by network jocks), it supports all the features of routing that other routers do, including running a routing protocol of some kind. The physical path that is used to disseminate routing protocol updates is via the VLAN ports that are members of the VLAN specified in the RSM interface VLAN configurations. Suppose we have defined an interface VLAN 1 in the RSM, and within the Catalyst (actually within the Supervisor), we have defined ports 3/1-20 to be in VLAN 1. Routing protocol updates for the subnet associated with VLAN 1 will be sent out these ports. In Figure 5-8, we see a sample network with two Catalysts—Catalyst 5000 #1 and Catalyst 5000 #2—and two routers. For example, Catalyst 5000 #1 sends out routing updates to router 1 via IGRP broadcasts send on VLAN 1; similar broadcasts are sent on VLAN 2 and VLAN 3.

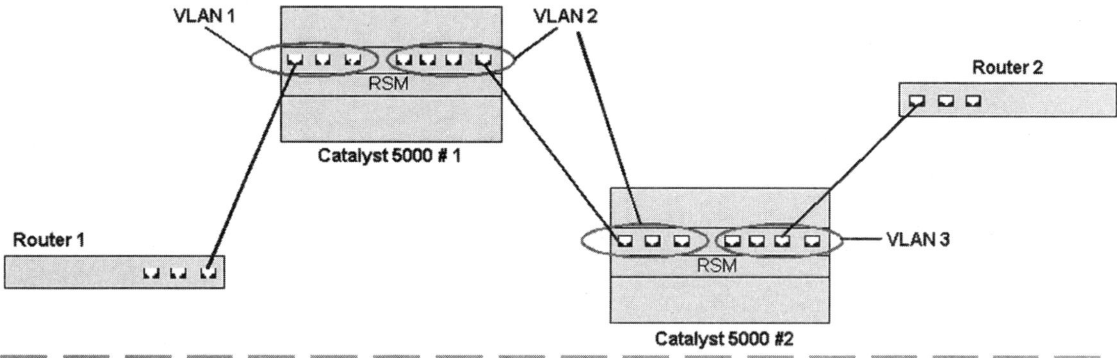

Figure 5-8 Routing protocol updates in an RSM network.

Even though there are no physical connections from the RSM out to the external routers, the RSMs in Figure 5-8 still send routing updates out the Ethernet module ports for each respective VLAN. To send, for example, an IGRP routing update, the RSM sends a single update to the broadcast address of the VLAN. This is then flooded out of every port configured for that VLAN. It is like having one router Ethernet interface connected to a hub: that Ethernet interface will send out broadcast IGRP updates that will be seen by all other devices on that hub.

RSM Boot Process

Like any Cisco router, the RSM has NV (nonvolatile) RAM and flash memory, as well as a boot ROM, which contains the usual low-feature IOS set. (All these router functions are described in detail in the *Cisco TCP/IP Routing Professional Reference.*) By default, the RSM will boot from the flash memory stored in the PCMCIA card in slot 0. Generally, no action other than plugging in the RSM to the Catalyst is necessary to get the RSM to boot. Only if the configuration register has been changed from the hexadecimal value of 2102 will the RSM try to boot from another location. The current configuration register setting can be obtained by viewing the output of the `show version` command:

```
Router>show ver
Cisco Internetwork Operating System Software
IOS (tm) C5RSM Software (C5RSM-ISV-M), Version 11.2(12a.P1)P1
Copyright (c) 1986-1998 by Cisco Systems, Inc.
.
.
Configuration register is 0x2102
```

The bulk of this display is not relevant to this discussion and has been omitted. The configuration register value is given on the last line of the display. The last four bits of the configuration register form the Boot field, and if those bits match the following patterns, the RSM knows where to get its operating system file from:

- 0000 forces the RSM into ROM Monitor mode, from which an operating system image can be manually loaded.
- 0001 forces the RSM to load the restricted image found in the boot ROM.
- 0010 or 0011 directs the RSM to the `boot system` commands listed in the configuration file. If there are no `boot system` commands in the configuration file, the RSM will search for a system image stored on a network server.

To set the boot image location, we have to change the value of the last hexadecimal digit of the configuration register setting. This is done with the `config-register` command in configuration mode. If, for example, we wish to change the value of this digit to 1, to load from boot ROMS, the following commands are executed:

```
Router#conf t
Router(config)#config-reg 0x101
Router(config)#^Z
```

This can be verified by again using the `show version` command and viewing the last line of the display, as follows:

```
Configuration register is 0x2102 (will be 0x101 at next reload)
```

As you can see, a reload of the RSM is necessary for the change to take effect. Generally, you will only want to have the RSM boot with a full system image (IOS file), rather than the Boot ROM or ROM monitor. Given this is the case, there are two locations that can hold a full image: the PCMCIA slot and a network server. It is preferable to have the primary source as the PCMCIA slot to minimize the effect of any network link outages; clearly, you would not want to take out the ability for the RSM to reload if the link to the network server goes down.

To load from the flash memory, it is simplest to use the `boot system` configuration command. To configure the RSM to load in preference from PCMCIA slot 0, then slot 1, then from a TFTP server at 200.200.25.14 using the file named config-file, we issue the following in configuration mode:

```
Router(config)#boot system flash slot0
Router(config)#boot system flash slot1
Router(config)#boot system tftp config-file 200.200.25.14
```

There is one other option: You can specify that the RSM load from onboard flash memory. The contents of this memory can be examined by looking at the `bootflash:` contents as follows:

```
Router#dir bootflash:
-#- -length- ---date/time--- name
1     2677800 Jan 01 2000 00:02:29 c5rsm-boot-mz.112-12a.P1
4924248 bytes available (2677928 bytes used)
```

To configure the RSM to boot using this image, use the following command:

```
Router(config)#boot system flash bootflash:c5rsm-boot-mz.112-12a.P1
```

Configuration File Management

The RSM uses ASCII configuration files just like any other router and can source that configuration file from flash or a network server. The usual `conf net` command will load a configuration file from a network server; however, you can use a `boot network` command to have the RSM take its configuration from a network server on startup. Of course, these commands load the configuration file into running memory. To execute this configuration, use the following commands:

```
Router(config)#boot network rsm-config 200.200.25.14
Router(config)#service config
Router(config)#^Z
```

This tells the RSM to get its configuration file from the TFTP server with IP address 200.200.25.14, using the file named `rsm-config`. The `service config` command enables this capability.

Catalyst 5K Token Ring Implementation

As discussed in earlier chapters, token ring refuses to die, and now technologies like Direct Token Ring (DTR) that require neither a token nor a ring to operate have renewed interest in this method of LAN access. To that end, we'll cover how to configure the features discussed in Chapter 2 on a Catalyst 5K switch. The default configuration that arrives on a Catalyst 5K token ring module allows a certain level of plug and play.

Basic Token Ring Configuration

Just as with the Ethernet module, where all ports belonged to the default VLAN 1 so that any device plugged into any port could communicate with a device on another port, the same is true for the token ring module. Upon delivery, all ports are assigned to the default TR-CRF, which is in turn assigned to the default TR-BRF. This is fine if you do not want to segment your token ring module. However, as you can't assign new TR-CRFs to the default TR-BRF, you need to create a new TR-BRF to segment the token ring module. As a recap, a TR-CRF identifies multiple ports that are part of the same ring. The TR-BRF switches packets between multiple rings by either source-route bridging or source-route transparent bridging.

So to add a new TR-BRF to which you can assign new TR-CRFs members, go to enable mode on the 5K and type the following:

```
Cat5K#set vlan 10 name brf10 type trbrf bridge 1
```

This configuration can be verified by issuing the `show vlan` command, which will generate an output similar to that below:

```
VLAN  Name                      Status        Mod/ports     Vlans
----  ------------------------  ------------- ---------     -----
1     default                   active        4/1-4
10    brf10                     active
```

This `set vlan` command defines the new TR-BRF to have the name trbrf10 and to belong to VLAN 10. The type can identify the VLAN as type Ethernet, FDDI, TR-BRF, or TR-CRF. The bridge parameter is an optional one that sets the identification number for the bridge, which can be between 1 and F in hex. Note that the token ring module is in slot 4, and the default TR-BRF has ports 1 through 4 assigned.

The next step is to assign a TR-CRF to this TR-BRF, which can be achieved with the following command:

```
Cat5K#set vlan 11 name crf11 type trcrf ring 1 parent 10 mode srb
```

Again, we can verify this configuration with the `show vlan` command as follows:

```
VLAN       Name                Status        Mod/Ports     Vlans
---------- ------------------- ------------- ------------- -----
1          default             active        4/1-4
10         brf10               active                       11
11         crf11               active
```

As we now see, we have introduced another VLAN—VLAN 11 of type TR-CRF—which has VLAN 10 as its parent. The parent relationship is seen by the entry for VLAN 10, showing that VLAN 11 belongs to it. This use of the `set vlan` command is quite similar to the first; the differences being that this time we are specifying a TR-CRF on ring 1, with a parent of VLAN 10, using SRB to switch packets with the parent TR-BRF.

To complete this sample configuration, we will create a second TR-CRF function and show the TR-BRF bridging between two TR-CRFs. The physical network we are creating with this configuration is illustrated in Figure 5-9. As we can see, the default TR-BRF is only used to connect to the default TR-CRF and does not really do much; it is there really as a convenience for making the module a somewhat plug and play device for those that do not need to configure multiple TR-CRFs on their network.

The more interesting part is when we consider ports 5 and 6, then ports 7 and 8 in Figure 5-9. Here, we have configured the devices on port 5 and 6 to be part of the same ring, which can bridge across to the devices on ports 7 and 8, which are part of their own ring. So let's create the second TR-CRF, assign it to the same parent TR-BRF, and give each TR-CRF the appropriate ports, starting with the second TR-CRF:

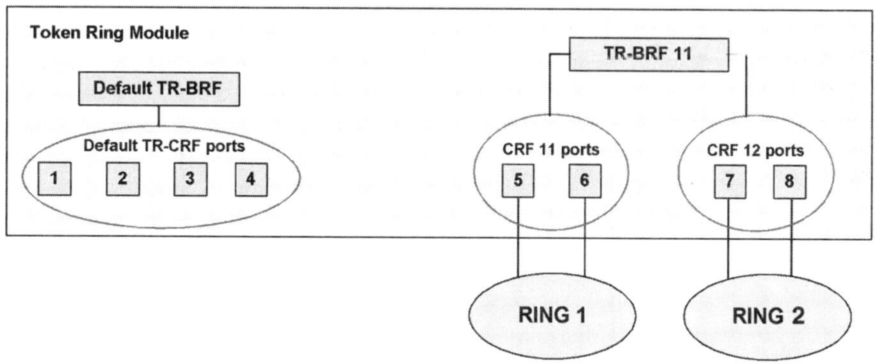

Figure 5-9 Physical connections in multiple CRF example.

```
Cat5K#set vlan 12 name crf12 type trcrf ring 2 parent 10 mode srb
```

This time we have created VLAN 12, which will support the workstation attached to ring 2. Again, we have configured VLAN 10 as the parent and source-route bridging to exchange packets with the TR-BRF function. To assign ports 5 and 6 to the first TR-CRF and ports 7 and 8 to the second TR-CRF, issue the following commands:

```
Cat5K#set vlan 11 4/5-6
Cat5K#set vlan 12 4/7-8
```

We can see the effect of these commands by now issuing the `show vlan` command as follows:

```
VLAN     Name        Status      Mod/ports            Vlans
-------- ----------- ----------- -------------------- ------
1        default     active      4/1-4
10       brf10       active                           11, 12
11       crf11       active      4/5-6
12       crf12       active      4/7-8
```

Customizing the Token Ring Configuration

One of the features that does differentiate token ring and give it some appeal is the ability to assign different priorities to ports on a ring. The first point is that there are potentially two priorities that you can set for a port. These are different from the port priorities that were set for spanning tree priorities. With spanning tree priorities, we configured the priority for individual ports to ensure that the Spanning Tree Protocol selected the ports we wished for forwarding packets for individual VLANs. With the priorities we are about to set, we are configuring how the port handles priority setting in the frames received and how the port itself can request the token.

The first priority is the *priority threshold.* Incoming packets can be placed into either a high- or low-priority transmit queue. The switch will decide to place an incoming frame into the low- or high-priority queue depending on the token ring frame priority in the Frame Control Field of the frame. By default, an incoming frame with a priority of 3 or less will go into the low-priority queue. These priority values are set by the token ring station and can range in value from 0 to 7.

The second priority is the *reservation priority* when requesting a token from the ring. This is set to 4 by default and can range in value from 0 to 6. It is often a good idea to increase this priority for a switch port on a busy token ring. So let's look at the command to do this:

```
Cat5K#set tokenring priority 4/9 threshold 5
Port 9 priority threshold set to 5
Cat5K#set token ring priority 4/9 minxmit 6
Port 9 minxmit set to 6
```

With this configuration, we are placing more of the incoming frames into the low-priority queue and setting the switch port to the highest priority when requesting a token. It is possible to customize settings for 4- or 16-Mbit/sec operation and full or half duplex (full duplex is used for Dedicated Token Ring [DTR] and uses Transmit Immediate, or TXI, to bypass waiting for a token). However, I prefer to leave the ports set to `auto` for both speed and duplex. If the settings have been changed for some reason, you can reset them to `auto` with the following commands:

```
Cat5K#set port speed 4/1 auto
Cat5K#set tokenring portmode 4/1 auto
```

A useful feature that is enabled by default for 16-Mbit/sec media (and not available on 4-Mbit/sec media) is Early Token Release (ETR). Under normal token ring operation, an endstation needs to wait until the packet it sends off around the ring has returned before it can transmit a new token onto the ring. With ETR, an endstation can send a new token immediately after it has finished transmitting a packet. The idea behind token ring is that only one device will have the token at a time (implying only one device can transmit at a time), and, therefore, collisions do not occur. Typically, the station with the token can transmit, and when the transmitted packet is returned from its travels around the ring, the transmitting station lets another station have the token. As there is only one path around the ring, this wastes possible ring transmission time. It is clearly safe to transmit a new token directly after a data packet is transmitted, since that packet will have passed through a neighboring endstation before that endstation gets the new token, thus avoiding any possible collisions.

In Chapter 2 we discussed the operation of the all-routes explorer packet in source routed networks. This feature of token ring has the ability to generate a significant amount of traffic, as the explorer packets multiply throughout the network. With the 5K range of switches, there is the option to enable All-Routes Explorer Reduction (ARE). This ensures that the explorer packet multiplication discussed does not bring a network to its knees. With ARE reduction enabled, the switch ensures that only one of these packets is accepted per VLAN, rather than allowing multiple copies of the same packet. This feature can be enabled as follows:

```
Central> (enable) set tokenring reduction enable
```

As well as these customizations, the token ring module also supports port naming and STP customization, just as we have already discussed for the Ethernet modules.

Token Ring RSM Operation

The RSM provides routing between token ring VLANs as well as between Ethernet VLANs. As we discussed in the RSM section, the RSM itself does not offer any useful external network connections; however, with the addition of the VIP2 (versatile interface processor) board, external network connections for the RSM do become available. The VIP2 card makes the RSM more like a 75xx router. One notable exception is in effect however: There is no support for VTP with token ring VLANs on the RSM.

A VLAN is a broadcast domain. That is a simple concept in Ethernet networks. In token ring networks, however, that simple definition turns out to be not so simple. In token ring there are broadcasts that are contained within one physical ring (equivalent to a TR-CRF) and broadcasts that travel throughout a bridged domain (i.e., within a TR-BRF). With Ethernet VLANs, we enabled the RSM to route between those VLANs by defining VLAN interfaces that had an IP address with the `interface vlan` command in configuration mode. For token ring routing, we create an interface to a specific TR-BRF VLAN within the RSM (assuming that the TR-BRF has already been defined on the supervisor). Before we delve into configuring the RSM, we do, however, have to review one new protocol that runs on the RSM in a token ring environment: the Duplicate Ring Protocol, or DRiP.

DRiP issues advertisements about the status of all the TR-CRFs it knows about. Another RSM will hear these advertisements, and by processing them, it will be able to appropriately filter ARE packets that have already been on a ring once. DRiP also enables an RSM to detect duplicate TR-CRFs across multiple RSMs and switches.

The advertisements that DRiP uses are multicast, so that they are heard by neighboring devices but not passed on by the normal bridging functions. Each RSM has to generate its own advertisements. These advertisements are sent at 30-second intervals by the RSM.

RSM Configuration for TR-BRF Routing

Remember, the default TR-BRF cannot have new TR-CRFs assigned to it, so when creating multiple TR-CRFs (these are the ones that actually have physical ports assigned to them), a new TR-BRF must be created. Before illustrating the command sequence in detail, let's discuss what we are going to do first.

Our goal is to support IP routing on the RSM between multiple token ring VLANs that exist on the switch. Within the RSM, we are going to create separate VLAN interfaces that equate to the TR-BRFs in existence. Within the switch, the `set vlan` command is used to create the TR-BRF VLANS and the TR-CRFs that belong to them. The `set vlan` command is also used to define which physical ports are assigned to the TR-CRF VLAN number. So, referring to Figure 5-10, let's put some numbers together in an example and show how it's done.

The RSM configuration will be something like this:

```
Interface vlan10 type trbrf
      Ip address 172.7.6.5 255.255.255.0
Interface vlan20 type trbrf
      IP address 172.7.7.5 255.255.255.0
```

Within the Catalyst 5K, the expected configuration will be as follows:

```
Set vlan 10 type trbrf
Set vlan 40 type trcrf parent 10
Set vlan 20 type trbrf
Set vlan 50 type trcrf parent 20
Set vlan 40 3/1-2
Set vlan 50 3/3-4
```

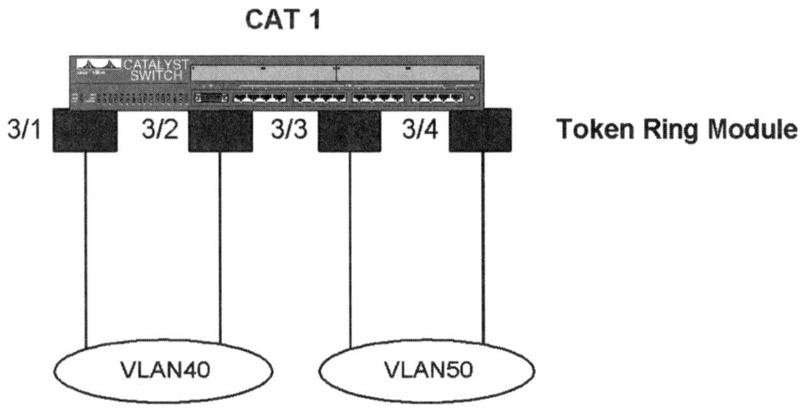

Figure 5-10 Routing between token ring VLANs and an RSM.

VLAN#	PORTS
40	3/1, 3/2
50	3/3, 3/4

BRF LANS CREATED ON RSM; 10, 20

PARENT LAN	CRF CHILD VLANS
10	40
20	50

There are many combinations that may be needed in practice, such as routing between token ring and Ethernet VLANs on the RSM. This is quite easy to add; all that need be done is ensure that IP routing is turned on and that the RSM is aware of all the VLANs that require routing. All the VLANs defined as interfaces on the RSM are in effect directly connected as far as the routing table is concerned, and routing between them is therefore a simple task. Suppose we want to add a VLAN 60 in operation on an Ethernet module and route between that and the two token ring VLANs 40 and 50 defined above. What we need to add to the configuration is on the RSM:

```
Interface vlan60 type ethernet
      IP address 172.7.8.5 255.255.255.0
```

Then on the switch, we need to define the Ethernet VLAN and the ports within that VLAN as follows:

```
Set vlan 60 4/2-5
```

This now defines VLAN 60 as having Ethernet ports 2 to 5 on module 4 and VLAN 60 as a routable interface on the RSM.

ISL For Token Ring

We have previously noted that token ring interfaces do not support the ISL trunking protocol. That does not mean, however, that token ring VLANS cannot participate in trunking at all. It is possible to have ISL trunks carry token ring VLAN information over the normal Fast Ethernet ISL links, although this does require different headers in the ISL frame. With Ethernet, it was simple; the ISL tags identified each packet as having originated from a single Ethernet VLAN. With token ring, there is another level of hierarchy. The VLAN tags for token ring ISL must identify the TR-CRF and TR-BRF from which the packet originated. This also opens up the possibility of the token ring ISL frame listing a source and destination VLAN ID, since packets can be destined for another port that could be part of the same TR-CRF, and another TR-CRF within the one TR-BRF. To travel to a completely different TR-BRF, access to a router or RSM is required.

TR-ISL is quite a neat feature for those already operating token ring networks. It is one way of making a 100-Mbit/sec backbone available to token ring networks without changing anything on the token rings themselves. The 100-Mbit/sec option is cheaper and simpler than going to ATM LANE, currently the only other real alternative for high-speed backbones for token ring networks. It is believed that 100-Mbit/sec token ring will be available soon, but as a new technology, it will not be as mature as 100-Mbit/sec Ethernet, it will be more expensive, and it will have limited vendor support, particularly in the early stages.

So let's look at how to configure TR-ISL in a network. The example we will use is a router with a token ring interface connected to an existing token ring. This router also has a Fast Ethernet interface that is set to ISL encapsulation for a link to an ISL encapsulated Fast Ethernet port on a Catalyst 5K. This Catalyst has a token ring attached, and we want to use the ISL link to transport packets between the two token rings at either end of the ISL link. The key to this configuration is that the token ring attached to the router and the token ring on the switch must be considered as part of the same VLAN, which means part of the same TR-BRF. If you require more information on the router configuration, full explanation of token ring bridging on routers is given in the *Cisco TCP/IP Routing Professional Reference.*

First let's look at the network, as depicted in Figure 5-11. In this figure, the Catalyst has a token ring connected to port 4/1, and the Ethernet port 3/1 is configured as a trunk that connects to interface E0 on a router. The router also has an attached token ring on interface T0.

The enabler for all this to happen is the ability to define a subinterface on the ISL link that will carry the token ring encapsulated packets. Now then, let's decide that the token ring VLAN that will be used for PC1 to PC2 communication is VLAN 100. This is a TR-BRF, as we are necessarily creating multiple TR-CRFs since we are connecting PCs on different

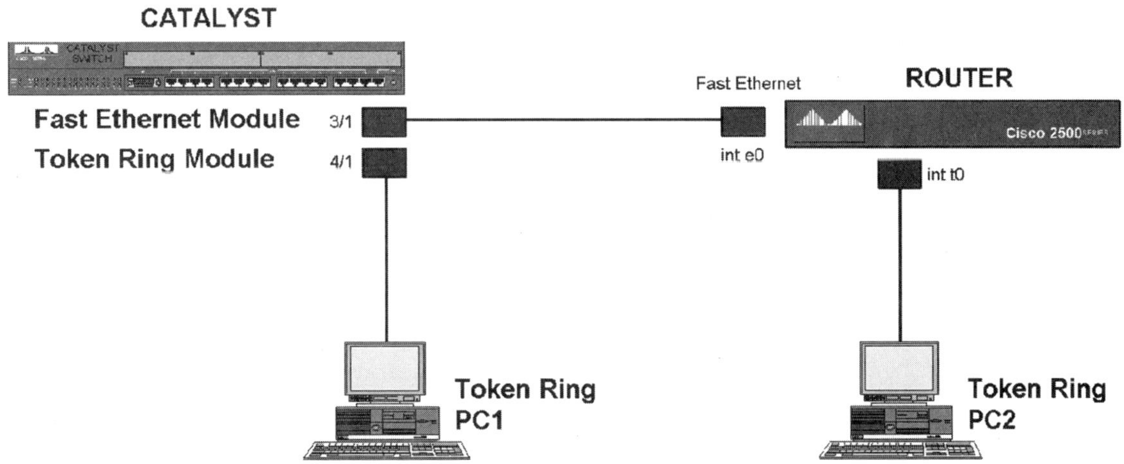

Figure 5-11 Network connectivity for token ring ISL.

devices. On the switch, we therefore have to define a TR-CRF that has VLAN 100 as its parent in order to be able to assign physical ports on the switch. We'll call this VLAN 200. In the following configuration, we need to configure a bridge number on the router, which must be unique on the network. For this example, we'll use 15.

The switch configuration will contain the following:

```
Set vlan 100 name trbrf100 type trbrf stp ieee
Set vlan 200 name trcrf200 type trcrf mode srt
Set trunk 3/1 on
Set vlan 200 4/1
```

Correspondingly on the router we will create the following (which identifies the token ring and Fast Ethernet ports in use as belonging to the same spanning tree via the bridge-group association):

```
Bridge 1 protocol ieee
!
interface fastethernet 0.1
      encap tr-isl trbrf-vlan 100 bridge-num 15
      bridge-group 1
!
interface tokenring0
      bridge-group 1
```

Note that we have forced both the switch and router to be using IEEE-type spanning tree and are using the universal source-route transparent bridging on the switch. With this configuration, packets are being transparently bridged, so specification of IP addresses is not essential. Should routing be required, IP addressing can be added to the token ring 0 interface on the router as normal.

Catalyst 5K FDDI

FDDI and, later, CDDI (which is the FDDI set of protocols running over copper rather than fiber-optic cables) were the first commercially available 100-Mbit/sec backbone technologies and found their way into many campus and corporate networks. In fact, if you buy into the idea of full-duplex Fast Ethernet giving you 200 Mbit/sec, you could argue that FDDI provides 200 Mbit/sec of throughput, since it consists of two counter-rotating rings, each operating at 100 Mbit/sec.

The FDDI frame type is not compatible with Ethernet, and therefore unless your network is FDDI end to end (very few are), the network will need to translate frames from FDDI to Ethernet when the packet needs to change from one medium to the other. In fact, that is what the FDDI module is, an Ethernet packet translation bridge. These days, it is questionable whether you would want to employ an FDDI ring, given the lower cost of 100-Mbit/sec Ethernet that can use Fast EtherChannel to improve throughput. One point in favor of FDDI is that by using fiber connections, the cables are not susceptible to electromagnetic interference. In fact, that point made 10BaseF cabling (10-Mbit/sec Ethernet over fiber) perform significantly better than 10BaseT cables in some environments. However, if you think that fiber cables are justified, it may be worth looking at early deployment of Gigabit Ethernet over fiber. That is simpler to understand, does not have the latency involved in packet translation, and has upside throughput ability.

If FDDI needs to be supported in your existing network, however, the Catalyst 5K can do it. Let's see how. The translation that is performed is to take in Ethernet VLAN packets and convert them to 802.10 packets with a per-VLAN SAID value (the specifics of 802.10 and SAID were discussed in Chapter 2) for transmission onto the FDDI ring. The opposite translation takes place with packets going from FDDI to Ethernet. Of course, this means that every Catalyst involved maintains a VLAN-to-SAID value list. On the Catalyst 5K range, the VLAN and SAID numbers do not have to be the same value to reference the one VLAN. That is not the case with all switches (for example, the old Catalyst 1200), some of which come with a fixed SAID-to-VLAN mapping. Care must therefore be taken in planning this in a mixed environment.

Before we look at the most common application of FDDI—a trunk that carries multiple VLAN traffic across a backbone—we'll examine the configuration of native VLANs on FDDI. This would typically be used if the FDDI interface is connecting FDDI-attached workstations to the Catalyst and we want those workstations to be part of a VLAN. This is illustrated in Figure 5-12.

The option to map a VLAN to the native FDDI VLAN on a nontrunk FDDI port is only available for Ethernet-type VLANs on the Catalyst 5K. We create a VLAN for use on the FDDI module with the following (assuming the FDDI module is in slot 4):

```
Central> (enable) set vlan 99 4/1
VLAN 99 modified.
VLAN 1 modified.
VLAN Mod/Ports
---- ---------------------------
99   4/1
```

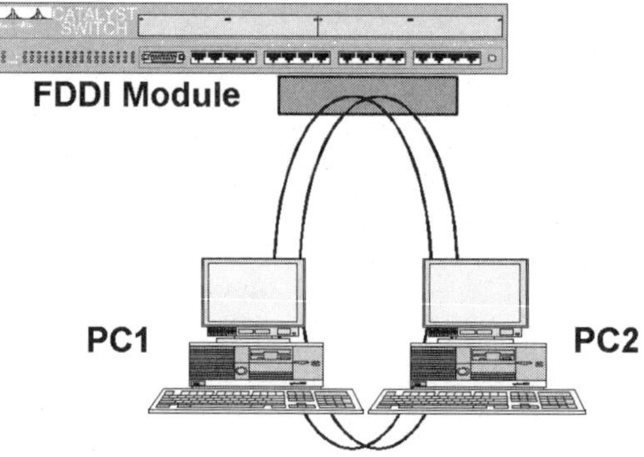

Figure 5-12 Network configuration for making FDDI-attached workstations part of an Ethernet VLAN.

PC1 and PC2 are on VLAN 99

This can be verified by issuing the `show vlan` command, which generates the following display:

```
Central> (enable) show vlan 99
VLAN Name                            Type  Status    Mod/Ports
---- -------------------------- ----- --------- ----------------
99   VLAN0099                        enet  active    4/1-2
VLAN SAID       MTU   RingNo BridgeNo StpNo Parent Trans1 Trans2
---- --------- ----  ------ -------- ----- ------ ------ ------
99   100099     1500  0      0        0     0      0      0
```

This is a fairly trivial exercise and one that will only be used very rarely. Let's move on to the FDDI as a trunk, a much more real scenario.

Assuming that our physical connections to the FDDI are operational (i.e., that we have FDDI cables to ports A, and B with the Ring, Thru A, and B LEDs lit on the FDDI module), it should not be possible to connect the FDDI cables the wrong way round, as they are keyed to only make connections with the right cable. However, it is possible for the cables to be forced to the wrong connection and it does not take much effort to check.

Having established physical connectivity, the first job is to create the FDDI VLANs that will exist on the trunk and be used to transport packets across the trunk for the Ethernet VLANs at the end of the trunk. The second job is to create the translation between each FDDI VLAN and its corresponding Ethernet VLAN. We are going to create the configuration to support the network depicted in Figure 5-13.

Just as we have to create VLANs 10, 20, and 30 on Cat 1 and Cat 2, we have to create VLANs 100, 200, and 300 on Cat 1 and Cat 2 also. Of course, this means the Ethernet-to-FDDI VLAN translation has to exist

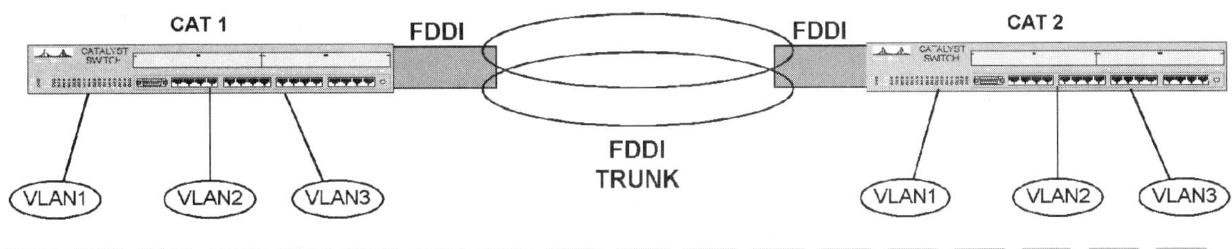

Figure 5-13 Network connectivity for using FDDI as a trunk.

on each Catalyst. To make it easy to manage, we will translate VLAN 10 to 100, 20 to 200, and 30 to 300. The commands executed are illustrated on Cat 1 as follows (these configuration commands assume the Ethernet VLANs 10, 20, and 30 already exist):

```
Cat1> (enable) set vlan 100 type fddi
VTP: vlan addition successful
Cat1> (enable) set vlan 200 type fddi
VTP: vlan addition successful
Cat1> (enable) set vlan 300 type fddi
VTP: vlan addition successful
```

Now that the FDDI VLANs are created, we can establish the translation mappings. It does not matter which VLAN we put first in this command, the ethernet or FDDI VLAN. What we are establishing is a bidirectional translation:

```
Cat1> (enable) set vlan 10 translation 100
VTP:vlan modification successful
Cat1> (enable) set vlan 20 translation 200
VTP:vlan modification successful
Cat1> (enable) set vlan 30 translation 300
VTP:vlan modification successful
```

The last thing is to make sure that the FDDI trunk is on with the following:

```
Cat1> (enable) set trunk 4/1 on
```

This configuration sequence enables the ethernet VLANs to communicate from Cat 1 to Cat 2 over the 802.10-encapsulated FDDI trunk.

ATM Operation on Catalyst 5K Switches

The Catalyst 5K range has a nice ATM LANE module that incorporates all the functions of the LAN Emulation Client. It is assumed that you have read and digested Chapter 3, so we won't replicate the information in that chapter here. Of course, to establish an ATM link, one needs an ATM switch and in this instance, we will be using a LightStream 1010 box. (LightStream configuration is covered in the next chapter.) Before we discuss any configuration, or anything else in any detail, let's look at what we are trying to achieve, which is illustrated in Figure 5-14.

Planning the Implementation

To get LANE functioning in the network shown in Figure 5-14, we need to complete the following tasks:

- Configure the ATM interface for VPI/VCI signaling and ILMI.
- Configure the LES/BUS per ELAN.
- Configure the LEC for *each* ELAN on *each* Catalyst.

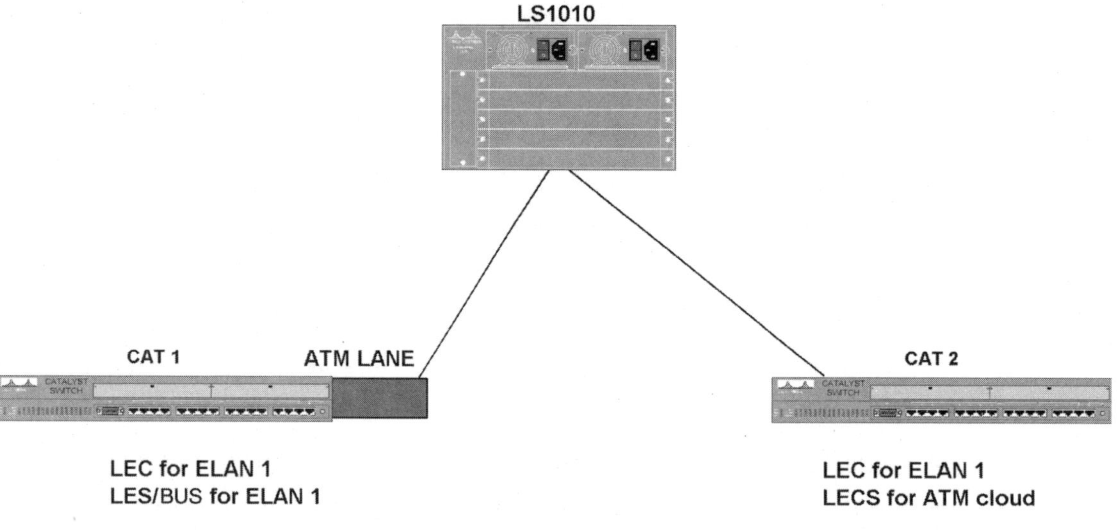

Figure 5-14 Network connectivity for LANE deployment.

- Configure the LECS (LAN Emulation Configuration Server) on Cat 2, which will serve the entire ATM cloud, irrespective of the number of ELANs created.
- Tell the LS1010 the address of the LECS.

Clearly, for each ELAN we want to be running on the Catalyst (we generally map one ELAN per VLAN, just as we did with mapping Ethernet to FDDI VLANs in the previous section), we have to create another instance of the LEC. This is required because the LEC can only be a member of one ELAN, and it is likely that we will want to trunk multiple VLANs over the LANE trunk connection. So, you need to plan the number of LECS per Catalyst, which Catalyst will be the LES/BUS for each ELAN, and which Catalyst will be the LECS for the whole ATM cloud.

To access the ATM LANE module, use the `session` command as before. For example, if the ATM LANE module is in slot 5, access to it will be gained by issuing the following commands:

```
Central> session 5
ATM>
```

This module operates a cut-down version of the ATM software that runs on routers. As such, one enters privileged mode by the `enable` command, and to change the module's configuration, we must enter the `conf term` command.

Basic Catalyst 5K ATM LANE Configuration

Not that we will repeat much of Chapter 3, but a brief list of definitions here will be helpful when executing the configuration commands that follow:

- LAN Emulation Client (LEC) is the interface for address resolution requests between the ATM world and the non-ATM world on a per-emulated LAN basis.
- The LES/BUS consists of two functions. First is the LAN Emulation Server, which registers LECs in the ELAN and handles LE_ARP requests and responses. The second part, the BUS, is the Broadcast and Unknown Server, which handles replicating broadcast and multicast packets through the connection-oriented ATM cloud.
- The LAN Emulation Configuration Server (LECS) is consulted just once when a LEC first comes up on the ATM network. The LECS tells

the LEC which ELAN it belongs to. To do this, the LECS maintains a database that is used to tell the LEC the ATM address of the LES for its particular ELAN.

Given that we have physical connectivity between the ATM LANE module and the LS1010 (this can be via numerous forms, typically fiber at varying rates, or UTP using 155 Mbit/sec), the first job is to ensure that the ATM module has the configuration to enable it to signal to the LS1010 that a switched virtual circuit (SVC) is required. Remember, in all ATM communication, cells are transmitted along virtual circuits, either of the permanent or switched variety. This is admittedly a general statement. However, the majority of cell traffic takes place via SVC connections, which are established for the duration they are needed and torn down immediately afterwards.

As well as the ability to signal SVC requirements, the ATM module needs an ILMI connection for exchanging network configuration information with the LS1010 switch (ILMI is like SNMP). We are now going to create those two required PVCs: one that will be used to signal SVC requirements as they arise (i.e., this connection is being used to set up other temporary SVCs) and one for the ILMI communication. This is completed as follows:

```
ATM#conf t
ATM(config)#int ATM 0
Atm(config-if)#atm pvc 1 0 5 qsaal
Atm(config-if)#atm pvc 2 0 16 ilmi
```

This display requires a bit of explanation. The first two lines are self-explanatory; we are getting into configuration mode for the ATM interface (this presupposes that we have used the `session` command to get to the ATM LANE module). The `atm pvc` command, however, has several options. This command first defines the Virtual Circuit Descriptor (VCD), which is a local value that we can define as anything we like. The next two values define the Virtual Path Identifier and Virtual Channel Identifier and, in this case, use the default values for the respective functions. In fact, in some versions of the ATM software, these two PVCs are already created in the module's configuration.

The final fields used here (the `qsaal` and `ilmi` arguments) define the AAL encapsulation for each PVC. The options are `ilmi`, `qsaal`, and `aal5snap`. The `ilmi` option is the clear choice for its function, and `qsaal` is used for the PVC that will be used for call setup and termination.

Now we'll configure the LES/BUS for the default ELAN. In Figure 5-14 we see that for this ELAN we are going to configure the LES/BUS on Cat 1. For each subsequent ELAN that maps to a separate VLAN, we will have the option to choose which Catalyst hosts the LES/BUS function for that ELAN. Because each ELAN can be considered its own broadcast domain, we configure each ELAN on its own subinterface on the ATM interface. So on Cat 1 we perform the following:

```
ATM(config)#interface atm 0.1
ATM(config-subif)#lane server-bus ethernet ELAN1
```

This is all there is to it. You now have the combined LES/BUS operational for ELAN 1 on Cat 1. The next stage is to define the LEC function on Cat 1 and Cat 2. The goal here is to use the `lane client` command to map VLANs to ELANs on each of the Catalysts. In the following example, we'll show the command to map VLAN 1 to ELAN 1 on Cat 1. (The same logic can be used to map other VLANs to other ELANs on either Catalyst.) Specifically, we'll have to replicate this mapping on Cat 2:

```
ATM#conf t
ATM(config)#interface atm0.1
ATM(config-subint)#lane client ethernet 1 ELAN1
```

Two things are immediately worthy of note. First, we have to map VLAN numbers to ELAN names, which may seem inconsistent to some people. Second, we are only illustrating the mapping of Ethernet VLANs. The reason is that at time of writing, this mapping is only available for Ethernet VLANs. Should we need to do this for subsequent VLANs, like VLAN 2, 3, 4, etc., all we need do is specify a new subinterface, define a LEC for that subinterface, and map the VLANs to an appropriately named ELAN.

Now comes the slightly tricky part. Tricky, I think, not because of the complexity of the configuration or of the concepts involved, but because you have to enter a series of 40-digit numbers that represent the ATM addresses of network components in ESI format. (I have yet to get this right the first time; data entry is not my strongest skill.) What we want to do is build a database within the LECS. This database will list the LES address for each ELAN and enable the LEC to find this database on the LECS. That's it. That's all we are accomplishing with the following commands. The only thing that makes it tricky, as I said, is that you have to enter 40 digits, which is prone to error, and determining what those 40-digit addresses are requires a bit of effort also.

Remember that the LEC interrogates the LECS to determine which LES to connect to, which by association defines the ELAN the LEC belongs to. In order for the LECS to return the LES address, we must configure that information into the LECS. Of course, the LEC needs to know where the LECS is also. We accomplish this as follows.

First of all make sure that the ATM 0 interface (the one that connects to the LS1010) is not shut down by issuing the `no shut` command when in interface configuration mode. Then exit configuration mode, and enter the `show lane default-atm-address` command, which should generate an output similar to the following:

```
ATM#show lane default-atm-addresses
interface ATM0:
LANE Client: 47 .00918100000000E04F2F2A01.00E04F2F2631.01
LANE Server: 47. 00918100000000E04F2F2A01.00E04F2F2632.01
LANE Bus: 47. 00918100000000E04F2F2A01.00E04F2F2633.01
LANE Config Server: 47. 00918100000000E04F2F2A01.00E04F2F2634.00
```

These ESI addresses are derived from MAC addresses as described in Chapter 3. On the Catalyst providing LECS services, there is a pool of MAC addresses from which the addresses above are generated. In the list of MAC addresses, the first is used for the LEC function, the LES uses the second, the BUS uses the third, and the LECS uses the fourth.

So now we have to configure the LECS with this LES address. The commands to set up the LANE database are as follows on Cat 2 (as that is the LECS for the network):

```
ATM#conf t
ATM(config)#lane database table1
ATM(config)#name ELAN1 server-atm-address
4700918100000000E04F2F2A0100E04F2F263201
ATM(config)#default-name elan1
```

The first configuration command creates a LECS database called `table1` on Cat 2. The second configuration command places an entry in that database. This entry is the 40-digit ATM address of the LES for the named ELAN, that being `ELAN1`. This process is called *binding* an ELAN name to a LES address. The final command defines `elan1` as the default ELAN, meaning that if a LEC is not explicitly bound to an ELAN, it will assume membership of ELAN 1.

This database must now be bound to the specific ATM interface in use for this ATM cloud, which in this case is the ATM 0 interface, still on Cat 2:

```
ATM(config)#interface atm 0
ATM(config-if)#lane config table1
ATM(config-if)#lane config auto-config-atm-address
```

The first line defines the interface we will use. The second specifies the name of the LECS database. The third line here means that ILMI will be used to automatically calculate the LECS address.

With this complete, we set up the LECS address in the 1010 switch as follows:

```
LS1010#conf t
LS1010(config)#atm lecs-addr 4700918100000000E04F2F2A0100E04F2F263400
```

Note that because the last two digits of these ESI addresses define the subinterface in use, the LECS is specified for the whole cloud and is therefore not specified per subinterface but for the whole interface. This allows all the ELANs to gain access to the one LECS.

We now have a base configuration that maps a single VLAN to a single ELAN. This can be extended using more subinterfaces to match additional VLANs to more ELANs should we wish. As you can see, LANE is by no means a plug-and-play technology, and it really is questionable in my mind when it is justified.

An alternative to LANE is setting up PVCs directly on the Catalyst. This can be a useful alternative if your utilization of LANE is only for a small part of the network. By this I mean if you only have a small number of LANE-connected devices, like two or three, it may be simpler to establish a fully meshed PVC network than rely on LANE to establish the SVCs, since they are needed to communicate between ATM devices. In my opinion, setting up more than four or five ATM devices with fully meshed PVCs is a pain and justifies the LANE configuration, so that SVCs can be created on an as-needed basis.

Before we do that, let's look at some commands we can use to verify the configuration.

Useful `Show` Commands for Lane

As long as we keep in mind the process of LEC going to LECS to get the address of the LES/BUS and take care with the addresses, we can use the following commands to verify the operation. The best place to start is the `show lane client`; secondary commands are `show lane config`, `show lane database`, and `show lane default-atm-address`. All these should agree about who is the LECS, who is the LES/BUS, and so on. The output of the `show lane client` command is as follows:

```
ATM#show lane client
LE Client ATM0.3 ELAN name: elan3 Admin: up State: operational
Client ID: 1
HW Address: 00C0.0cdf.0340 Type: ethernet Max Frame Size: 1516
ATM Address: 47.00000055001234567890A0055.00400CDE1230.03
VCD   rx    tx    Type        ATM Address
0     0     0     configure 47.000000444444444400550055.000123456789.00
14    3     4     direct     47.000000444444444400550055.000123456789.01
16    0     8     send       47.000000444444444400550055.000123456789.01
```

The first four lines of this display show the information specific to this LEC, which subinterface it is on, ELAN membership, address, etc. The remainder of the display is a table that shows for every Virtual Channel Descriptor (i.e., for active virtual channel connections currently active on the LEC), the cells received and transmitted, the type of connection (can be `configure`, `direct`, `distribute`, `send`, `forward`, or `data`), and the ATM address of the device at the other end of that connection.

The `show lane client` command is useful for making sure all required connections are made and that they are to the correct ATM addresses. The remaining `show` commands described above provide verification of the ATM addresses used in the configuration.

Establishing Direct PVCs

Many engineers do not like the complexity of setting up and maintaining a LANE environment. An alternative if ATM forms only a small part of your network, which could be the case if you subscribe to a commercially available ATM network for high bandwidth purposes, is to configure PVCs directly on the Catalyst. This solution can be thought of as subscribing to a high-bandwidth Frame Relay service, except due to the nature of ATM, the performance guarantees are real. Figure 5-15 shows how this may be deployed to bridge together two parts of VLAN 1 that exist in different geographic locations.

The way this works is that the ATM network vendor will define the PVC on their switch, which is connected to your Catalyst. You then define the PVC information in the Catalyst, and you get the cell-based service over the ATM cloud from your Catalyst to whatever the destination is at the other end of the PVC. This type of connectivity uses the RFC-1483 LLC/SNAP encapsulation discussed in Chapter 3.

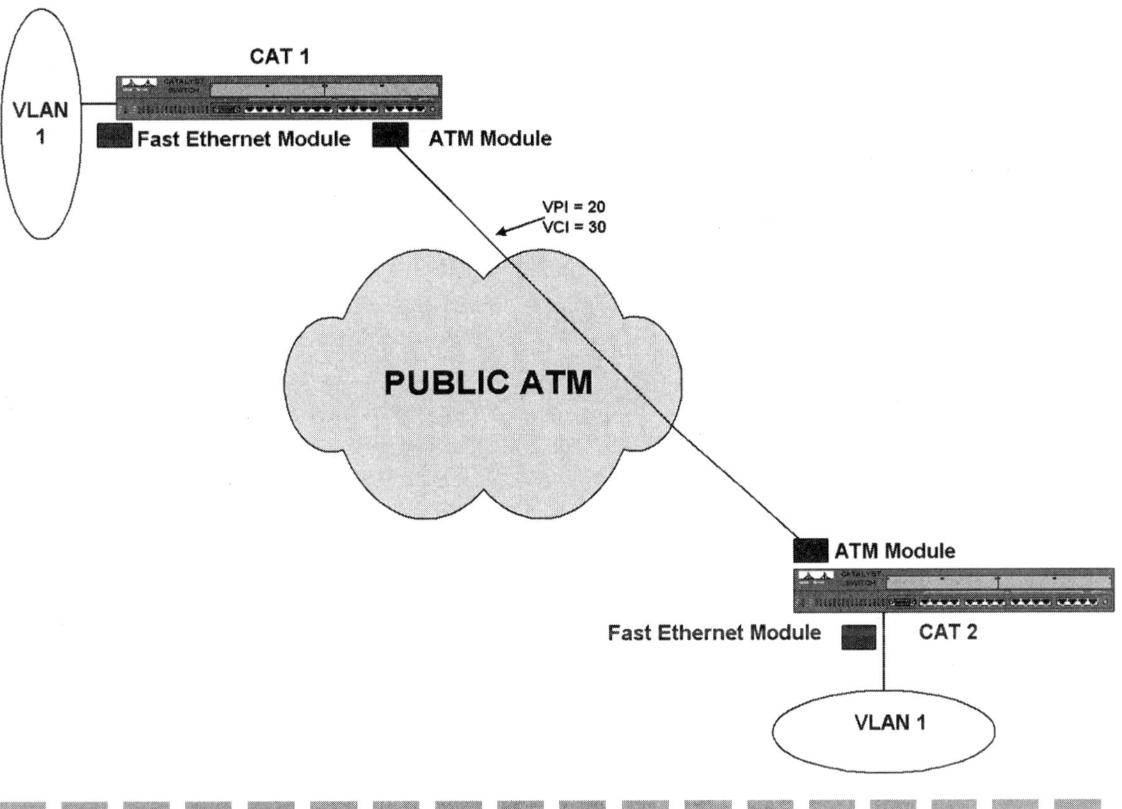

Figure 5-15 Physical connectivity for a public ATM network.

Assuming that the ATM network vendor has told you the VPI/VCI number of the PVC (in the case of Figure 5-15, we are taking 20 and 30), you can map a VLAN to use that PVC with the following commands:

```
ATM#conf t
ATM(config)#interface atm 0
ATM(config-if)#atm pvc 10 20 30 aal5snap
ATM(config-if)#atm bind pvc vlan 10 1
```

After getting into configuration mode for ATM interface 0, we specify the local VCD as 10, for the VPI of 20 and VCI of 30 supplied by the ATM network vendor, with the LLC/SNAP encapsulation. Next, we bind VLAN 1 to the VCD of 10 to map the VLAN to the VCC that will carry traffic across the ATM cloud to its destination.

Because the VCD is something that is defined locally, it is wise to check that you are not about to use a VCD number already configured on the Catalyst; this can be done using the `show atm vc` command as follows:

```
ATM# show atm vc
Intfc. VCD VPI VCI Type AAL/Encaps Peak Avg. Burst
ATM0     1   0   5  PVC   AAL5-SAAL 0      0     0
ATM0     2   0   16 PVC   AAL5-ILMI 0      0     0
```

In this case, the useful information is that VCD 1 and 2 are already in use. To verify that the PVC connection has been set up correctly, use the `show atm vlan` command as follows:

```
ATM#show atm vlan
VCD          VLAN ID
10           1
```

Summary

This chapter covered most of the configuration issues that will be met during initial Catalyst 5K deployments. We started with a review of the hardware, describing each module, the different supervisors, the Ethernet and group Ethernet switching modules, RSM, LANE, FDDI, and backplane configurations. The larger members of the 5K range were identified as switches and an LS1010 in the same chassis. We then discussed the internal operation of the 5K, discussing key subcomponents such as the SAMBA, the EARL, the NMP, and the MCP. We also discussed the process for how the Catalyst 5K range switches a packet from input to output.

The initial configuration file that comes with a 5K switch was explained in detail, and the process for software upgrades was illustrated. The command-line interface was illustrated as being substantially different from the regular Cisco IOS command structure, and navigation between modules using the `session` command was discussed. The initial setup of the SC0 interface, which is unique to the 5K range, was shown as well.

We also discussed how to boot the Catalyst using different image and configuration files. In addition, establishing multiple VLANs, VTP modes, and pruning was shown, along with the creation of ISL trunks to carry multiple VLAN traffic between switches. The operation of VMPS for dynamic VLAN membership was discussed, as well as customizing the configuration for port names, priorities, and so forth. We showed how

EtherChannels can be established to boost the available bandwidth above 100 Mbit/sec and how to speed up STP convergence using Uplink Fast and Backbone Fast.

The RSM's boot process and configuration to route between multiple VLANs was shown as well. Token VLANs were covered, with explanations of how to create TR-BRFs and TR-CRFs and how these are handled on the RSM. Also, FDDI was discussed as both a trunk option and as a medium for native VLANs.

Finally, we covered configuration of the ATM module for both LANE and direct PVC mapping for the transport of VLAN packets.

CHAPTER 6

Implementing ATM Switching

Introduction

This chapter looks at implementing ATM functions within Cisco routers and the LightStream (LS) 1010 ATM switch. The discussion on the LS1010 is also applicable to a LS1010 operating in the bottom slots of a 5500 series Catalyst, which contains the five-slot LS1010 backplane within its chassis. Note that at the time of writing, connectivity between the LS1010 cards in the bottom five slots of the 5500 and the rest of the cards in the 5500 is only via external connections. There is not currently a backplane connection between the Catalyst 3.6-Gbit/sec bus and the LS1010 5-Gbit/sec bus. This, of course, limits throughput between the two buses to the speed of the external link between the Catalyst and LS1010 cards. It has been announced that backplane connectivity within the 5500 will be available soon, which will remove this limitation and provide backplane throughput between the two 5500 buses.

The hardware we will look at includes the ATM Interface Processor (AIP) card found in Cisco 7xxx series routers, the ATM Network Processor Module (NPM) for the 4x00 series routers, and the LS1010 itself. The functions available on the AIP and NPM are similar to the Catalyst ATM LANE module discussed in the previous chapter. The features that we will explore include SVC and PVC provision, Circuit Emulation Services (CES), Point-to-Point Protocol (PPP) and Classic IP Over ATM (CIOA) for router ATM devices, and then PNNI (Private Network-Network Interface), LANE, 1 and Multiprotocol Over ATM (MPOA).

Overview of ATM Processors for Cisco Routers

Here we'll look at the different modules available for the 7xxx and 4xxx routers to natively generate ATM cells.

The AIP for 7xxx Routers

The ATM Interface Processor (AIP) for 7xxx series routers comes on a plug-in card and provides native cell-based services to the router. Previously, the most common form of ATM connection had been via an

ATM Data Service Unit (DSU) connecting to a Cisco High-Speed Serial Interface (HSSI). This connection used ATM Data Exchange Interface (DXI) encapsulation of frames, leaving the ATM DSU to convert the frames to cells. Now with the AIP, routers interface using ATM user-network interface (UNI) directly, generate cells natively, and connect at a physical level to SONET/SDH fibers.

The AIP Hardware The AIP has three LEDs that show the operational status of the unit:

- *The RX Carrier LED*—If this is lit, it means that carrier is seen, which in the case of the fiber interface indicates that light is seen on the fiber.
- *The Enabled LED*—This indicates that the AIP is ready for action, but not necessarily that the ports are configured for operation.
- *The RX Cells LED*—This flickers during normal operation to indicate that valid cells are being received.

There are a number of things you must consider on the hardware and physical connection level when deciding to implement an AIP. The first is to make sure that the backplane bus your router is using has enough aggregate throughput available for the ATM traffic you expect to pass through it. The 70xx routers have just over 500-Mbit/sec throughput available using the CxBus, the 7505 has just over 1 Gbit/sec with the CyBus, and the 7507/7513 have just over 2 Gbit/sec available with a dual-CyBus architecture. As a rule of thumb, single-bus routers should have a maximum of two AIPs.

The various physical interfaces that the AIP supports are implemented in Physical Layer Interface Modules (PLIMs) that slot on to the AIP. There are PLIMs available for the following:

- SONET/SDH for MMF up to 3 km and SMF to 15 km with a single-duplex SC connector or two simplex SC connectors
- TAXI 4B/5B on MMF for links up to 3 km, using MIC connectors for FDDI-like encoding of data onto the fiber (note that if the AIP is communicating via the ATM cloud with a router using DXI on a HSSI, the AIP requires NLPID encapsulation).
- 34-Mbit/sec E3 and 45-Mbit/sec DS3 on RG-59 coaxial cable for transmission up to 50 m.

Care must be taken when ordering, as these PLIMs cannot be swapped out in the field. One point of interest is that the maximum transmission unit (MTU) of the AIP is set to 4470 to avoid unwanted fragmentation when FDDI is in use; however, it can be expanded to 9188 to accommodate the maximum IP MTU of 9180. MTU settings and their effect on high-speed communications is discussed in the *Cisco TCP/IP Routing Professional Reference.* Although the AIP only has one physical interface, it does support the use of subinterfaces as used on the Catalyst ATM LANE module so that multiple ELANs can be supported in a LANE environment. The most common adaptation layer accessed over the AIP is AAL5, which is used for RFC1483, CIOA, and LANE, with AAL3/4 for Switched Multimegabit Data Service (SMDS).

In the section on network design we will cover the traffic shaping feature of the AIP, which reduces congestion. As will be explained, congestion control is more significant in ATM networks than in other networks. The reason is the small size of the cell. If a single 53-byte cell is lost when transmitting a FDDI packet over the ATM cloud, that will cause the retransmission of up to 93 cells. Cell loss has an exponential effect on bandwidth consumed.

The ATM NPM

The ATM Network Processor Module does for the 4x00 series what the AIP does for the 7xxx series routers, in that it allows the router to generate cells natively, obviating the need for an ADSU (ATM DSU). The NMP also supports the same AAL3/4, AAL5, and LANE services the AIP does, including support for AIP like traffic shaping. The NMP supports over 1000 simultaneous VCs, SONET at 155 Mbit/sec on MMF and SMF, and DS-3/E-3 physical layer interfaces.

Circuit Emulation Services

The Circuit Emulation Services (CES) are there to provide constant bit rate services to devices that require it, such as PBXs. In Chapter 3 we covered how CES allocated a cell slot every so often in the cell stream to give the impression of a fixed bandwidth and latency link.

Typically a CES port adapter will have interface connections for four T-1 or E-1 connections (these would go to the PBX, for example), plus an OC-3 fiber or DS-3/E-3 link to an ATM network. The CES connections use AAL1 adaptation for that traffic; however, the DES module also supports AAL5 for data traffic. If your carrier supports channel activated signaling, it is possible to release the CES bandwidth when no voice traffic (or whatever has been set up to use the CES service) is present. When no CES traffic is present, the bandwidth is returned to the pool of available cell transmission for variable bit rate traffic to use. A typical application of CES is illustrated in Figure 6-1.

Basic ATM Processor Configuration

Configuration of the ATM processor is quite straightforward, if the necessary parameters are known. In this section we'll examine the commands you need to execute in order to get a router ATM interface working. A point to note is that when we look at the AIP configuration, there is only one interface on it, which is always numbered 0. So to access this interface, we use the convention of slot/port number, and if the AIP is in slot 4, we access the AIP port via the reference 4/0.

ATM Rate Queues

The main difference between the AIP and the ATM NPM is in the creation of rate queues, something that we have not covered up till now and need to clarify. The AIP has eight rate queues: 0 through 3 are high pri-

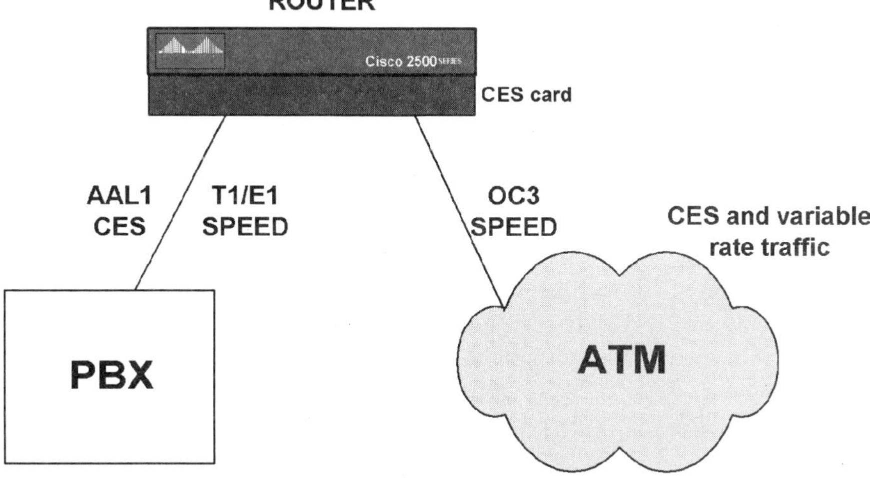

Figure 6-1 CES and variable-rate traffic.

ority and 4 through 7 are low priority. Cells in the AIP low-priority queues do not get processed until the high-priority queues are cleared. The NPM has up to four rate queues. Over time the requirement for rate queue configuration has changed with different versions of IOS. Currently you can manually configure rate queues, leave it to the IOS, or perform some combination of both. Let's take the AIP configuration to illustrate what needs to be done.

The role of a rate queue is to limit the speed at which any of the virtual circuits (VCs) assigned to that rate queue can transmit. Think of the rate queues as different categories of connection, each referring to the peak rate available for that queue. For example:

Rate queue 1 might be set to 100 Mbit/sec.

Rate queue 2 might be set to 45 Mbit/sec.

Rate queue 3 might be set to 10 Mbit/sec.

When a VC is created, either as a PVC through manual configuration or a switched virtual circuit (SVC) setup by the switch for a temporary connection, part of the configuration or negotiation process for that VC is to define the peak rate that will be transmitted on that VC. That peak rate will define which rate queue the VC is made a member of. For example, a VC that requests a peak rate of 100 Mbit/sec will be assigned to rate queue 1, a VC requesting 10 Mbit/sec will be assigned to rate queue 3, and so on.

The simplest approach is to not concern yourself with rate queues and leave rate queue creation to the IOS. An example of this interface configuration is as follows, which creates a PVC on interface 4/0, with VPI = 5 and VCI = 40:

```
ATM(config)#interface 4/0
ATM(config-if)#pvc 5/40
```

That's it, no permanent rate queues have been configured. The IOS dynamically creates a rate queue when a `pvc` command creates a PVC that does not have a peak rate that matches any of the existing rate queues in existence. In this instance no traffic shaping has been specified and a rate queue set to the maximum value of throughput supported by the PLIM (for example 34 Mbit/sec if it is an E-1) is created. Essentially this means that all VCs will be assigned to this rate queue.

Where you may be concerned about rate queue configuration is if you decide to implement traffic shaping. An example where traffic shaping is used to force the software to create a rate queue is as follows:

```
ATM(Cconfig)#interface 4/0
ATM(config-if)#pvc 5/41
ATM(config-if)#vbr-nrt 155000 50000
```

In this case, we have created a PVC with VPI = 5 and VCI = 41, set up for variable bit rate nonreal-time traffic with a peak rate of 155 Mbit/sec and an average rate of 50 Mbit/sec. If a rate queue does not exist to service these connection characteristics, the IOS will create it. So we can implement traffic shaping without having to manually edit the rate queues.

If you do wish to have a fine degree of control over how the rate queues are formed, it is possible to create a rate queue manually. In older versions of the IOS, this used to be a required feature. If no rate queues were defined before PVCs were created, an error message would be generated. Thankfully this is no longer the case. Should you wish to allocate a larger portion of the available bandwidth to one of the rate queues, you can define its peak rate manually as follows:

```
ATM(config-if)#atm rate-queue 1 1000000
```

This sets the peak rate for rate queue 1 to 100 Mbit/sec.

Where the AIP and NPM differ is that with the NPM the rate queues are all the same priority.

Configuring a Static PVC on Router Interfaces

It should be understood that to use a PVC, it must be configured in the router ATM interface and the ATM switch it is connected to. In the later section on the LS1010, we'll cover PVC creation for the switch. The PVC will remain active until it is taken out of the configuration of either the router or the switch.

To configure an ATM PVC on a router is quite similar in concept to setting up a Frame Relay DLCI (Data Link Connection Identifier). The DLCI must be mapped to a destination IP address. Just as in Frame Relay, we considered the DLCI as a pipe that led to a particular IP address, so the ATM PVC is set up to access one specific remote IP address. In Figure 6-2, we show the PVC 20/30 being switched through an LS1010 to the remote address 188.2.3.4. Note that on the first link in the chain, both the router and the LS1010 know the PVC by the same identifier; however, on the second link (from the LS1010 to the destination machine) a different identifier is used.

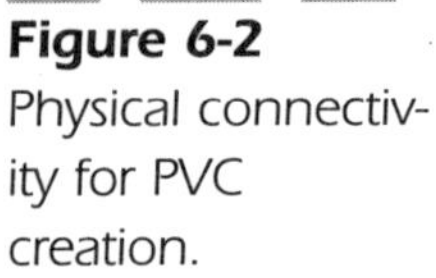

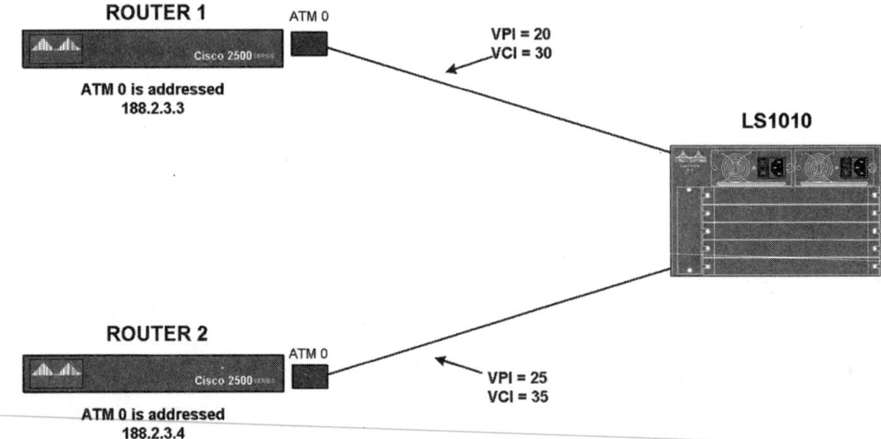

Figure 6-2 Physical connectivity for PVC creation.

It is possible to use PVC discovery so that manual configuration into the router ATM interface is not required; however, we will cover manual creation here and follow that with a brief look at PVC discovery. To create PVCs, we use the `atm pvc` command, which has some compulsory, but many optional, arguments.

When configuring a PVC, you must configure the VCD, VPI, and VCI along with the encapsulation that will be used. Optionally you can configure peak, average, and burst cell rates, as well as whether the PVC will use OAM (Operation, Administration, and Maintenance) cells for maintenance purposes. If you do not specify the cell rates, the PVC will default to connecting to the highest rate queue available. As an aside, if you wish to view the list of configured rate queues, it is displayed in the third-from-bottom line in the `show atm interface atm` command for the interface you are interested in. The relevant parts of this display are as follows:

```
Router# show atm interface atm 4/0
ATM interface ATM5/0:
Rate-Queue 1 set to 100Mbps, reg = 0x4EA DYNAMIC, 1 VCCs
ATM5/0.1:AAL3/4-SMDS address c111.1111.1111 Multicast
e222.2222.222Config. is ACTIVE
```

In this example, there is only one rate queue configured, which is typically the configuration for data only applications.

Now back to creating an ATM PVC that will function like the more familiar Frame Relay DLCI. Using the `ATM PVC` command, we must specify the VCD (or some other name we wish to use to identify the VPI/VCI pair), followed by the VPI and VCI the PVC will use, then the encapsulation. The encapsulation can be of the following types:

qsaal—Used by the signaling PVC.

NLPID—When a HSSI is set for ATM-DXI and uses an ATM DSU to access an ATM network, the encapsulation is NLPID. If the AIP is going to communicate with an HSSI in this configuration at the other end of the PVC, its encapsulation must be set to NLPID also.

aal45smds—for PVCs over SMDS transport.

ilmi—for the SNMP like ILMI PVC.

aal5snap—Used for PVCs that will be used to transport multiple network layer protocols over the one PVC. This is the encapsulation that must be used for PVCs using inverse ARP.

aal5mux—Requires an additional argument that specifies the network layer protocol that will use this PVC. Options are IPX, IP, decnet, vines, xns, apollo, and appletalk.

In most instances, the encapsulation to use will be clear. The only time when choice enters into the picture is when you are deciding between aal5mux and aal5snap. For PVC use I prefer aal5mux for keeping each protocol to its own PVC, thus simplifying troubleshooting and management. However, the drawback is that you lose inverse ARP.

The optional commands are to define the peak and average Kbit/sec rates and the burst cell rate for the PVC. An example to create a PVC with VCD = 10, VPI = 20, VCI = 30, using aal5mux encapsulation for IP, is as follows:

```
ATM(config)#interface atm 5/0
ATM(config-if)#atm pvc 10 20 30 aal5mux ip
```

Of course, this is no real use to us yet; we have to map a destination protocol address for the device at the remote end of the PVC to make it usable by the AIP. You should consider the mapping of a PVC to a protocol address as an integral part of PVC creation. When we map the VCD to a destination IP address, it is assumed that the ATM switch the AIP is connected to will be switching this virtual circuit to an interface with that IP address on the destination machine. This configuration just shows you what needs to be done on one end of the connection. To complete the connection, the ATM switch has to switch the circuit to the correct destination, and the remote end needs a similar configuration also.

To map destination protocols to ATM PVCs, you must first create a map-list of a specific name. This will put you into map-list configuration mode, which will allow you to enter a list of protocol address-to-PVC VCDs. Then you enter interface configuration mode for the ATM interface the PVC is defined on and associate the map-list created (via the `map-group` command) with that interface. The command sequence is:

```
ATM(config)#map-list ippvc
ATM(config-map)#ip 1.2.3.4 atm vc 10 broadcast
ATM(config-map)#int atm 5/0
ATM(config-if)#map-group ippvc
```

With this command sequence we have created a list called `ippvc` for the PVC with VCD = 10 above. In the map-list we have mapped the destination address 1.2.3.4 to the VCD and specified the broadcast argument. This is similar to the broadcast command that was used when configuring Frame Relay DLCIs in that it enables broadcast routing protocol updates to be sent over the PVC that would otherwise be dropped. Next we have defined the `ippvc` map list to be operative on the ATM interface 5/0. This concept can be extended to multiple destinations via multiple PVCs coming in via the one physical interface and by using subinterfaces to accommodate multiple subnets on the one physical interface.

To complete this configuration, we assign an IP address of something like 1.2.3.3 to the ATM interface 5/0, and we should then be able to ping across the PVC. This completes the simplest case of PVC configuration, which, in effect, is using straight RFC1483 encapsulation and static mapping to create the PVC-to-destination IP address mapping.

The next step is to look at using ATM ARP, by setting up the ARP server configuration and the ATM ARP client configuration, which will eliminate the need for manual mapping. This is moving the network to the Classic IP Over ATM model, as specified in RFC 1577. However, the configuration for ATM ARP services is slightly different for a SVC environment compared to a PVC environment, so before we configure CIOA, let's configure the AIP for SVC operation without ATM ARP services.

Configuring SVC Operation on Router Interfaces

This process requires more steps than PVC creation and is also more prone to error, since we must use the 40-digit ESI addresses in the configuration (this address is referred to as the *ATM NSAP* for the interface). The process is as follows:

- Create a signaling PVC between the AIP and the ATM switch.
- Create an ILMI PVC between the AIP and the switch.
- Define the NSAP of the interface being configured.

- Create map-groups and map destination IP addresses with destination NSAP addresses.

The reason we have to get involved with the 40-digit addresses this time is that, because the SVC is created on an as-needed basis, there is no VPI/VCI pair already defined that we can use in the configuration to reference the connection.

In Figure 6-3, should the AIP interface 5/0 in router 1 need to contact the AIP interface 4/0 in router 2, UNI signaling is used to negotiate a connection with VPI/VCI identifiers. The NSAP 1 and NSAP 2 addresses are used during this signaling process, but not in the cells that are sent from router 1 to router 2. The LS1010 A and B will use PNNI to exchange NSAP address information for the calculation of route paths. So the first tasks are to create the signaling and ILMI PVCs between router 1 and LS1010 A as follows:

```
ATM(config)#interface 5/0
ATM(config-if)#atm pvc 1 0 5 qsaal
ATM(config-if)#atm pvc 2 0 16 ilmi
```

Now we have to assign the NSAP for this interface and the IP address it will use, which is accomplished with the following commands:

```
ATM(config-if)#atm nsap-address
47.0081.a9.876543.2100.0000.fedc.ba98.7654.3210.01
ATM(config-if)#ip address 1.2.3.4 255.255.0.0
```

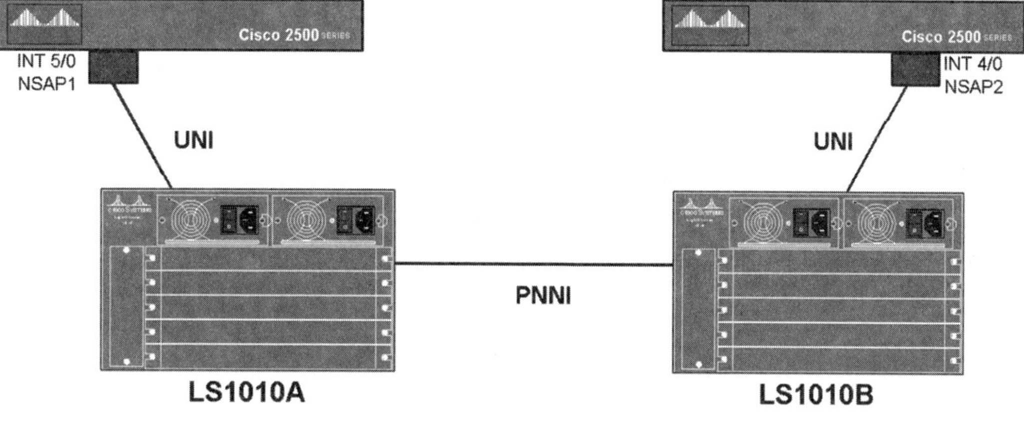

Figure 6-3 Use of UNI signaling to negotiate a connection with VPI/VCI identifiers.

With the addressing of this interface complete, we turn to defining the destination IP address to the destination NSAP address. With that in place the interface is then able to receive a request to contact the destination IP address, know what NSAP address that maps to, and use the signaling PVC to request a VPI/VCI pair that identifies the VCC that will reach the desired destination. So while still in interface configuration mode, we add the map-group that will contain the mapping for the destination IP and NSAP addresses, then add the map-list `dest1`:

```
ATM(config-if)#map-group dest1
ATM(config-if)#exit
ATM(config)#map-list dest1
ATM(config-map)#ip 1.2.3.5 atm-nsap
47.0081.a9.876543.1111.1111.2222.2222.3333.3333.01 broadcast
```

Of course, providing static mappings of this type for all the SVCs that may be necessary on even a modestly sized ATM network becomes very burdensome. This static mapping using RFC 1483 encapsulation is significantly improved upon by the introduction of an ATM ARP server à la RFC 1577, which is the subject of the next section.

Configuring Classic IP Over ATM on ATM Router Interfaces (RFC 1577)

The change that we introduce to the network with RFC 1577 operation is to define one ATM ARP server per logical subnet. This eradicates the need for any `map-list` or `map-group` configuration statements. Of course, this requires that an ATM ARP server is available. Any AIP or NPM can be used as both an ATM ARP server and ATM ARP client. ARP was designed to supply a layer 3 address, given a layer 2 address, like a MAC address. We will supply a layer 3 address (in this example, an IP address) and request a layer 2 address (with RFC 1577, IP subnet rules apply and ATM addresses are effectively used as layer 2 addresses), which is serviced by the ATM ARP server.

The process is for each ATM interface to be configured with the same address of the ATM ARP server, on a per-subnet basis. When a client establishes a link to the ATM ARP server, the server sends inverse ARP requests to the client to learn its IP and ATM address. These addresses are stored to service future requests for ATM address information.

Starting the ATM ARP Server Process

In ATM ARP, there is a client and server process. Starting the server process involves starting the client functions as well. The ATM ARP server is a nonredundant device and, as stated, is configured on a per-subnet interface, so each subinterface on an AIP or NPM will have its own ATM ARP server defined. Once the NSAP and IP address for the interface (or subinterface if multiple subnets are to be addressed on the one ATM interface) are defined, a single-line entry to start the ATM ARP server is needed:

```
ATM(config-if)#atm arp-server nsap self
```

This sets the interface being configured as the ATM ARP server for the subnet.

On other ATM interfaces in the same subnet, the keyword `self` will be replaced with the NSAP address of the interface configured as the ATM ARP server. Thus the `atm arp-server` command is utilized on every interface, whether it is the ATM ARP server or not.

Essentially, this is all that is required to enable an interface for SVC operation. We will now look at the configuration for PVC operation.

PVC Operation with Inverse ARP

Having an ATM ARP server available simplifies the configuration of SVCs. With PVCs we have a permanent connection, and it is not necessary to refer to an ARP server to resolve address issues. This function instead is handled by inverse ARP:

```
ATM(config-if)#atm pvc 10 20 30 aal5snap inarp 10
```

This creates the PVC with VCD = 10, VPI = 20, and VCI = 30, using the `aal5snap` encapsulation, which is the only encapsulation that supports inverse ARP for PVCs. In addition, we enable inverse ARP with a timeout value of 10 minutes. The timeout value specifies how often inverse ARP datagrams will be sent down this VCC; the default is 15 minutes. This inverse ARP process returns the IP address of the device at the other end of the PVC connection.

Of course, inverse ARP only works for IP. Other network protocols, such as IPX or XNS, will require separate `map-list` statements.

Sample Network Configurations

There is virtually a limitless variety of network configurations we could choose from to illustrate the practical application of the commands discussed above. What we will do is show how three router interfaces could be connected via an ATM cloud using AIPs (the configuration for NPMs is the same). The first example will illustrate more commands; we will just use straight RFC 1483 configuration, with no RFC 1577 ATM ARP server, and enable the interfaces for PVC communication. This is likely to be the first application many corporate network managers use ATM for. In this instance, ATM is used as a fast pipe between a limited number of locations. Often this is done by accessing a commercial ATM network, such as British Telecom's CellStream. In this situation, the VPI and VCI values are defined by the ATM vendor, and all that is left is for the AIP (or NPM) to be configured to access the predefined VPI/VCI pairs.

The second configuration will set one of the routers to be an ATM ARP server and also explore SVC configuration. The network we will configure is illustrated in Figure 6-4.

In this network, our job is to configure each router to use the two PVCs the ATM cloud is presenting us with. Clearly we will need to know the VPI and VCI numbers for each PVC that is set on the ATM network before commencing configuration. For router 1, the PVC to router 2 is set to VPI = 10, VCI = 10, and the PVC to router 3 has VPI = 10, VCI = 11. This yields a configuration for router 1 (using subinterface 1 for this subnet) as follows:

```
Interface atm1/0.1
Ip address 142.8.1.1 255.255.255.0
Atm pvc 1 10 10 aal5snap
Atm pvc 2 10 11 aal5snap
Map-group r1-pvcs
!
map-list r1-pvcs
ip 142.8.1.3 atm-vc 2 broadcast
ip 142.8.1.2 atm-vc 1 broadcast
```

This pulls together the configuration for router 1; we have identified the PVCs, addressed the interface at the IP level, and mapped the PVCs to the destination IP addresses. We now proceed in a similar fashion for router 2, given that PVC 10/20 goes to router 1 and 10/21 goes to router 3:

```
Interface atm1/0.1
Ip address 142.8.1.2 255.255.255.0
Atm pvc 1 10 20 aal5snap
Atm pvc 2 10 21 aal5snap
```

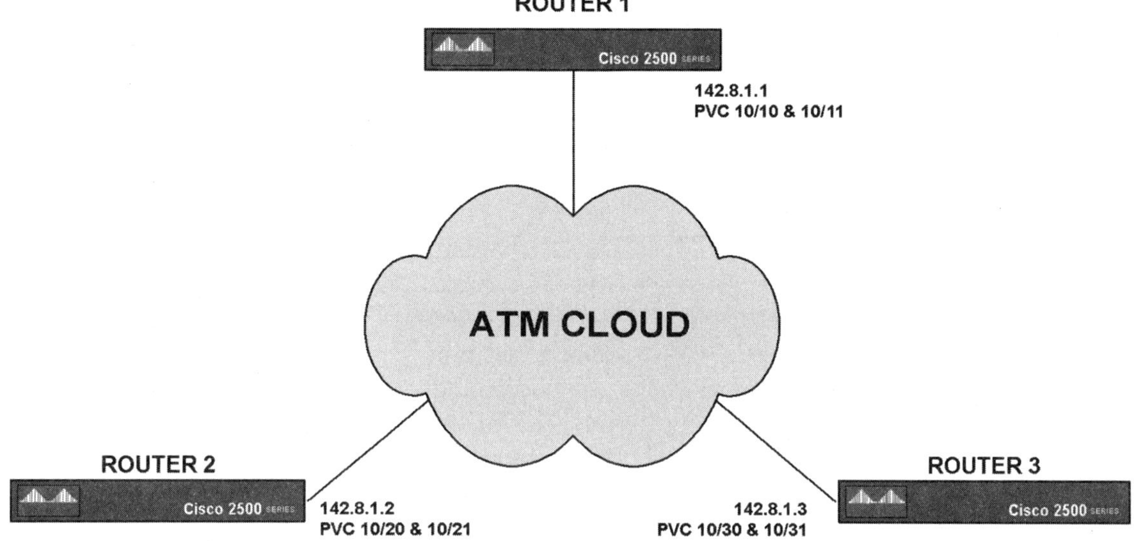

Figure 6-4 Simple ATM network connectivity.

```
Map-group r2-pvcs
!
map-list r2-pvcs
ip 142.8.1.3 atm-vc 2 broadcast
ip 142.8.1.1 atm-vc 1 broadcast
```

To complete the network, we configure router 3 with PVC 10/30 to router 1 and 10/31 to router 2 as follows:

```
Interface atm1/0.1
Ip address 142.8.1.3 255.255.255.0
Atm pvc 1 10 30 aal5snap
Atm pvc 2 10 31 aal5snap
Map-group r3-pvcs
!
map-list r3-pvcs
ip 142.8.1.2 atm-vc 2 broadcast
ip 142.8.1.1 atm-vc 1 broadcast
```

It is also worth considering how the routers would be configured if an ATM ARP server was on the network. For illustration purposes, we could designate one of the routers—say, router 3—as the ATM ARP server and look at how both SVC and PVC configuration is affected. The connections we will establish are as follows:

- *Router 1*—PVC using inverse ARP for IP address resolution to router 2 and SVC when communication with router 3 is necessary
- *Router 2*—PVC using inverse ARP for IP address resolution to router 1 and SVC when communication with router 3 is necessary
- *Router 3*—Will host the ATM ARP process, using a PVC with inverse ARP for communication with router 2 and an SVC to communicate with router 1 when necessary

It is important to be clear on the difference between inverse ARP and ATM ARP. Inverse ARP is used in a PVC environment to determine the IP address of the device at the other end of the PVC; this obviates the need for `map-group` and `map-list` commands in the configuration. ATM ARP is used in SVC environments, where it is only necessary to configure the NSAP address of an interface, plus the NSAP of the ATM ARP server. With ATM ARP, the ATM ARP client maintains a connection to the ATM ARP server and requests ATM-to-IP address mapping information whenever necessary.

For each router we perform the following:

- For SVC communication, assign the interface NSAP and IP address, and the address of the ATM ARP server (either self or the server's NSAP address).
- For the PVC connection, assign the interface IP address, use `aal5snap` encapsulation, and set the inverse ARP timer. This negates the need for `map-group` and `map-list` statements.

For router 1 this translates to the following configuration:

```
Interface atm 4/0.1
Ip address 142.8.1.1 255.255.255.0
Atm nsap-address 7.1111.22.333333.4444.55555.6666.7777.8888.9999.01
Atm pvc 1 0 5 qsaal
Atm pvc 2 10 10 aal5snap inarp 5
Atm arp-server 47.1111.22.333333.4444.55555.6666.7777.8888.aaaa.01
```

With this configuration we have defined the IP address and mask as normal and set the NSAP address for the interface. We also created a signaling PVC for requesting SVCs, defined a PVC to contact router 2 (using inverse ARP, so no map statements are required), and specified the NSAP address of the ATM ARP server to that of router 3.

For router 2 we generate the following configuration:

```
Interface atm 4/0.1
Ip address 142.8.1.2 255.255.255.0
Atm nsap-address 47.1111.22.333333.4444.55555.6666.7777.8888.bbbb.01
Atm pvc 1 0 5 qsaal
Atm pvc 2 10 20 aal5snap inarp 5
Atm arp-server 47.1111.22.333333.4444.55555.6666.7777.8888.aaaa.01
```

This is essentially the same configuration as for router 1. The change comes when we look at router 3:

```
Interface atm 4/0.1
Ip address 142.8.1.3 255.255.255.0
Atm nsap-address 47.1111.22.333333.4444.55555.6666.7777.8888.aaaa.01
Atm pvc 1 0 5 qsaal
Atm pvc 2 10 31 aal5snap inarp 5
Atm arp-server self
```

Here the configuration is to use itself as the ATM ARP server and a PVC to communicate with router 2. This is a more typical configuration as the network grows. It can be useful to establish PVCs for connections that are heavily used and rely on SVCs for establishing connections on an as-needed basis for infrequently contacted destinations. This is the same concept as having a leased line available for permanent connections and dial-up for infrequently contacted destinations.

Useful `Show` and `Debug` Commands

There are many, many `show` and `debug` commands for ATM configurations. The most useful are as follows:

- `show atm vc`
- `show atm int atm`
- `show atm map`
- `show atm ilmi`
- `debug atm events`
- `debug atm errors`
- `debug atm packet`

The `show atm vc` command is straightforward; it lists on a per-interface basis the VCD, VPI, and VCI numbers of all SVCs and PVCs in operation at that time. Clearly, if there is difficulty using IP ping to contact a remote location, the place to start is here, in order to determine if there is indeed a VCC that can carry the ping packets to the requested destination. If an appropriate VCC is not available, you need to delve further to determine what is stopping a VCC from being established. Problems of this nature are normally resolved by confirming NSAP addresses in the configuration and looking at the output of the debug commands.

Before looking at `debug` commands, it is worth issuing the `show atm map` command, the output of which is as follows:

```
ATM#show atm map
Map list ATM:
142.8.3.1 maps to VC 10, broadcast
142.8.4.2 maps to NSAP
47.1111.22.333333.4444.55555.6666.7777.8888.aaaa.01
```

This clearly shows the destination for each of the VCCs listed in the `show atm vc` command and can alert you to a VC being mapped to a destination you do not expect. The `show atm int atm` was discussed earlier when we were looking for a way to display the rate queues set.

Of all the `debug` commands, `debug atm events` is potentially the most useful and should be enabled when you are configuring ATM. If you are configuring from the console port or have issued the `term mon` configuration command on a telnet session, issuing this `debug` command will alert you to the progress of configuration changes or failures that may occur as a result of trying to establish VCCs.

Clearly, if a VCC that you expect to be established is not available, the `debug atm errors` is most likely to list the cause. Typical entries in this display show if the OAM cells are not being responded to by a remote device or if an encapsulation type is set incorrectly for communication.

The `debug atm packet` is rarely used; it displays header and initial packet contents for all inbound and outbound packets, which can generate a significant overhead and, in extreme cases, render the ATM processor and even the whole router useless until a reload is issued.

Overview of Configuring PPP Services on ATM Router Interfaces

For many network engineers, PPP has several attractions when they are implementing connection-oriented services. As its name suggests the Point-to-Point Protocol has been designed with connection orientation in mind. PPP can encapsulate multiple layer 3 protocols and provides a simple method of implementing the Challenge Handshake Authentication Protocol (CHAP). ATM is a connection-oriented protocol, which leads some network designers to look at taking advantage of PPP's features, implementing them over an ATM transport.

The key to understanding what is happening with PPP over ATM configuration is the virtual access interface. For PPP over ATM, a virtual template is created that lists the familiar PPP settings (PPP is dealt with more fully in the *Cisco TCP/IP Routing Professional Reference*), such as IP unnumbered and CHAP authentication. This virtual template is then applied to the encapsulation for a PVC on a router ATM interface. The following configuration shows what might be put in to the ATM interface on router A in Figure 6-5:

```
interface virtual-template 2
encapsulation ppp
ip unnumbered ethernet 0/0
ppp authentication chap
!
interface atm 2/0.2
point-to-point pvc 0/34
encapsulation aal5ciscoppp virtual-template 2
```

Of course, the CHAP username and password set on this router and the router at the other end must agree for the CHAP authentication to

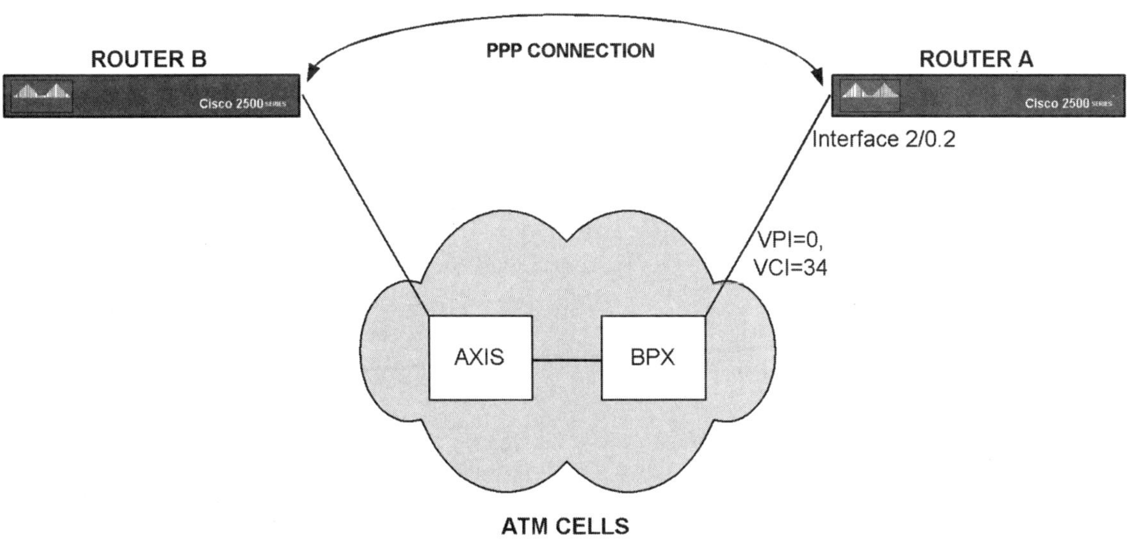

Figure 6-5 Network connecting for PPP over ATM.

complete (as discussed in the *Cisco TCP/IP Routing Professional Reference*). The other end of this PPP connection is terminated in a frame-based PPP encapsulated interface connected to a StrataCom Cisco AXIS shelf, as shown in Figure 6-5. The AXIS shelf is a means of connecting lower-speed links into the ATM core.

Introduction to the LS1010

The LightStream 1010 (LS1010) ATM switch is Cisco's current workgroup and campus ATM switch product, although it is believed this line will be discontinued at the end of 1999. The LS1010 is a five-slot device, much like a Catalyst 5000 in appearance, connecting line cards via a 5-Gbit/sec backplane. The ATM Switch Processor (ASP) must be inserted in slot 3. When in a 5500, the ASP must be in slot 13.

The LS1010 supports all the usual interface standards for ATM, from 25 Mbit/sec up to OC-12, 622 Mbit/sec via Port Adapter Modules (PAMs). The open four slots in the LS1010 can be filled with Carrier Modules (CAMs), each capable of supporting two PAMs. Given that each PAM can have several ports, the first thing to become accustomed to with LS1010 configuration is that we have three levels of specification to address a port: We have to identify slot, then PAM, then port on PAM, so port 0 in PAM 0 in CAM 0 is 0/0/0.

In addition to the usual ATM ports, the LS1010 PAMs support E-1/T-1, E-3/T-3, and Circuit Emulation Services at T-1/E-1 speeds.

Basic LS1010 Configuration

The LS1010 switch can be considered a plug-and-play system. We discussed the ATM address construction in Chapter 3, which lends itself to forming complete ATM addresses from device MAC addresses, if an address prefix is defined. The LS1010 comes with preset Cisco prefixes, thus allowing all the ATM address configuration to be performed via ILMI, with no manual intervention. What technically happens is that the LS1010 sends the prefix to an endstation (a Catalyst or router with an ATM processor), which will then form its complete ATM address from that prefix and its own MAC address.

Once this is done, the switch configures itself as a single-level PNNI routing hierarchy and for many small (fewer than six switches) installations, this is adequate. The ATM address of the LS1010 itself is generated in the same way.

Autoconfigured ATM Addresses

Let's imagine that we take our LS1010 fresh out of the box and connect it via a T-3 link to a router AIP. Using the Cisco auto-addressing prefix, the address that the AIP constructs looks something like that shown in Figure 6-6.

The MAC address in this figure is supplied by the endstation the LS1010 connects to, ensuring that this address will be unique among devices connecting to the LS1010. Of course, the endstation connected to the LS1010 will need the default PVCs for ILMI and signaling configured, but given that they are, the ATM address autoconfiguration should take place.

There will also be a slightly different setup in the AIP or NPM to accept the LS1010-supplied prefix. In the previous section we used the `atm nsap` command to specify the complete ATM address for the AIP interface. If we want the AIP to accept the LS1010 prefix, but supply the rest of the address according to our specification, we must use the `atm esi-address` command, as follows:

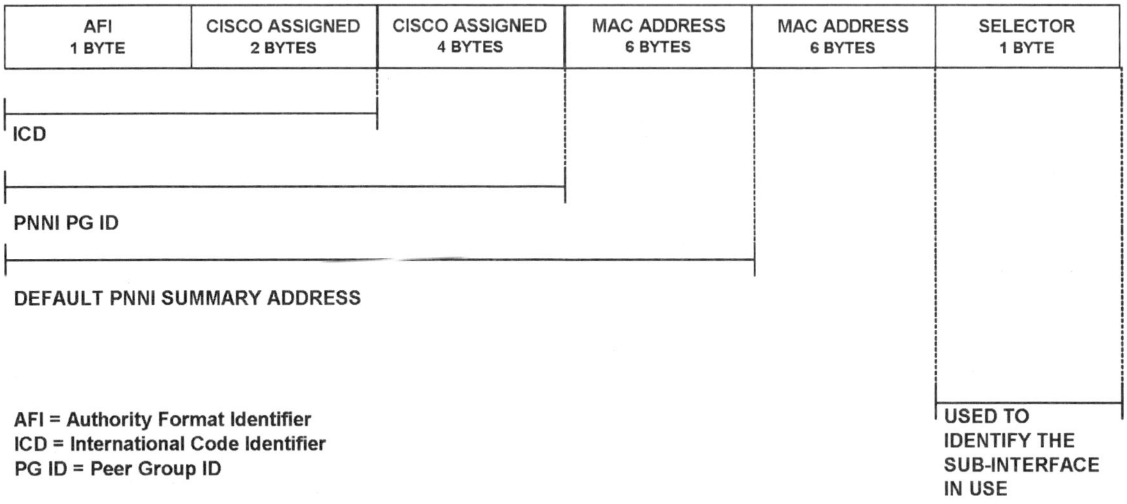

AFI 1 BYTE	CISCO ASSIGNED 2 BYTES	CISCO ASSIGNED 4 BYTES	MAC ADDRESS 6 BYTES	MAC ADDRESS 6 BYTES	SELECTOR 1 BYTE

Figure 6-6 ATM addressing in an auto-addressing environment.

```
interface atm 5/0
atm pvc 1 0 5 qsaal
atm pvc 2 0 16 ilmi
atm esi-address 123456789012.01
```

In this configuration we have the usual ILMI PVC established with the switch (the ATM prefix from the 1010 is supplied via ILMI), followed by the `atm esi-address` command. If we want the endstation to accept the prefix from the LS1010 and complete the rest of the ATM address using an internal MAC address, we just leave the interface configuration with the signaling and ILMI PVCs configured and do not insert any address-specific commands. This is the most common configuration, since it generates the least work.

Of course, establishing the ATM address through autoconfiguration is fine, and with the endstation able to signal for SVCs, communication across the ATM cloud as represented by the LS1010 switch should be possible. However, there is a lot more available, particularly if the LS1010 is being connected to an existing ATM addressing hierarchy. Auto-address configuration is also a problem if you are mixing ATM switches from different manufacturers together, as they will have different prefixes and a single-level PNNI hierarchy will not be established without manual intervention.

We can configure the ATM address manually in these scenarios, when we need to override the default prefix. We can do this on a per-interface basis by assigning a new ATM prefix that is different to the default 13 bytes, as follows:

```
Ls1010#conf t
Ls1010(config)#interface atm 0/0/2
Ls1010(config-if)#atm prefix 47.1111.2222.3333.4444.5555.6666
Ls1010(config-if)#
```

In this case, port 2 in PAM 0 in the CAM in slot 0 will use the prefix entered for assigning its own and attached endstation's ATM addresses. The `show atm address` command will display all the switch addresses, prefixes in use, and LECS address if we are operating in a LANE environment. If you are going to generate a nondefault PNNI scheme, refer to the later section on PNNI configuration.

Types of Connection Available

We have discussed PVC and SVC creation for ATM processors in routers; however, when we look at VCC creation on an LS1010, we find that other types of VC circuits do exist, including PVP switching, PVP tunneling, soft PVC, and soft PVP. First, let's describe PVC creation in the LS1010.

When creating a PVC with AIP and NPM processors, we were defining the VPI/VCI pair and mapping a destination address to that. This enabled the router ATM processor to send data for the destination IP address out on a particular VPI/VCI channel. The router does not care how the VPI/VCI is switched through the ATM network; however, the LS1010 does. So configuring PVCs on the LS1010 is a different concept than that of PVC creation on the router ATM processor. What we want to achieve with the LS1010 PVC configuration is to configure it to take an incoming VPI/VCI pair on a particular interface and send it out on another VPI/VCI pair on a different interface. So for PVC creation on a LS1010, we need to specify the source interface, VPI and VCI, followed by the destination interface, VPI and VCI, as follows:

```
Ls1010(config)#interface atm 0/1/1
Ls1010(config-if)#atm pvc 10 20 interface 0/1/0 30 40
```

The effect of this command is to switch cells coming into the LS1010 on interface 0/1/1 with VPI = 10 and VCI = 20, out of interface 0/1/0 with VPI = 30 and VCI = 40, as illustrated in Figure 6-7.

This is somewhat like MAC addresses being changed as a packet travels through a router; the ultimate destination is the same, just part of the local addressing alters on a hop-by-hop basis. In this example, router A and router B would be using different VPI and VCI numbers to contact each other, but the router interfaces that connect to the LS1010 would be configured for the same IP subnet.

The operation we have described above is referred to as *VCC switching*. This mode has the LS1010 switching connections based on the VPI

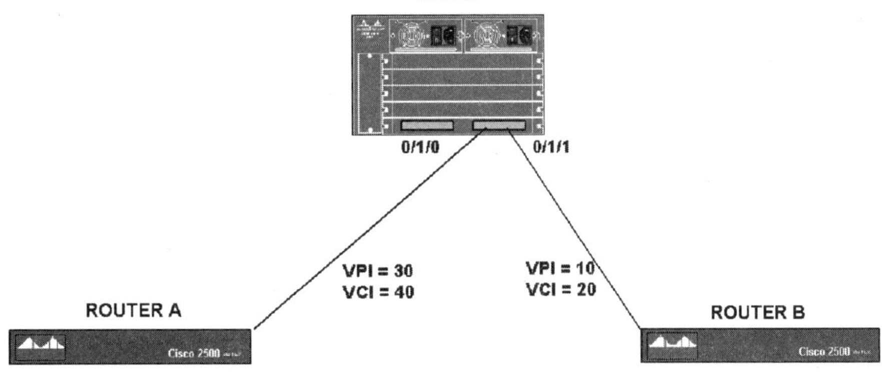

Figure 6-7 Network connections for a PVC in and out of an LS1010.

and the VCI. In larger networks with multiple LS1010s, there is another mode, called *VP switching,* where the LS1010 maps connections based just on the VPI. The segment of the connection that is switched based just on the VPI number is known as the *virtual path connection* (*VPC*), illustrated in Figure 6-8. In this figure LS1010_2 only looks at the VPI value in determining where to switch a connection to.

To configure a switch such as LS1010_2 in Figure 6-8 to operate in this fashion, we make use of the `atm pvp` command. This command can be used to configure both regular VP switching and PVP tunneling, which is used when a public network is used to connect two LS1010 switches together. First, let's look at the command syntax for regular VP switching. In the following configuration, we will be telling the switch to take in any connections with a VPI of 10 on 0/1/1 to send them out of 0/1/0 with VPI of 20. The VCI value will remain constant during this switching process:

```
LS1010(config)#interface atm 0/1/1
LS1010(config-if)#atm pvp 10 interface atm 0/1/0 20
```

There are many options for this command, but this will suffice for the basic functionality.

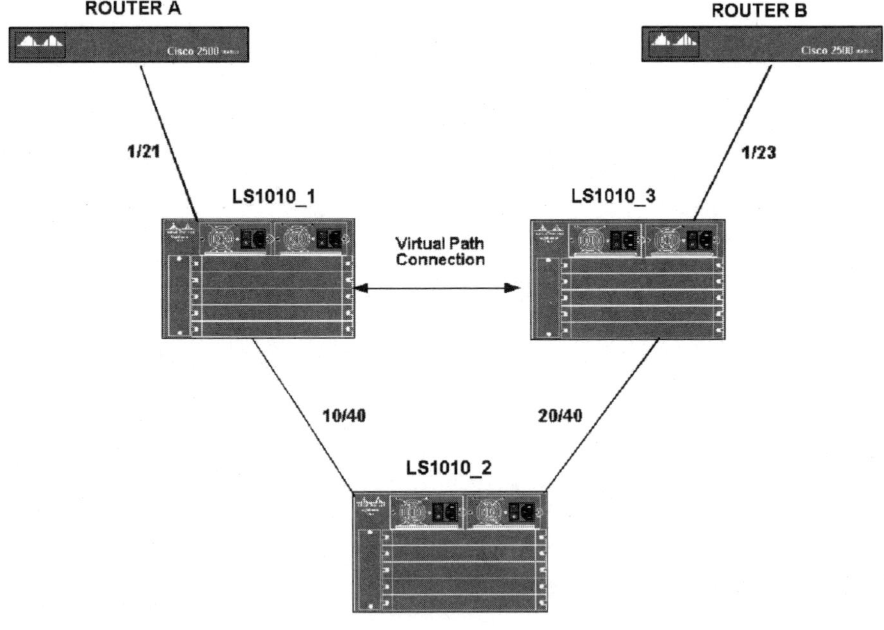

Figure 6-8
VP switching.

The VP tunnel feature is implemented a little differently. What we are trying to achieve with PVP tunneling is shown in Figure 6-9. Essentially, we are getting the two LS1010s connected via a public network that only supports PVCs and configuring them to communicate signaling information across this link so that SVCs can be set up also.

This makes the public network transparent to the rest of the network connected to these two LS1010 switches. Typically, the public ATM network will only support PVCs, but with PVP tunneling, SVC capability between LS1010_1 and LS1010_2 is restored. In the example below, we will configure the virtual path tunnel on both the LS1010_1 and LS1010_2 in Figure 6-9. For LS1010_1, the interface 0/1/1 is used to connect to the public network. We will give the PVP tunnel the ID of 50, which means we have to create a subinterface on 0/1/1 numbered 50 to create the tunnel. On LS1010_2 we have to create a PVP similarly numbered.

```
LS1010_1(config)# int atm 0/1/1
LS1010_1(config-if)#atm pvp 50
LS1010_1(config-if)#interface atm 0/1/1.50
```

Figure 6-9 Network connections with PVP tunneling.

This is followed by a similar configuration on LS1010_2:

```
LS1010_2(config)# int atm 0/1/1
LS1010_2(config-if)#atm pvp 50
LS1010_2(config-if)#interface atm 0/1/1.50
```

So much for straight PVC connection. However, wouldn't it be nice if we could assign PVCs but have them adapt to network failures by rerouting? Adapting to a link or switch failure is not possible with the configurations used so far, as we have hard-coded the interface and VPI/VCI pair that will be used to send cells out of every LS1010 in the PVC path. There is, however, an alternative, known as the *soft PVC,* that configures the endstation (router or Catalyst switch) to use a PVC connection to the LS1010 it connects to. But from there on, within the ATM network, the cells are transported over SVCs that can adapt to link failures. This also reduces the setup required, as each LS1010 in the path from source to destination no longer needs to be explicitly configured for the PVC path.

The information we need to gather before we can execute the necessary commands is as follows:

- Source interface
- Source VPI/VCI pair
- Destination ATM address for the soft PVC
- Destination VPI/VCI pair

These values are shown in Figure 6-10, which illustrates soft PVC operation, highlighting the PVC parts between the ATM switches and endstations that are connected to the SVC operation between LS1010 switches.

Because we have to configure the long ATM addresses, once again, this configuration is prone to a lot of errors when you are entering those addresses. The destination ATM address (as perceived from LS1010_1) will be an ATM address on LS1010_2. Once we create the soft VC, it is a bidirectional connection, so we enter the configuration on LS1010_1 with the soft PVC address of LS1010_2 as the destination.

The IOS does simplify the identification of soft VC addresses, as they are explicitly listed in the `show atm addresses` command output. Each interface will have its own soft VC value. So to configure PVC 10/20 on 0/1/1 on LS1010_1 to use a soft PVC to connect to 30/40 on interface 0/0/0 on LS1010_2, we do the following. First, determine the soft VC address for 0/0/0 on LS1010_2:

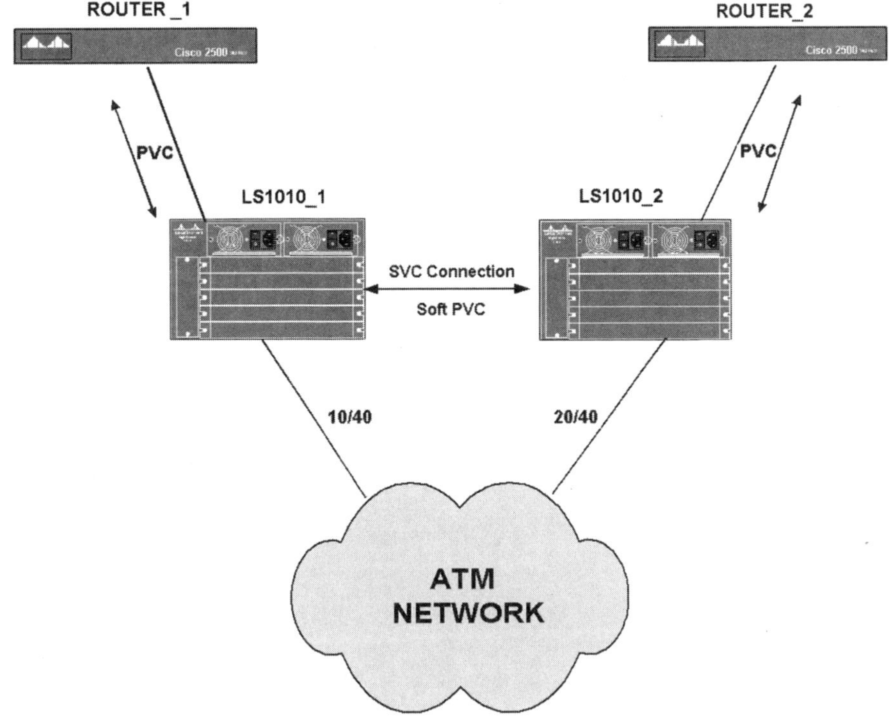

Figure 6-10 Network connections for soft PVC operation.

```
LS1010_2#show atm address
.
soft VC addresses
47.0091.8100.3333.4444.5555.6666.7777.8888.9999.00 ATM0/0/0
```

Now we have the information to go to LS1010_1 and complete the configuration:

```
LS1010_1(config)#int atm 0/1/1
LS1010_1(config-if)#atm soft-vc 10 20
47.0091.8100.3333.4444.5555.6666.7777.8888.9999.00 30 40
```

So we have established soft PVC operation between LS1010_1 and LS1010_2. To complete this network configuration, router_1 in Figure 6-10 needs to be configured with a PVC with VPI/VCI of 10/20, and router_2 needs a PVC configured with VPI/VCI 30/40. It should be noted that the soft PVC is available for both VC and VP switching. VP switching for soft PVCs is invoked by use of the `atm soft-vp` command being used in place of the `atm soft-vc` command in the syntax above.

Simple IP Configuration

First of all, the LS1010 is not a router, nor does it support a router module inserted in one of the available slots. As such, the support for IP really comes down to configuring an IP address on the LS1010 Ethernet port, setting up the LS1010 to participate in RFC 1577 CIOA, or making the LS1010 part of the LANE configuration. In Chapter 5 we covered setting up the Catalyst 5000 modules and all the devices needed for CIOA or LANE operation (like an ATM ARP server for CIOA, and a LES/BUS or LECS for LANE). We can actually configure the LS1010 to perform the same functions, as long as we know what devices we have in the network and what load they are running with. In some networks it will make sense to configure the Catalyst for these functions; in another, it will make more sense for the LS1010 to take on the additional load. We'll cover LANE configuration in a later section. Here we'll examine how to set the LS1010 Ethernet IP address and the ASP CPU IP address so that we can telnet to it, along with how to configure the LS1010 as an RFC 1577 ATM ARP server.

The LS1010 ATM Switch Processor (ASP) is located in slot 2 of the chassis (slot 13 if we are using a 5500 Catalyst) and has an Ethernet interface, which is located as 2/0/0 on the LS1010. To assign an IP address to this Ethernet interface, we perform the following commands:

```
LS1010(config)#interface ethernet 2/0/0
LS1010(config-if)#ip address 142.8.7.4 255.255.255.0
```

To complete the IP configuration for the LS1010, we should add a couple of commands in global configuration mode as follows:

```
LS1010(config)#ip host-routing
LS1010(config)#ip default-gateway 142.8.7.5
```

The first command enables ARP and proxy ARP services, and the second identifies the IP gateway that will be used to access IP addresses not on the local subnet.

This is only part of the story. We have already said that the LS1010 can be configured to perform network services, such as an RFC 1577 ATM ARP server, or as one or more of the LANE components. If we want to telnet to the LS1010 from another device, we will need to configure the ASP CPU as either an RFC 1577 client or a LANE client, depending on the IP-to-ATM address mapping methodology in use on the network.

This is an important point. By setting up the LS1010 as an RFC 1577 client or a LANE client, we are enabling IP connectivity for management purposes of the switch only—by that I mean the ability to telnet to it or send SNMP commands to it. By addressing the ASP Ethernet port with an IP address, we have not enabled IP connectivity to attached devices.

Say we want to telnet to the LS1010 from an attached router. Provided the router has a means of mapping the destination IP address (the IP address we will give to the ASP) to an ATM address either by static commands, CIOA, or LANE, the router will have the information it needs to establish a connection. For the LS1010 to be able to respond, it too needs a way to get destination ATM addresses. We will provide this functionality by configuring the ASP as a CIOA (RFC 1577) client or as a LANE client.

When configuring the CIOA client on the ASP interface, we again use the 2/0/0 identification as we did for the Ethernet interface, but this time specify ATM and a subinterface as follows:

```
LS1010(config)#interface atm 2/0/0.1
LS1010(config-subif)#atm nsap-address
47.0091.8100.1111.2222.3333.4444.5555.6666.7777.01
LS1010(config-subif)#ip address 142.5.4.3 255.255.255.0
LS1010(config-subif)#atm arp-server nsap
47.0091.8100.0000.0000.3333.4444.5555.6666.7777.00
```

This is, of course, the same set of commands we used on the AIP to set that as a CIOA client. Remember, the process for IP connectivity over ATM is that once the destination IP address is defined, that address must be mapped to an ATM address, and either by manual configuration of PVCs or signaling for SVCs, a VPI/VCI pair is identified that defines the connection to reach the desired destination.

We can follow a similar line of reasoning by using the LANE client commands used on the AIP and Catalyst to define the LS1010 ASP as a LEC:

```
LS1010(config)#interface atm 2/0/0.4
LS1010(config-subif)#ip address 142.7.6.5 255.255.255.0
LS1010(config-subif)#lane client ethernet LAN1
```

Here we have addressed the subinterface in question, then attached it to the Ethernet ELAN named LAN1.

This is all we need do to enable remote devices to establish IP connectivity to the LS1010 for management and configuration purposes. Configuring the LS1010 as an ATM ARP server is a relatively simple process as well. We use the `atm arp-server self` command as we did on an AIP. It is questionable whether this would be done in a real-world network, as generally you would want to leave the LS1010 configuration as bare as possible to leave it free for cell-switching duties. Endstations like the 7200 AIP are better prepared to run the ATM ARP server function.

Clocking Considerations

In Chapter 4 we discussed the need to define a network clock source when we were using Digital Voice Modules on the 3810 concentrator. When we come to using constant bit rate and real-time services over ATM, similar issues apply. With data-only applications, deriving a clock on a hop-by-hop basis is fine, but with voice and video services, we have to be more careful. The way it works is that each port derives its receive clock from the incoming data, allowing it to understand what it has been sent. But what about the transmit clock? If we are carrying delay-sensitive traffic, having the clock differ on a hop-by-hop basis can cause degradation of the transmitted signal. The choices we have for defining the clock source for transmitting signals are as follows:

- Loop-timed, when the transmit clock is derived from the receive clock
- Network-derived, when a hierarchy of clock sources is defined
- Free-running, when the clock is derived from the onboard PAM oscillator

So what we need to do is configure the LS1010 to use transmit clocking for all its interfaces from the same source, and, of course, list prioritized alternatives should that primary source fail. The clocking is generally derived from one interface and distributed to other interfaces via the backplane. The best way to explain this is via an example.

In Figure 6-11, we have LS1010_A set as the reference clock source. There is no particular setting that goes into LS1010_A to define it as the reference; it is just that all other LS1010 switches will be configured to take their clock from an interface that is derived from LS1010_A. In this example, LS1010_C has been configured to derive its transmit clocking from interface 0/0/0. The clock on this link is supplied by LS1010_B, which is configured to take its clock from LS1010_A. The question is, what happens to the ability of LS1010_C to transmit if the link to LS1010_B fails? The proper thing to do is create a hierarchy of clock sources that maintains a single clock source during link failures. Of course, the clock of final resort could be set to an interface that is using the oscillator on the PAM; that way at least the LS1010 will be able to transmit cells in the worst of cases.

In the case of LS1010_C in Figure 6-11, we will configure the clock source with highest priority from interface 0/0/0 and second-highest priority from interface 0/0/1. There are two stages to this process. The first is completed in global configuration mode and details the prioritized list of interfaces. The second is on a per-interface basis, which identifies

Figure 6-11 Network configuration for single-source clock.

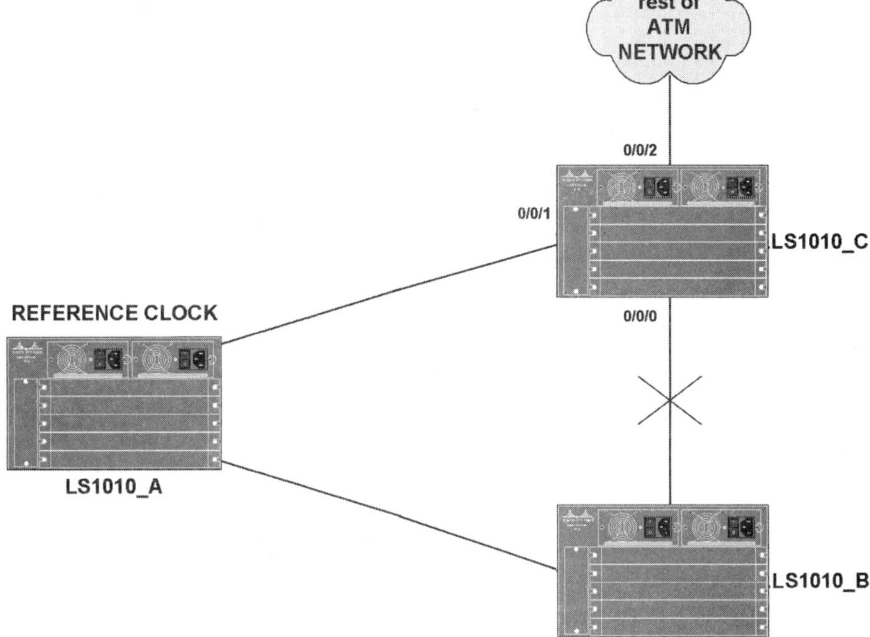

whether the interface will use network-derived clocking, the onboard oscillator, or clocking from received signals. For our interface 0/0/0 to be configured as described, we enter the following:

```
LS1010_C(config)#network-clock-select 1 atm 0/0/0
LS1010_C(config)#network-clock-select 2 atm 0/0/1
LS1010_C(config)#interface 0/0/2
LS1010_C(config-if)#clock source network-derived
```

Thus the configuration for interface 0/0/2 to use transmit clocking sourced primarily from 0/0/0, then 0/0/1 is complete. If you attempt to use ATM switching for CES or other real-time traffic without a single clock source, you are likely to end up with line errors due to clocking differences on a hop-by-hop basis.

Overview of ATM Routing

We have discussed the construction of ATM addresses and the Peer Group ID portion, as illustrated in Figure 6-6. It is now worth considering how several LS1010 switches connected together will decide to route a call from one endstation to another. ATM routing is only used during the call setup phase. Think of an SVC being established. The endstation will be attempting to contact a remote ATM address; signaling is used to identify a VPI/VCI pair that is the only destination identifier used in the cells carrying data from source to destination. The endstation is, in effect, saying to the LS1010, *tell me what VPI/VCI I can use to contact my destination ATM address.* The LS1010, of course, has to decide how it is going to contact the destination ATM address. There are two mechanisms for the LS1010 to use: static routing with the Interim Inter-Switch Signaling Protocol (IISP) or PNNI.

IISP basically uses static routing to define next-hop switches for destination ATM addresses, and UNI signaling assigns VPI/VCI information. PNNI is a more complex protocol that is more like a traditional OSPF routing protocol with automatic dissemination of routes and best-route selection based on numerous criteria. For small LS1010 networks of up to 10 or so switches, IISP is normally adequate. However, it must be said that because PNNI is the default mode for the LS1010 and it is the simplest to implement, PNNI should be considered the preferred method even for small networks. The only time IISP and static routing is preferred is if two PNNI domains are being connected together and you do not want them to share complete knowledge of each other's topology. This is similar in concept to when static routes were used to connect different autonomous systems together in IP routing.

We will discuss routing more fully in a later section; however, the entry of a static route is quite simple and can be illustrated with the `atm route` command. This is the same concept as adding a route with the `ip route` command in a router. With the `atm route` command we are going to tell the LS1010 which interface to use when trying to contact a given 13-byte prefix (remember from Figure 6-6 that the first 13 bytes is the default summary address). An example is as follows:

```
LS1010(config)#atm route 47.0091.1111.2222.3333.4444.5555 0/0/1
```

As we shall see, we will treat PNNI as a dynamic interior routing protocol, like OSPF, and static IISP as an exterior protocol, much like IP static routing.

IISP and PNNI for the LS1010

IISP and PNNI are the static and dynamic ways that ATM switches determine the route a particular SVC will take through the network.

This really only refers to the routing of ATM signaling requests. Once the signaling is complete and a connection established, VPC/VCI references define the physical path followed. Should that physical path be disturbed, the SVC may be reestablished using signaling for reestablishment of the connection. In the case of PNNI, ATM routing tables will be adjusted to route around failures in a dynamic fashion. With IISP, the routing tables are static and do not adjust to topology changes without manual intervention.

A point worth noting is that most endstations, such as a router AIP, use only one physical connection into the ATM network. This, of course, is a single point of failure. In many ways it is like connecting a single site into an IP backbone; there is generally only one local access point into the network. The difference is that in today's networks, single sites are generally connected into an IP backbone at speeds that are low enough to make an ISDN connection using multilink PPP a realistic backup for that single access point. The speed of ATM access usually is such that a dial backup is not feasible. If a backup is required for the single line into an ATM backbone, another router AIP is required, with its own connection to the backbone. For the endstation network to adapt to a link failure into the ATM backbone, some sort of regular routing protocol, such as IGRP or OSPF, must be used to notify other routers of a link failure to the ATM backbone. Of course, in this instance, the endstation network is not aware of ATM and only views the ATM link as it views any other IP link.

However, what we are talking about in this section is routing within an ATM backbone, and within that backbone, the ATM routing will only have an effect on SVC connections (OK, it will affect soft PVCs also, but those are SVCs when within the ATM backbone). PVC connections are, of course, by their nature predefined in terms of the route through the network.

Static IISP Routing

The default condition regarding ATM routing on the LS1010 switch is for PNNI to be enabled. If we want to set up static routing, we have to manually turn off ATM routing, save the configuration, and reload the box. This is because the command to turn off routing will only take effect at boot time. This is the exact opposite of routers, which have no routing protocols enabled in the default configuration and only know about directly connected networks at the IP level.

The construction of an ATM routing table is different to the more familiar IP routing table. An IP routing table lists destination network numbers (or subnets if netmasks are applied) against next-hop router addresses. This makes sense. Imagine, for example, several routers being connected on the same LAN segment; on any given router, it will use the same interface to access any of the other routers. We therefore tell each router the list of remote networks available by each of its neighbors.

ATM is purely a connection-oriented protocol, and the physical connections in an ATM backbone are always of the point-to-point type. There are no shared media hubs in the ATM world. In this case, we specify destination ATM prefixes that can be accessed via a given interface on the switch, as shown in Figure 6-12.

In this figure the 13-byte destination ATM prefixes are represented by ATM_A, ATM_B, and ATM_C, and we see that each routing table lists these destination prefixes as reachable via one of its own interfaces. To

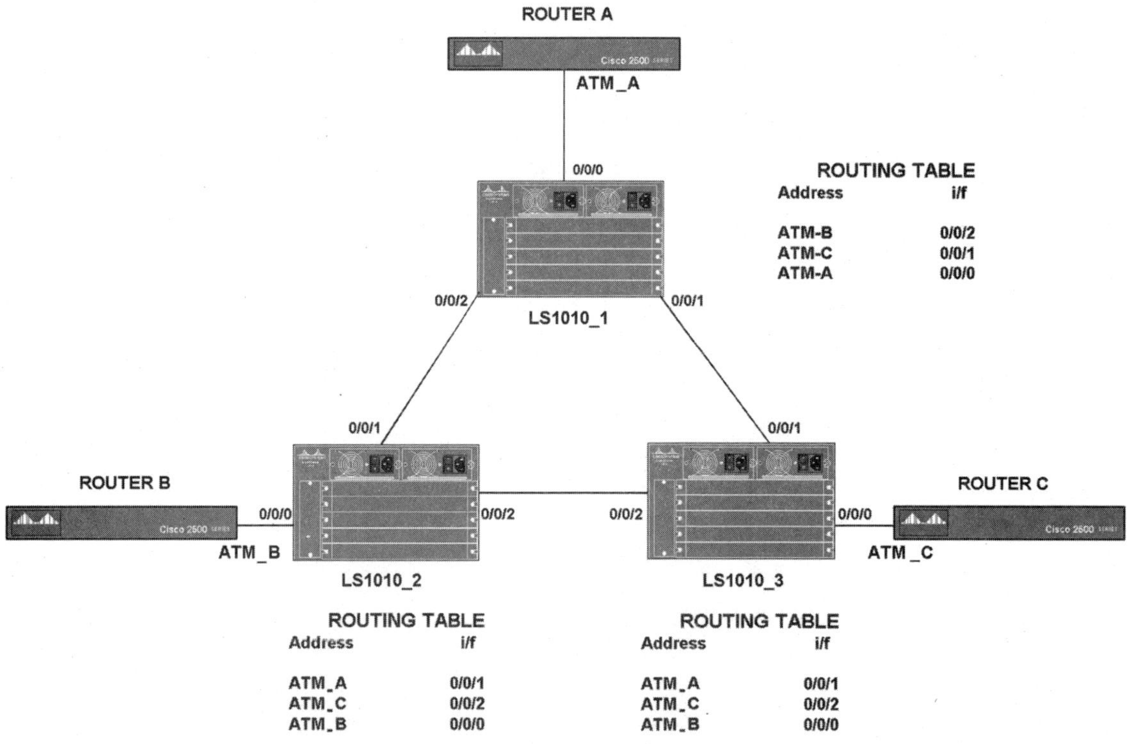

Figure 6-12 Destination ATM prefixes.

set this up in a set of LS1010 switches, we have to complete the following steps:

1. Turn off ATM routing.
2. Define the ATM address and disable ILMI autoconfiguration.
3. Define an interface as user or network in IISP terms.
4. Add static routes with the `atm route` command.

The first step is self-explanatory. The second is necessary if you are not going to use the default Cisco addresses. The only time you should use the Cisco default addresses is if you have a small isolated ATM network that will never have a PNNI hierarchy or be connected to another ATM network. The third step is necessary; it does not matter which end of a switch-to-switch link you configure as the user end or which is the network end, as long as you assign one to each. The final step is to add the static routes to the ATM routing table, which requires you to know the destination prefixes and which interface they will be accessed via.

Let's go through a complete configuration:

```
LS1010(config)#atm routing-mode static
This configuration will not take effect until next reload
LS1010(config)#copy system:running-config nvram:startup-config
Building configuration...
LS1010(config)#reload
LS1010(config)#interface atm 0/0/0
LS1010(config-if)#no atm auto-configuration
LS1010(config-if)#atm prefix 55.1111.2222.3333.4444.5555.6666
LS1010(config-if)#atm iisp side user
LS1010(config-if)#exit
LS1010(config)#atm route 47.0091.2222.3333.4444.5555.6666 0/0/0
```

So to start with we made the ATM routing mode static, saved that in the switch configuration, and reloaded. Next we configured the ATM 0/0/0 interface to *not* autoconfigure its ATM address and gave it the prefix we want it to use. The last 6 bytes are provided by a MAC address. The final interface configuration was to set the IISP mode to `user`, meaning the switch at the other end of this link needs the command issued with the network argument instead of `user`.

Of course, changing the ATM prefix of one interface means that the prefix of the ATM device that interface is connected to needs to be changed also to match. Of course, if the attached device is an endstation, it will take the prefix from the switch; however, if the attached device is another switch, they need to match prefixes.

Configuring PNNI

For simple applications with no hierarchy, there is no LS1010 configuration required to get PNNI operational; it is enabled by default. PNNI does a number of things, however. These can be categorized as:

- Quality of service (QoS) routing
- Designed with address and routing hierarchy in mind
- Route information exchange via a link state mechanism

PNNI does not commit to provide the best service available through the network, just one that meets the QoS parameters requested by the connection during call initiation. PNNI uses source routing to ensure that a connection travels the negotiated path from source to destination and receives the negotiated QoS. QoS parameters are specified by the ATM endstation and are configurable. The three parameters that are most commonly specified are the cell loss ratio (CLR), the cell delay variability (CDV), and the cell transfer delay (CTD).

The CLR is the number of cells lost in the network divided by the number transmitted into the network. Usually this is a very small number. The CDV is the change in amount of time that cells can be delivered that are part of the same connection. The CTD is the latency of the connection—that is, the time between the first bit in and the last bit out. Normally the default values are adequate.

As we stated earlier, the 20-byte ATM address is made up of a 13-byte prefix made up of 7 bytes of Cisco information, plus 6 bytes of switch MAC address, which ensures all default ATM addresses are globally unique. If you have a desire to assign your own ATM addresses, you should obtain a prefix from a national authority. In the United States this is ANSI; in the United Kingdom, this is FEI.

Hierarchy is supported within PNNI by use of the organizational scope. In practice, ATM interfaces are assigned a level that will identify the number of bytes that will be used to define the prefix, which will always be less than 13. A level of 72 uses 9 bytes as the prefix, and 64 uses 8. Within a hierarchy, individual switches are elected as peer group leaders (PGLs) for their groups within the hierarchy, and others as logical group nodes (LGNs) that will connect to other groups within the hierarchy. The level is configured using the `atm pnni` command and the `node x level y` subcommand, which identify the node in use and the level you are going to assign it. In this case the node value *x* identifies a node on the switch, and the level value *y* is the level we discussed (either 72, 64, or however many bits will be subtracted from the usual 13-byte prefix). (*Note:* It is recommended that hierarchy within PNNI not be explored without in-depth analysis and probably consulting assistance from Cisco.)

Being a link state mechanism, the PNNI neighbor discovery via the Hello protocol, database synchronization, and PNNI topology state elements (like OSPF LSAs) should be familiar concepts to those who have used OSPF. Essentially, PTSEs (PNNI topology state elements) are flooded through the network, which are then used by the nodes to compose topology databases. The Hello protocol sends small packets every 15 seconds, as long as no topology changes have taken place. If a topology change, like a link-down, occurs, PTSEs are sent immediately to reflect the change.

Configuring LANE on the LS1010

We have discussed the concepts of LANE already. In this section we'll look at the configuration necessary to have the LS1010 operate in a LANE environment. The job is to decide which LANE tasks will be performed by the LS1010s and which will be performed by other endstations, such as Catalyst ATM LANE modules. To allow the ATM network to emulate a LAN (in effect, making the ATM cloud look like another segment on a LAN), it must provide ATM multicasts to emulate LAN broadcasts. To do this requires the generation of the LES/BUS and LECS previously discussed. For the sake of completeness we will provide a brief summary of LANE here before moving on to LANE configuration.

Summary of LANE Operation

LANE operation is supported via many virtual circuit connections, or VCCs. The goal of LANE operation is to generate the data-direct VCC, which is the VCC that carries data from one LANE client to another. To reach this end goal, three stages must be completed beforehand:

- Initialization
- Registration
- Address resolution

During initialization, the first job of a LANE client (LEC) is to contact the LECS. The LEC determines the address of the LECS either by its own configuration, ILMI, or the well-known LECS address. The connection from the LEC to the LECS is called the *configure-direct VCC.* Once this VCC has been made, the LEC knows which LES to contact and which ELAN it is a member of. The LEC starts a bidirectional control-direct VCC to the LES for purposes of joining the ELAN. The LES will inform the LEC of the BUS address (in a Cisco environment the LES and BUS are normally on the same machine). Now the LEC will create a multicast-send VCC to the BUS, which enables the BUS to add this new LEC to the multicast-forward VCC, so that it receives ATM multicasts carrying the LAN broadcast packets.

During registration the LEC registers its MAC address and ATM address with its LES so that it can participate in the LE_ARP process for address resolution. This is done via the LES, adding the new LEC to the point-to-multipoint control-distribute VCC that forwards all unresolved LE_ARP requests to all LECs on the ELAN.

During address resolution, the LEC requests the ATM address for a specified MAC address (remember, the originator of these requests will have been on a LAN and so is trying to contact a specific MAC address). If there is an entry in the LES for this destination MAC address, it will supply the corresponding ATM address to the LEC. If not, the LES will use LE_ARP to all LECs to determine if the desired address is available. Once the LEC has the ATM address of the destination it must contact, a data-direct VCC carries the data from source to destination. These VCCs are summarized in Figure 6-13.

Configuration Tasks for LANE

When we come to configuring these functions on an LS1010, there are some simple rules to follow. We must always configure the LECS on the major interface rather than a subinterface. The LEC and LES/BUS are always configured on subinterfaces. This makes good sense, as the LECS must service multiple ELANs, but the other components are specific to one ELAN. Of course, one physical interface can be a member of multiple ELANs, whereas we use subinterfaces on a per-subnet basis, with each ELAN being on its own subnet.

So, now we will illustrate the major interface and subinterface commands necessary to configure a LEC and LES/BUS, followed by the global configuration commands and major interface commands to configure a LECS. The LECS is the only LANE component to be configured on the major interface. In all the following configurations we will assume that we are using the default Cisco ATM addressing. To set up a LS1010 as a LANE client, we need to complete the following steps:

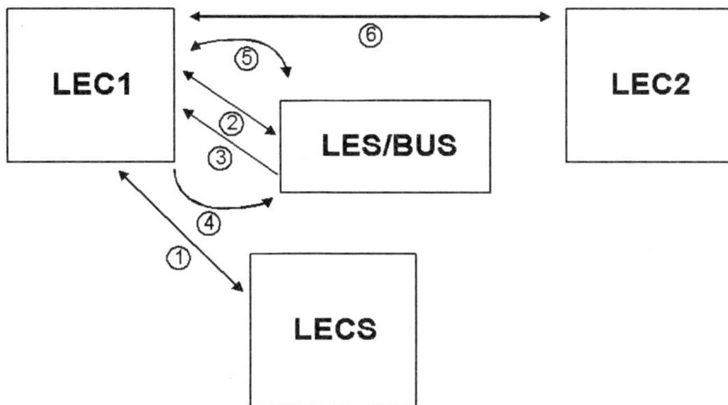

Figure 6-13 Virtual circuit connection in LANE.

1. LEC contacts LECS for ELAN membership information using a configure direct VCC.
2. LEC establishes a control-direct VCC with the LES.
3. LES adds LEC to the control-distribute VCC.
4. LEC uses multicast-send VCC to register with BUS.
5. BUS adds LEC to multicast-forward VCC to receive LAN broadcasts.
6. Data-direct VCC is established for LEC1-to-LEC2 communication.

- For the major interface, specify the ILMI and signaling PVCs and the Cisco method of computing the LECS address.
- On the subinterface in question, start the client for that ELAN and specify an IP address.

We achieve this with the following:

```
LS1010(config)#interface atm 2/0/0
LS1010(config-if)#atm pvc 1 0 5 qsaal
LS1010(config-if)#atm pvc 2 0 16 ilmi
LS1010(config-if)#lane config auto-config-atm-address
LS1010(config-if)#interface 2/0/0.1
LS1010(config-subif)#lane client ethernet ELAN1
LS1010(config-subif)#ip address 172.6.4.3 255.255.255.0
```

In this configuration we specified the signaling and ILMI PVCs for interface 2/0/0 and used the `config` optional parameter to restrict the auto-address configuration command to the LECS only. For the subinterface 2/0/0.1, we made it a member of the ELAN 1 emulated LAN and applied an IP address compatible with this subnet. The only time it really makes sense to go to the trouble of making an LS1010 a member of a LEC is if you have a desire to telnet to the LS1010 on a network that is using LANE to resolve IP-to-ATM addressing issues.

To make the LS1010 perform LES/BUS services, we must ensure that the same major interface commands for PVC and automatic address calculations are made. The only change is to add in one line to the configuration of the subinterface. So, given we have configured ATM interface 2/0/0 already, to make subinterface 2/0/0.1 capable of supporting the LES/BUS function, we add the following to the above configuration:

```
LS1010(config-subif)#lane server-bus ethernet ELAN1
```

So far, nothing in the LANE network will work, as we have not specified the information necessary for the first part of LANE to function, i.e., the ability to contact the LECS. We have told each interface to use the Cisco automatic method for determining the LECS address, which is to obtain that address from the switch. The alternative is to configure the ATM address of the LECS into each client. If the endstations are routers, this would be via the `lane global-lecs-address` command, followed by the NSAP address of the LECS.

To tell the LS1010 which address to advertise to endstations, we use the `atm lecs-address-default` command. This is a global configuration command that sends the LECS address to every LEC that connects via ILMI. The `atm lecs-address` command can be used on a per-interface basis to take priority over the global default if required.

The process we are about to follow to establish LECS operation on the LS1010 is as follows:

1. Create the LECS database.
2. Define the ILMI and signaling PVCs as usual.
3. Add ELAN name to LES NSAP address entries.
4. Specify auto-addressing for the LECS.

The first stage is to create the database in global configuration mode and specify auto-addressing as follows:

```
LS1010(config)#lane database db1
LS1010(lane-config-database)#name elan1 server-atm-address
47.0091111122223333444455555.666677778888.01
LS1010(lane-config-database)#default-name elan1
```

The first command created a LECS database and placed us in database configuration mode. Once in this level of configuration mode, we can enter the ATM address of the LES for each ELAN. This configuration is concluded by assigning `elan1` as the default ELAN, in case a LEC requests a connection to an ELAN not listed in the LECS database.

From here we move to the configuration of the major interface in question. In this example, we will use 2/0/0 as before. Assuming we have assigned 0/5 to signaling and 0/16 to ILMI on this major interface, we have to add the following:

```
LS1010(config)#interface atm 2/0/0
LS1010(config-if)#lane config elan1
LS1010(config-if)#lane config auto-config-atm-address
```

The `lane config elan1` command starts a LECS process using the database configuration file named (in this case, `elan1`) on the interface we are configuring.

As stated earlier in this chapter, it is more common to have endstations perform all LANE components, including the LECS. Following that model does not require any alteration of the LS1010 configuration, other than that required to allow a telnet session to the switch. In fact, it is more common to not even telnet to the LS1010 over the ATM network. If LS1010s are in the campus, it is more common to connect the Ethernet interface to a separate network so that telnet access is available even if the ATM network is down. If remote access to the LS1010 is required, connecting a modem to the AUX port provides adequate out-of-band access.

LANE Component Redundancy

LANE version 1.0 does not support automatic fault tolerance. If a LES goes down, that ELAN is out. If a LECS goes down, all your ELANs are dead for LECs that want to join them. LECs that have already joined their respective ELANs can continue to operate if a LECS fails.

To provide backup for these critical network components (while we wait for LANE version 2.0 to be widely available), Cisco has introduced a proprietary protocol called the *Simple Server Redundancy Protocol* (SSRP) for LANE. The first thing to look at is providing multiple LECS on the network. For SSRP it is important that all switches have the same list of LECS addresses in the same order. The simplest method for assigning LECS addresses to endstations is to configure the LECS address into the switch and let ILMI deliver that address to the endstation. With this method, we define multiple entries in the switch for the LECS default address, giving each one a priority order. In the following example, we define two LECS addresses on the switch (LS1010). The first LECS address has the highest priority and will be the preferred LECS, with the second its backup:

```
LS1010(config)#atm lecs-address-default
47.0000.1111.2222.3333.4444.5555.6666.7777.8888.00 1
LS1010(config)#atm lecs-address-default
47.0000.1111.2222.3333.4444.5555.6666.7777.9999.00 2
```

A similar process is required for redundant LES/BUS operation. The LES/BUS is always on the same machine in a Cisco implementation on a per-ELAN basis. What we need to do to provide redundancy is specify alternate addresses for the LES in the LECS configuration database for each ELAN. Again, it is imperative that this database is identical on all LECS. As before, we configure the database by creating it and naming it, then adding entries for the LES ATM address for each ELAN name. The only difference is that we have multiple entries for each ELAN, each with a different index value that signifies its priority order. The configuration commands to create a database called `db2` with prioritized LES addresses per ELAN are shown below for the ELAN named `elan2`:

```
LS1010(config)#lane database db2
LS1010(lane-config-database)#name elan2 server-atm-address
47.009111112222333344445555.666677778888.01 index 1
LS1010(lane-config-database)#name elan2 server-atm-address
47.009111112222333344445555.666677779999.01 index 2
```

Overview of LANE 2.0 and MPOA for the LS1010

So far we have illustrated the configurations associated with LANE version 1.0, which has the ATM communication bound by the normal subnet rules for IP communication. MPOA uses LANE as one of its building blocks to enable ATM communications to cut through the normal IP subnet rules and allow subnet-to-subnet communication without recourse to an IP router. There are other shortcomings of LANE version 1, such as:

- Lack of built-in redundancy for LANE components
- Requires a separate VCC for each flow (leading to excessive numbers being required on even moderately sized networks)
- Poor support for multicast services, as they must flow through the BUS (which leads to ELAN clients seeing multicast traffic even if they have not registered for it)

In this section we'll review the enhancements available with LANE version 2.0 and the components of MPOA, and we will illustrate how each component is configured on Cisco equipment.

Overview of LANE 2.0

LANE version 2.0 uses two distinct protocols: an enhanced UNI for LANE endstation-to-LANE server communication and a new NNI for server-to-server communication. These relationships are illustrated in Figure 6-14.

The new LUNI specifies how a LEC will communicate with the LANE servers. Specifically, the following features are now available:

- A more scalable multicast solution
- Sharing of VCCs by multiple traffic flows
- Improved QoS functions, supporting the eight user priorities defined in 802.1P

The LNNI protocol enables primary servers to communicate with their backups. For example, the primary LECS will communicate with its backup, and the primary LES will communicate with its backup. The LNNI protocol governs how these server pairs communicate with each other and manages a controlled swap-over from primary to backup, keeping only one server out of the pair active at one time.

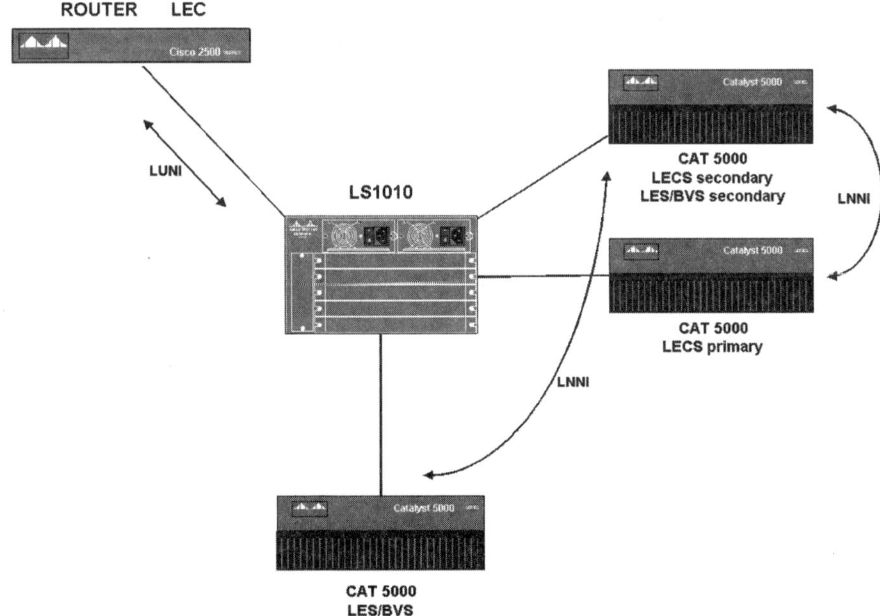

Figure 6-14 LANE version 2.0 LUNI and LNNI communication paths.

MPOA Operation

We discussed the basics of MPOA (Multi-Protocol Over ATM) in Chapter 3. In this section we'll start with a recap of MPOA before we look at configuring the main components. MPOA can be considered a combination of LANE, NHRP (Next Hop Resolution Protocol), and MARS (Multicast Address Resolution Server), as it brings the NHRP functionality of being able to break IP subnet boundaries to LANE. Essentially, NHRP allows an ATM endstation to contact its destination directly, whether that destination is in the same IP subnet or not.

The work that NHRP does is actually quite clever. With regular routing protocols, routing information is summarized at the subnet level. By this I mean that a routing table keeps track of how to reach subnet rather than individual workstations on a network. This enables routers to control quite large networks, as they do not have to keep track of all the endstations. Of course, for NHRP to cut through subnet boundaries, it needs detailed knowledge down to the ATM address of the endstation. In IP terms, it means that NHRP needs layer 2 information, when most routing protocols, like IP, do not carry layer 2 information. It is the job of MPOA route servers to provide the layer 2 information that enables NHRP to perform subnet cut-through. This is illustrated in Figure 6-15, which shows a direct ATM connection from endstation 1 to endstation 2, even though they are on different IP subnets.

MPOA actually delivers layer 2 functionality via LANE and marries that to layer 3 functionality via NHRP and MARS. For a host or any other ATM endstation to participate in MPOA communication, it requires a stack that understands MPOA operation. With just LANE, the layer 3 stack in endstations did not require any special version. The MARS part of MPOA is fully specified in RFC 2022 and enables endstations to dynamically register for IP multicast groups.

MPOA is implemented in two processes: the Multi-Protocol Client (MPC) and the Multi-Protocol Server (MPS). The MPS performs several functions, first being the route server, which resolves the destination ATM address for MPCs, even if they need to cross subnet boundaries. The MPS also acts as a default forwarder for packets that cannot be assigned to a virtual circuit. The final responsibility of the MPS is to deliver MARS functionality. The MPC is a user of these MPOA server services and resides in the ATM edge device (typically a router with AIP, or Catalyst 5K with an ATM card). MPS services need to be run on a device with layer 3 functionality to allow routing protocols to be run, typically a router or RSM module in a Catalyst.

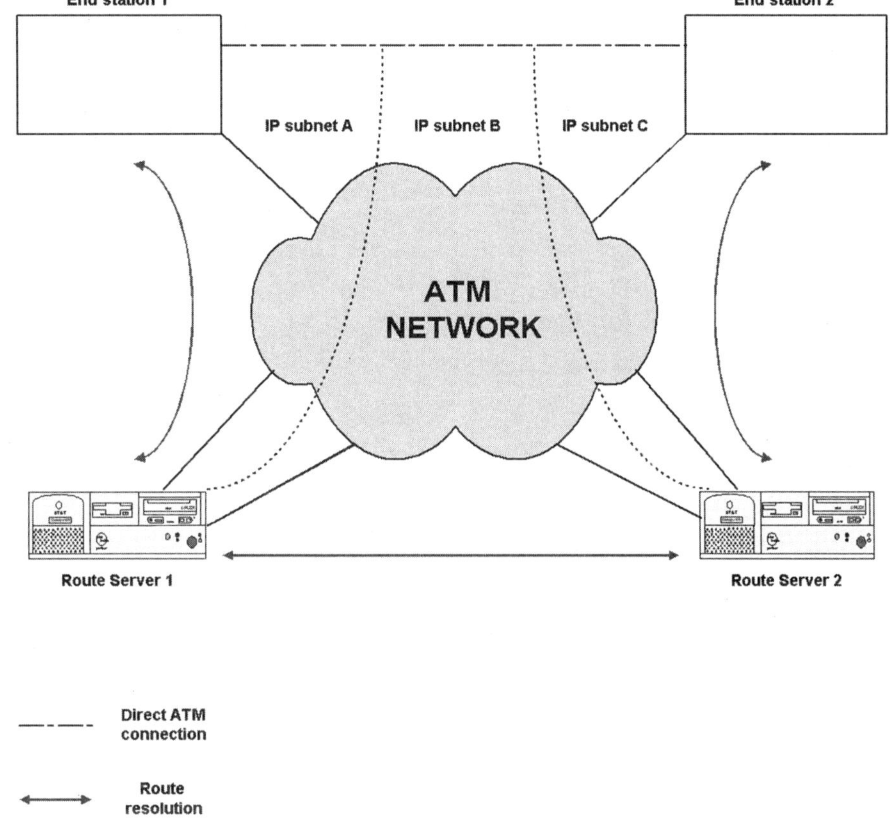

Figure 6-15 Overview of NHRP connections.

MPOA Client Configuration

The job of the MPC is two-fold: to contact an MPOA route server and to establish a cut-through connection once the destination ATM address has been received. An MPC actually gets access to the ATM network via a LEC, although the MPC and a LEC often reside on the same physical interface. Think of the LEC in MPOA as supplying layer 2 connectivity to the ATM network; the LEC is like a client to the MPC. This is illustrated in Figure 6-16.

We will start our configuration of the MPC on the basis that a LEC has already been created and made a member of `elan1` on the ATM network. The first job is to associate an ELAN ID with an existing ELAN name. In configuration mode on the device performing LECS operation, assuming we have already created a LANE database and associated an

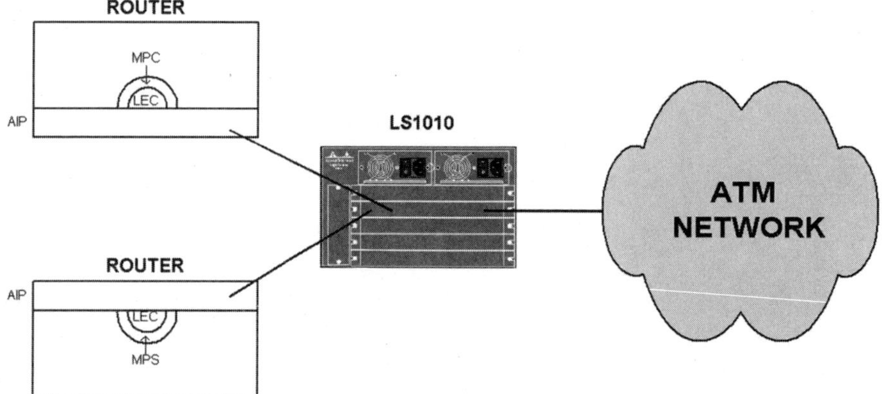

Figure 6-16 MPS and MPC use a LEC to gain access to the ATM network.

ELAN called `elan1` with the ATM address of the LES for that ELAN, we perform the following:

```
LS1010(lane-config-database)#name elan1 elan-id 10
```

We also need to configure the LES with the ELAN ID we are going to use in the MPC configuration:

```
LS1010(config-subif)#lane server-bus ethernet elan1 10
```

This needs to be placed in the subinterface where the LES is resident.

We are now in a position to create the MPC. The process is as follows:

1. Create an MPC client process.
2. Specify the ATM interface the MPC will be associated with.
3. Bind the MPC to the ATM interface.
4. Bind the LANE client to the MPC.

This is illustrated in the following IOS commands:

```
LS1010(config)#mpoa client config name mpc1
LS1010(config)#interface atm 2/0
LS1010(config-if)#mpoa client name mpc1
LS1010(config-if)#interface atm 2/0.1 mul
LS1010(config-subif)lane client mpoa client name mpc1
```

So, this configuration creates an MPC called `mpc1` on ATM interface 2/0, using the LEC configured on ATM interface 2/0.1. Note that in this configuration, I have simplified the display and not shown the entries necessary for configuring the ATM interface (ILMI and signaling PVCs) or shown the configuration of the LANE database.

MPOA Server Configuration

The MPS has the responsibility of providing the destination ATM address across subnet boundaries to the MPCs. In essence, this can be conceptually split into two tasks. The first is to determine what the destination ATM address should be by use of NHRP; the second is to deliver that address to the requesting endstation (or in the case of shortcut domains, optionally decide not to). The MPS accepts MPOA requests from the MPCs and converts them to NHRP requests for passing on to route servers, as illustrated in Figure 6-15.

Should it be decided to split up a large MPOA network into shortcut domains, that is possible via the network ID configuration option. The concept here is that shortcuts are only possible to endstations configured with the same network ID. By default, all MPS on a Cisco network will have a network ID of 1 and, therefore, permit communication between all of them. The network ID features can be a benefit if you are interested in MPOA but want to segment one group of users off from the rest of the network.

The configuration tasks for the MPS are quite similar to those for the MPC. It is required that signaling and ILMI PVCs be established on all required interfaces and that LANE be set up also. We have to assign an ELAN ID for both the LANE client and LES, as we did for the MPC. Given those conditions, the setup commands are as follows:

```
LS1010(config)#mpoa client config name mps1
LS1010(config)#interface atm 2/0
LS1010(config-if)#mpoa server name mps1
LS1010(config-if)#interface atm 2/0.1
LS1010(config-subif)lane client mpoa server name mps1
```

MPOA does offer some advantages for very large networks; however, for the majority of smaller networks, it just adds complexity for very little gain.

LS1010 Applications

So far we have looked at the basics of LS1010 configuration and what the key parameters are. We have examined the configuration specifics for the various ATM modes of operation available to this platform.

Now we will look at using the default configuration of the LS1010 as it comes out of the box. We will include useful show commands for the

1010 and the attached endstations that can be used to illustrate the effects of our configuration and to check the operation of the network. My choice here is to create what is still the most common application of IP networking on top of ATM in existence today—the RFC 1577 Classic IP Over ATM (IOA) operation.

Implementing the Default LS1010 Configuration

This section pulls together some of the individual configuration items we have been discussing so far and illustrates the most common `show` commands. Still, the most common initial application of ATM in the corporate world is as a high-speed WAN transport. As such, CIOA as specified in RFC 1577, is still the most common implementation and the one we will explore here.

The network we will configure is essentially that shown in Figure 6-2. We have two routers equipped with AIPs that need to transport cells between them via the LS1010. As far as the LS1010 configuration is concerned, it is a plug-and-play operation; no extra configuration is required. If you suspect the configuration has been altered, the best thing to do is to erase it before configuring the endstations. We will achieve the following, with reference to Figure 6-2:

- Configure the ATM interface on router 1 with IP address 188.2.3.3.
- Assign an ESI (End System Identifier) to the ATM interface on router 1.
- Configure the ATM interface on router 2 with IP address 188.2.3.4.
- Assign an ESI to the ATM interface on router 1.
- Configure router 1 as the ATM ARP server.
- Verify the configuration with reference to `show` commands.
- See the relevant LS1010 default configuration commands.
- Illustrate some pertinent LS1010 `show` commands.

The pertinent configuration details for router 1 are as follows:

```
interface ATM3/0
 ip address 188.2.3.3 255.255.255.0
 atm pvc 1 0 5 qsaal
 atm pvc 2 0 16 ilmi
 atm esi-address 111111111111.00
 atm arp-server self
```

The pertinent configuration details for router 2 are as follows:

```
interface ATM3/0
 ip address 188.2.3.4 255.255.255.0
 atm esi-address 222222222222.00
 atm pvc 1 0 5 qsaal
 atm pvc 2 0 16 ilmi
 atm arp-server nsap 47.0091810000000060630A1401.111111111111.00
```

The only tricky part of this is determining the NSAP address to use to define the location of the ATM ARP server. The NSAP address above is split into four sections by periods. The first two sections are provided by the LS1010 as a prefix, and we have specified the ESI to be 111111111111.00 on router 1 and 222222222222.00 on router 2. So to get the ATM ARP server working, we told router 1 to be the ARP server and router 2 to look at the NSAP address of the router 1 ATM interface.

The first question is how to determine the NSAP address of interface ATM 3/0 on router 1. The correct command to use is as follows:

```
Router1#sh atm ilmi atm3/0
Interface                  ATM3/0         ILMI VCC:      (0, 16)
ILMI Keepalive:            Disabled
Address Registration:      Enabled
ILMI State:                UpAndNormal
Peer IP Addr:              0.0.0.0       Peer IF Name:   ATM12/0/0
Prefix(s):
47.0091810000000060630A1401
Addresses Registered:
Local Table :
47.0091810000000060630A1401.111111111111.00
Remote Table :
47.0091810000000060630A1401.111111111111.00
```

Not exactly intuitive, but this command does give you the correct result. The next thing of interest is to look at the virtual circuits generated, as illustrated in the following command:

```
Router1#sh atm vc
Interface VCD VPI VCI Type Encapsulation Kbps Kbps Cells Status
ATM3/0      1   0   5  PVC   AAL5-SAAL      0    0      0  ACTIVE
ATM3/0      2   0  16  PVC   AAL5-ILMI      0    0      0  ACTIVE
ATM3/0     12   0  39  SVC   AAL5-SNAP      0    0      0  ACTIVE
ATM3/0     15   0  43  SVC   AAL5-SNAP      0    0      0  ACTIVE
ATM3/0     16   0  42  SVC   AAL5-SNAP      0    0      0  ACTIVE
```

This, of course, shows the signaling and ILMI PVCs; however, there are more SVCs active. These are there due to pings generated from another device. If we look at the `show` command for a particular VC, we will see the remote device that initiated this SVC connection:

```
Router1#sh atm vc 12
ATM3/0: VCD:12, VPI:0, VCI:39, etype:0x0, AAL5 - LLC/SNAP, Flags: 0x50
PeakRate: 0, Average Rate: 0, Burst Cells: 0, VCmode: 0x0
OAM DISABLED, InARP DISABLED
InPkts: 12, OutPkts: 13, InBytes: 1244, OutBytes: 1296
InPRoc: 12, OutPRoc: 10, Broadcasts: 0
InFast: 0, OutFast: 0, InAS: 0, OutAS: 0
OAM F5 cells sent: 0, OAM cells received: 0, TTL: 4
interface = ATM3/0, call remotely initiated, call reference = 6
vcnum = 12, vpi = 0, vci = 39, state = Active
 aal5snap vc, point-to-point call
Retry count: Current = 0, Max = 10
timer currently inactive, timer value = 00:00:00
Remote Atm Nsap address: 47.00918100000000060630A1401.222222222222.00
```

There is one more command of interest for router 1 and that is to look at the ATM ARP server itself, as below. This display shows the ATM-to-IP address map:

```
Router1#sh atm arp-server
Note that a '*' next to an IP address indicates an active call
      IP Address TTL ATM Address
ATM3/0:
    * 188.2.3.4 17:28 4700918100000000060630A14012222222222222200
    * 188.2.3.3 17:28 4700918100000000060630A14011111111111111100
```

This concludes what we have to do to look at router 1. Turning our attention to router 2, we can see the same outputs; the only change is that there is no ATM ARP server process. This base configuration can be added to quite easily to support tens of ATM nodes with very little configuration. On the LS1010 side, we leave the configuration as default, and if we add more LS1010 switches to the network, the default operation of PNNI will handle ATM route information. In addition, using the default method of having the switches assign prefixes keeps all the ATM nodes in the same level of the hierarchy. In this instance, new endstations, like more router AIPs, will be added with a configuration very similar to that of router 2. The normal troubleshooting tools like ping and the `show` commands illustrated should be enough to get a simple ATM network of this type operational.

Congestion and Traffic Management

ATM was designed for carrier class networks where QoS is of paramount importance and sophisticated protocols are required to ensure service levels are met. By contrast, most corporate networks utilize a very simple method of meeting service levels: providing more than enough bandwidth. The distinction here is quite important. A carrier with a very large national or global network traditionally makes money by charging users for connection time or fixed-cost leased lines. The carrier does not design the network to cope with all users trying to connect and use the network at the same time.

With a large network this works well, since, for example, the probability that every telephone subscriber will pick up the phone and make a call at the same time really is zero. However, the carrier does have to make sure that even under heavy loads, the network will route connections so that the expected QoS is delivered. Typically, if connections are requested that will overload capacity, those connections are denied access. (If you call internationally on a regular basis, you will know what I mean.) In the corporate world, typically those kinds of safeguards have not existed, if a user starts a big FTP transfer over a low-capacity link, existing users of that link will suffer a performance hit.

The *Cisco TCP/IP Routing Professional Reference* covered protocols, such as RSVP and RTP, that add a measure of QoS functionality to existing corporate networks. These protocols are, however, limited in their usefulness in a LAN environment and only really work on point-to-point links.

This brings us to one of the only two real advantages ATM offers over existing solutions to corporate networks (ATM for carrier-class networks offers many benefits). ATM only makes sense in the corporate world for a high-speed technology if the network either needs sophisticated end-to-end QoS or needs high-speed links over 5- or 6-miles distance. In the rest of this section we'll look at the QoS features of ATM and see how they can be mapped to an IP network.

Handling Congestion in an ATM Network We have touched on how cell loss can have an exponentially bad effect on some ATM networks. Let's use a bit of simple math to illustrate that point, which will show why congestion management on ATM is more important than on other networks. If we are using TCP as the transport protocol over ATM, a single dropped cell will cause the retransmission of all the packet data that is left unacknowledged in the TCP sliding window. As an example, with RFC 1577, you could have an IP packet size of 9180 bytes, which equates to 192 cells. If one of those cells is dropped, the packet checksum fails and TCP will rerequest the whole packet. If that cell was dropped because of congestion, the rerequest mechanism of TCP makes things even worse, and instead of allowing you to recover from transmission errors, it actually takes the whole congested area of the network out of operation.

To prevent this, the LS1010 has a lot of traffic management capabilities, including:

- Intelligent discarding of packets, rather than the indiscriminate cell dropping described above
- Routing connections based on available QoS capacity via PNNI
- Traffic policing by enforcing traffic contracts for differing ATM traffic types
- Buffering in shared memory
- Traffic shaping
- Management of available bit rates (ABR)

Before we look at the traffic management features of ATM during and after call setup, it is necessary to list the various acronyms that will be used to describe ATM service parameters:

- Available bit rate (ABR)
- Burst tolerance (BT)
- Connection Admission Control (CAC)
- Constant bit rate (CBR)
- Cell delay variation tolerance (CDVT)
- Cell loss priority (CLP)
- Cell loss ration (CLR)
- Explicit Forward Congestion Indicator (EFCI)
- Generic cell rate algorithm (GCRA)
- Generic connection admission control (GCAC)
- Intelligent packet discard (IPD)
- Maximum burst size (MBS)
- Minimum cell rate (MCR)
- Maximum cell transfer delay (MCTD)
- Peak cell rate (PCR)
- Sustainable cell rate (SCR)
- Unspecified bit rate (UBR)
- Variable bit rate nonreal-time (VBR-NRT)
- Variable bit rate, real-time (VBR-RT)

These acronyms will be used to simplify the reading of the following text.

Let's deal with call setup first, which, of course, relates to establishing an SVC. Generically this breaks down into three parts. The first is the traffic contract that specifies the nature and value of parameters like CBR, VBR-NRT, etc., which define both traffic requirements and required quality of service, such as PCR and SCR. Next, the switch receiving this new call will check its CAC. If the request is admitted, it passes the request on to the third stage, PNNI, which calculates a route through the network that can meet the required traffic contract.

The LS1010 uses CAC to decide whether a connection may be established or not. CAC may be done on the basis of a resource base, or it may be a policy-based CAC in which you can define a best-effort option. In essence, the CAC checks to see if there are enough local resources to meet the requirements of the traffic contract requested by the connection. If there are, PNNI will then be used to determine a source route through the network. It is termed GCAC (generic connection admission control) in the case where QoS features are checked along the route identified by PNNI, as illustrated in Figure 6-17.

When the connection is, in effect, a different set of mechanisms, take control to make sure that the connection does not attempt to break its traffic contract and disturb other connections on the network. Primarily,

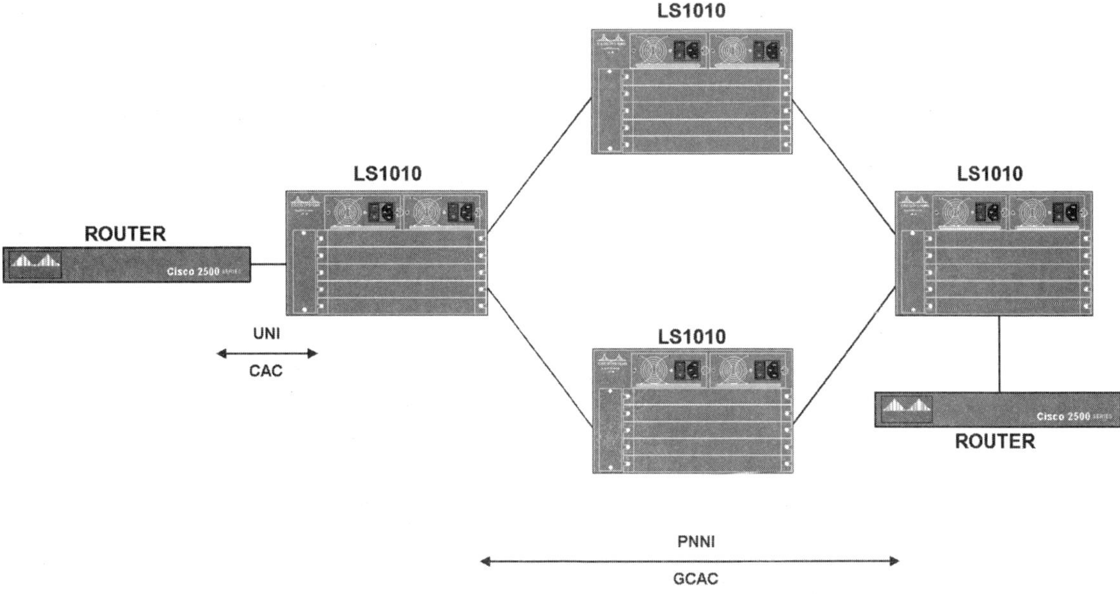

Figure 6-17 CAC as a local feature and GCAC as an end-to-end feature.

traffic policing takes on this responsibility, which uses the ATM Forum GCRA to check conformance for specific VCCs. This is enforced at the LS1010 interface that connects to the AIP or NPM. Cells are examined at the input to the switch and normally passed if the cell rate is within the traffic contract. If the traffic contract is exceeded, the LS1010 will mark cells with the CLP bit so that they can be discarded if congestion is experienced further on in the network, or in extreme cases, they are dropped altogether.

ABR is the specification that defines how endstations and intermediate switches will behave during times of congestion. It is a complex specification that is only worth looking at in overview. All of ABR is based around a flow of resource management (RM) cells from source to destination that are occasionally injected into the VCC data stream. The early implementation of ABR was termed *EFCI mode,* with intermediate switches setting the EFCI flag during congestion. This EFCI flag is set in the header of cells being forwarded through a switch. The destination endstation receives this flag and uses return RM cells to tell the source about the congestion.

This, of course, has potential latency problems. In the relative rate marking mode of ABR, a switch experiencing congestion will not set the EFCI flag in the header of packets going to the destination, but instead will reduce latency by marking backward RM cells being returned to the source endstation. This reduces latency by alerting the source endstation to slow down sooner.

My recommendation is to not change the QoS variables from the default values, particularly on the LS1010 for traffic pacing. Until you have a specific problem to solve on the network, the default values are generally fine. As for traffic shaping on a router AIP or similar ATM processor, if you are connecting to a public ATM network, you may wish to have the AIP settings match those of the public network. In this instance, commands you may wish to explore include the following, which will be part of a map-class:

`Atm forward-peak-cell-rate-clp0 (rate)`—To set the peak rate of high-priority cells

`Atm backward-sustainable-cell-rate-clp1 (rate)`—To change the sustainable rate of low-priority cells coming back from the destination router

`Atm forward-max-burst-size-clp0 (cell-count)`—To set the maximum number of high-priority cells at the burst level of an SVC

In each of these examples, `clp0` relates to high-priority cells and `clp1` relates to low-priority cells. Each command can be applied to either high or low priority and in the forward and backward direction (from the view of the AIP you are configuring).

IP over ATM QoS Issues As mentioned in Chapter 3, there are issues when mapping IP class of service (CoS) to ATM quality of service (QoS) features. Cisco makes available a feature that can be configured on ATM endstations called IP-to-ATM CoS, which lets you configure parameters on the router endstations that will take effect on CoS across the routed IP and switched ATM portions of a network. The goal of this technology is to enable you to give mission-critical traffic priority over noncritical traffic so that even during times of congestion the critical traffic will get through.

The feature used to deliver these benefits is the precedence field in the IPv4 header, which is a 3-bit value in the Type of Service byte. The mechanism is that different classes of IP traffic will be given different values in the IP Precedence field, which will be driven by more familiar mechanisms such as the committed access rate (CAR) or any policy-based routing enforced. These values are then carried forward into the ATM network, with different probabilities regarding whether they are dropped or not. This is achieved via a facility called Weighted Random Early Detection (WRED) groups, which are configured on the endstation router, which sets the drop conditions on a per-VC basis across the ATM network. WRED is just an algorithm for deciding which packets to drop should congestion occur. The WRED group we will illustrate shows how you can customize the parameters that control that algorithm.

Figure 6-18 illustrates an example where the CAR for a given stream is set within the routed IP network, which is translated by the endstation ATM router using WRED. This feature is only available on the 7500 series router equipped with a VIP2 card or PA-A3 ATM adapter. With this configuration, it could be that one of the types of queuing available within a Cisco network has been implemented to prefer some UDP traffic over TCP traffic by setting of the IP Precedence field. The goal is to have that preference extended across the ATM cloud.

Within the PA-A3 adapter, buffers are allocated on a per-VC basis to create queues for each VC. WRED is then applied to determine what traffic should be eligible for discard. In terms of configuration, we have to define a WRED in global configuration mode, then configure actions to take for each level on IP Precedence encountered. IP Precedence is set in route-map configuration mode. The process is to define an access control list that identifies the traffic you want to set precedence for (access lists were covered in the *Cisco TCP/IP Routing Professional Reference*). Then, in route-map configuration, you set the precedence for that access control list. Let's suppose we have created an access control list numbered 120. This is how we set the precedence for the traffic identified:

```
router(config)#route-map test1
router(config-route-map)#match ip address 120
router(config-route-map)#set ip precedence 5
```

The next stage is to apply that route-map to an interface as follows:

```
router(config)#int s0
router(config-if)#ip policy route-map test1
```

So, if we have all our SAP servers on one subnet, we have our access list 120 identify packets destined for that subnet. We can use the `route-map` command to set the precedence and apply that policy to a router interface.

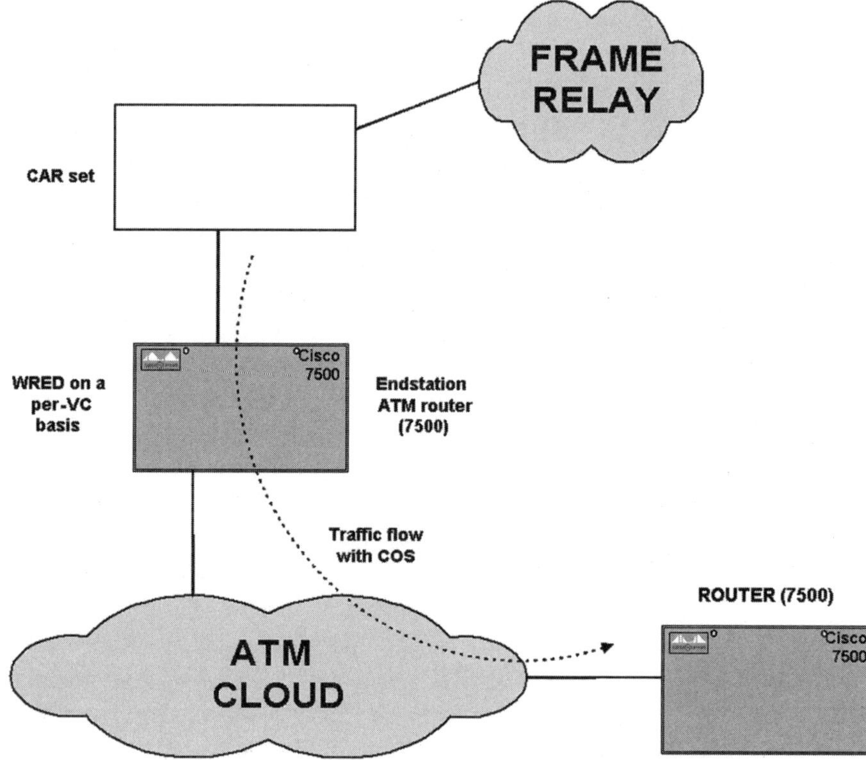

Figure 6-18 Network configuration illustrating location of WRED operation.

As IP Precedence is a 3-bit field, the possible values it can have are from 0 to 7. For each precedence value, we will define the minimum threshold for the WRED algorithm to start dropping packets in the queue. This is specified by a number of packets. We also have to specify a maximum threshold number of packets in the queue (the per-VC queue of packets) whereby if this number of packets is reached, all further packets are dropped. We can also specify a mark-probability-denominator that says if the average queue length meets or exceeds the maximum threshold, one out of the number of specified packets are dropped. For example, if the mark-probability-denominator is 50, one in 50 packets is dropped when the average queue length meets the maximum threshold value. It is important to remember that all these figures are based on packet rather than cell values.

Following is an example:

```
Random-detect-group
      Precedence 0 100 800 50
      Precedence 1 150 800 50
      Precedence 2 200 800 50
      Precedence 3 250 800 50
      Precedence 4 300 800 50
      Precedence 5 350 800 50
      Precedence 6 400 800 50
      Precedence 7 450 800 50
```

So, looking at what will happen to IP packets that come into the 7500 for transport over an ATM network that have IP Precedence set to 4, we see that packets will start to be discarded when the input queue for this precedence level reaches 300 packets. If the queue reaches 800, all packets will be discarded, and when the average queue length is 800 packets, one in 50 packets will be discarded.

Summary

In this chapter we started with a review of router ATM processors, the AIP for the 7xxx series, and the NPM for the 4x00 series. This included a look at the hardware features and rate queue configuration. We took the AIP as an example to illustrate ATM endstation configuration for SVC and PVC operation, showing the setup of the signaling and ILMI PVCs necessary for SVC operation. The first example of ATM communication setup used RFC 1483 encapsulation and had static IP-to-ATM address maps to facilitate address resolution across the ATM cloud.

Classic IP Over ATM as defined in RFC 1577 was discussed and its component configuration illustrated, particularly with reference to the ATM ARP server. Once the ATM ARP server is established and all clients can reach that server, no further static maps are required. At this stage we listed some of the more common `show` and `debug` commands that can be used to analyze ATM processor operation. From here we covered an interesting option of carrying PPP services over ATM, which gives network connections simple access to the CHAP.

The LS1010 was introduced as the ATM switch of choice in the Cisco environment. Even though this is scheduled for discontinuation in the next year, it is still a very popular device. The Cisco auto ATM address registration was described, and we illustrated how PVC configurations were made. The difference between the LS1010 ATM switch and AIP endstations were highlighted with this PVC configuration, as the job of the switch is to take in a PVC cell and switch it out another interface—clearly, a different job than the endstation. We covered simple IP configuration that allows a telnet session to the LS1010 to be established over the ATM network, either by use of static configuration, ATM ARP, or LANE, which, after all, are only different ways of resolving IP to ATM addresses.

After the LS1010 configuration, we looked at single-source clocking issues when the LS1010 is used to transport delay-sensitive traffic, such as voice and video. For data-only applications, this is not such a concern.

We moved on to look at ATM routing, using both static IISP and the dynamic PNNI protocol. We concluded that the default PNNI protocol was far preferable and recommended. IISP is useful only to connect two disparate PNNI domains, much like static routing as an exterior gateway protocol in IP routing. With that covered, we moved on to configuring LS1010 interfaces to participate in LANE as a LEC, LES/BUS, and LECS. We concluded that section with a discussion of LANE component redundancy.

Next, we looked at the enhancements available in LANE version 2.0, in terms of multiplexing multiple conversations down one VCC, and better QoS and multicast operation. After that we moved on to MPOA, which uses LANE as a component, plus NHRP and the MARS multicast capability. For MPOA, we illustrated the physical network connections necessary and configuration of both MPS and MPC devices.

The next section provided an overview of all the configuration used in the most common ATM application currently: router endstations communicating with an LS1010 with CIOA. We used this configuration as the base for typical `show` commands. We concluded the chapter with a review of QoS features available in ATM and how by the use of WRED we could examine IP Precedence levels and have the priorities set by that mechanism carried forward through an attached ATM network.

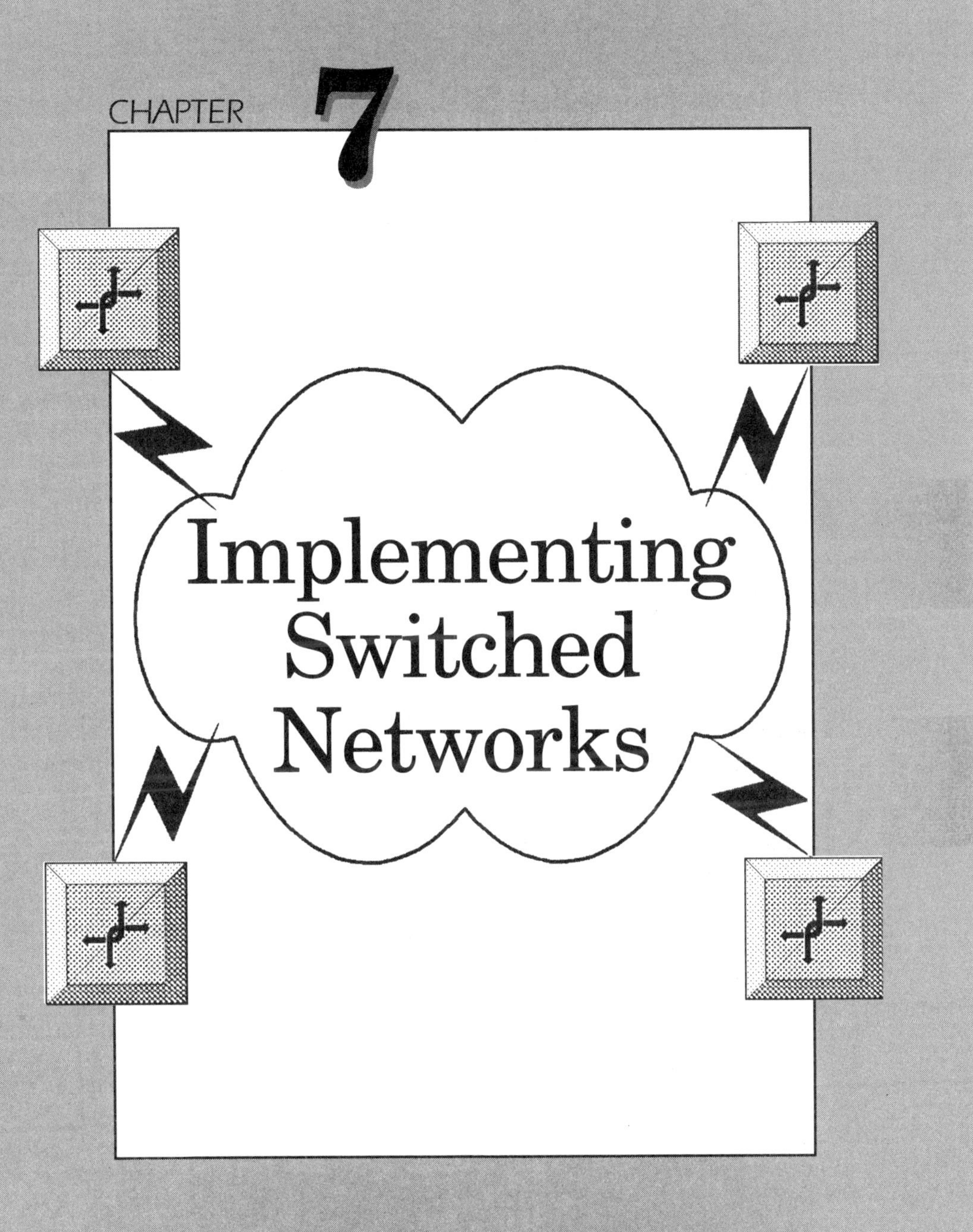
CHAPTER 7
Implementing Switched Networks

Introduction

I chose not to call this chapter Network Design, as I do not perceive network design as a separate, discrete, and once-off task. I do not believe in a once-off process that will accommodate all your current and future network needs and that reduces a network manager's job to one that continually expands upon a fixed formula of how to add capacity and workstations. Every network is different, and each network is constantly changing. In my opinion network design is part of an ongoing process of network implementation. In essence, a network manager has to continually redesign his or her network to meet the ever-changing demands that are placed on it. That is not to say that there is not a sensible jumping-off point of interconnections from which to start. We will present a blueprint switched network design that is a good starting point for the vast majority of implementations.

Although this chapter will present a basic framework for switched network design that makes sense for most networks with today's technology, the focus here really is to generate thought about the benefits and pitfalls of implementing different solutions in a network, depending on the nature of the network traffic. My message here is be cautious of leaving your network design to someone who has not or will not be managing networks on a day to day basis. The best preparation for network design is network management. The most useful information in network design is that of the traffic usage on the network in question. Examples are as follows:

- What type of traffic is there: unicast, multicast, broadcast?
- How much traffic and at what time of day are the major traffic flows generating?
- What levels of service are required by the applications being served?
- How are users that need to work together geographically located?

If a network is already in place, this information is clearly easier to obtain, so that the current design can be replaced with a better one. Making estimates of traffic flows is fraught with danger, and if you are implementing a completely new network, or one that will be servicing dramatically different applications, prototyping is normally the best way forward. Once you have a feel for the traffic on the network, it is essential to fully understand how each network device and link between devices affects the traffic and its flow. In the generic blueprint for a switched network that we will present, the most important point is that packets will be switched from client PC all the way through the network to the server. This minimizes the changes that occur to the packet headers (remember that packet headers are rewritten every time they go through a router, which takes time to do) and makes the network perform well and in a scalable fashion.

In the preceding chapters we have looked at the theory and operation of all the features and functions you need to deploy a well-designed and -implemented network. The goal of this final chapter is to bring that together to discuss how they can be assembled in one network

Network Implementation Goals

The following sections discuss my personal classifications for switched network designs. Others will classify it differently. The whole point is that there are no absolutes in this field. There are many different views, which are in many cases equally valid. These classifications are not presented in priority order; each network will have its own priorities for each of these aspects. Here we will state the demands that each of the classifications places on the network. The next section will explain how a generic switched network deals with these demands.

My classifications are as follows:

- *Scalability*—Ensuring that network performance is maintained as the network grows
- *Redundancy*—Maintaining service in the event of component failures
- *Class of service*—Making sure essential traffic gets through in times of congestion
- *Security*—Ensuring only the people you want to access data can.

Even these classifications overlap significantly; however, we have to impose some separation of these interrelated topics in order to present the text, so here goes.

Scalability

When implementing a network design, we want to do all that is possible to ensure that we can cope with growth on the network. The old adage of what goes up must come down has not applied to network traffic yet. For network traffic, it seems the only way is up. However, we have to be clear about what we are scaling. The idea that we only have to plan for more users adding to network traffic is way out-of-date. What is driving network traffic are newer applications, like multicast and multimedia, remote access, and interaction with partner company networks and the Internet.

In addition to these concerns we must also think of how increased complexity or size in the network will affect the operation of the network itself. A short historical perspective is appropriate here. As flat shared media networks grew in size, they experienced collision and traffic limitations. These shared networks were broken up with bridges to localize problems with traffic and collisions. As broadcasts on these growing networks became a problem (particularly during link failure conditions), routers were introduced to split interconnected networks into broadcast domains. Additionally, adding routing into the network allowed address hierarchy at a layer 3 protocol level that allowed significantly greater scalability.

As routed networks grew, the mechanisms for dealing with link failures (Distance Vector Routing Protocols) became troublesome. In some large routed networks, the behavior of routing protocols and their effect on route table calculation presented almost insurmountable problems. In addition to the size of routing tables and the processing power required to recalculate when a failure occurred, the distance vector practice of regularly sending the complete routing table contents in routing updates could flood network links alone during route advertisements.

Switching VLAN traffic eliminated some of these problems by placing a lot of the software routing functions into specialized hardware, thus increasing performance; however, we must face the fact that we have not reached the final iteration of network devices and probably never will. Network demands appear set to continue to grow and change, presenting new challenges that will be met with new solutions.

For your network to be scalable, hierarchy of some kind is an absolute necessity. In a pure IP network, that means you have to split the network into separate network numbers, or subnets. To discuss this we will introduce the accepted three-tier classification of core, distribution, and what are referred to as *access,* or *edge,* devices. This concept is illustrated in Figure 7-1.

The core of the network typically handles the most traffic and must have the highest availability. Edge devices connect to the end users and typically have multiple connections towards the core, but only a single one to the user. Distribution devices connect the edge devices to the core.

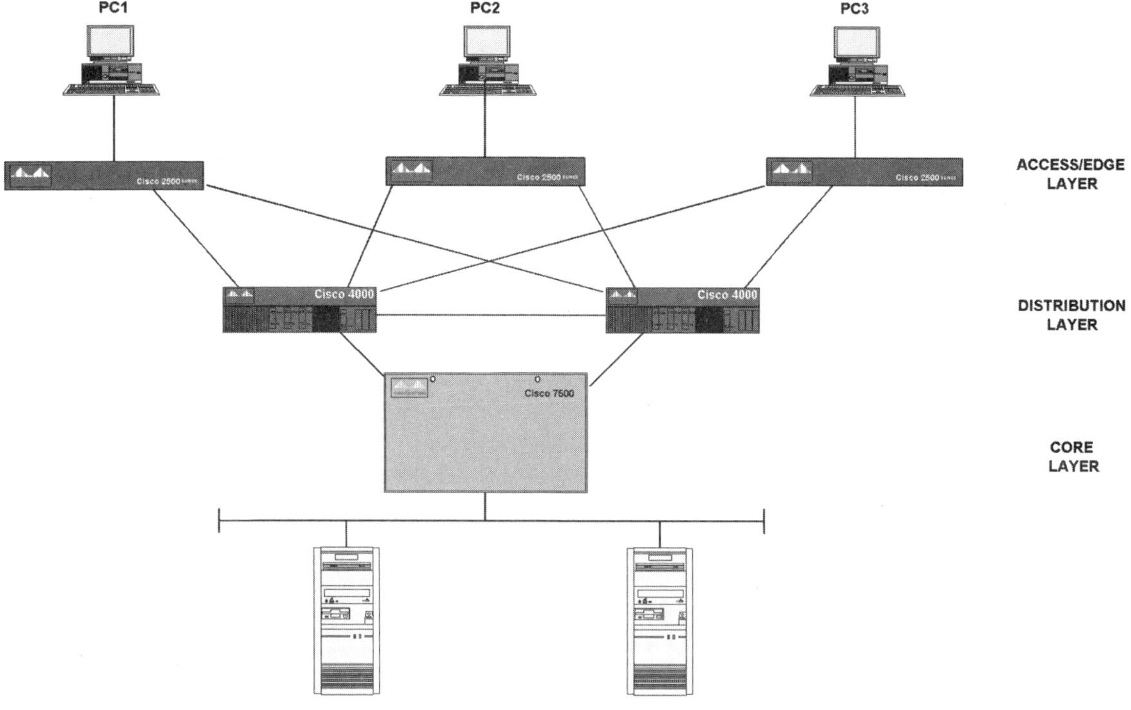

Figure 7-1 The three-layer classification of core, distribution, and access layer devices.

The characteristics of the core devices are that they need to have high availability and have the highest levels of throughput in the network. Core devices must also support mechanisms for failover in the event of link or device failure, so they need a layer 2 (for example, STP) rerouting protocol. In terms of scalability, we must design the network such that the addition of endstations or applications does not affect the performance of the core in any meaningful way. This can be achieved either by planning the addition of capacity within the core to handle new loads or by minimizing the effect that new clients and applications have on the core.

Distribution devices will perform the packet manipulation required within the network, such as routing between VLANs and security access/priority lists, and so forth. This level is scaled by adding more devices as needed.

So, in summary, scalability in network implementation means that new traffic can be added to the network without any of the following:

- Layer 2 or layer 3 routing protocol consuming inordinate amounts of bandwidth

- Overloading of links or devices within the network
- Running out of layer 3 addresses

Redundancy

Everyone wants their network operational all the time. That can be accomplished—at a price. Determining the level of redundancy appropriate for your network comes down to the needs of the application in question. It's up to the person responsible for your business to determine the level of redundancy justified for the network applications. In this respect, every network is different and needs to be judged on its own merits.

To help with the decision making, we can split the question of redundancy into the following categories:

- Servers
- Networking devices
- Data paths
- Physical locations

Servers Of course, I assume that a data backup operation exists whereby the backed up data is stored at an alternate location. We then have to consider two further parts of server redundancy: backup for the hardware the server processes run on and physical location of that backup server.

When we look at backup hardware, we must consider how quickly it is required for the backup server to take over from the primary in the event of a primary failure and what action needs to be taken by endusers to attach to the backup. These options will vary depending on the operating system your server runs on. NetWare, Windows NT, and UNIX all have different schemes for server backup. Generally, in order to design server backup into your network, you need to understand how the primary and backup server maintain synchronization of the services they are providing to the user. If this requires a dedicated high-speed link between the servers (as in fault-tolerant NetWare), this may restrict where you can place the backup server in the network. If this high-speed link uses proprietary communication mechanisms and can only be of a fixed length, your backup server placement is obviously limited. However, if this link can be transported over network devices that can utilize Gigabit Ethernet, or ATM, you obviously have more flexibility.

Apart from placing the backup server in your network, you have to consider how the endstations will connect to the backup in the event of a primary server failure. There are many different ways that an endstation can determine the server address that it is going to connect to and each one has an impact on your network configuration. The most common is for the endstation to be configured in some way to determine the server it will connect to. Generally, this is in the form of a server name that one of the network operating system processes resolves to an address. In the case of NT, this will be a NetBIOS call to a server name that may be resolved to an IP address by WINS (discussed in the *Cisco TCP/IP Routing Professional Reference*). In NetWare the endstation will issue a broadcast Get Nearest Server query, and the server responding will supply the address of the preferred server.

If your network operates in this way, clearly, the endstations do not know about a backup server to contact in the event of the primary failing. With this type of operation, the primary and backup servers need to communicate between themselves, and the backup needs to take over if the primary stops responding. This means that the backup has to be a mirror of the primary, including the addresses it uses, so that the endstations are unaware of any difference in their communication with the backup server. This has implications for your network implementation. Clearly, if you want your backup server in a geographically different location than the primary (either a different equipment room or even a different building), your network design has to easily accommodate addresses from the same IP subnet appearing in two different places. So although you may have subnets appearing in two different physical locations, you need to implement the network such that these different physical locations are considered the same in the logical sense. This is illustrated in Figure 7-2.

In this figure, there are two connections from the servers to their attached Catalysts. The first (link 1) is for endstation access, and the second (link 2) is for primary to backup server communication. For this type of scheme to work, the primary and backup communicate and synchronize data during normal operation. If the primary server fails, the backup will take over, using the same addresses (probably both the layer 2 as well as the layer 3 address.) This will cause the Catalysts to recalculate the STP and provide access to the server MAC address at the new location. To STP it will look like the device has moved on the network. As far as the endstations are concerned in this scenario, there has been a short break in communications, but they are still talking to the same server using the same layer 2 and layer 3 address.

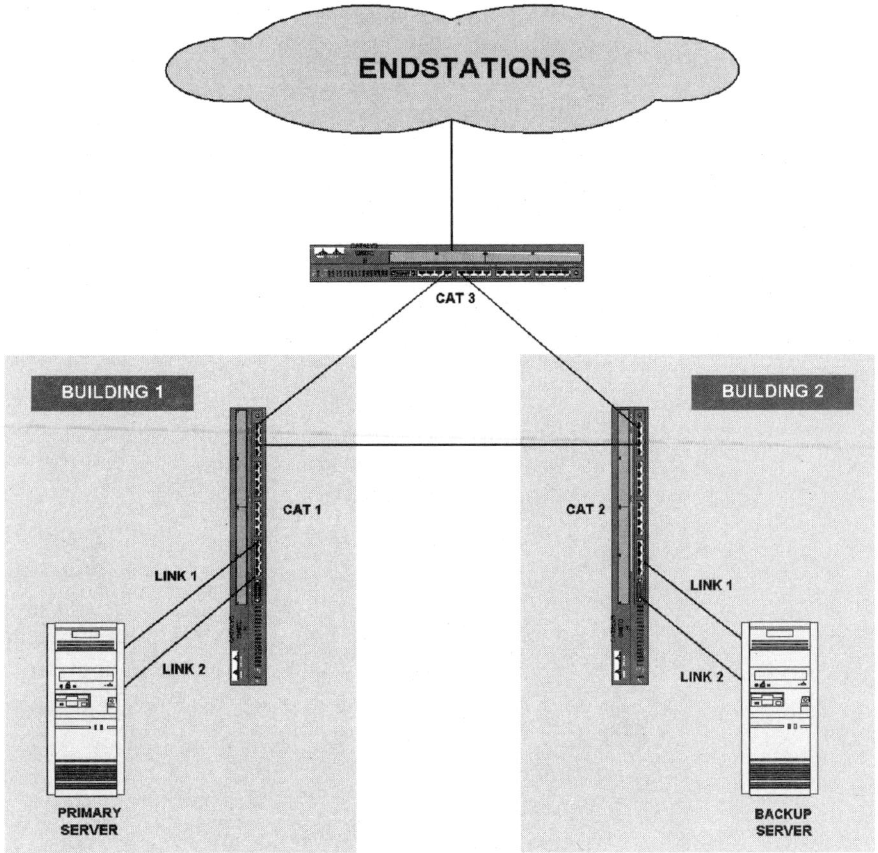

Figure 7-2 Placing primary and backup servers in different buildings.

The alternate approach puts more onus on the endstations. Some backup schemes have backup server addresses configured into the workstations. For this to work, the endstation must be aware that a connection to the primary server is no longer available and must initiate a connection to the backup. This obviates the need for duplicate addresses to be used by the primary and backup servers.

Clearly, the downside to each endstation knowing a name or address of the primary and/or backup server is that if you have to reconfigure the servers with new names or addresses, you face an arduous task of changing the configuration of all the endstations that connect to these servers at the same time. This can be a real headache.

Another option that I have seen in use on some UNIX server platforms is to leave the endstations without any explicit configuration of server names or addresses in them, thus leaving the flexibility to reconfigure servers without concern for endstation configuration. To put this into practice requires the endstations to be able to listen on specific UDP port numbers for a broadcast from the server. Once the workstation hears the broadcast, it has the source IP address of the server and can initiate a logon. All the endstation needs to be configured to do is listen on a specific port number for the primary and a different port for the backup.

With this mechanism, your network must be preconfigured to carry these broadcast messages to all the subnets that have endstations on them that may want to logon to the servers in question. In the event of a primary server failure, the endstation realizes that no traffic has come from the primary for a predetermined amount of time, and then decides to listen for packets coming from the backup server (clearly, during normal operation the backup server has to send out a small amount of broadcast traffic so that the endstations have enough information to log on to it should the primary fail). Once the endstation hears a packet from the backup server (typically sent on a different UDP port number from the primary), it can log on to the backup, and as long as the primary and backup servers were synchronized, resume normal operation.

Networking Devices So, assuming we have a suitable mechanism for users accessing a backup server in case the primary goes down, we next look at what happens if a networking device fails. By “networking device” I mean a router, switch, or hub. Of course, it is assumed that redundant power supplies, supervisor engines, and fans are resident in each core and potentially each distribution device to make the device itself reliable in the event of single-component failure.

Generally, network devices are only provided with automatic backups in the distribution and core of a network. Providing backups for the access, or edge, devices (I’ll call them access from now on) requires redundant physical paths to the workstation, which is not commonly provided. Redundancy for access devices is generally of the form of swapping out devices. Clearly, having a TFTP server with a current copy of all access device configurations will help in quickly being able to reconfigure replacement devices and getting them operational. In critical areas where backup access devices are not provided—for example, in a financial dealing room—it is typical to feed alternate users on a desk from different access devices. With an implementation of this nature, even if one access device does go down, the worst that happens is a user has to look over the shoulder of his or her neighbor until the faulty device is replaced.

An alternate solution in networks that truly require complete redundancy is to have two network interface cards (NICs) in a PC. Those two NICs can be connected to different access switches. An interesting point is that these two NICs will need to be configured for the same subnet and attached to ports on different switches that are configured for the same VLAN. In this configuration, the endstation should share its traffic across the two NICs and transfer all traffic off the NIC connected to a failed switch, should that occur. The endstation will know an attached access switch has failed, since the line protocol will fail on the NIC. Fortunately, endstation operating systems allow this IP configuration, whereas a true routing device would not.

In my opinion, this setup is probably more trouble than it is worth. There are far more failures at the endstation PC level than there are at the access switch level. As long as there is good redundancy provided by the distribution and core layers, you have satisfied most redundancy questions. In the core and distribution sections of the network, network device redundancy is a must-have. Failure of an access device will only affect those directly connected to it; failure of a distribution or core device will typically affect many more users.

One of the fundamental design decisions you have to make when implementing a switched network is where you will have layer 3 routing functionality. Access devices (in most cases, 2916XL or newer 2948G switches) will not support layer 3 routing. The access devices are dedicated to switching at layer 2 and merely recognize which VLAN traffic is destined for, switching it out the correct port. Access switches need to support VTP for dynamic learning of VLAN information and multiple high-speed uplinks to the distribution devices. Clearly, there needs to be more than one uplink to the distribution level, or you cannot achieve distribution device redundancy. The 2948G, which should be available by the time of publication, has two Gigabit Ethernet uplinks and 48 ports of 10/100 Ethernet for workstation connections, which make it ideal for wiring closet applications.

However, back to the distribution layer. Do we want to have the distribution layer devices perform the routing between VLANs, or do we want to have them send packets back to the core for that functionality? This has an effect on how we deliver redundancy within the distribution layer network devices and how those devices recover from outages.

Refer to Figure 7-1. If PC1, PC2, and PC3 are all on different VLANs, we can provide them with the ability to communicate either with routing at the distribution or core layers. If we choose to leave routing purely to the core, we get more traffic there; however, we do maintain performance of the distribution layer, as it does not have to support routing processes/protocols and their inherent processing overhead. The question of redundancy is also affected. If we do not provide routing at the distribution layer, we use STP to redirect packets in the event of link failure.

For the blueprint network design we will deal with a little later on, we bring the routing function within the distribution layer; however, an alternate is presented that uses separate routes between the core and distribution switches.

So far we have said that device replacement is generally suitable for the access layer, and multiple device redundancy supported by STP (or in the case where the distribution layer has routing functionality, OSPF, or similar) is appropriate for the distribution layer. At the distribution layer, Uplink Fast and Backbone Fast are enabled to speed STP convergence time. The switched core relies upon multiple links between devices and, typically, STP to converge should one of those links fail.

Data Paths When discussing device redundancy, we have already alluded to some of the issues related to data path redundancy. The reality is that all of these issues are interrelated. There are three aspects to delivering redundant data paths that we will discuss here. The first is that the paths taken by all cabling and land lines must be completely diverse. There is little point in having two cables going through the same cable run or access point to a building. Equal care must be taken when ordering diverse routes for lines from telcos. It is best to use different telcos for both lines to ensure complete redundancy; otherwise, you are unlikely to get redundancy within the telco network.

The second aspect is how the rerouting protocols will make use of these diverse routes in the event of a failure. Designing a network that will reroute traffic over an alternate path is all well and good, but does that alternate path have sufficient capacity to handle both its usual load and the additional rerouted traffic? In more than one network design, I have seen the potential for the rerouting of traffic over already fully utilized links that would have saturated the link carrying both its regular and the newly rerouted traffic. This is, of course, worse than not providing an alternate path, as you are taking two links out of action with only one failure.

The third aspect is to consider how a given link failure will affect the layer 3 routing protocol and STP. Generally, if a link failure occurs within a layer 2 switched fabric, STP will reroute around the failure by unblocking switch interfaces. The only time a link failure causes a routing protocol to recalculate routes is if the link is directly connected to a router interface. When we get to designing a combined switched and routed network, we will examine how various link failures cause protocol routing recalculations.

Physical Locations Physical locations are important at two levels. First, all networking equipment should be in secured locations. This means wiring closets for access devices and equipment/communication rooms for core and distribution. We then need to be confident in the power and environmental conditions the equipment is kept in, typically AC and UPS. This is all basic stuff. Of more interest is when we consider disaster recovery for the network. How does a disaster in one building on our network affect service to other parts of the network—particularly if the disaster happens to the building housing the central servers?

The key to providing physical redundancy for central servers is to have a completely redundant physical path from the endstation devices back to the alternate location housing the backup central servers. In addition, you need the dynamically rerouting protocols that will detect those failures and route around them. We will discuss this in the context of an example in a later section.

Class of Service

There are a lot of choices here, and we will look at the main ones individually. Essentially you have to decide on what is going to receive priority treatment and how your network is going to handle a condition where traffic of different priorities are competing for the same resource. It can be reasonably argued that class of service defines all of the objectives for network implementation, in that the network is there to service application needs. Routing protocols, STP, and backup devices all have an impact on class of service. However, in this section we'll take a more narrow focus: the ability of the network to provide better service to predefined traffic. We will look at the queuing and signaling methodologies within Cisco solutions that enable this to happen.

The key concept within the overall framework of class of service is that of end-to-end service levels. This is particularly challenging for IP-based networks. In the ATM world all communications are based around connections. This makes it simpler for the call setup process to negotiate a path through the network that has guaranteed that it will meet the required service level. In IP networks, some traffic is connectionless, and we therefore have a different approach. In IP networks we have to look at reserving a specific amount of bandwidth for some traffic types and giving priority to some traffic over others. The priority-handling mechanisms within IP networks set priority on a packet as it gets sent, then rely upon programming of intermediate devices to ensure service levels are met. We cannot follow the ATM model completely and be assured that if a connection is made, the network has guaranteed to meet its requirements.

So within a Cisco IP network, we have to rely on the queuing mechanisms available within the intermediate devices to get the traffic marked as important through in times of congestion. Let's look at those now.

Class of Service Queuing Options The queuing mechanisms available in Cisco software involve the following:

- First in, first out queuing (FIFO)
- Priority queuing (PQ)
- Custom queuing (CQ)
- Weighted fair queuing (WFQ)

As you would expect, the list is presented in ascending order of complexity, with FIFO as the simplest.

FIFO is the queuing method that most network engineers are familiar with. It relies on the network device storing packets during times of congestion, then releasing them at a rate the network can handle. This storing mechanism is provided by the buffers and the hold queues within the IOS. The *Cisco TCP/IP Routing Professional Reference* covered optimizing the configuration of these features. FIFO is obviously limited, as it does not differentiate between high- and low-priority traffic. This type of operation is a nightmare for delivering any type of delay-sensitive traffic, such as voice. This is particularly so if the path being traversed goes from a high-speed LAN to a low-speed leased line, as bursts of data traffic will consume all available buffers, typically on a regular basis.

Priority queuing is a step up and is based upon packets being placed into one of four queues: high, medium, normal, or low priority. There are many options to prioritize packets into one of these queues, including source or destination address, protocol type, or incoming interface. The mechanics of configuring priority queuing are to create a `priority-list` in global configuration and to apply that list to an interface as a `priority-group`. An example is as follows:

```
priority-list 1 interface serial 0/1 high
interface e1/1
priority-group 1
```

Custom queuing was designed to provide guaranteed bandwidth for an identified set of traffic at a given point within the network. Custom queuing uses a different mechanism than priority queuing; it assigns a different amount of space for each of the queues holding traffic, then services each queue in a round-robin fashion. The net effect of custom queuing is to guarantee performance by guaranteeing a portion of the available bandwidth to specified traffic. Custom queuing is implemented in a similar fashion as priority queuing and never in addition to it. With custom queuing, a `custom-queue-list` is applied to an interface, and the contents of that list is defined on a queue list as follows:

```
Queue-list 2 byte-count 2000
Interface serial 0/1
  Custom-queue-list 2
```

The overall operation is that several `queue-list` commands will be entered in the configuration. When a packet comes through an interface with a `custom-queue-list` defined, the `queue-list` specifications will be searched until a match is found. This enables a packet to be placed in a specific queue. Let's say for argument's sake we want to give better treatment to telnet sessions in a network. In the configuration so far, we have a list 2 operational on serial 0/2.

First we need to define what queue 2 means. By default, all queues created have 1500 bytes of queue space, so if we are going to put higher priority traffic in that queue, we need to make it bigger. So, what we will do is identify telnet sessions by TCP and port 23, then allocate that to a specific queue number and give that queue 2000 bytes, which is accomplished as follows:

```
Queue-list 2 protocol ip 1 tcp 23
Queue-list 2 queue 1 byte-count 2000
```

The first line says that custom queue list number 2 will apply to packets destined for port 23 that use the IP protocol TCP. These packets will be sent to queue 1. The second line assigns a byte count of 2000 bytes to queue 1.

The most current form of queuing, though, is Cisco's weighted fair queuing (WFQ). The goals of WFQ are to deliver good response time to all users and share the remaining bandwidth between the high-bandwidth consumers. This has the effect of allocating all the available bandwidth to the traffic flows that need them, yet still providing light users of network bandwidth a reasonable piece of the bandwidth pie.

WFQ achieves its aims by giving low-volume traffic streams preferential service and sharing out what remains of the bandwidth to high-volume traffic streams. WFQ is an adaptive mechanism that allocates bandwidth among flows dynamically. As such, it has some similarities to the ATM model of multiplexing. Just as ATM does, it will give more bandwidth to the flows that need them, without the need to allocate fixed-sized chunks of bandwidth (as time-division multiplexing, or TDM, does). TDM will leave the preallocated chunks of bandwidth unused if its owner is not transmitting. With WFQ, the dynamic allocation of bandwidth gets around that.

The mechanisms that input to WFQ are the IP Precedence field and the Resource Reservation Protocol (RSVP). WFQ can assign a faster response to higher-priority packets. This is achieved by assigning more bandwidth to packets with higher precedence values. What happens is that WFQ will identify the precedence value for each flow, sum them, then decide how much each flow will get of the available bandwidth by dividing each flow's precedence by the summed value. With RSVP, WFQ is used as the mechanism to allocate buffers and schedule packet transmission and as such is part of the process to guarantee service.

WFQ is enabled on an interface by the `fair-queue` interface command.

Class of Service Signaling Options We discussed signaling in the sections on ATM as a way for an endstation to request a connection to its destination through the network. As such, signaling is a communication mechanism for a network device to get what it needs from the network as a whole.

Signaling in QoS or CoS is a similar concept. QoS signaling is a means for a network device to request something from the network. So far we have discussed QoS features that apply at discrete points within the network. By that I mean that each router or switch has been configured to provide a certain level of service in isolation. It is far more preferable to attempt to emulate the ATM model and provide service levels on an end-to-end scale, with all devices in the path from source to destination coordinated for service levels.

The end-to-end coordination is primarily delivered by a combination of IP Precedence and RSVP. IP Precedence is defined in the packet and, therefore, is present end to end. RSVP has the signaling mechanisms necessary to reserve bandwidth end to end as a traffic flow is established.

Configuring IP Precedence based on extended access lists was covered earlier. We'll now look at the configuration of RSVP on network devices. For RSVP to work, all devices in the data paths from source to destination need to be RSVP-capable, and that includes the endstations also.

Generically, the tasks when implementing RSVP are to enable RSVP on the device, define the traffic flow characteristics.

The first thing is to decide the amount of bandwidth on an interface to reserve for RSVP and define the single-flow limits for each RSVP flow. For example, you may want to allocate 100 Kbit/sec on an interface for use by RSVP and have no single flow within that 100 Kbit use more than 20 Kbit/sec. RSVP-aware hosts send an RSVP PATH message when they want to establish an end-to-end RSVP flow. The receiver will send back an RSVP RESV message that specifies the service characteristics required of the connection. If all the intermediate devices can support the requested bandwidth, the guaranteed path is made; otherwise, the reservation attempt is rejected.

It is possible to configure the intermediate devices to generate their own RSVP RESV and RSVP PATH messages to always have bandwidth reserved whether endstations are generating them or not, but this is a little-used feature. So to configure RSVP on intermediate routers and set the bandwidth reservations, we only have to implement one command on the interfaces that will participate in the RSVP process. Here we specify that for a total of 100 Kbit/sec on interface serial 0, no more than 20 Kbit/sec is reservable per traffic flow:

```
Interface serial 0
  Ip rsvp bandwidth 100 20
```

Security

Security is, of course, a vast topic that involves enough material to justify multiple volumes being written about it. In the context of this chapter, we will restrict the discussion of security to examining who can get on the network (network devices as well as users) and how we ensure that traffic is not altered in transit. Of course, two of the goals of network design—security and ease of use—are typically opposing; often the more secure a network is made, the more difficult it becomes to use. The choice, as always, comes down to individual circumstances.

The type of security that most users are familiar with is a network logon that is administered via a server, typically NT or NetWare. Before an endstation is allowed to access any resources on the network, the user must supply a registered username and password that the server recognizes. The password authenticates that the user is who he or she claims to be, and the permissions set up on the server define what that user is authorized to access.

Within the LAN environment, it is unusual for network devices to add any layers of authentication; however, dial-up users are typically required to supply CHAP usernames and passwords to authenticate themselves on the dial-in access device prior to logging on to a server. In most cases the CHAP username and password can be the same, and the network logon carries this through to the server, thus making the two-step process transparent to the user. Setting up CHAP on dial-in devices and network device security is covered extensively in the *Cisco TCP/IP Routing Professional Reference.*

The most common forms of network security found in networks are firewall devices, which can be one of the following devices:

- A router with access lists preventing certain source, destination, or traffic flow types from traversing the router (for example, a two-interface router)
- A network address translation device that hides the IP addressing scheme from devices connected to either side of it (for example, the Cisco PIX firewall)
- An application proxy server that has two instances of HTTP, FTP, or other common applications, one for each side of the firewall, and that carries data from one application instance to the other (for example, the Apache proxy server)
- A circuit-level proxy server that has separate instances of communications-level protocols, such as TCP, one for each side of the firewall (for example, a SOCKS proxy)

So, if we get to the stage where we feel comfortable with the authentication and authorization of users on the network, we still have to consider data security, which can be addressed by encryption. Encryption is normally one of two types: symmetric or asymmetric. A computer implementing *symmetric encryption* uses a secret and distinct key for each conversation with every computer it talks to. For example, if computer 1 talks to two other computers, it will have a different key for each of the two computers it talks to. This is the basis for the Data Encryption Standard (DES). This method does work, but it has scalability problems when implemented in a large network where each workstation talks to a large number of other computers.

Asymmetric encryption uses the concept of public and private keys. As an example, computer 1 may give its public key to any computer wanting to talk to it. The public key is used to encrypt the data, and only computer 1's private key can unlock that data. This form of encryption is used in RSA (Rivest-Shamir-Adleman) and DSS.

Either symmetric or asymmetric encryption can be used to encrypt the actual data sent over the network wire, but there is one other form of encryption that is much more processor-intensive and is used to encrypt passwords sent over network media: secure hashing. This is implemented in MD5 (Message Digest Algorithm 5), which is used when CHAP authenticates a user (typically using PPP encapsulation). As far as the specifics of network device configuration go, encryption is only configured on PPP links where CHAP is implemented.

A simple aspect of switched networking that enhances security is that only those users configured for VLAN membership will see traffic for that VLAN. In shared media networking, all users saw all traffic on the same segment. So, clearly, if a cracker cannot sniff the packets on the LAN, it is more difficult to compromise security.

Common Switched Network Design

So, enough of the generalities. In this section we'll describe an existing network implemented using routers and hubs, then we'll look at the issues this implementation causes and the challenges it will face when you implement new applications. We will then present a blueprint for switched network design that will allow us to overcome the current network problems and accommodate the new applications. This blueprint is a good starting point for almost any network design, but of course, it requires customization for each implementation.

A Typical Router Network

Our fictitious network is depicted in Figure 7-3. This network supports two major buildings for the company (we'll call it Acme Inc.) that house its central databases. Acme also has five regional branches.

Each of the major buildings has around 500 users and the regional offices around 100. The major buildings are connected via two T-3 lines, and each regional office is connected via two T-1 lines, one to each major building. Within each major building, departmental LANs are connected to shared media hubs, each with its own router interface. The major building LAN deployment is shown in Figure 7-4.

The original design met the needs of the time. Daily backups of the central servers were taken, and in the event of a major disaster with those databases, the plan was to point everyone to the backup servers,

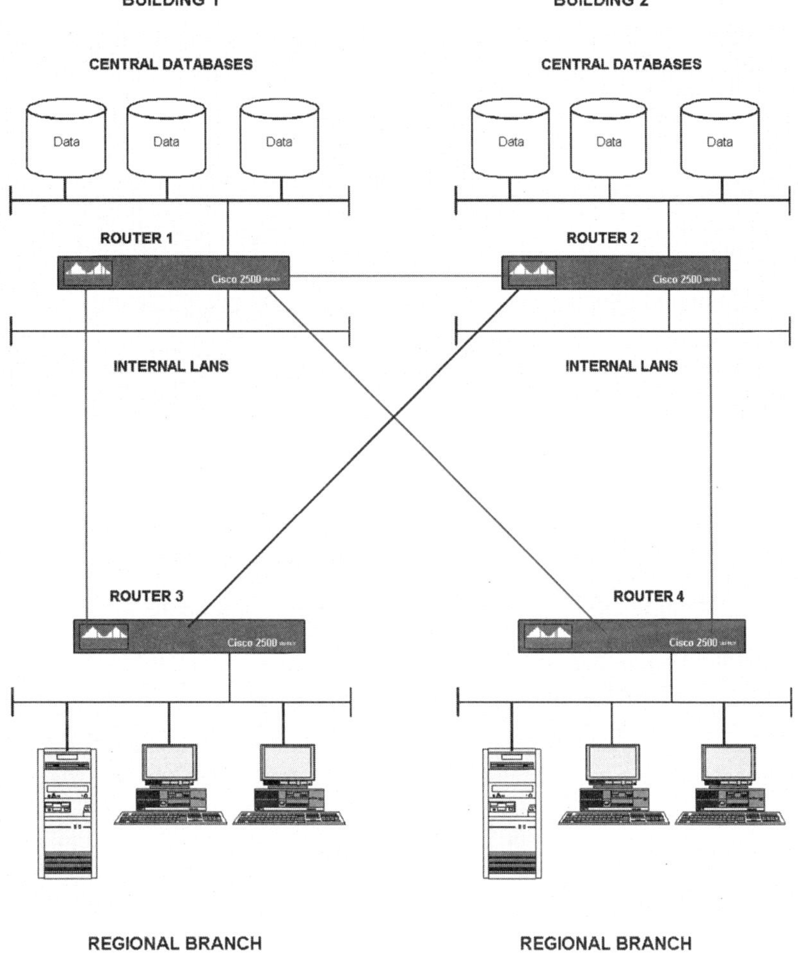

Figure 7-3 Overview of Acme's routed network.

which would be, at most, a day out of date. In this design each leased line had a backup, and the IGRP routing protocol rerouted around communications line failures. Departmental servers have been deployed to meet disparate needs and local resource.

The problems of this network are as follows:

- The collisions on shared media hubs are an increasing problem performance-wise.
- The whole network can be brought down with the failure of the central router in building 1.
- There is no link redundancy for LAN links within the major buildings.

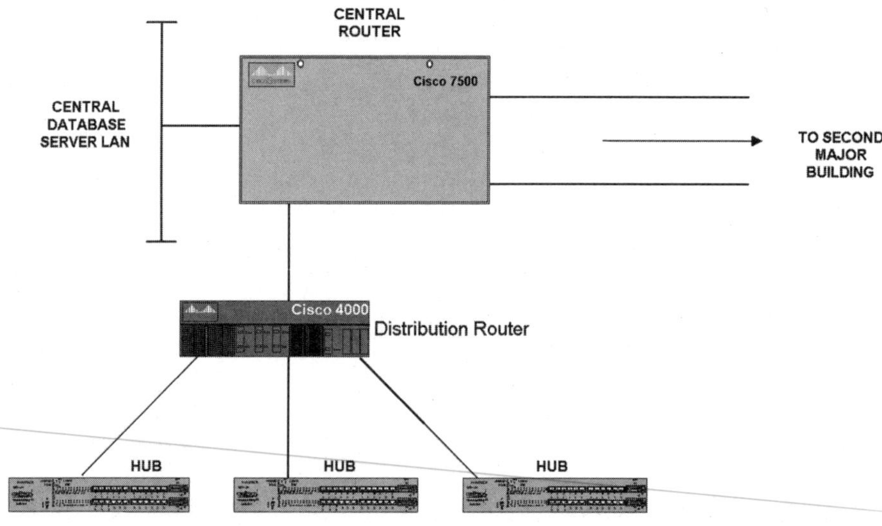

Figure 7-4 Major building network design for Acme.

- Users are constantly moving location within the major buildings, which is leading to a lot of access to departmental servers via traffic that has to pass through the central router.
- The information held on servers in regional branches is now being accessed by users in the major buildings and other branch offices.
- The departmental and branch office servers are not being properly backed up and managed by the users that had them installed.
- The central routers are becoming overutilized with cross-department and cross-branch traffic.

Additionally, there are new challenges of how to deliver multimedia services to users on this network and how to deliver more throughput for what seems to be an ever-increasing demand for network bandwidth.

This is a fairly common situation, and one that can be addressed with the switched network blueprint quite well.

A Switched Network Blueprint

Our goals for the switched network design are as follows:

- Wherever possible, place the high-volume traffic through fast switches rather than slower routers.

- Utilize low-cost switches instead of shared media hubs.
- Provide the throughput to allow central database servers to be mirrored.
- Centralize all departmental servers.
- Provide an alternate path within the distribution and core layers to cope with any single-device or link failure.
- Provide a VLAN hierarchy that will allow for easy relocation of users without a major disruption to network traffic.

There are a number of trade-offs that we are making with these goals. First, we know we cannot implement a network without some routing. We cannot have one broadcast domain cover all users, so our first piece of judgment comes in when we have to decide how many VLANs to create and how they will be distributed throughout the network. The centralization of all servers will increase the amount of traffic in the distribution and core, but it will make the management of these servers and the relocation of users far simpler. Centralizing departmental servers also allows several smaller servers to be collapsed into one larger server. This tends to be beneficial on cost grounds and provides a higher level of service overall. Providing alternate paths to cope with device and link failures is expensive; it can double the number of interfaces needed within core and distribution devices and leased lines purchased. This, however, needs to be justified against the business expense of losing service, which is getting increasingly high in today's world.

OK. Now we will get down to addressing the architecture within each layer of core, distribution, and access devices.

Access Layer The access layer is the simplest part to design in the switched network. Our main job is to make sure that endstations have access to a switched port rather than a shared media hub. In most cases the endstations will only have one NIC and, therefore, one port assigned; however, in some cases it is required to assign two connections for the endstation, each going to a different access layer switch. For the majority, though, we will consider the following as the issues for the access layer:

- Endstation connection
- Handling multicasts
- Uplink connections
- Required protocol support STP, VTP, and CGMP/IGMP snooping

Very few installations are being performed at the time of writing that are not 100 Mbit to the desktop. There is little reason not to go for this speed, because all the leading NICs support this speed and the cost of 10/100 switching ports is equivalent to the cost of shared media ports of only a couple of years ago. Making the leap to providing switched port rather than shared media access allows the provision of one switched port per user, which brings full-duplex operation into reality.

Of more interest is how each access device will connect to the distribution layer at a physical and protocol level. By the time of publication, the trunking modules for the 2916XL range should be available, so we can assume that for new networks at least, we will be able to connect access layer switches to distribution via trunk connections using ISL or 802.1q encapsulation. It is unclear whether Cisco will continue to develop the ISL standard as the newest switches, the 4000 range, do not support ISL for trunking and rely upon 802.1q. This is not really as important as it first may seem; it is still perceived that VTP is the important protocol that will distribute VLAN information irrespective of the layer 2 encapsulation for the trunks. VTP works equally well over either encapsulation. As such, using 802.1q rather than ISL encapsulation is of the same order of selecting Ethernet_II or Ethernet_SNAP as an encapsulation type for Ethernet communication.

Another important issue to be addressed within the access layer is the handling of multicasts. If you are using the 2900XL range, CGMP is really the way forward. However, a newer approach is that of IGMP snooping. Clearly, when an endstation issues an IGMP `join` message, that `join` message carries enough information for an intermediate switch to determine the MAC address of the endstations that should receive particular multicast group traffic. To enable a switch to use IGMP snooping (it is called *snooping* because it enables the switch to snoop into the contents of an IGMP packet to get the information it needs), issue the `set igmp enable` command in global configuration mode. That should be all you need to do to allow dynamic IGMP operation (statically configuring multicast router entries and group memberships is possible, but not recommended). With switches that support both CGMP and IGMP snooping, you can only have one operational at a time.

In summary, at the access layer we will not perform any layer 3 routing. We will, however, provide a redundant layer 2 trunk path through the distribution layer, support VLANs across multiple-access switch devices, and support the distribution of VLAN information via VTP. As such, our access layer will look like that shown in Figure 7-5. In this figure we see endstations on different VLANs. Should a device on VLAN 2

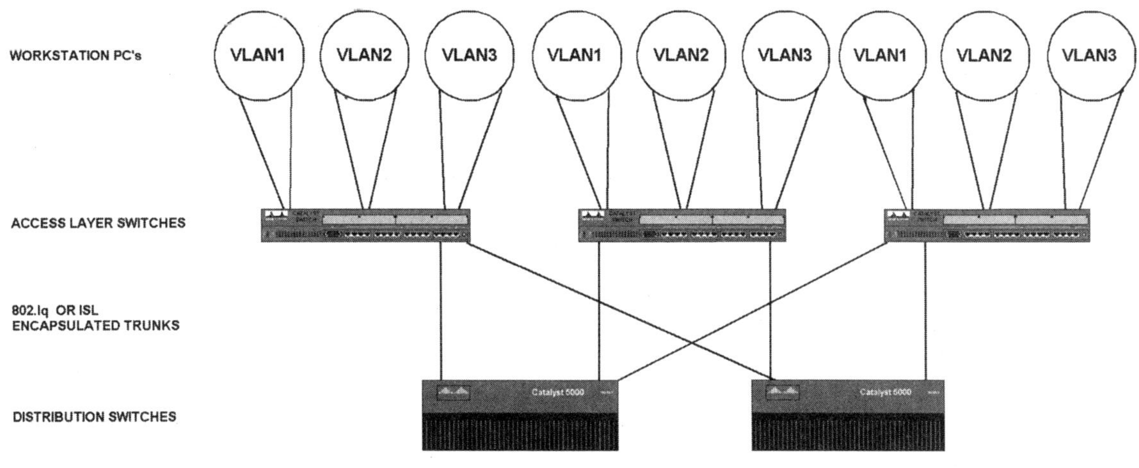

Figure 7-5 Typical access layer connections.

wish to communicate with another endstation on VLAN 2 that is connected to a different access switch, that communication will be accommodated through the distribution layer switches. For a VLAN 3 device to communicate with a VLAN 2 device, recourse has to be made to layer 3 routing, which is addressed in the discussion of distribution layer switches that follows.

The hardware choices are 2900 (either the 2900 range fixed-configuration switches based on the 5000 architecture or the XL range) or the new 4000, which offers significantly more backplane throughput. For higher-density LANs, the 4000 is probably a better choice. It does not support ISL, though, and multicasts are best handled with IGMP snooping. The 2900XL range offers good performance for smaller LANs and supports ISL and CGMP.

Distribution Layer If we allocate our resources and users wisely between VLANs, we should minimize the amount of nonserver-related traffic that needs to be routed between VLANs. The main job of the distribution layer is to "fan out" connections from the core to the individual access switches; however, in our design, it will also route between VLANs via internal RSMs.

As well as providing multiple connections to each access layer device, the distribution layer has to provide redundant connections to the core network. This is as we would expect. One potential physical layer connection for this is shown in Figure 7-6.

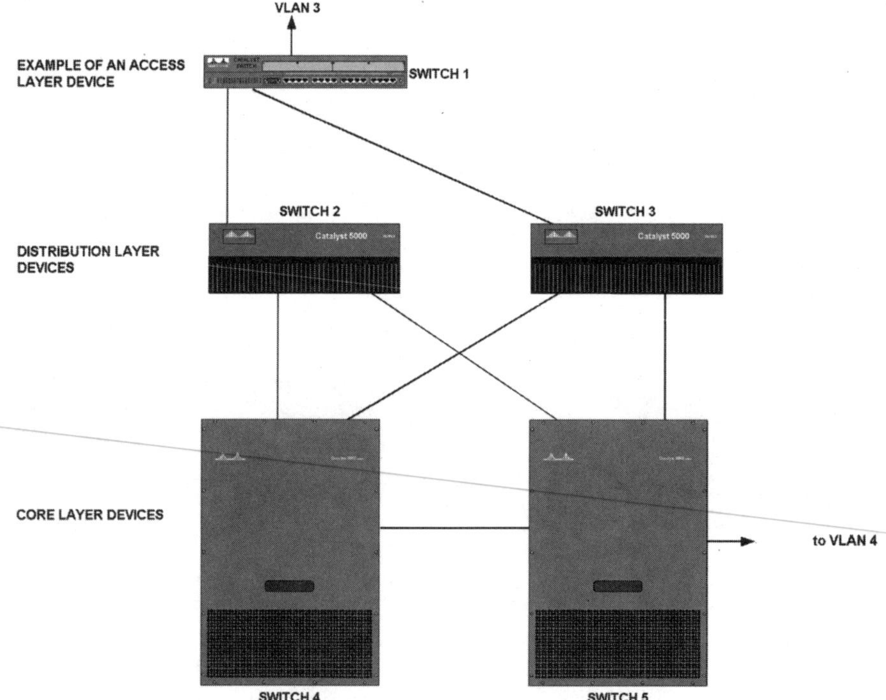

Figure 7-6 Typical distribution layer connections.

Let's just talk through how this configuration will react during normal and fault conditions. For this discussion we'll assume that the endstation illustrated as being on VLAN 3 has to communicate with another endstation that is on VLAN 4. The physical path from VLAN 3 to VLAN 4 is via the core switches. The RSM within switch 2 in Figure 7-6 will have to know that to get to VLAN 4, it must go via switch 3, which is only contactable via the core.

Within Figure 7-6, each of the links shown (with the exception of the link connecting the endstation to switch 1) are trunks that carry multi-VLAN traffic. In addition, each VLAN will be running its own copy of spanning tree to select switch ports in the forwarding and blocking state. In this discussion, it is assumed that Uplink Fast and Backbone Fast are in operation to speed convergence in link failures.

So, for argument's sake, let's say that for VLAN 3, spanning tree has selected the route from switch 4 directly to switch 1 to the endstation on VLAN 3. Should any device or link fail in that path, spanning tree for VLAN 3 will recalculate and change the status of ports from blocking to forward as appropriate to make a new path available. In the network illustrated, this will be via switch 4.

Given that we have said our preferred option is to have routing handled at the distribution layer, a Route Switch Module within the switch rather than an external router will allow two main benefits. The first is to allow the router to switch traffic to pass across the switch backplane, rather than an external link. Clearly, this is both quicker in terms of latency and has greater throughput. The second is less obvious. A router will only allow one interface to be configured for a subnet. If you try to configure two interfaces to be within the same subnet, a message similar to the following appears:

```
Router2(config-if)#ip address 172.27.209.61 255.255.255.224
172.27.209.32 overlaps with Loopback0
```

In a routed network, this is not a problem, as, generally, alternate paths are provided from source to destination via different intermediate subnets. In an environment where we may have a router that we want to connect to multiple distribution layer switches, each with a path to the same VLAN (each VLAN is a subnet), this could cause problems in router configuration. By this I mean that you cannot have two router interfaces directly connected on the same VLAN.

So if you are going to have discrete routers in the network, they can only be connected to each VLAN at one point. This has implications for the physical connections you can make in the network. With discrete routers you will only provide one access point from each router into the layer 2 meshed network. Should a link from a router into the meshed layer 2 switched network fail, you have to rely on a routing protocol to reroute traffic from the router with the failed link to the router that now has a path into the switched network. This causes a greater disruption to traffic flows and potentially a longer time for convergence. Not only will the routing protocol have to recalculate to be able to reach all the VLANs via a different router, but STP will also have to converge to route VLAN traffic over new paths. This is illustrated in Figure 7-7.

In this figure let's say that the routing protocol has decided that router 1 provides the best path to the user VLANs. Should the link from router 1 to switch 1 fail, the routing protocol will have to detect this failure and start to route traffic to router 2. This will, of course, mean that each STP for each VLAN that was sending traffic over the switch 1 to router 1 link will also have to recalculate.

One way around this is to have router 1 and router 2 present equal-cost paths for the user VLANs to the core; then traffic will be shared between router 1 and router 2 during normal operation, with all traffic switching over to one link if the other should fail. This can be an attrac-

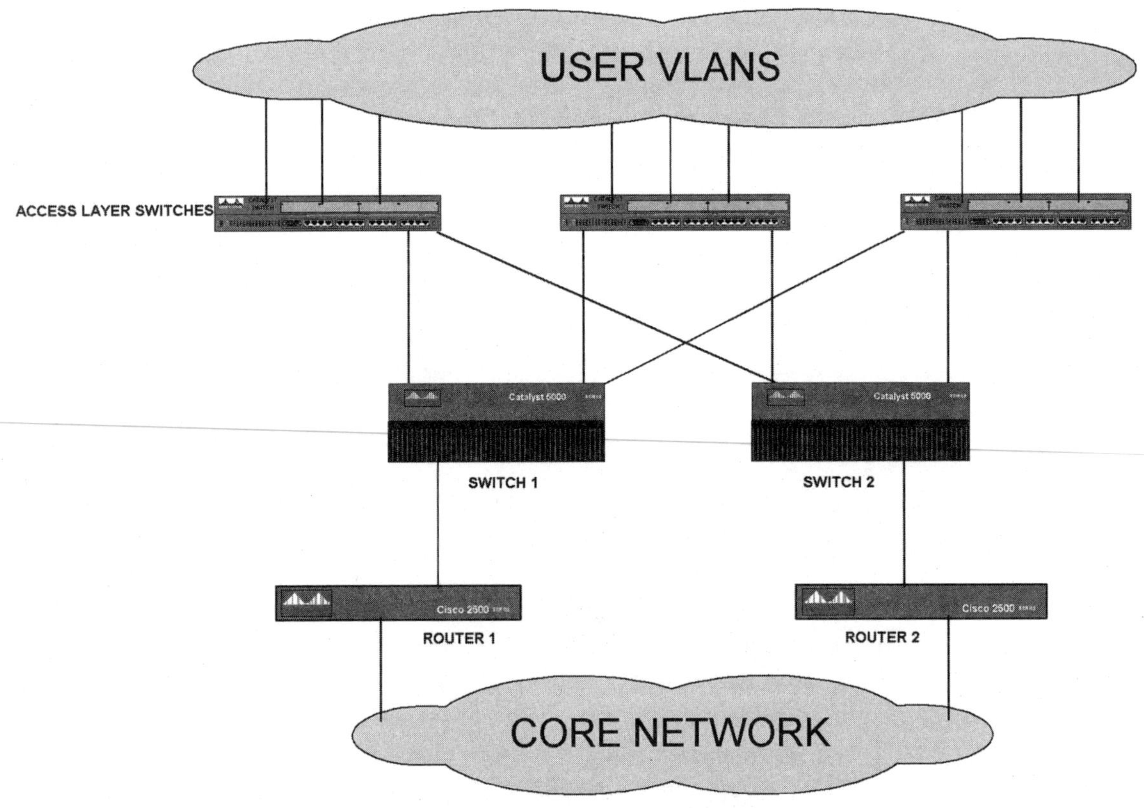

Figure 7-7 Physical connections for discrete routers in between the distribution and core layers.

tive option in that it makes the best use of available devices and bandwidth, but you need to be sure that the applications using this mechanism can support out-of-sequence packet delivery. This is not a problem for TCP, which handles such things, but applications that use UDP need additional intelligence at the application level to ensure packets are processed in the correct order. If the routing function is provided within the switch via an RSM card, router 1 and router 2 disappear from the network in Figure 7-7 and link failures within the distribution to access layer only cause an STP recalculation.

In the preceding discussion when we considered separate routers and switches at the distribution layer, the router-to-switch links need to be made with some type of trunk encapsulation that will support subinterfaces on the Ethernet connections and allow traffic multiple VLANs down the one physical link. If you do decide to go with routing at the distribution layer, you have to use the 5000/5500 or newer 6000 series switches for routing support. If routing is kept at the core, it is feasible to go with 4000 series switches for this layer, which have high-capacity 32-Gbit/sec backplanes. It all depends on the scale and budget of your network.

There is a strong argument to place some routing functionality with the distribution layer switches. If there are print servers connected to the access layer switches that receive print jobs from a number of VLANs, it is clearly advantageous to have this traffic only get as far into the network as the distribution layer, rather than going all the way back to the core for routing. It is better to restrict the traffic going back to the core to that which needs to go to the central servers (this will be most of the traffic, in any case, but we don't want to send anything there unnecessarily). By putting the print server on its own VLAN and enabling the distribution switches to route print requests from other VLANs to it, you are saving lots of work for the core. This is quite a common scenario when you have one large printer shared between users that are sitting close together but have different job functions and, hence, different VLAN memberships.

Core Layer The core layer is based around high-performance switches that carry the bulk of traffic on the network. The links between these switches are trunks that carry the aggregated traffic from all the VLANs used at the access level to the central servers. In a properly designed network, each distribution layer switch will only carry traffic from a portion of the total number of VLANs on the network, whereas the core switches have them all.

In terms of connecting servers to these core switches, we have two options. The first is to put the servers on their own VLAN and have the core switches maintain some routing functionality so that users from several VLANs can have access routed to these servers. The second option is to have the servers connect to the core switches via links that support trunking. This option gets around the need for the core to support routing functionality. The downside is that the servers need NICs that support trunking capability, and more processing overhead is experienced on the server to handle that functionality. It all comes down to where you want to place the processing load.

Two Alternatives in Putting the Three Layers Together

In this section we'll look at two approaches that differ mainly with respect to where routing functionality resides within the network and how the central servers are connected to the core switches. The first takes the approach of each server being connected to the core switches via a trunk link that will carry multiple VLAN traffic. The second puts the servers on their own VLAN and relies on routing devices to route traffic to and from the endstations.

The first approach is illustrated in Figure 7-8. In this figure, there are two dotted lines that show how an endstation on VLAN 1 would have its packets routed to a central server (connected via a trunk that supports multi-VLAN traffic to a core switch) and to a print server on VLAN 2. The advantage of this design is that, as far as possible, all packets only traverse switches. There is no need for a router to be involved for endstations to contact central servers. The only time a router process is used is for an endstation to communicate with anything else is if communication with a device such as a print server located on another VLAN is necessary.

This design works best if the VLANs are evenly distributed between the access layer switches. In practice this does not happen. No matter how well the initial design meets the needs of the users, users change locations, get different applications, and generally move on in their business life. The fortunate thing with this design is that EtherChannel links can be used to supplement any of the switched links that experience bandwidth constraints.

The downside to this design is that servers need to do more processing to service requests from multiple VLANs via the trunk links and it is not cheap in terms of capital cost. However, in my opinion, with the cost savings in moves, adds, and changes, and the ability of this network to scale to meet increasing needs, over the long term a network of this kind for any sort of business-critical environment turns out to be cost-justified.

An alternate design that makes use of what may well be existing router equipment to facilitate cross-VLAN communication and places the central servers on their own VLAN is shown in Figure 7-9. This design

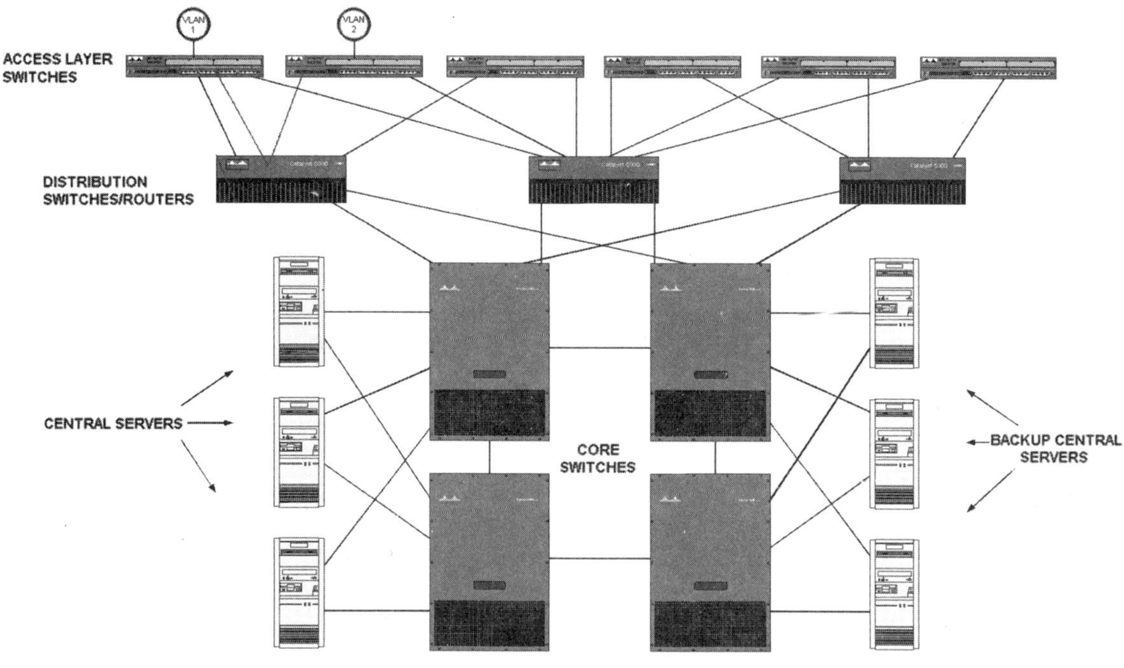

Figure 7-8 A complete switched network with routing at the distribution level and switching at the core.

only produces minimal improvement over what was probably already in place with a more traditional routed network. The improvement here is in providing more collision domains at the access layer. For any communication between the central servers and endstations, the path has to go through the core routers. This is, of course, what we want to avoid, as routers are slower at forwarding packets than switches.

I have seen designs similar to this one that introduce another layer of switches between the core routers and the central servers. The advantage is that the central servers have their own collision domain. I do not like this approach very much, as it adds another layer of switches in with little purpose. If you do decide to go with redeployment of equipment and implement this type of network, I would rather put the central servers on separate interfaces to the core routers to give them their own collision and broadcast domains.

The recommendation is therefore to go with networks similar to that depicted in Figure 7-8. Despite the plethora of interconnections, this is a simple design. Essentially, each network device has at least two paths

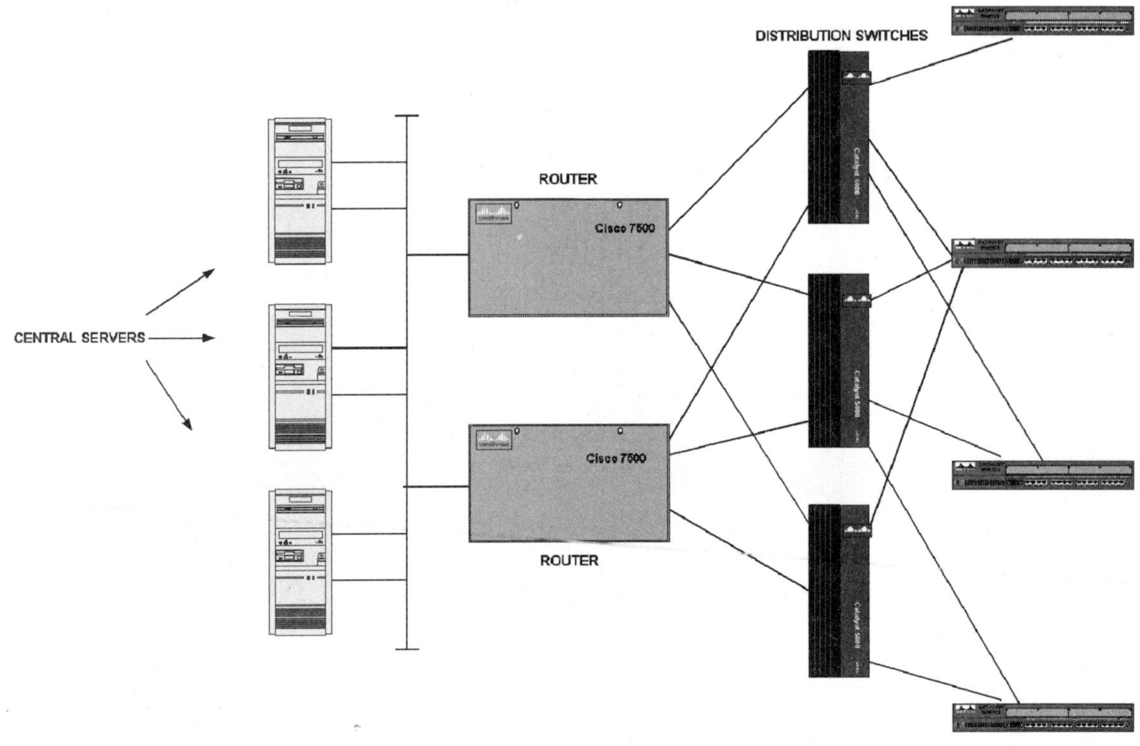

Figure 7-9 *Alternate design of switched network using existing router equipment, which places central servers on their own VLAN.*

through the network, and no single device failure causes an outage within the core and distribution layers. The main advantage is that packets can travel an exclusively switched path between endstation and server, and that routing is only used for endstations to communicate with devices at the access layer that are members of a different VLAN. This leaves packets unaltered as they travel from client to server (the bulk of the traffic), thus producing the best performance and scalability.

Redesigning the Routed to a Switched Network

It is increasingly becoming a common task for network managers at all kinds of organizations to look at how they should redesign their existing routed networks to take advantage of switched technologies. The main concern seems to be how a VLAN hierarchy can be best designed to suit the network's needs. The way to look at it is that a VLAN is a subnet. So at its most simple, the question of how to design a VLAN hierarchy is really the more generic question of how is the addressing hierarchy going to be organized.

In a typical routed network, such as the network used at Acme, shown in Figure 7-3, we could implement a VLAN hierarchy that mimics the existing subnets in use. This, of course, means that the central servers are on their own subnets, and all traffic to and from endstations must be routed. If we were to maintain the existing address scheme, the main benefit of introducing switched technology would only really come at the access layer, where we replace shared media hubs with switches that introduce multiple collision domains and open up the possibility of full-duplex Ethernet operation for directly connected endstations.

Making the Most of Switched Network Designs

To really make the most of a switched design, you need to have as much traffic switched as possible, with the minimal level of routing. Of course, we cannot have the whole network on one VLAN, as in a network of any reasonable size, the broadcast would kill us. That was the problem in the old days of large bridged LANs.

The network blueprint of Figure 7-8 provides the maximum amount of switching, with the minimal level of routing. The only downside is that the servers need to be able to directly talk to endstations that are on different subnets, which requires a host NIC and driver software that is capable of supporting either ISL or 802.1q trunking. In this design there are options with EtherChannel and, ultimately, Gigabit Ethernet that will happily transport far more traffic than any server currently marketed today can handle. The job, then, becomes one of splitting users between servers and adding the VLANs to support that.

Moving to this type of VLAN deployment is a shift in thinking from the more traditional router-based networks. With the traditional router networks, there was a simply understood hierarchy. Central servers were on one subnet, a separate set of subnets linked the core devices to the distribution routers, and user groups had yet another set of subnets. The route from one endstation to the central server was up the hierarchy and back down, through the subnets. With the network type shown in Figure

7-8, the path from endstation to central server is all within one subnet. So, instead of a hierarchy, we have multiple parallel paths from endstations to servers, in terms of the subnets traversed.

Redesigning Acme's Routed Network

Let's now set down some goals in redesigning Acme's routed network to become a higher-performance, higher-availability switched network. Our goals will be as follows:

- New applications are coming onstream that will utilize multicasts and make greater demands on the available bandwidth.
- These greater bandwidth demands require class of service facilities to be implemented on the network to ensure critical traffic always gets through.
- With newer business-critical applications being deployed, the need for redundancy and automatic failover is significantly greater.
- It is expected that Acme is about to undergo dramatic growth, and the network must be able to scale to twice its size without degradation in performance.

Head Office Configuration

The network blueprint of Figure 7-8 can be adapted to Acme's situation to meet all of the stated demands of the previous section. Figure 7-10 shows how the new network is configured in building 1. Building 2 will have a mirror image for backup server connection and connections to user LANs.

In this design, each access layer switch has two connections to the distribution layer. The distribution layer performs any routing required, as shown in Figure 7-8, and the core switches have trunk links to the central servers. There is one case not shown in Figure 7-8, and that is if an endstation needs to connect to a device that is also connected to the access layer but not connected to the same distribution switch. An example of this is if an endstation like those shown on VLAN 3 and VLAN 4 in Figure 7-10 need to communicate. In this case the only physical path is via the core switches.

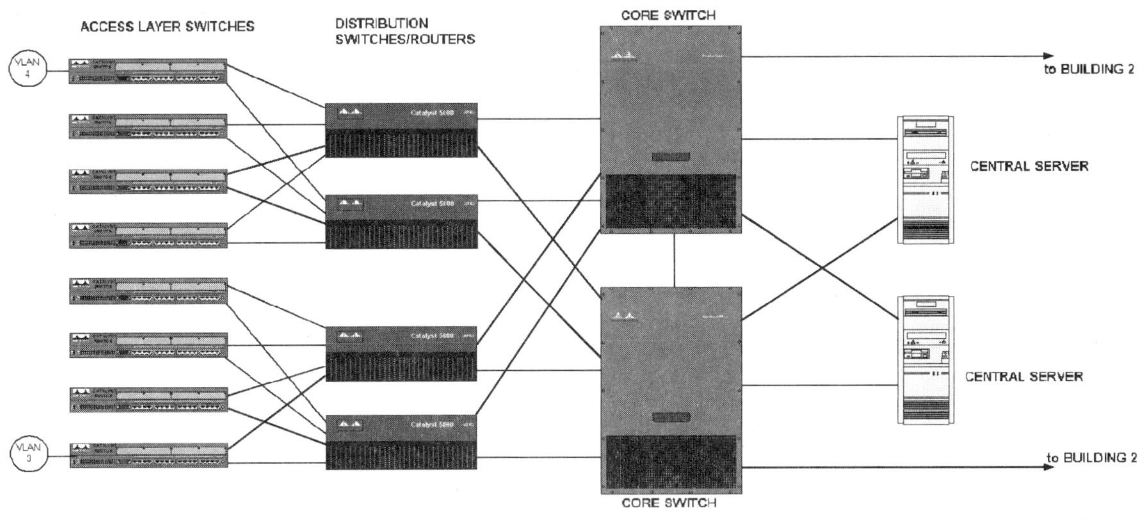

Figure 7-10 Network for building 1 in Acme's new switched design.

Of course, in this design the core switches do not perform routing functions for the distribution layer switch that is connected to VLAN 3. The RSM in the distribution layer switch must have received a routing protocol update telling it that a route to VLAN 4 exists via the RSMs in each of the upper two distribution switches. Depending on the routing protocol in use and the speed of the links involved, the RSM in the switch connected to VLAN 3 will either pick one of the upper two switch's RSMs as its preferred route to VLAN 4, or in some cases, deem them equal-cost routes and send traffic to both. In either case, it is the destination MAC address of the RSM that is used to get the packet from the lower to upper distribution switches, and the core switches can direct packets based on destination MAC addresses.

In essence, this gives an overview of the way the network performs as a whole. We will now look at each layer in turn.

Core

At the core we form an interconnected network of four of the highest-powered switches we can afford, connected via the highest-speed links available. These switches must have excess capacity under all conditions, or the network is doomed to failure. In the case of Acme, we have chosen to split the core switches between the two major buildings within the network. This provides good redundancy in that each building can operate independently in the event of a disaster (the backup servers are located in building 2).

The main question is what speed and of what type should the links be that interconnect the core switches. The links in this core network are of two types: the connection between the two switches within the same building and the connection that travels between the buildings. Given that even the endstations are probably going to be connected at 100-Mbit/sec Fast Ethernet, it does not make much sense to deploy a new network with FDDI at the core, so we really have the option of ATM or some type of faster Ethernet technology, like Fast EtherChannel or Gigabit Ethernet.

In this case, the most common connection between the two core switches in the same building is to use UTP and Fast EtherChannel to take the core network to whatever bandwidth is necessary. Also, until recently, ATM would have been the logical choice for high-speed, building-to-building connectivity. Now, however, we have the realistic option of Gigabit Ethernet, which can be used in either case of intrabuilding or interbuilding connections.

Being based on optical technology is an additional benefit for Gigabit Ethernet, in that the physical medium is not susceptible to electromagnetic interference. The choice between Gigabit Ethernet and multiple UTP Fast EtherChannel links, in many cases, may come down to an economic one of whether the budget will stand the higher cost Gigabit links. It is, however, the preferred option.

Deciding between ATM and Gigabit Ethernet for the interbuilding connections is a little more involved. The advantage of Gigabit Ethernet is its simplicity, both in terms of device configuration and common frame format with the LAN traffic. It is also a known technology that does not require much retraining. There are two downsides to consider, though. First is that Gigabit Ethernet is limited to a few kilometers, whereas ATM does not have distance limitations. The second is that if your plans include multimedia traffic over the interbuilding links, ATM has all the built-in class of service features.

For a technology like Gigabit Ethernet to really offer the same class of service as ATM is a real challenge and the best method of assuring that is to make sure that there is plenty of bandwidth on these links to accommodate even peak loads. We have discussed RSVP, IP Precedence, and the other protocols added to IP networks to provide better class of service, but they still do not quite measure up to what is available within

ATM. The choice will be different for each network. If you really need the class of service guarantees built into ATM and can justify the complexity and retraining, your choice is clear. However, I believe that for the majority of enterprise networks, Gigabit Ethernet will provide sufficient bandwidth and, hence, service levels for a long time to come and allows network managers to take advantage of the bandwidth of optical communications, without the retraining needed to support ATM.

Having selected the interconnecting links between the core switches and having determined to place the switches in two locations, we just have to decide how the core switches connect to the distribution switches. In each building the core switches are configured to support two links to each server. It is assumed that within the application layer there is intelligence within the endstations to determine if a primary server is unavailable and initiate a connection to the backup server. For most networks, having two server connections to the core switches when there is a live backup server available is overkill. Most networks can stand a swap to the backup system while a NIC is replaced in the primary server. However, we show the most complex case here, which can be simplified if need be.

Distribution Switches The distribution switches incorporate the only routing capability for the LAN side of the network. Existing routing devices can be used to interface the major building networks to regional branches. In this case there is no real benefit to introducing switching technology to the WAN, as the network is not of the size or throughput that justifies a switched WAN.

It is in these distribution switches that we have a route processor that will run the routing protocol (probably OSPF or EIGRP) that will reroute around failures in the inter-VLAN communication links. The distribution switches have redundant paths both into the core and into the access layer. The multiple paths between these switches and the core are far more important than the redundant paths between the core switches and the central servers. It is true that if we were to implement the network with only one link from each of the distribution switches to the core switches, failure of that one link will not necessarily take out access to the core. It is conceivable that STP will recalculate and work out that for traffic destined for the core; a physical path is available to another distribution switch via an access level switch. This will, of course, redirect the traffic, but it could well overload an access layer switch and not provide an effective backup under all load conditions.

A third alternative would be to only have the distribution switches utilize one connection to the core switches, but to chain the distribution layer switches together. In this case, if the distribution to the core link goes down, STP can reroute traffic to its neighboring distribution switch to reach the core without recourse to the access layer. The advantage is that fewer ports are needed on the core switches, thus saving costs. The downside is that a single link that goes from the distribution switch to the core now needs to carry twice its normal load, both its regular load and the redirected load. This could cause capacity problems.

At the end of the day, the number of core switch ports you want to buy and the level of redundancy you are happy with is an economic decision.

Access Switches

Access switches have the simplest job. They perform no routing and only have single connections to the attached endstations. Having trunk interfaces on the access layer switches is essential for the design presented in Figure 7-10. The protocols that need to be supported are STP and either CGMP or IGMP snooping for efficient routing of packets and handling of multicasts. The selection of CGMP or IGMP snooping will come down to the access layer switch chosen. This will also most likely be the deciding factor for what encapsulation you use for the trunk links, probably 802.1q or ISL.

Beyond these requirements, it is simply a matter of selecting the access layer switch that will meet your throughput requirements and fit into the overall budget level. The new 4000 series switches offer the highest level of throughput for the access layer, at 32 Gbit/sec. The 2924 and other fixed-configuration switches in the 2900 range have the same 1.2-Gbit/sec throughput of the Catalyst 5000, and the new 2900XL range have a 3.2 Gbit/sec switching fabric.

General

When implementing a switched network, your prime concern in deciding how to arrange the collection of devices that will form your network is understanding the packet flow and what each device will do to the packet flow. Beyond that, you must have a clear understanding of how the devices will behave under different fault scenarios and how they will affect the operation of the network.

The two most common flaws I have seen in network implementations are inserting devices that do not add value and not sizing links or devices to cope with additional traffic during fault conditions. Let's look at a few such mistakes.

Switches are more expensive than shared media hubs and use more processing power. It is often assumed that implementing a switch is preferable to implementing a hub in all cases; however, this is not always true. A common implementation is that a server sending out UDP broadcasts, such as might be used for a stock or news feed, might be sent out to 30 or 40 machines. Connecting these endstations to the server via a switch is not the best solution. Connecting them via a standard hub will be cheaper and provide better performance. The reason is that a switch has to take each packet in, and if, as in this case, a broadcast is going to each endstation, then the switch has to use processing time to replicate each packet out each interface. The hub, as it is a shared media device, will be sending each packet out each interface by default without any processing overhead. Depending on the power of the switch and the number of endstations receiving the broadcast, it is possible for a relatively modestly sized UDP broadcast to overwhelm a switch, whereas a hub would perform without problems.

Another common mistake with switched network design is to try to make use of existing routers within the new switched network where they do not add any benefit. Commonly I see existing routers being redeployed to connect central servers to the core switches. This really does not do much for the network overall, as it means every packet to and from the central servers has to be routed and will suffer the performance hit that implies.

As far as planning capacity to deal with network outages, we have the same issue as was faced in the routed network world. If you deploy links that you expect to carry traffic in the event of an outage, those links (and by implication the attached network devices) must not run at more than 50 percent load during normal operation. Otherwise, they will not be able to accommodate the new traffic. If you do provide alternate paths without this capacity, it is worse than not providing the alternate path. By overloading a path with redirected traffic, you are taking that out of operation also, resulting in two links down rather than one.

In cases where network congestion cannot be accommodated by adding more bandwidth, or where there are peaks of delay-insensitive traffic interrupting delay-sensitive traffic, class of service features can help considerably. IP Precedence in the IP Type of Service field is gaining popularity, and we discussed some of the options that can be implemented on a network to make use of that. RSVP is generally seen as the way forward, with WFQ (weighted fair queuing) quite popular, although

WFQ is not the answer to all situations. If your high-priority traffic is the low-volume traffic, WFQ will not service your needs well. In that instance custom queuing is a better bet.

As in most things when you get to this level of network implementation, there are no hard-and-fast rules. You have to experiment with different settings to gauge their effect in your environment. Clearly, a test network is a must to avoid messing with mission-critical systems in production.

The last general point is to briefly discuss scalability in the design we have presented for Acme. Should the network grow, our game plan is to add more distribution-level switches for more access-level switches that will bring on the users. We can also increase the number of VLANs by adding new central servers to service these new users. This should be accommodated with the design shown until you run out of either interfaces or throughput at the core-level switches. With devices like the 8500 and 12000 switches now available, that means a very large network, indeed.

Summary

We started this chapter by stating that network design and implementation are part of network operations. Networks have to continually meet changing demands and, therefore, need to be continually redesigned to meet those new demands. This sort of constant redesign includes adding links and new nodes, which must be done with the knowledge of how that will affect the operation of the network as a whole under normal and fault conditions.

To effectively implement new network equipment, knowledge of traffic types, time of flows, required service levels, and geographic location of users make up the most basic of required information. The goals of network design were identified as implementation of a scalable, secure platform that provides redundancy for link and device failure, while delivering required service levels with the appropriate levels of security.

Redundancy requirements include servers, network devices, data paths, and locations. Since levels are met by configuring class of service features that were examined as queuing options, such as FIFO, priority queuing, custom queuing, and weighted fair queuing. Class of service signaling focused on the RSVP protocol as a way to signal throughput requirements across a network. Security options of different types of firewalls and both symmetric and asymmetric encryption were described.

Two common designs for a switched network were presented, with the options that minimize the amount of traffic that needs to be routed selected as the preferred. If you want to implement something other than the preferred method presented, you need to be very clear on why you have an unusual case and how better your proposed network design will be than the blueprint given.

We moved on to look at an existing network that was experiencing difficulties meeting the needs of its users regarding throughput, redundancy, and the capacity to expand. The new design centralized servers, switched traffic from source to destination for client/server communications, and provided far better redundancy and scalability. This switched network design focused on splitting the network into three hierarchical levels: core switches, distribution switches, and access-level switches. The access-level switches provide multiple collision domains, support multiple VLAN assignments and multiple uplinks to the distribution layer, and handle multicasts via either CGMP or IGMP snooping. The distribution switches link the core to the access layers and deliver all the routing functionality within the network. It is at the distribution layer that any packet manipulation in terms of class of service features go on.

Elsewhere, the speed of switching is available, such that the packet is carried from device input to device output in an unaltered state. The core network utilizes high-powered switches that support Gigabit Ethernet or multiple Fast EtherChannel links. We briefly discussed the selection of Gigabit Ethernet as a preferable technology to ATM in most instances, except where very high-speed links are required between locations several miles or more apart.

Finally, we redesigned the existing routed switched network to the new switched model and illustrated how the connections were made in the new environment.

INDEX

B

C

D

E

F

G

H

I

T

U

V

W

ABOUT THE AUTHOR

Christopher S. Lewis is vice president of ILX Systems, the leading provider of networked real-time financial information, where he runs a large international Cisco-powered network. Mr. Lewis frequently contributes articles to leading technology journals, including *Network Computing Magazine*, for which he is a contributing editor.

Cisco Technical Expert

Advanced

IP Routing

IN Cisco

Networks

- PREP GUIDE FOR THE CCIE EXAM
- HANDS-ON TROUBLESHOOTING
- INTEGRATING MULTIPLE ROUTING PROTOCOLS
- VLSM IN CLASSLESS IP ENVIRONMENTS

TERRY SLATTERY, CCIE #1026 & BILL BURTON, CCIE #1119

Advanced IP Routing in Cisco Networks

Terry Slattery, CCIE & Bill Burton, CCIE

0-07-058144-4 $55.00

Covering all the protocols that run on Cisco IP routers, this clear, illustrated guide provides all the expertise needed to design, configure, manage, and troubleshoot this vital technology. Features a wealth of network examples and actual router configurations.

Cisco Technical Expert

Cisco

Router OSPF

Design & Implementation Guide

- PREPARATION GUIDE FOR THE CCIE EXAM
- CONFIGURATION AND DESIGN OF A NETWORK FOR OSPF
- CRITICAL DESIGN ISSUES AND CONSTRAINTS OF OSPF
- OSPF TROUBLESHOOTING AND REPAIRS

WILLIAM PARKHURST, PH.D., CCIE #2969

Cisco Router OSPF Design and Implementation Guide

William Parkhurst, Ph.D., CCIE

0-07-048626-3 • $55.00

The CCIE exam demands full knowledge of Open Shortest Path First (OSPF). This guide reveals step-by-step how to configure, design, and implement a network using OSPF. Discusses the latest protocol OSPF2.

Cisco IOS Essentials

John Albritton, CCIE
0-07-134743-7 • $55.00

This comprehensive and easy-to-use reference provides invaluable information on Cisco's Internetwork Operating System (IOS) used by administrators to manage Cisco equipment. From initial IOS setup to the most complex multi-protocol configurations, the author shows how effortless it is for anyone with a basic understanding of computer networking.

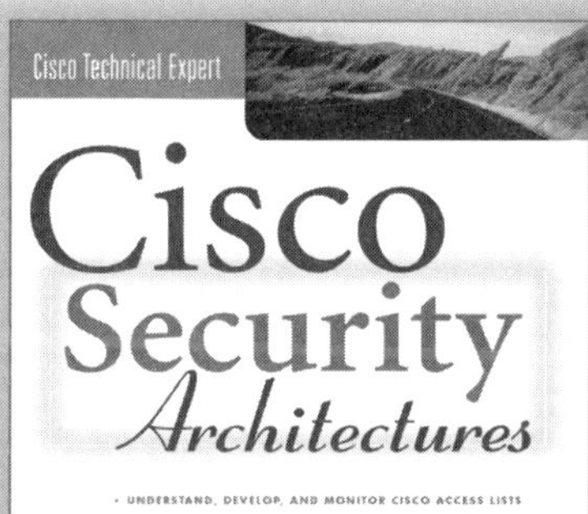

Cisco Security Architectures

Gilbert Held & Kent Hundley, CCNA
0-07-134708-9 • $55.00

This important, comprehensive guide shows you how to avoid common mistakes that result in network vulnerability and provides numerous examples of practical methods to secure your network.

Configuring Cisco Routers for ISDN

Paul Fischer, CCNA
0-07-022073-5 • $55.00

Ideal as an on-the-job reference or supplement to Cisco-related courses, this indispensable resource shows how to install, troubleshoot, and solve real-world configuration problems. Spotlights specific cases of Cisco router connections and offers detailed descriptions of real products.

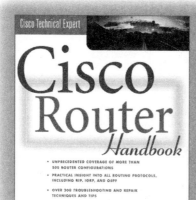